The Movie Game

The **Movie Game**

The film business in Britain, Europe and America

MARTIN DALE

Cassell
Wellington House
125 Strand
London WC2R 0BB

PO Box 605
Herndon
VA 20172
USA

First published 1997

British Library Cataloguing-in-Publication Data
A catalogue record for this book is available from the British Library.

ISBN 0-304-33386-7 (hardback)
      0-304-33387-5 (paperback)

Cover design by Inês Ferreira
Cover illustration by Xavier Monsalvatje

Printed and bound in Great Britain by Biddles Ltd, Guildford and King's Lynn

To Meni and Eva

Contents

Illustrations

Acknowledgements

I would like to thank Jane Greenwood at Cassell for her commitment to this book during its long gestation, and Terry Ilott for his incisive editorial advice.

I am grateful to the many people who granted me interviews, including Frans Afman, Agustin Almodóvar, Kimmo Aulake, Chris Auty, Tim Ball, André Bonzel, Paul Bricault, Paul Brooks, Colin Brown, Caitlin Buchman, Deborah Burton, Frances Cairncross, Jean Cazès, Hugues de Chastellux, Adriena Chiesa, Larry Chrisfield, Bo Christenson, Sesto Cifola, Frédéric Comtet, Diana Cosbrooke, Peter Cowie, Anatole Dauman, Andrew Davis, Mark Devoraugh, John Dick, Sean Dromgoole, Didier Duverger, Jake Eberts, Tabitha Elwes, George Faber, Pere Fages, Chris and Breda Fahey-Thomas, Luigi Ferrara, William Field, Angus Finney, Richard Fox, Julian Friedmann, Jorge Gallegos, Fernando de Garcillan, Dieter Geissler, Paulo Glisenti, Daniel Goldman, Alain Goldman, James Green, David Hancock, John Heyman, Sally Hibbin, John Hopewell, Janice Hughes, Mona Jensen, Duncan Kenworthy, Nadine Luque, Jorge Marecos, Cristina Martins, Pedro Martins, Neil McCartney, Cameron McCracken, Kip Meek, Dieter Mentz, Sophie Migraine, David Morrell, Bertrand Moullier, Tino Navarro, David Norris, Jonathan Olsberg, Jordi Parcerisa, Mercedes Perez-Desoy, Bruno Perrin, Simon Perry, Paula Picado, Paco Poch, Antonio Portero, Ricky Posner, Nik Powell, John Ptak, David Puttnam, Peter Read, Brian Reilly, Simon Relph, Alain Rocca, Conrad Roeber, Antonio Saura, Michel Schmidt, Andrew Sharp, Adrian Scrope, Mark Shivas, Wolfram Skowronnek-Schaer, Bernie Stampfer, David Stephen, Stewart Till, Judy Tossell, Jacqueline Touchard, Juliette Towhidi, Patrick Uden, Colin Vaines, Tarcy Vanhuysse, Antonio-Pedro Vascencelos, Andres Vicente Gomez, Jean-Paul de Vidas, Kent Walwin, Neil Watson, Antonio Weinrinter, Mark Westaway, John Wolstenhome, Caroline Wood, Steve Woolley and Colin Young. Special thanks to everyone at Spectrum, SP Filmes, Bonne Question and Nuit de Chine.

The design and layout of the book is the work of Inês Ferreira. Rictor Norton and Kenneth Burnley were excellent in copy-editing and proof-reading the text. I also greatly benefited from the visual genius of Xavier Monsalvatje and J. C. Suarès.

For my research, I had the invaluable support of Maria de Jesus Santos and Isabel Durana at the library of the Cinemateca Portuguesa.

I would also like to thank all my friends and family. My parents gave me their love and also very valuable editorial suggestions. Finally, the most special thanks to Meni and our daughter Eva.

Preface

Not a half dozen men have been able to keep
the whole equation of pictures in their heads.
F. Scott Fitzgerald

THIS BOOK IS A REFERENCE GUIDE to the motion picture industry in all its various guises – from micro-budget to blockbuster and from Europe to America. The 'game rules' of each sector are outlined, followed by profiles of all the leading players.

Designed principally for film professionals, who want an overview of their mercurial industry, the text should also be of interest to all those fascinated by the film business, and who seek a better understanding of its inner workings.

There are many books on the Hollywood studio system and a significant number on low-budget film-making. But the connection between the different parts of the business, particularly that between Europe and America, is relatively unexplored territory.

Europe has always been the 'hidden' half of the American film equation. The Majors were built by native Europeans and have always been highly dependent on European talent and revenues. The Independents finance their films through pre-sales to Europe, and many of the leading producers are native Europeans who have relocated to the movie colony.

While the American Majors thrive on high-risk free-market capitalism, Europe's media groups are enmeshed in political straitjackets designed to defend the 'national interest'. Quotas and subsidies have herded European cinema into a cultural ghetto from which it is very difficult to conduct rational debate. The Union's MEDIA Programme seems to have only intensified the problem.

The film industry is more than just glitz and glamour. It is a key economic sector which is emerging at the heart of the new multi-media universe. This makes it ever more important to unveil some of its mysteries. The subject is of particular concern in Europe, because the existing nation states fear that their sovereignty will be usurped by Hollywood's growing media empires.

Europe's media groups are as wealthy as their American counterparts, but lack the vital entertainment software needed to protect their retail empires. Politicians would like to blame this crisis on unfair competition from America. This was a popular theme in the 1993 GATT debate and has led to repeated attacks on the American distributor UIP which in 1996 culminated in EU raids on UIP offices.

Such political fireworks hide a very genuine failure of European economies which could prove to have devastating effects in the coming years. America is surging ahead in the production of valuable software for the cyber age, while Europe is still catching her breath.

Economic realities are beginning to force changes and a reluctant admittance that it is perhaps the politicians and the state who are actually to blame. Companies such as PolyGram have been producing powerful new films which also perform well at the box office. Recent examples include *Trainspotting* in Britain and *The Eighth Day* in France. Even state subsidy committees are now emphasizing more 'commercial' projects.

The Berlin walls surrounding European media are likely to collapse in the near future. This will offer opportunities for new talent to emerge and a stronger industry to be built.

Inspiration can be drawn from the few European film-makers who have succeeded in rising above the 'subsidy trap' mentality. The book concludes with profiles of leading producers, including David Puttnam, Claude Berri, Pedro Almodóvar and Luc Besson. They are the human face of the industry and prove that however bureaucratic the world becomes, there will always be mavericks who stand out and make their voice heard.

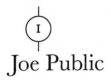

Joe Public

In this country, public opinion is everything.
Abraham Lincoln
The mob does not deserve to be enlightened.
Frederick III of Prussia

MAKING A MOVIE is as expensive as producing a private jet, and ultimately must be paid for by the public. This can be achieved through a 'democratic' system, involving the 'tyranny of the box office', or an 'aristocratic' model whereby the state decides what films to make, and the taxpayer foots the bill. America has chosen the former model, Europe the latter. One requires an intimate knowledge of the audience; the other tends to idealize the nature of the 'national public'.

Many would like to think that Europe has a more 'cultured' and 'educated' population than America. For example, avant-garde film-maker Peter Gidal claims that 'The average American reads three books in a lifetime, three works of literature (classified by God-knows-who as literature) as opposed to something on the best-seller list. Does that have any measurable effect in contrast to a culture like Germany where, just making it up, the average German probably reads thirty-seven works of literature, forty-seven philosophical essays and twenty-two books of left-wing politics.'[1]

In fact statistics show that patterns of 'cultural consumption' in America and Europe are surprisingly similar. America has the added advantage that half her population goes on to higher education compared to 20–30% in Europe. The main difference between the two systems is that while Europeans like to wear their cultural baggage on their sleeves, Americans tend to prefer designer labels.

People in Western societies are veritable media junkies. They spend most of their waking lives surrounded by electronic wallpaper – over nine hours a day.

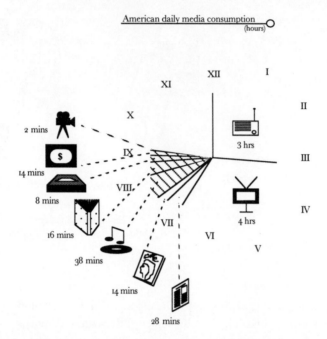

American daily media consumption (hours)

In Europe, the consumption pattern is very similar. 85–90% of this time is devoted to 'mass media' – television, radio, newspapers and magazines – with only 10–15% of time spent on more expensive 'premium media' – music, books and cinema. But it is the latter which soaks up 70% of our media spending.

The average person spends $445 a year on communications media in the US and a similar figure in the EU. This is under a fifth of all leisure spending. Larger categories are alcohol, restaurants and holidays.

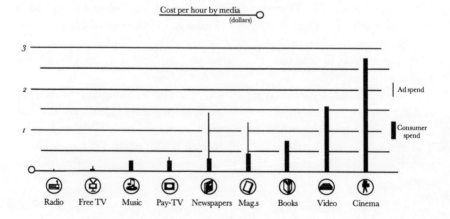

Cost per hour by media (dollars)

Each media has an effective 'price' which can be calculated by the amount we spend on it per year, divided by the hours of consumption. In addition there is an 'implicit' price, of the ad spend that tops up consumer expenditure.

Radio and television are by far the cheapest media. They cost the consumer virtually nothing. In America, free and basic cable TV costs under $0.02 an hour. In Europe, the licence fee pushes this up to about $0.06 an hour. The majority of the cost is borne by advertising. Advertising in the US is worth $0.04 an hour per person for radio and $0.10 for television, and about two thirds that level in Europe.

The contribution of advertising is even more obvious in newspapers and magazines, which are expensive media to produce but are sold cheaply. In the US, newspapers actually cost $1.35 an hour but are sold at $0.28. In Europe the ratio is slightly lower, especially for national newspapers.

Premium media are all sold in expensive units, but music, books and games can be consumed repeatedly, which reduces their effective cost. In the case of recorded music, the unit cost is often upwards of $10 but a high level of listening brings the price down to $0.24 an hour. The opposite is true of cinema, where the unit cost is relatively inexpensive, but its one-off nature makes it the most expensive form of media consumption.

Hollywood earns the bulk of its revenues in the two most expensive media – cinema and video – despite the fact that most people watch Hollywood films on free TV. This is comparable to the music business, where revenues are earned by selling compact discs and cassettes, but the most common way of listening is the radio.

The European Union has a slightly larger economy than that of America – $7.5 trillion against $7.2 trillion (50% of which is made up by Germany and France), and the two continents have similarly sized mass media industries.

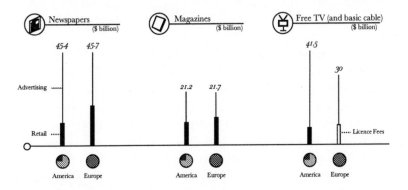

In relation to premium media, Europe's music and book industries are of comparable scale to those in America, but the film-related industries (cinema, video and pay-TV) are far smaller.

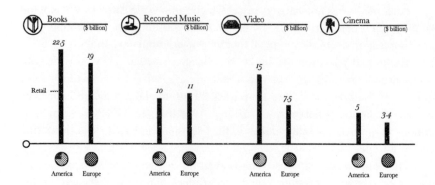

Europe continues to produce much of its software for mass media – especially journalism – but in premium software, is highly dependent on America. This gives Europe a very 'parochial' feel.

Mass media tend to be locally orientated, whereas premium media are very international. Europe exports only in niche 'cultural' fields. This means that for filmed entertainment, while Hollywood has market revenues of $16 billion, Europe earns little over $200 million (with another $1.2 billion provided by the state).

Europe excels mainly in journalism and advertising. The latter has grown spectacularly since the early 1980s, with Europe now spending around $65 billion a year in advertising (0.9% of GDP) compared to $90 billion in the US (1.3% of GDP). Europe has proved herself extremely adept at building a powerful advertising industry and yet she seems incapable of duplicating this success in premium media.

This is indicative of the cultural and political framework in Europe. Mass media are paid primarily by corporations and the state and politicians are deeply concerned with their control. This is possible because they are essentially journalistic in nature. Lobbying at the corporate and political level can easily make itself felt.

Premium media are much more difficult to control. They have a different 'culture' which is 'mythic' rather than journalistic. They are less concerned with day to day affairs, much more with themes and undercurrents of society. Industry analyst A. D. Murphy states this difference very clearly: 'Films succeed or fail on their own merits. No Ralph Naders, Moral Majorities etc. can impact the film business in the way that automobile tires, Corvairs or commercial advertisers are affected by consumer or advocacy pressures. Also, films of mass appeal are relatively impervious to "critics". Films that are going to be popular are popular.'[2]

History shows that when the state tries to control premium media this almost inevitably leads to its decline. Europe is increasingly orientated around mass media whereas social trends suggest that she should be doing the opposite.

'The era of mass media is over', says Caitlin Buchman of Film Strategies, 'We're now moving towards a choice-driven, individualistic culture. This should be wonderful for Europe because Americans tend to be so conformist. The next century could easily belong to the Europeans.'

The collapse of Europe's premium media is often blamed on the rise of television. But although the 'electronic hearth' has undoubtedly lowered the audience, television is no more capable of destroying the movies than radio was of destroying the music business. Startling proof of this is that American movies have enjoyed constant revenues in real terms in Europe since the 1960s, whereas European cinema has collapsed. The real tragedy of European cinema is that the state has encouraged a shift in commissioning strategies, abandoning what was previously the core audience.

THE FILM AUDIENCE

A third of all adults never go to the cinema and the core of the film audience are 'avids' who attend at least once a week and buy 40% of all tickets. A further 40% are sold to those who go at least once a month.

Avids are even more important for new releases, buying 60% of tickets sold. The film audience is therefore a very particular substratum of society. The number of cinema 'avids' is under 10 million in the United States (3.5% of the population) and under 5 million in the European Union (1.5%).

The cinema 'avids' have an intimate understanding of the medium and know what they do and don't like. They often supplement this interest by reading film magazines and pay great attention to upcoming titles. They are the key generators of 'word of mouth', the hunters and gatherers who spread the word to the rest of society.

Video and pay-TV also have 'avid' consumers, but with much larger numbers – about 30 million in the US and 10 million in Europe for each media. Thus the total premium 'avid' film audience is about 20% of the population in the US and 8% in Europe.

The 'heart' of the avid audience is young people, where there is the strongest rejection of European films. The few European films which achieve theatrical success are mainly targeted to a niche older audience.

On average, one third of the audience are teenagers, another third are those in their twenties and the rest are over thirty. Countries such as Germany and the UK have a very high dependence on the young audience. At the other extreme, France has 40% of the audience over thirty.

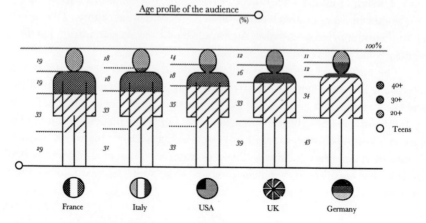

Age profile of the audience (%)

France	Italy	USA	UK	Germany

Source: Author's analysis based on US (MPAA 1983), UK (Caviar 1992), Germany (SPIO 1993), France (CNC 1988), Italy and Spain (*Screen Digest* 1990).

In recent years the cinema age profile has been skewing more to older audiences (known as 'greying' of the audience). But this actually returns it to the pre-television levels and maintains a very young mix. In France, for example, 44% of the audience was aged 15–24 in 1962, then shot up to 55% by 1973 but has now slipped back down again to under 45%.

The overall age profile of the cinema is reminiscent of rock music – where 65% of the market is under twenty-four. As with music, there are 'niche' films which appeal to an older audience, comparable to jazz and classical music where 72% and 81% of sales are to those over twenty-five.

As well as being highly dependent on the young, the cinema is also much more 'down market' than most arts. The average film-goer comes from a lower social class than the average theatre-goer. This is particularly true in Europe, where the average monies spent on theatres and concert per head is more than double that spent on the cinema. The 'down market' image means that ethnic groups are an important section of the audience. In America 17–20% of the audience is 'non-white', and has become an important 'niche' market.

Britain has the most broadly based film market, with 26% of the audience from the AB classes, 33% from C1 and 41% from C2DE. France has the most up market audience, with 44% having university education, 20.5% with technical education and 36.5% with only secondary education. Other countries lie in between.

This division hides the fact that more privileged groups actually attend the cinema far more frequently. In America, 27% of those with college education go to the cinema at least once a month, compared to 17% for those with only high school education. In Britain there are twice as many 'avid' filmgoers amongst AB classes than the rest.

An effective film industry must be aware of the lifestyle and tastes of its core audience. This requires intelligent use of advertising, critical reviews and word of mouth, and also respect for what the audience is actually looking for. For example, an audience survey by the CNC in 1989 showed that the main concern for French viewers is story and stars, with 70% of viewers citing story as the deciding factor. Critics' reviews and awards had a negligible impact, but it is the latter which tend to guide European production.

The Hollywood Majors have fine tuned their ability to cater to their core market, and release around 150 films a year. The Independents release a similar number of films and focus on more 'edgy' material, some of which will break out into the 'mainstream'. For the avid film-goer this means he or she has the chance to choose between five to six new films a week.

Inevitably certain films 'click' with a wide audience and trickle out from the avid audience to the general public, thereby becoming blockbusters. Other films bomb. In between there is a 'demand' curve, which is relatively stable every year.

In Europe, commissioning editors are far less concerned with appealing to the public, and therefore instead of a demand curve, there are 'pockets' of demand – a few local blockbusters, a narrow niche market, and the majority of films with zero box office. The resulting economic deficit is met by the taxpayer, because politicians assert that although nobody wants to see these films they represent high cultural value.

The Majors

*The cinema is nothing other than a new means of printing
and Louis Lumière is a new Gutenberg.*
Jean Renoir

THE INVENTION OF THE GUTENBERG PRESS signalled the end of the feudal era. It broke the monopoly of the Church on information and culture, and provided the basis for the construction of modern nation-states. This process reached its apogee in the nineteenth century with huge colonial empires, designed to disseminate 'national culture' throughout the world.

The electronic age has slowly undermined these national cultures and has created a new 'religion'. The growing multi-media empires are run by Machiavellian Princes who stand at the heart of the new Information Society. The cornerstone of their kingdoms is the movie business, over which the Majors have an increasing stranglehold. The nation-states of tomorrow may well be the seven sisters of the Motion Picture Association of America (MPAA) – Warners, Disney, Paramount, Universal, Columbia, Fox and MGM – whose interests extend from micro-chips to french fries.

The new empires have been made possible with the aid of the US government which has provided generous tax breaks and reversed the Paramount decree and Fin-Syn which prevented the studios from owning theatres and television networks. In 1996 Congress passed a telecommunications bill which will speed up the rate of convergence between the software, computing and telecoms industry.

Hollywood now represents giant 'keiretsu' groups ranging from broadcasting to theme parks. That influence will soon extend to all forms of communication, creating Big-Brother-sized information networks. As Michael Ovitz says, 'entertainment and sports will be the Trojan Horse that brings everything else into the home'. Each Major will offer a cradle-to-grave service, providing the nervous system of the post-modern society.

There are six big players in the business, followed by the 'sick man' MGM. The post-merger revenues of the Big Six are as follows:

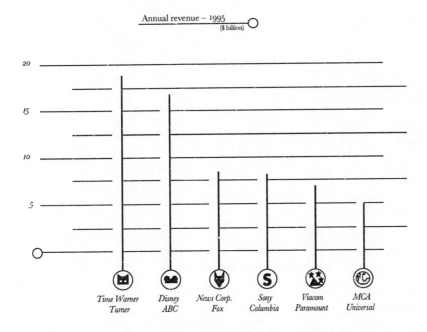

The movies are only a small part of each Major's business. The principal interests of each company cover a variety of different sectors:

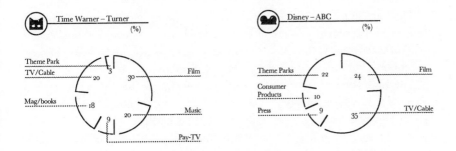

The most powerful players earn under a third of their total revenues from filmed entertainment. Those Majors with a higher dependence on film – MCA, Sony and MGM/UA – are much more vulnerable to fluctuation in global revenue.

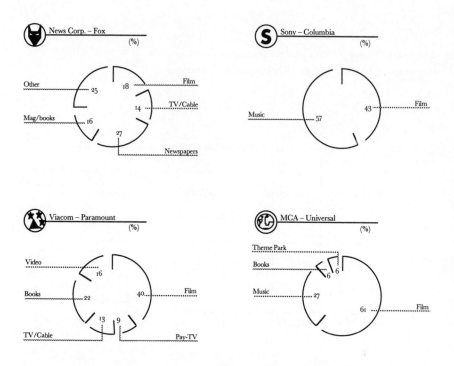

Source: Company Accounts
(Financial data are an average for 1993–95, aggregated for Viacom, TW/Turner and Disney/ABC)

The Majors are the focal point of the world's premium media industries. They have a world share of 80% in film, 70% in television fiction and 50% in music. In the US they also have an 80% share of pay-TV and 40% of books and magazines.

They are also the leading owners of theme parks and look set to control American broadcasting (as a result of the Fox channel, Warner's fifth network and Disney's merger with ABC). At various times the Majors have established joint ventures, but the trend is for separate 'empires'.

The high level of competition amongst the studios means that there is a tendency for average earnings per picture to even out over time. The distributor with the highest average grosses since 1987 has been Disney at $47 million, followed by Paramount at $44 million, but both have moved towards the industry norm in recent years. In the case of Disney this has also been the result of doubling the number of releases.

The weakest player of the Big Six is Sony, which has consistently grossed under $20 million in the US since 1987, with the exception of 1991 and 1992. MGM/UA's performance has been even weaker, but crept up to Sony's level ($18.5 million) in 1995.

The average grosses 1987–95 (adjusted for inflation) have been as follows. (NB: Sony acquired Columbia/TriStar in 1989.)

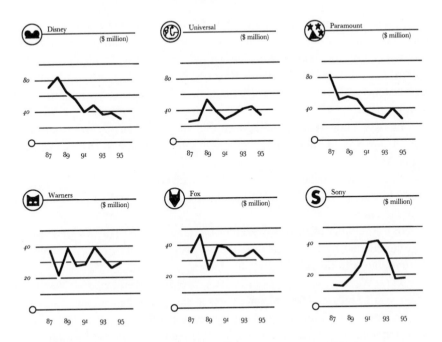

The Majors now seem to be all stabilizing around $34 million average gross per picture, except for Sony and MGM/UA.

The largest number of films come from Disney, Sony and Warners (37, 35 and 29 in 1995). The market shares in 1995 were 19% for Disney, 16.3% for Warners, 12.8% for Sony, 12.5% for Universal, 10% for Paramount, 7.6% for Fox and 6.2% for MGM/UA.

COMPANY PROFILES

Each Major has its own unique operating philosophy which is cultivated by its top management.

TIME WARNER – THE BAT STUDIO

Time Warner has been described as a 'Holy Roman Empire built on fiber optic cable, celluloid and glossy magazines with names like Vibe'.[1] The company is seen as a decentralized confederation of feudal city-states with one part of the empire frequently entering into conflict with another.

The blue-blooded Time acquired Warners for $13 billion in 1990. Visionary chairman Steve Ross died in 1993, and was succeeded by Gerald Levin. Overall,

Time Warner prides itself on stable management, especially in filmed entertainment where Terry Semel and Robert Daly have been running operations since 1980.

Warners is considered a hands-off studio and excellent at marketing its pictures. The company has several deals with European producers (including David Puttnam and Dieter Geissler) and between 1991 and 1993 had a high profile $600 million deal with Arnon Milchan's Regency Productions, Studio Canal+ and Scriba-Dehyle. Milchan continues to be the largest single supplier of films to the Warners slate.

In 1995 Time Warner announced that they were increasing their 19.5% stake in Turner to a full merger. This was in direct response to Disney's acquisition of ABC.

The deal was challenged by the FCC on anti-trust grounds and by telco US West who owns 25% of Time Warner Entertainment (a stake they bought for $2.5 billion in 1993).

In the summer of 1996, US West's objections were overruled and despite a recommendation by FCC staff to reject the deal, the FCC gave the merger its blessings, but with the rider that certain interests be sold off.

Time Warner's total debt burden is now pushed even higher – from $16.4 billion to $18.7 billion. These massive debts already limit the company's freedom of movement and eat into profits. The upside is that the merged company has a massive library, key strategic interests in cable television and considerable scope for rationalization.

DISNEY – THE MOUSE HOUSE

Disney was for many years an outsider, not even belonging to the MPAA. The company was in the doldrums in the early 1980s, and was finally taken over in 1984 by a new management team headed by Michael Eisner, Frank Wells, Jeffrey Katzenberg and Richard Frank.

'Team Disney' applied modern management techniques to revamp Disney. They built new theme parks, established a vast consumer products division, re-released the priceless Disney animated classics in cinema and video sell-through, and produced new animated films and adult live-action pictures.

The company had a 20/20 plan – 20% growth and 20% profit margin which it has broadly maintained since 1984. The $19 billion acquisition of ABC in 1995 establishes the company as the joint leader of the industry with its arch-rival Time Warner.

Disney's steady growth was based on stable management, with a key figure being studio chief Jeffrey Katzenberg, who has now moved to Dreamworks SKG. Katzenberg is a hard worker, known for his saying 'If you're not available to work on Saturday there's no point showing up on Sunday.'

For years, Disney had a reputation as Scrooge McDuck, keeping production budgets 30% lower than most studios and working with a large number of neophyte directors under close supervision from the 'suits'. But in the early 1990s Disney began to mellow out. The draconian cost and editorial controls were relaxed and the company began to court independent talent including a deal with Merchant Ivory and the $60–90 million takeover of leading indie distributor Miramax in 1993.

At the same time, cracks began to appear in Team Disney's walls. Theme park results were stalling on the back of the Euro Disney debacle, average grosses per picture began to fall and management began to leave.

The first to go was head of video, Bill Mechanic, who left for Fox in autumn 1993 and was followed by head of TV, Bob Jacquemin, in January 1994. Disney was then devastated by the tragic death of Frank Wells on 3 April 1994, which propelled further changes. Ricardo Mestres was dismissed from Hollywood Pictures along with half of his twelve-man team in May 1994.

A public feud then broke out between Eisner and Katzenberg which culminated in the latter's resignation in September 1994 and his replacement by Joe Roth. Katzenberg subsequently sued Disney for $250 million which he claimed was due to him as a 2% studio profit share stipulated in his contract. The fourth core member of Team Disney – Richard Frank – resigned in March 1995. These upheavals left serious questions over management succession, made even more serious by Eisner undergoing quadruple heart bypass surgery.

Such doubts were spectacularly silenced by the acquisition of ABC and the appointment of Michael Ovitz as president in August 1995. Eisner was buying the network where he began his career, and said that he made the ABC bid with Ovitz in mind as his new crown prince.

Ovitz duly began extending the Disney empire. One of his first initiatives was to announce the creation of a new advertising agency with Coke. He also set up a three-year licensing deal with toy manufacturer Mattel and a ten-year $2 billion cross-promotional deal with McDonalds. But the promised synergies have not been easy to achieve. ABC staff have complained of over interference from their Disney bosses and network ratings have fallen. It is still to be seen whether 'one plus one equals four'.

NEWS CORPORATION/FOX – INDEPENDENCE DAY

News Corporation is the opposite management model to Time Warner, but is considered by many to be the model media company because of its global reach and its presence in all major publishing areas.

The company has been compared to the classical Roman Empire, led by the vision and iron will of a single Emperor. One Fox executive said of Rupert Murdoch: 'He is like Caesar and his guys are like interchangeable governors. They will gladly go to the farthest reaches of the empire with the knowledge they will be brought back to Rome at some point.'[2] Murdoch tolerates flamboyant individuals while building core businesses but then tends to dispense with them, as shown by the dismissal of Barry Diller in 1992.

Murdoch is the man who breaks the rules. He once said that the only good regulator was a dead regulator, but his success has been built on canny diplomacy with politicians. He is brilliant at spotting an opportunity, from building the Fox network, to launching Star TV in Asia. The latest example was in 1996 when he first inked a digital alliance with Bertelsmann and Canal+, but after they dragged their heels, switched to the Kirch group. Over time, he is expected to own 25% of the European pay and digital TV market.

In 1995 Murdoch sold a 13.5% stake in News Corporation to telco MCI for \$2 billion, thus considerably boosting his cash reserves. He used these funds in 1996 to make the \$2.5 billion acquisition of New World Communications which boosts his production capacity and television station ownership.

Overall, the 'Boss' has a reputation as a right-wing conservative, but the secrets of his success have been to boldly go where no one else dared, his populist eye for a good story and his very tight financial controls.

VIACOM/PARAMOUNT – THE MOUNTAIN

Paramount was the leading Major in the late 1970s, when it included amongst its top management Barry Diller, Michael Eisner, Frank Mancuso, Dawn Steel, Jeffrey Katzenberg and Don Simpson. In 1983 Charles Bluhdorn – of parent company Gulf and Western – died and was replaced by Martin Davis who did not see eye to eye with existing management and led to a mass exodus.

Paramount seemed to lose direction and hit a low point in the early 1990s under the reign of TV supremo Brandon Tartikoff. In early 1994 Paramount merged with Viacom and Blockbuster, bringing Sumner Redstone into the driving seat. Redstone has established a strong personal hold over the group, confirmed by his firing of Viacom chief Frank Biondi in 1996.

Redstone has been reshaping the company to try to trim some of its \$10 billion debt. In 1996 he sold his cable services to TCI for \$2.2 billion and was rumoured to be considering selling the Blockbuster video chain. The conglomerate retains key strategic interests including 2000 screens, nine cable networks and pay-TV channels Showtime and the Movie Channel.

MCA/UNIVERSAL – JURASSIC PARK

Before Seagram's \$5.7 million acquisition of 80% of MCA in June 1995, the company had a reputation for conservative management, as symbolized by its corporate HQ – the Black Tower. Since then, most top management has been replaced, with Lew Wasserman, Sid Sheinberg and Tom Pollock all taking backseat roles, and a new company headquarters being built, which some already call the 'White Tower'.

Seagram's boss, Edgar Bronfman Jr. has appointed top CAA agent Ron Meyer as president, and former Viacom chief Frank Biondi as CEO. Meyer in turn recruited Sandy Climan, formerly head of CAA's ten-person corporate finance team, who advised clients such as Sony, Matsushita and Credit Lyonnais.

Studio management had been rankling under previous bosses Matsushita, who acquired the company in 1990 for $6.1 billion. The Japanese bosses lost money with MCA and also prevented it from making new acquisitions which provoked Wasserman and Sheinberg to threaten resignation in 1994.

The creative powerhouse at the studio is Steven Spielberg, formerly through Amblin Entertainment and now under a pact with Dreamworks SKG (see below). Spielberg's foreign gross alone for the company exceeds $3 billion.

The new Universal is flavoured by its Dreamworks relationship and by the youthful leadership of Bronfman, Meyer and Biondi. Early talent deals have been signed with Sylvester Stallone, Mike Nichols, and Richard Gere.

DREAMWORKS SKG – THE CYBER STUDIO

The 'digital studio of the 21st century' was founded in 1994 by Steven Spielberg, Jeffrey Katzenberg, and David Geffen. They put in $100 million of their own money as equity, raised a $1 billion credit line with Chase Manhattan and sold a third of the company for a total of $900 million to outside investors (including $500 million to Microsoft founder Paul Allen and $300 million to Samsung's Lee Family). Dreamworks is building a new campus-style studio complex at Playa del Rey and already employs 800 people with an annual overhead of $40 million.

The new studio stands at the cutting edge of multi-media synergies, using the latest technologies and capitalizing on Spielberg's and Katzenberg's skills in popular entertainment and animation films.

Spielberg heads the live-action unit, along with key staff from his production company Amblin. They plan to release three films in 1996, five in 1997, seven in 1998 and nine annually from then on. Katzenberg heads the animation unit (which includes a $50 million co-venture with Silicon Graphics) and will release a Christmas feature annually from 1998. Geffen heads the music arm which aims to set up an indie label and distribute through MCA (who acquired Geffen records in 1990 for $545 million). The TV arm, headed by former Disney TV chief Bob Jacquemin, aims to produce five primetime series by the year 2002.

By 1998 the venture plans to spend $800 million in film production, $200 million in animation, $125 million in TV production and syndication and $20 million on the record label.

Dreamworks will co-ordinate its own US theatrical distribution and MCA/Universal will handle international theatrical sales, worldwide video and music, ancillary rights and theme park franchises. US pay-TV is with Time Warner's HBO, TV programming with Disney's ABC (a $200 million joint venture) and interactive entertainment with Microsoft.

The main weakness of the start-up studio is the absence of a film library and diversified distribution activities. They aim to be theatrical distributors which is the most risky part of the business. The talent behind the venture is nonetheless impeccable and there are important franchises such as *Jurassic Park, Casper,* and *The Flintstones* to build upon. The team has to prove that they can overcome the many 'barriers of entry' within the business and establish themselves as a fully fledged Major.

SONY (COLUMBIA/TRISTAR) – LAST ACTION HERO

Sony acquired Columbia and TriStar in 1989 and despite a $2.7 billion loss in 1994 have reaffirmed their commitment to the business, albeit with a massive shake-up in management.

The parent company, Columbia Pictures, has a turbulent history. The troubles began with a cheque forgery scandal in 1978 involving Columbia chief David Begelman, which led to his resignation. The company suffered disappointing results in the late 1970s and was sold to Coca-Cola in 1982 but continued to underperform.

This led to the appointment of David Puttnam in 1986, who promised to give Coca-Cola 'a studio it could be proud of'. Puttnam switched the emphasis of Columbia to smaller, more 'worthy' pictures and was accused of ignoring 'franchises' such as *Ghostbusters*. He also suffered the debacle of Bill Cosby's *Leonard Part 6*.

The slate of films greenlighted by Puttnam had disastrous returns, with an average US box office of $7 million. Coca-Cola were disillusioned by the experience and sold the company to Sony in 1989 for $3.4 billion. Sony also assumed debts of $1.5 billion and paid an additional $700 million in compensation to get Jon Peters and Peter Guber to head the studio. (Sony had earlier paid $2 billion in 1987 to acquire CBS Records.)

Early results were poor and Jon Peters resigned in 1991. By far the best years were 1991 and 1992, followed by a slump. The studio emphasized that it was about 'quality' movies and the cutting edge, but some claimed that a negative atmosphere prevailed. According to one producer, 'It's obvious to me now that the problem is the culture. It's not positive enough . . . But the movies are good, and the deals are good.' Others criticized the CEO, one source saying 'Guber brilliantly exploited the Japanese. He took their concept of loyalty and management and turned it into loyalty without accountability.'

The year 1993 was of crucial importance. Sony produced the expensive flop of the *Last Action Hero*, and in November the legendary Sony chief Akio Morita suffered a major stroke. Morita resigned a year later and Sony announced that it was writing off $2.7 billion against the studios – 47% of its book value. This resulted in a major shake-up of staff including the exit of SPE group president Jonathan Dolgen, CEO Peter Guber and TriStar chief Mike Medavoy. In 1995 Sony US president, Michael Schulhof, was dismissed.

New SPE chief is Jeff Sagansky, who had been chairman of TriStar pictures in the late 1980s. He inherits a studio where average US grosses per film are predicted to slip to $13 million for 1996. As a result, Sagansky has introduced massive restructuring, including the dismissal of studio chiefs Alan Levine and Mark Canton, along with the production heads at TriStar and Columbia and the president of worldwide marketing. Sagansky and new chariman John Calley, recruited from UA, will now try to rebuild the studios.

MGM/UA – HEAVEN'S GATE

MGM, which once boasted 'more stars than the heavens', seemed to lose its way in the 1960s, and in 1967 was acquired by Edgar Bronfman Sr. of Seagram. The studio exited distribution in 1973, and agreed to release pictures through United Artists. Las Vegas high roller Kirk Kerkorian began buying stock, securing a majority stake by 1977, and Kerkorian subsequently acquired UA from Transamerica in 1981 for $380 million.

During the 1980s, the studio seemed to be permanently up for sale. In 1985 Kerkorian sold Disney the worldwide rights to the MGM name and logo in connection with theme parks and then sold the entire company in 1986 to Ted Turner for $1.45 billion. Turner stripped out the 3600-title MGM library and then sold the MGM lot and lab to Lorimar for $190 million, and the rest of the company back to Kerkorian in 1987 for $0.3 billion.

In 1988 a 25% stake was sold to Guber-Peters and MGM went through a $400 million restructuring. Kerkorian then bought back the shares and in April 1989 sold the studio again, this time for $1 billion to Australian Group Quintex but the deal fell through after the latter's bankruptcy.

In November 1990 MGM was sold once more, for $1.3 billion plus $600 million in assumed debts to Giancarlo Parretti's Pathé Communications backed by fellow Italian, Florio Fiorini. Thus began MGM's blackest era, chronicled in a 1993 book by French conservative MP François d'Aubert, *Dirty Money*.

D'Aubert hints that Parretti and Fiorini had links with the Mafia and money-laundering, commenting that 'Their mysterious financial network is in the process of crumbling like a house of cards. It raises doubts, questions and suspicions.' Aubert laid many of these suspicions at the door of French state-owned bank Credit Lyonnais and thereby the Socialist government. The sacked head of the bank, Jean-Yves Haberer claimed that many of the suspect loans were the result of direct political pressure from ministers under the pretext that certain strategic sectors had to be supported regardless of the cost.

Giancarlo Parretti began his career as a waiter in Orvieto and made his way up to become the owner of hotels, newspapers and a football team. He had close links with Italian businessman Florio Fiorini who according to d'Aubert 'was pulling the strings'.

Parretti was introduced to Credit Lyonnais in 1987 by Cannon Films (at the time run by Menahem Golan and Yoram Globus). Credit Lyonnais started to bankroll Parretti's Pathé empire which quickly extended to Cannon and their extensive European theatre chain.

In his short rein, Parretti was considered to barter away what was left of the studio's future and in six months spent $150 million in 'unrecorded disbursements', while MGM was unable to pay its bills and labs refused to release the negatives for key releases.

Credit Lyonnais removed the Parretti team from MGM after a prolonged court case in Delaware in 1991, which accused Parretti of 'gross neglect, gross inefficiency' and entering into 'improper-related party transactions'.

On the first day of hearings, Parretti called bank chief Gille a liar and said that CL were involved in fraudulent activities. These echoed claims by Kirk Kerkorian, who sued CL for 'fraud, racketeering and conspiracy' to counteract a class-action lawsuit accusing him of leaving MGM in a debt-ridden shambles.

Parretti was indicted in the US in 1991 for perjury and tampering with documents but fled the country for Italy, where he had already been convicted of fraudulent bankruptcy. In 1992 Florio Fiorini was arrested in Switzerland on fraud charges after the bankruptcy of Geneva-based Sasea to which Credit Lyonnais had lent $1.5 billion. The company's total liabilities were $3.4 billion.

From jail, Fiorini began to make a series of devastating revelations about corruption scandals in Italy including illegal party financing to the tune of over $1 billion by state petroleum company Eni, of which he was CFO, and $7 million of illegal kickbacks to the Socialist Party channelled via the Vatican bank Banco Ambrosiano shortly before Robert Calvi's mysterious death.

In the meantime Credit Lyonnais bought control of MGM in 1992 and now owned 98.5%. MGM then borrowed a further $489 million above its credit line of $395 million. On an annual turnover of $1 billion the studio lost $100 million in 1990/1, $350 million in 1991/2 and $270 million in 1992/3.

In 1993 Credit Lyonnais hired Creative Artists Agency to oversee its $3.1 billion entertainment portfolio and gave MGM a new $190 million credit line to fund new production. Alan Ladd Jr. was replaced by Frank Mancuso in July 1993, and John Calley and Mike Marcus (from CAA) were appointed to run separate studio operations. Results began to improve with successes such as *James Bond: Goldeneye* and *Get Shorty* and in October 1995, Guy-Etienne Dufour put MGM/UA up for sale.

The principal attraction of the studio was its library, and the final short list included News Corp., PolyGram, and Morgan Creek. But in keeping with the

MGM saga, the company was sold back to Kirk Kerkorian who had settled his lawsuit with CL in 1995 by paying $125 million and emerged as the last-minute backer of the management group led by Frank Mancuso. The total deal was worth $1.3 billion with Kerkorian agreeing to put up $650 million in equity, Australia's Seven Network $250 million and the management group $400 million with an additional $400 million in loans.

The main challenges for the company will be to survive alongside its larger rivals and to halt the constant losses that have haunted the studio in recent years.

HOW THE MAJORS DO BUSINESS

A Major is a giant software publishing house with most revenues earned in distribution and retail. The Majors cover several media areas, each fed by labels run by separate commissioning editors. Product is supplied by in-house talent locked into first-look deals, and independents who retain some rights.

The new Napoleons who run the Majors now have a sphere of influence far wider than that of the movie moguls of old, but they are nonetheless constrained by the fact that their companies are public corporations and they must answer to their shareholders. This requires a high level of professional management, particularly in filmed entertainment because of the high risks and modest profits.

The main attraction of the movie business is that it has a high growth rate and offers market muscle and synergies with other media. The Majors have been growing at a real annual compound growth of 9% since 1980.

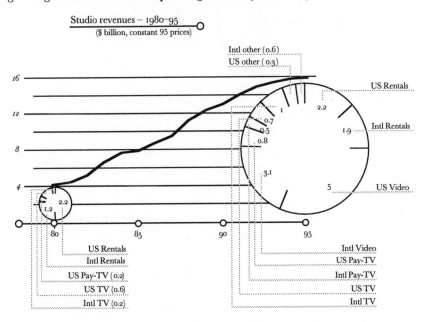

Studio revenues – 1980–95
($ billion, constant 95 prices)

The biggest growth area in the 1980s was video, but has now shifted to the overseas market. Tom Pollock recently emphasized: 'The international market-place represents about six billion people. That's where growth is going to be. In this country, we're just stealing markets from each other.'

The healthy growth rates for film have caused a high level of competition. As a result, film profit margins (operating income divided by sales) at the Majors have been progressively pushed down, from an average of 15% in the 1970s, 10% in the early 1980s to around 5–6% in the late 1980s.

In the early 1990s the profit squeeze forced most independents out of the business, which allowed the Majors to recover profitability to around 7–8%. Profit margins nonetheless remain lower in film than in comparatively low risk mass media areas such as television and the press.

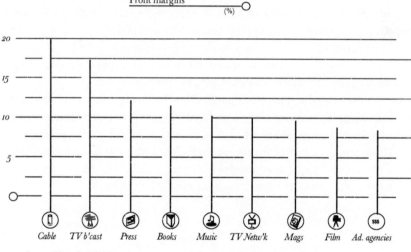

Profit margins (%)

| | Cable | TV b'cast | Press | Books | Music | TV Netw'k | Mags | Film | Ad. agencies |

Source: Veronis & Suhler, 1992

Disney, Fox and MCA have enjoyed profit levels of around 10% in recent years. Time Warner and Viacom have scored close to zero profits because of 'goodwill' write-offs and servicing charges on their high debt mountains, and Sony has incurred losses because of poor average returns and appreciation of the yen. In cash flow terms, the companies are much healthier. For example, Time Warner's cash flow was $3.3 billion in 1995 but the company recorded a $218 million loss.

The high-cost/low-return equation for film means that much of the Majors' business is to do with risk management. Like other areas of American business, the Majors are now run in an MBA technocratic management style which tries to transform the art of making movies into a science. This has tended to result in a climate of fear, creative sclerosis, and what Jeffrey Katzenberg has described as an 'invisible wall between power and talent'.

The movies produced by the studios sometimes seem to be very formula driven, and audience surveys have suggested a frustration with the new movie diet.

'I think the business is in a state of crisis for a lot of reasons' says one studio distribution exec, 'I don't see a lot of hot young talent coming up, and I see too much biz and not enough show. It's become very assembly line.' This is confirmed by Peter Bart of *Variety*: 'The present studio bureaucracies, with their fervid phalanxes of development executives and script-note providers are not coming up with the answers.'[3]

One of the problems is the lack of a new talent wave. The New Hollywood was built on the crest of the American New Wave – propelled by movie brats such as Spielberg, Coppola and Scorsese. In today's Generation X era, there has been nothing like the same explosion of talent. It seems that the present generation has neither a voice, nor anything to say.

Hollywood will survive only if it is brave enough to spot new talent and back projects which capture public opinion. In many cases this has been the motivation of buying up indies such as Miramax, because these often seem to be at the cutting edge. Cross-over hits such as *The Crying Game, Four Weddings* and *Pulp Fiction* demonstrate that the audience is eager to support fresh perspectives.

The migration of the top talent agents such as Michael Ovitz, Ron Meyer and Mike Marcus to the studios may make them more 'talent friendly'. But the need to protect the bottom line will mean that risk management will continue to be a key preoccupation in Hollywood.

The tools of risk management are the same as those of any other multinational business. They include:

- Barriers to entry
- Diversification
- Vertical integration
- Portfolio strategy
- Quality control
- Research and development
- Proven talent
- Cost control
- Marketing
- External suppliers
- Off-balance-sheet financing
- Cross-collateralization

BARRIERS TO ENTRY

The film business is often presented as a high risk casino-style environment in which 'nobody knows anything'. This has led some to compare the business to oil exploration.

In fact the risks are far more manageable than they first seem. The most important aspect of the business is that there has been a consistent and faithful level of demand over the last thirty years.

The most important part of the business is 'theatrical' – release in the movie theatres – because box office success will determine revenues in all other media. As a consequence the Majors will typically make a loss in theatrical in order to reap profits in other media.

The theatrical market has the steepest 'demand curve' of all media because of its high price. The Majors release around 150 films a year and dominate the 'demand curve' for films. The 1995 US box office per film was as follows:

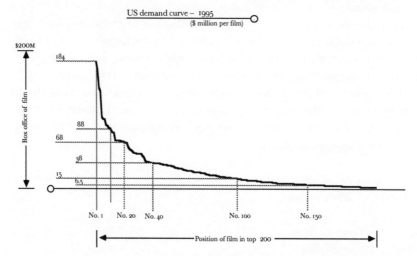

US demand curve – 1995 ($ million per film)

This 'demand curve' has remained fairly stable since the 1960s. Under ten films gross over $100 million, another ten films gross over $50 million and a further forty gross over $20 million. The last fifty films (a third of the total) have meagre grosses.

In the pre-television era, the Majors used to release over 300 films a year – averaging almost one a day. This high level of production was necessary because of high attendances and the common practice of double-bills. Production levels were cut back in the early 1970s as the Old Hollywood suffered a severe financial crisis and the New Hollywood emerged. The Majors released 277 films in 1970, but only 157 in 1975. The number of releases fell to around 130 a year during the 1980s but has now risen back to 150–160.

The dominance of the theatrical market by the Majors means that although certain studios will do better than others, there is a surprising level of stability in the business overall. In order to protect this stability each Major tries to secure its own position and prevent competition from outsiders. This is made possible because of the formidable barriers of entry into the business – including high overhead, and the importance of a library and a wide production slate.

High overhead

The Major distributors have huge overhead costs, which reflect massive staff and in-house facilities. The absolute minimum annual overhead costs for a US distributor is $100 million, but is typically much higher. In 1992, the average cost structure for a Major distributor was 36% for negative costs, 8% for video duplication, 30% for overhead and 17% for prints and advertising. This left 9% for profit. Hidden within these figures is the R&D level, i.e. development spending on scripts, which is between $300–500 million for the Big Six Majors combined.

The total number of permanent employees within the film divisions of the Majors is around 15,000–20,000. This is the backbone of the 'industry', including all those responsible for administration, development and distribution. Alongside this in-house staff is the total freelance labour force available for work in film and television, whose size is around 150,000 in the US.

Despite this high employment level, there is an extremely steep pay pyramid, with Hollywood's top 200 earning over a third of all salaries. In contrast, the average wage rate for film and TV overall was only $34,268 in 1993 which was well below other sectors such as mining, aerospace, finance, computers, transportation and engineering.

Libraries

The growing number of channels, or 'windows', through which films can be exploited, make it increasingly important to have a strong library, and keep it replenished with attractive new films.

The Majors' film libraries give them huge leverage power in the market and also a constant source of income which can be used to balance out the annual income stream from film production.

The value of the Majors' film libraries has been expanding rapidly with the growth of television channels and new media. An indication of this rise is the Majors' film inventory (including library titles and current releases) which increased in value from $840 million in 1973 to $5 billion in 1988.4

David Morrell of KPMG, who has been responsible for the revaluation of a significant number of libraries, estimates that after adjustment for residuals and inflation, film libraries have increased in value 15 to 20 times since 1980 and television libraries 30 to 50 times. In 1993 alone, libraries were adjusted upward by 70%.

The main US film libraries are approximately as follows:

Time Warner/Turner

Warner	3200
Turner (MGM pre-1986, Warner pre-1950, RKO pre-1948)	3522
New Line (RHI/Hal Roach and Nelson)	1600

Viacom/Paramount

Paramount	908
Viacom	500
Republic	1000

Other Majors

MCA (Universal, Paramount pre-1948)	3101
Sony	2327
Fox	2077
Disney	348
Miramax	200
MGM/UA	1523

Independents

Metromedia (Orion, AIP, MCEG, Goldywn)	2400
Credit Lyonnais	900
PolyGram	500

Source: *TBI*, Vogel, *Variety*, Annual Reports

The annual income from libraries is considerable. The 1500 MGM/UA library is estimated to earn $70–80 million in annual revenues. On this basis the combined annual library earnings for the Majors is probably well in excess of $1 billion worldwide.

The value of film libraries has not always been recognized. In 1958 Lew Wasserman of MCA paid $10 million for the ownership of Paramount's pre-1948 library. A week later the value of TV sales from the same library was $30 million. A similar piece of deft footwork was Ted Turner's stripping out of the MGM library in 1986 for $1 billion.

It is difficult to get a true value for film libraries, but company accounts give an indication. In Turner Broadcasting's accounts the value of non-current film assets in 1992 were $1.2 billion. Warners have a figure for 'library less amortization' in 1992 of $0.9 billion. 20th Century Fox has a value for 'non-current film costs net of amortization' in 1992 of $0.8 billion and Orion's 'film inventories' in 1993 were $0.5 billion.

The total accounted value of the Majors' 16,000+ titles is probably $6–8 billion. This is by far the most important component of most film companies' assets. The value of Hollywood's libraries is higher than the total production and promotion cost of the annual film slate and provides a very bankable asset upon which the Majors can obtain finance.

Wide production slate

A Major distributor needs ten to twenty films a year, ideally backed by an extensive library. Each film requires an average production and advertising investment of over $50 million. This means that a company must have annual resources well in excess of $500 million to even begin competing.

In order to negotiate attractive terms with retail arms, a distributor must be committed to at least five years in the business. The combined effect of overhead, library and production costs means that a company must have annual resources of around $1 billion and a five-year plan involving close to $5 billion. These high stakes explain why the Majors' position is virtually impregnable and that the only way into the business is to acquire a Major.

DIVERSIFICATION

The high risk/low reward equation of the movies means that it is very difficult to establish a viable studio based on cinema alone. The intelligent strategy for a Major is to establish other more stable sources of income which can offset annual variations in film – a classic example being Disney.

The true value of the film business is not the profits generated by the films, but the synergies that movies provide with other areas. These include television production, theme parks, consumer products, soundtracks, books, videogames and interactive entertainment. All of these areas have lower costs, lower risks and higher returns. Feature films provide the key to this magic kingdom.

VERTICAL INTEGRATION

Following the same logic, a Major can stabilize its cash flow and control costs by controlling each section of the value chain. The heart of the Majors' business is software – the production of feature films – but the bulk of profits are earned further down the value chain, in distribution and retail.

Hollywood's founding fathers began in retail – cinema exhibition – and diversified into production in order to combat the Edison Trust and to secure more popular films. Exhibition had always been the cash cow of the film business, but in 1948 the studios were forced to sell their theatres and concentrate on production and distribution. The federal government also provided incentives to start television production by preventing the networks from supplying most of their shows.

The result has been huge film and television publishing houses, whose motto is 'content is king'. In the 1980s, ownership restrictions over retail outlets were relaxed and the Majors have consolidated their control over the value chain – from theatres, to video stores, to pay-TV, the networks and cable.

PORTFOLIO STRATEGY

The Majors share a relatively 'captive audience' between them, but the performance of each individual Major will depend on where they score down the 'demand' curve.

In order to protect themselves, the Majors produce a wide portfolio of films including in-house labels, different budget levels and sequels.

Labels

Film is increasingly resembling the music industry, where the Big Six Music Majors (Warners, Sony, MCA, PolyGram, Bertelsmann and EMI) control the business, but each has several labels feeding into their network.

Labels at the studios include separate commissioning divisions and also in-house and independent production entities which stamp their 'label' on product. For example, at Disney there is Touchstone, Walt Disney and Miramax; and at Fox – 20th Century Fox, Fox Family, Fox 2000 and Fox Searchlight.

Different budget levels

Even within a distinct label, production is split over a range of different genres and budgets. For example, in 1990 the MPAA's 155 releases were divided as follows according to budget:

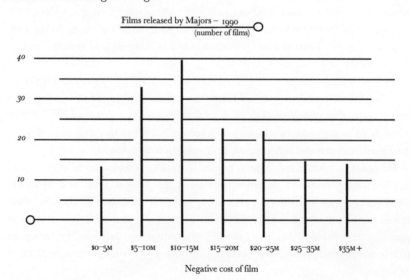

Films released by Majors – 1990
(number of films)

Negative cost of film

Source: MPAA

Locomotives

Each studio will produce one or two 'mega budget' pictures, aimed to guarantee a place in the Top Ten (or ideally Top Five) pictures of the year. These films are usually loss leaders, but are important because it is the top hits which act as 'locomotives' for the rest of the slate.

There have always been blockbusters – such as *Gone With the Wind* – but locomotives have become increasingly important as distribution has become a volume business. The Major sells 'packages' of ten to twenty films to television buyers, whose value depends on the lead titles.

The add-on benefits of locomotives mean that the Majors will often be willing to sink large sums of money and offer generous profit shares on these films.

Sequels

It is extremely difficult to predict the box office success of a new film, but much easier for a sequel. Studios will always be interested in exploiting a hit film through a series of sequels, although obviously not all films are appropriate for such treatment.

Sequels are usually dependent on a lead character who can be followed through a series of adventures. This character thereby becomes a 'franchise' which can be exploited for future films, and also for television series, consumer products and theme parks.

Every studio is interested in discovering franchises because they offer huge synergistic revenues and also help minimize risk in the production slate. Classic franchises include Batman, Ghostbusters, Freddy, Jason and Aliens.

QUALITY CONTROL

The Majors live or die according to the ability of their studio chiefs to commission and nurture winning films, and it has been their consistent capacity to produce 'A' titles which has enabled them to beat off competition from Independents.

In the early years of video there seemed to be a new market for 'B' movies in the action, violence, soft porn genre. However, once the Majors recognized the enormous potential of this new market they dominated the market with their 'A' titles. Today each 'window' – whether theatrical, video, pay-TV or free TV – is dominated by 'A' titles.

The heart of the business is the small number of individuals whose editorial judgement is trusted – basically the studio heads and top agents. Within each Major, there is a chain of decision leading up to the critical step of the 'green light'.

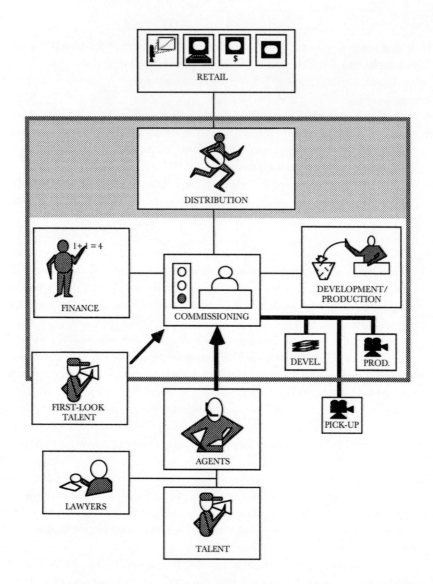

Hollywood was built by moguls who exerted a very high level of editorial control over production. The classic example was Irving Thalberg, who centralized production. Even decentralizers such as David O. Selznick exerted a high level of editorial input. More than distribution, or star power, it is this 'editorial expertise' which is the 'genius of the system'.

In today's Hollywood, the most successful Majors have been those with stable management and strong editorial skills. Classic examples are Terry Semel and Robert Daly at Warners, and until recently Jeffrey Katzenberg at Disney.

RESEARCH AND DEVELOPMENT

Every industry is dependent on R&D and Hollywood is no exception. The Majors spend around $300–500 million per year on script development and acquisition of literary rights, equivalent to about 10% of annual production expenditure.

Development departments are the 'eyes and ears' of the studio bosses. They include a hierarchy of script readers and development executives, and movies will rarely be put into production before being subjected to a series of rewrites and development committees. One studio executive commented, 'If a script isn't sent through the wringer at least 15 or 20 times, it's not worth the pages it's scribbled on.'

It is this development approach which is the source of Hollywood's strength and weakness. On the positive side, it leads to great discipline in scriptwriting. UK writer David Pirie says, 'I feel a chill of fear when I watch American films, thinking how much has gone into the script. When the ending works you know that it has probably been done 70 times.' On the negative side, development committees can easily lead to clichéd 'formula movies' and require a very strong director to protect his vision. One production chief recently admitted, 'With all the layers that exist at studios today, the pictures have become like the people – homogenized.' Peter Bart added: 'Think back for a moment to those regimes that produced the most hits and biggest profits. All appear to have these common denominators. They had very small staffs and uniquely unbureaucratic operating styles. By contrast present-day studios, stymied by creative gridlock, employ layers of as many as 60 development and production executives, but often fail at their primary task, turning out a flow of viable product.'[5]

Over half of Hollywood films are based on original scripts, which represent the greatest creative risk. The rest are adaptations of books and stage plays, remakes and sequels, which provide the security of prior success and notoriety.

The average film development deal per script is between $300,000 and $400,000 with top writers earning over $1 million. The ratio of developed projects to films is considered to be around 10 to 1, which means that the majority of scripts spend their lives in development hell. A studio buys an option on material for a specified length of time, after which it is put into 'turnaround', meaning that it may be acquired by a third party. It is not uncommon for a script to take many years before it sees the light of day. *Platoon* (1986) took ten years to get to the screen, *Carrington* (1995) took twenty.

PROVEN TALENT

Louis B. Mayer used to say that what distinguished the film business was that its major assets go home every night. Films are sold on the basis of their stars, who have a 'marquee value' in opening a film. As a consequence talent agents can command huge fees for their name actors.

Certain directors also have a marquee value, as well as serving as magnets for attracting the best actors and crew.

The studios try to protect themselves as much as possible by securing tried and tested talent. In the golden age of the studios, leading talent was under contract to the studios, and actors were obliged to follow the studio's wishes under threat of suspension and extension of their contract. Today the studios try to lock in talent by 'first-look' deals, by which they put up overhead and development spending in return for first right of refusal.

This makes it very difficult for outside players to break into the business. In the 1980s, independent producers could claim that stars were attached to a project on a 'credits not contractual' basis, but today agents demand a 'pay or play' deal, which means that if the film isn't made the talent still gets paid. This operates in favour of the Majors with their deep pockets, and represents a further barrier to entry.

EXTERNAL SUPPLIERS

The Majors are known as 'studios' but in fact the heart of their business is publishing and distribution. It is therefore very attractive to offload some of their production cost, particularly for high budget 'loss leaders'. Only half of the films released are produced in-house, the rest are acquired from third parties and are known as 'negative pick-ups'.

Pick-ups enable the studios to lower their cash outlay and access favourable union deals. The disadvantage is that they may force the studio to cede valuable rights. Pick-ups can be of three kinds – US rights, foreign rights or world rights. A split rights deal is more attractive to producers since it provides leverage, that can be used to acquire a share of the film's equity.

The studios are attracted to split rights deals when their cash reserves are low. For example, Fox was very much in favour of securing only US rights in 1993 and 1994, but announced in 1995 that they wanted to buy world rights.

Historically Hollywood has always been strapped for cash and is likely to continue to be interested in joint ventures with third parties. Half of the Majors' films are supplied by 'independents' but most of these companies are in fact satellites of the studios. They offer a 'loop hole' because independents are able to negotiate lower union wages under an agreement known as Article 20 (22 films in 1993) and also to produce non-union productions (37 in 1993).

COST CONTROL

One of the main causes of concern for Hollywood in recent years has been cost control. In the early 1990s there were industry memos by Jeffrey Katzenberg, Peter Dekom and Peter Hoffman predicting future crisis. Ironically one of the early movers in this campaign was David Puttnam who targeted high talent salaries and thereby became immediately unpopular.

Budgets have been spiralling in recent years, as a result of booming global revenues, but as revenue growth begins to tail off, it becomes increasingly important to control budgets. The fact that key agents have now moved into the studios should help such cost containment.

High budgets are not in themselves unhealthy for Hollywood. They actually represent an additional 'barrier to entry' and secure Hollywood's place in the world film market. MPAA budgets and advertising costs have grown spectacularly in recent years, in line with revenue growth:

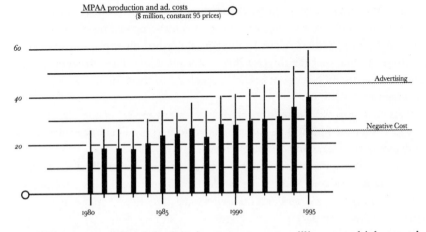

MPAA production and ad. costs
($ million, constant 95 prices)

Advertising
Negative Cost

1980   1985   1990   1995

The average MPAA budget in 1995 was $39 million, to which must be added $20 million in US advertising and $9–11 million for foreign advertising. The total is therefore around $70 million. But this 'official' figure slightly inflates the true figure because it excludes 'pick-ups'.

Most pick-ups involve cheap union deals and have a lower average budget. For instance, in 1989 the average in-house production budget was $23.5 million whereas the average pick-up budget was $8.4 million (often this only includes the value of US rights), bringing the average cost of all releases down to $15 million.

MARKETING

Although film development and production continues to have an artisan flavour, marketing and distribution are fully industrialized processes with comparable techniques to that of any other consumer product – from Coca-Cola to Compact Discs.

A film begins as a 'prototype' – comparable to the draft version of a book, or the blueprint for a new car – but during release, it becomes a 'product'. It will be duplicated into thousands of film prints and millions of video copies and will be transmitted into more than a billion homes.

The Majors' distribution arms do everything in their powers to guarantee the most effective release of their films. The Majors are aware that if they left film promotion to film critics, many of their most popular films would be killed at birth. They therefore spend millions in film advertising and only really pay attention to the critics for certain 'quality' films which need a strong write-up.

Market research

In order to maximize the effectiveness of any film release, the film will be tested with the public in order to gauge its audience appeal, and advertising campaigns will be tested for their awareness and effectiveness.

As a consequence of film previews, films will often be re-edited and in rare instances the ending may even be changed (most famously with *Fatal Attraction*). The right to 'final cut' will depend on the director's negotiating clout. The studios aim to nurture their relationship with established directors and will rarely impose an ending that the director does not want. Many directors actually find previews very useful because it brings them closer to the audience and can help them mature in their art.

Preview tests will be used to predict the 'want to see' of the film and the likelihood that the film will be recommended to friends. This will contribute to the design of the marketing campaign, which in turn will be tested.

As the film approaches release, extensive opinion polls will be designed to test the 'awareness' and 'want to see' of the film. These are a fairly accurate test of a film's likely success and can be used to fine tune the ad spend in order to achieve maximum impact.

Blitzkrieg marketing

In the pre-television era, films were slowly rolled out from city to city over a period of months. In today's advertising-soaked world it is much more cost effective for most films to make a massive nationwide release backed by saturation advertising.

A pioneer of blitzkrieg marketing was Joe Levine who released the Italian film *Hercules* in 1959 on 600 screens. At the time everybody thought he was crazy, but he grossed $20 million (equivalent to over $100 million at today's prices). The Majors embraced these techniques only two decades later, with the 460-theatre opening of *Jaws* in 1976.

The number of 800+ screen releases was 121 in 1993, 130 in 1994 and rose to 153 in 1995. These films now earn over 95% of all theatrical revenues. Wide release patterns are an additional 'barrier to entry' and make the film market very ruthless. A blockbuster will be allowed to stay on the screens for eight to ten weeks, but a low performer will be removed almost immediately.

The wide release pattern separates the Majors from the niche players. It is extremely rare for a narrow release to 'cross over' into the mainstream, but has been achieved recently by Miramax with *The Crying Game* and Gramercy with *Four Weddings*.

A famous saying in Hollywood is that if it sells in Peoria it will sell everywhere. The movie colony was built by European immigrants who from the very beginning tried to sell their films as widely as possible. Once films have been produced and packaged for the United States it is easy to export them abroad.

Foreign sales can often cushion failure in domestic markets, and represent almost half of a film's revenue stream. All films are dependent on foreign sales in order to recoup.

The main foreign markets are Europe (59%), the Far East/Australasia (30%) and Latin America (9%). The key territories are the Big Five European countries plus Japan.

Foreign theatrical revenue by territory is as follows (based on 1992 data):

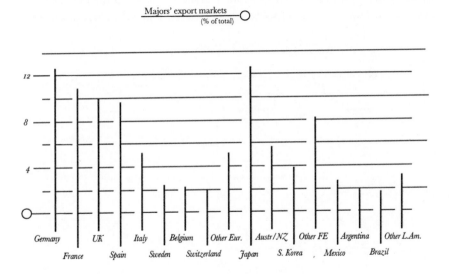

Majors' export markets (% of total)

OFF-BALANCE-SHEET FINANCING

The Majors preside over the circulation of billions of dollars of costs and revenues worldwide every year. They try to organize this flow in the most tax effective way. They take advantage of tax breaks, tax havens and favourable double taxation treaties. In this way, millions of dollars can be saved and used for other areas of expenditure. This is known as 'off-balance-sheet' financing.

Leading experts are John Heyman who is believed to have raised $2.4 billion in off-balance-sheet funding for the Majors, and Lewis Korman who raised over $300 million for Columbia Pictures in the 1980s before setting up Savoy.

Independents use the same techniques of 'financial wizardry' and they are explained in detail in Appendix A.

CROSS-COLLATERALIZATION

Perhaps the most notorious aspect of studio business is that 'net profits' are rarely paid out, despite blockbuster films. This has led to accusations of 'creative accounting'. In fact it is the ability of the studios to retain revenues in-house which is the key to their viability. Otherwise they would pay out on the 'winners' and have to soak up the losses of the 'losers'. In this respect the business is like gambling, where the bookie takes the bulk of the takings.

In order to understand how a studio allocates revenues between films and thereby 'cross-collateralizes' winners and losers, it is necessary to have a detailed understanding of studio accounting.

A film is sold across a series of different media, each with a different price and with a separate time 'window'. This is comparable to the book business where many books are first released at a higher price in hardback and subsequently at a lower price in softback. A typical film revenue stream is as follows:

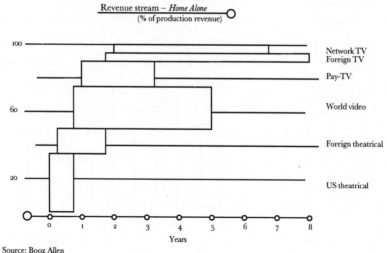

Revenue stream – *Home Alone*
(% of production revenue)

Source: Booz Allen

A film will be licensed across all media for a period of five to eight years. Nearly 100% of all revenues for the film will be sourced in the first four years, and from an accounting point of view, the film's cost will be written off (amortized) against this revenue. After the initial licence period the film becomes part of the Major's film library.

Production revenue

The film's revenue will be allocated across the Major's corporate structure, including retail, distribution and production activities. Net profits concern the small amount of revenues which trickle through to the production account. Each corporate filter between the consumer and the end producer will take a cut of revenues.

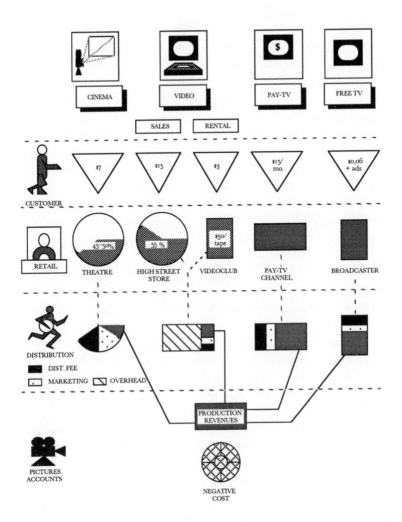

There are also additional ancillary earnings in music, consumer products and theme parks, but these are rarely allocated to the production revenue of a film.

Each revenue chain has its own types of deal (for full details see Appendix C). In theatrical release, the exhibitor keeps an average of 55% of the box office, and the rest is returned to the distributor as 'rentals'.

In the case of video, there are two systems – renting and sell-through. In the former, the distributor makes a single one-off sale to video stores at an elevated wholesale price. In sell-through, cassettes are sold in retail stores and the retailer retains around 45% of revenues.

For free television, films are normally sold in packages of 10 to 20 films and for pay-TV, the Majors are able to negotiate sliding scale deals, whereby a film with a high box office will earn a premium.

From these revenues the distributor will then make certain deductions. The first deduction is the distributor fee which is normally 30% for the US, 35% for the UK and 40% for the rest of the world. The distributor will then recoup all release costs (P&A) and a 10% charge for overhead. There is also a crucial additional deduction for video, whereby only 20% of revenues are considered for production revenue.

The high level of distributor deductions means that only one in ten films break even on production revenues. Very few films therefore earn net profits, but a much higher number make a profit for the distributor. The typical breakdown of production revenues by source is 60% from theatrical, 20% from video and 20% from TV. This is despite the fact that over 50% of the distributor's revenue actually comes from video.

Negative cost

Total production revenues are matched against the production investment or 'minimum guarantee' that the distributor has put into the picture. If the distributor put up the entire budget, this investment is called the 'negative cost' of the film.

The negative cost is 66% higher than the production budget – it is the total of all the various costs, charges and expenses incurred in producing the negative master of the motion picture. This is one reason why Hollywood budgets seem so high. Additional costs are overhead, interest, residuals, deferrals and talent gross participations. (See Appendix C.)

These additional costs will dramatically increase the cost of each picture. For example, a recent 15-picture slate of one Major had an average production budget of $23 million, but an additional $16 million in extra costs pushed the full negative cost to $39 million, broken down as follows:

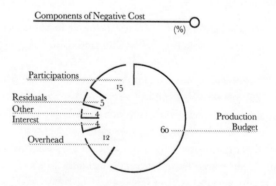

Components of Negative Cost (%)

Participations 15
Residuals 5
Other 4
Interest 4
Overhead 12
Production Budget 60

Source: US Major internal budget

Net profits

The surplus of production revenue over negative cost is known as 'net profits'. Net profits are designed to give producers and talent the impression that they will participate in the film's success. They are especially important for independent production, where financiers put up an equity stake in the picture.

One of the first net profit deals was between Mae West and Universal in 1939 under which she would receive 25% of the net profits from *My Little Chickadee*. In 1984, four years after West's death, it was discovered that Universal had not paid a cent. The studio was sued for $1 million and tried to defend itself by claiming that all accounting records were lost in a 1970 flood.

Another famous net profit deal was negotiated by Lew Wasserman in 1950 for Jimmy Stewart who agreed to accept 50% of the net on *Winchester '73* in lieu of his normal salary.

Net profits are mainly paid out on films which have a huge theatrical success, but cost relatively little to make. One example is Disney's *Three Men and a Baby*. The film earned approximately $250 million worldwide theatrical gross and probably $750 million in total retail income. This translated into 'picture revenue' of $150 million. Because the cost was low, the film earned $27 million in net profits:

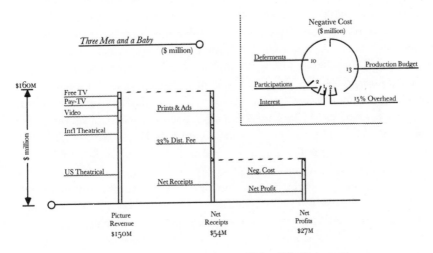

Source: Disney's profit participation 30 September 1991 (P&A = all distribution costs)

A similarly successful film such as *Four Weddings and a Funeral* would have generated even higher net profits because of its extremely low cost ($4.5M). However, a more successful film, such as Disney's *Who Framed Roger Rabbit*, actually resulted in a $20 million net loss because of its high budget:

Who Framed Roger Rabbit

Picture Revenue	$205M	*Production cost*	$50.6M
33% Distribution Fee	$68.3M	*Overhead*	$7.6M
P&A	$64M	*Interest*	$17.5M
		Participations	$17.1M
Minus Negative Cost	($92.3M)	*Total*	$92.3M
Net loss	($19.6M)		

Source: Disney's profit participation 31 December 1990 (P&A = all distribution costs)

Of course the Major's distribution fees and retained earnings in video means that the film was profitable for the studio.

Such examples of blockbuster successes which generate official 'losses', have led to a series of accusations against the Majors of 'creative accounting'. One of the most publicized attacks was by columnist Art Linson who claimed that Paramount had stolen his treatment for *Coming to America* and should pay him a fair share of the film's profits, rather than the official losses that the film had recorded. The story of the case was told in the book *Fatal Subtraction*, and resulted in a $0.9 million award against Paramount, pending appeal.

A more recent attack on net profit accounting was by the heirs of the late James Garrison – the man who investigated the JFK conspiracy. Warner Brothers claimed that despite *JFK*'s $210 million worldwide gross the film still had earned no net profits. The Garrison family mounted a class-action lawsuit at the end of 1995 against the seven major studios and the MPAA alleging 'an illegal conspiracy among the major studios that suppresses competition, fixes prices and violates the law'. The suit cited examples such as *Forrest Gump* and *Indecent Proposal* which have still not earned net profits. If the lawsuit is successful it may revolutionize Hollywood accounting practices.

Even if the net profits formula is changed, the studios' overall profit margins are still very tight. They cannot afford to pay out higher net profits unless they can claw back production or promotion costs, which is very difficult for them to do. What is most likely is an attempt to create a 'fairer' formula which still limits pay-outs.

3

What is Commercial?

Hollywood is a pay or play town.
John Ptak

THE MAJORS ARE HUGE INDUSTRIAL CONGLOMERATES that use the latest statistical methods to try to eliminate risk from their business. But there are no laws governing which films will be a success. In most high-cost industries, such as automobiles or computing, new product launches tend to be annual, with a long lead time and a reasonable margin for predicting consumer demand. In other areas of software publishing, there are a large number of 'new titles' every month but with far lower unit costs.

A Major releases a new $50 million film at least once a month, knowing that within the first week it may gross anywhere between zero and $100 million. The movies therefore remain a 'people business', and the decision to 'green light' a film is ultimately a question of instinct. The Majors directly employ 15,000 people in their film divisions and provide work for another 150,000, but commissioning rests in the hands of the studio chiefs.

The 'genius of the system' is the wider editorial apparatus that exists in Hollywood. There is constant dialogue between the senior studio executives, the top agents, the leading producers and the star talent which determines which projects feel 'right' or not. This is a community of around 200 top 'players'. The extreme example of this community at work is when a spec script is put up for auction and the players must decide within the space of 24 hours whether or not to shell out over a million dollars.

'The business is all about relationships with talent' says one top agent. 'You learn to quickly form an opinion – is someone still "in the business" or not. People can disappear overnight. A bit like a restaurant that nobody goes to anymore, but nobody can explain why. That's what happened when Parretti owned MGM, or Puttnam ran Columbia, the supply of good product dried up overnight.'

The top 200 players are divided into a series of fiefdoms which coalesce around each studio and the main agencies. But each fiefdom has feelers which stretch throughout the movie colony. There is constant feedback and sometimes even a housemaid can have an important influence on who gets cast in a leading role. This vibrant sounding-board of opinions helps the business keep in touch with the public. 'When I look at a project, I try and be as honest as possible about what I think about it' says John Ptak of Creative Artists Agency. 'Ultimately it's the same principle I used way back at college when I decided which movies to screen for our film club. That's the great advantage Americans have over Europeans. We think of ourselves as just one more member of the general public. If we like a project, maybe lots of other people will too.'

Hollywood tends to be typecast between the 'suits' – lawyers, agents and executives – and the 'creatives' - the directors, screenwriters and key craftsmen. But at the top, players need to use both their left and right brain. The producer is the editorial linchpin of the system. 'It's the producer whose vision – which he eventually shares with others – that eventually ends up on the screen', wrote Robert Evans in *The Kid Stays in the Picture*. 'He's the one who hires the writer and director. When a director hires a producer you're in deep shit. A director needs a boss, not a yes man.'

The producer is the dynamo who energizes the system, and often makes his opinions heard at high decibels. Many producers are known for their tough talking and brusque manners, making the town sometimes feel like 'holler'-wood. One producer remarked that it's lucky the town is divided between the coast and the valley – because enemies can escape from each other across the mountains.

This makes Hollywood very different from European cinema where each country likes to cultivate a 'village' atmosphere – calm and genteel at the surface but riddled with Twin Peaks-style resentments and gossiping underneath.

Hollywood was built by a group of East European hustlers who came out of the twilight world of *fin de siècle* popular culture. This new universe was born from the growing urban masses and the latest inventions such as electricity and motion pictures.

The new popular culture, thriving on both sides of the Atlantic, was viewed with great suspicion by the Establishment. Establishment hostility was increased because a large number of the new moguls were Jewish. This was particularly important in Europe, and fed into the rising tide of anti-Semitism that was to dominate the twentieth century.

Growing anti-Semitism in Europe at the end of the nineteenth century was one of the main causes of high levels of emigration to the United States, and it is no accident that the movie moguls were virtually all born within a 500-mile radius of Warsaw – the same epicentre which was the principal target of the Holocaust.

Despite a succession of attacks by the American Establishment, the colony has survived as a haven of popular culture. The business has nonetheless undergone a major shift in recent years as young MBAs have taken over. According to Mark Litwak, 'It is as if the studios are barreling down a highway with their eyes fixed on the rearview mirror.' This sentiment is confirmed by Steven Spielberg: 'The great gamblers are dead. And I think that's the tragedy of Hollywood today. In the old days the Thalbergs and the Zanucks and the Mayers came out of nickelodeon vaudeville, they came out of borscht-belt theater, and they came with a great deal of showmanship and esprit de corps to a little citrus grove in California. They were brave. They were gamblers. They were high rollers.'[1]

The attempt to produce assembly line hits reached its height in the 1980s with 'high concept' movies built around a marketing hook. Films were commissioned on a one-line or two-line pitch. Today there is a trend away from media hype. Audiences are increasingly screening out the quick sell, and are aware that the West, in particular America, has become an 'oversold' society – in the words of Earl Shorris, 'a generation bankrupted by salesmen'.[2]

THE ROAD TO THE GREEN LIGHT

Projects that get made in Hollywood have a snowball momentum behind them. As Mark Litwak puts it, 'Successful film-makers are distinguished not only by their command of the medium but also by their political savvy.'[3] The system will only spare you the time of day if it thinks you have something to sell. This takes confidence, skills, chutzpah and most important of all – a track record.

The advantage of the Hollywood studios is that they offer 'one stop' shopping. If a studio chief likes a project he will put up the entire production and marketing budget. The disadvantage is that thousands of people are competing for the same scarce resources.

Nobody will fund a film simply because it has a wonderful script, although a powerful screenplay can secure a development deal and help launch a career. To move from script stage to funded film requires a 'package' – a script with 'elements' attached. The crucial 'elements' are the director and the lead stars.

These 'packages' normally require 'pay or play' deals, which mean that they must be funded by producers with deep pockets – usually those linked to the studios. The vital role of talent also places much of the industry's power in the hands of the agents. 'It's an open secret in Hollywood that most top stars are not exactly avid readers', writes Judy Brennan in *Variety*, 'and that their agents, in lining up the best material and the richest offers, ultimately tilt the final decisions.'[4]

Studios and producers will not even look at a project unless it has been submitted by an agent, in order to avoid both wasting time and being sued. The agents thereby cement the system together. They evaluate scripts, put together packages and advise clients that already have first look deals with the studios. Since they are not tied to any one studio they also provide a vital medium of communication. 'When you work for William Morris, CAA or ICM you are in the nerve centre of the film business' commented agent Greg Moscoe. 'It's like working for the CIA.'[5]

TALENT AGENTS

Just as the studios have diversified into different areas of the media, the agents have extended talent management to include all types of 'celebrity' from movies to sports.

There are two kinds of talent which are critical to Hollywood – behind the screen and on-screen. The former depends on the ability to produce excellent products, but does not require public recognition. There are many executives, directors and writers who can command high talent fees because of their work and yet they remain unknown to the public.

On-screen talent requires charisma and screen presence. The best-paid actors are those who have 'marquee value' – their appearance in a film will attract a loyal following and help the film to 'open'. This is the definition of a 'star' and usually means that the actor has qualities that ignite the public's imagination and their dreams.

A star is one of the few 'brand names' in the business. Most industries revolve around brand names such as Coca-Cola or Levi's. In movies the only company with a significant brand name is Disney. Actors are the main selling tool, followed in rare cases by star directors such as Steven Spielberg.

Stars have a high level of media exposure and advertising poured on them. They cease to become simple human beings and become instead 'characters'. The 'character' may be quite different from the true personality of the star, but is a value which can be 'licensed' to many different activities. A film is sold on the basis of its stars, and is in effect a form of character licensing, whereby the stars 'endorse' the film. This licensing can be spread to many other areas – from restaurants to charity drives.

Licensing also exists for 'virtual' characters, such as Mickey Mouse, who are highly valued because they are less temperamental and do not demand a share of the gross. As computer animation develops, it is possible that one day all movie actors will exist only in our imagination.

In the golden age, each studio had its own team of players locked into long-term contracts, the most famous being MGM. The system began to change with David O. Selznick, who started to hire his talent out to the other studios. In effect, he shifted the business towards 'agenting'. The Paramount Decree further weakened the finances of the Majors and forced them to operate increasingly with independents.

The agent system was energized by Lew Wasserman (b. 1913) who was promoted to president of MCA (Music Corporation of America) by Jules Stein in 1946. Wasserman pioneered the packaging business – beginning in radio and then extending the principle to the movies. His first million-dollar deal was a seven-year contract with Warner Brothers for Ronald Reagan.

Wasserman understood that talent management was now split between agent and studio and created a powerhouse which one federal judge described as an 'octopus that virtually controls the business'. In the climate of the McCarthy witch-hunt and the blacklist, this led some to resent MCA's presence. In the late 1950s, MCA started producing television films, and in 1962 an anti-trust case obliged the company to choose between being an agent or a studio. Wasserman chose the latter.

The talent agents have become key powerhouses within Hollywood, but they have also eaten into the Majors' bottom line. Much of the increase in global revenues has been siphoned off into higher star salaries by the 'tenpercenters'. But for several years Hollywood has been suggesting that star salaries have to be brought into line and some have even suggested a salary cap, as has recently been introduced in baseball.

The agents were able to increase their leverage in the 1980s because of the proliferation of competition between the Majors and the Independents. The most spectacular success story is that of CAA which was set up in 1975 by a team of five William Morris agents led by the twenty-eight-year-old Michael Ovitz. The agency fought its way to the top, through tough negotiating and above all by attracting the best clients.

The pendulum may now be swinging back towards the studios, who no longer have such strong competition from the Independents. A key indication of this shift was a shake-up at CAA in 1995 in which Michael Ovitz and Ron Meyer left to become respectively president of Disney and CEO of MCA/Universal. Other former CAA studio chiefs include MGM president Mike Marcus and Joe Roth at Disney (who left CAA in the early 1980s).

The agency business continues to be dominated by the Big Three – CAA, ICM and William Morris – who in the early 1990s swallowed up two important independents, ITA and Triad. But new boutique agencies are always being opened up – such as the Endeavour agency set up in 1995 by four leading ICM agents.

Creative Artists Agency (CAA)

'The most influential person in Hollywood is not a star, a director or a studio head' wrote Mark Litwak in *Reel Power* (1987). 'While his name is rarely mentioned in the news media, and he never gets a screen credit, everyone who matters in the industry knows who he is. He is assiduously courted by producers and studio heads alike because they need his cooperation in order to gain the services of the best writers, stars and directors in the industry. He is Michael Ovitz, the president of CAA.'

CAA was established in 1975 by five former William Morris agents – Michael Ovitz, Ron Meyer, Bill Haber, Rowland Perkins and Mike Rosenfeld. They jumped ship after their mentor, Phil Weltman, was dismissed from WMA in 1975. The 'young turks' had become expert television packagers and now extended these principles to feature films.

CAA were hungry and aggressive deal-makers, and rivals complained that they acted like a 'pack of wolves' in stealing talent. Within ten years CAA were the smallest of the Big Three agencies (45 agents and 700 clients), but had established by far the most prestigious client list. Their near monopoly of key talent had been equalled only by Ovitz's idol – Lew Wasserman.

Like Wasserman, Ovitz advocated sombre suits and a low profile, but his management philosophy was very different. 'If CAA was in many respects an adaptation of MCA', wrote Connie Bruck in *The New Yorker*, 'it was MCA with a New Age twist: the ethos that Ovitz preached was collectivism – a blend of team sports and Eastern-style management techniques somewhat reminiscent of the human potential movement of the early seventies.'

Ovitz – the 'economic samurai' – practises an hour of *aikido* every morning, and like Gordon Gekko advises his disciples to read Sun Tzu's *Art of War*. His magnetic presence is legendary. 'He has an almost Rasputin-like ability to focus his eyes on you', said one colleague. 'He uses his voice in a soothing, harmonic way – it does something to your brain waves.'[6] Ovitz also likes to work in an aura of mystery which led MCA's Sidney Sheinberg to comment 'I accused him once of thinking he is a member of Mossad [the Israeli secret service].'

Critics accused CAA of becoming an obsessive cult, under which traitors to the cause would have their careers wrecked by 'attack teams'. In 1989 the screenwriter Joe Eszterhaus defected to ICM and claimed that Ovitz had then threatened 'My foot soldiers who go up and down Wilshire Boulevard each day, will blow your brains out.' Ovitz denied the allegations as a case of *Rashomon* false memory syndrome but later issued a statement via the Writer's Guild affirming that CAA would refrain from any such practices in the future.

Meanwhile Ovitz was playing corporate matchmaker. He was a member of the team that advised Sony in their takeover of Columbia-TriStar in 1989. He then played the decisive 'go-between' in Matsushita's acquisition of MCA/Universal in 1990, choosing the lawyers, investment bankers and public relations specialists that made the deal.

Ovitz then started to act as corporate representative for Apple, Paramount and Coca-Cola (with whom he later developed a joint advertising venture). In 1994 CAA appointed AT&T executive VP Robert Kavner to head a new multimedia division – indicating Ovitz's desire to be on top of new converging technologies.

CAA's most controversial consulting deal was struck in 1993, to oversee Credit Lyonnais's diverse entertainment portfolio (including MGM/UA). Jeff Berg of ICM tried in vain to overturn the deal on anti-trust grounds, likening Ovitz's position to that of Wasserman in 1962.

Ovitz is recognized as one of the few people who understand the 'movie equation' inside out. As an agent he often dictated terms to his studio clients. From the Sony takeover onwards he was wooed as a studio chief (referred to by the codename Superman), but he made it clear that he would only accept a dominion large enough to fit his ambitions. In 1995 he was tipped to take over MCA/Universal following the Seagram takeover (Edgar Bronfman is an old friend), but instead his number two, Ron Meyer took the job and Ovitz (aged forty-nine) became company president of Disney/ABC.

The twentieth anniversary of CAA saw its founding partners Ovitz, Meyer and Haber all leave. The new president is thirty-year-old Richard Lovett whose surname friends started to pronounce as L'Ovitz. Co-chairmen are Rick Nicita, Jack Rapke and Lee Gabler. The three ex-CAA partners signed an agreement under which they would receive around 80–85% of profits from all deals negotiated before 1 October 1995.

Not all of CAA's clients seemed impressed by the new regime. Early desertions included Sylvester Stallone, Alec Baldwin, Steven Seagal, Kevin Costner, Adrian Lyne and John Hughes. Corporate clients also fled the agency (including Coke which followed Ovitz to Disney). But CAA seems to have retained its leadership over the Big Three, even if in Hollywood's 'new world order', power has shifted significantly away from the agencies and back to the studios.

International Creative Management (ICM)

ICM is larger than CAA in billing terms and number of agents (220 agents and 2000 clients) and in 1995 was estimated to have billings over $1 billion and commissions over $100 million. The 'Machine' is divided into a series of baronial fiefdoms, with chairman Jeff Berg (b. 1947) topping the agency.

The agency went private for $71 million in 1988, and a subsequent share reshuffle in 1992 left Jeff Berg, Sam Cohn and Jim Wiatt with 60% of the company and Marvin Josephson with the rest. Berg is very different from Ovitz. He has a looser control over the agency and his cold and sometimes idiosyncratic manner has earned him the nickname 'The Iceman'.

ICM has a much more extensive international network than CAA, with offices in all European countries, including Duncan Heath in the UK and an informal relationship with Art-Média in France (after a formal alliance 1993–95). This network enables the company to be actively involved in seeking production finance and the agency has recently helped put together films such as *Braveheart, Leaving Las Vegas, Antonia's Line* and *The Usual Suspects*.

ICM agent Peter Rawley explains that 90% of his job is now seeking capital funding for projects that ICM clients wish to make. A good example is Polanski's *Death and the Maiden*. The film was developed by Warners but then put into turnaround. ICM decided to make it as a French production taking advantage of Polanski's Franco-Polish nationality. Rawley put together Flach film, TF1 and Jane Barclay's Capitol films as sales agent. The film was sold in the US only in the fifth week of pre-production.

The most significant deal orchestrated by ICM was James Cameron's multi-million nine-picture deal with Fox in the US, Nippon Herald in Japan, Associated Artists in Italy, Jugendfilm in Germany and UIP in the rest of the world. The deal took one and a half years to put together, but Cameron found it too unwieldy. In late 1994 Cameron announced he was leaving ICM in order to be represented solely by his lawyers.

ICM has already been the principal beneficiary of CAA's defections and may soon establish itself as the leader of the pack.

William Morris Agency

William Morris is the oldest and most 'gentlemanly' of the Big Three (150 agents and 2000 clients), founded in 1898.

In 1993 the more relaxed atmosphere was shaken up by the acquisition of niche agency Triad. Triad boss Arnold Rifkin was appointed head of the WMA motion picture department and has brought Morris in line with its two rivals.

TALENT RELATIONSHIPS

The studios have always been concerned with establishing good relationships with key talent, formalized through multi-picture deals and 'first look' development deals. These include overhead and development costs and often a site on the studio lot. Each studio has twenty to thirty housekeeping deals with key talent. Some of the main talent relationships in 1996 were as follows:

MCA/Universal	*Warners*	*Disney*
Dreamworks SKG	Kevin Costner (Tig)	Merchant Ivory
Ivan Reitman	Mel Gibson (Icon)	Miramax
Sylvester Stallone	A. Milchan (Regency)	Cinergi (A. Vajna)
Bubble Factory	Morgan Creek	J. Bruckenheimer
Imagine (R. Howard)	David Puttnam	Michelle Pfeiffer
D. and J. Zucker		Martin Scorsese
Danny de Vito		
Beacon		

Paramount	Fox	Sony
Neufeld/Rehme	James Cameron	Mike Medavoy
Scott Rudin	Chris Columbus	Mandalay (P. Guber)
Sidney Pollack	Ridley & Tony Scott	Castle Rock
Michael Douglas	Meg Ryan	Stanley Jaffe
Barry Levinson		
Marshall/Kennedy		

Each studio sees itself as a 'family'. It tries to remain on very good terms with those within the family and can offer many perks and sweeteners. To those outside the 'family' the studio can appear far less benign.

RULES OF THUMB IN HOLLYWOOD

Any 'rule' concerning what is commercial is made to be broken, and films often get commissioned not because they possess some magic ingredients, but because they have sufficient talent backing them.

Nonetheless, Hollywood has evolved a certain *modus operandi* which reveals key aspects of popular film-making. These principles are also interesting because governments in Europe have defined their 'national cultures' in opposition to these popular values.

MYTHIC JOURNEYS

'I felt the sounds from the screen wash over me, and I was overcome by the awesome rightness of things', wrote Jon Boorstin in *The Hollywood Eye* (1990). 'Engulfed by that dark space I indulged in glorious private pleasures, yet I was not alone. I was protected, but I was free. I felt my soul expand to fill the room.'[7] The ritual of film-going has often been compared to the dream experience, the religious drive and the need for illumination by the shaman. Stories ignite our imagination and send us on a journey into another world – the world of the unconscious.

The 'mythic' aspect of story-telling is universally accepted for children's tales, and commentators such as Bruno Bettelheim and Vladimir Propp have revealed their recurring themes and mythic structures. Children's tales revolve around immediately recognizable archetypes and offer moral lessons through the confrontation between the hero and the villain. They help children learn the language of the 'collective unconsciousness' at the same time as they are learning to identify the names and rules of the conscious world.

Fairy-tales are universal and told to all children irrespective of their social background. This is not true of adult stories, where there is a sharp division between popular and elite culture. Popular culture maintains the strongest link with folk tales, using archetypes, strong villains and moral conclusions.

The 'journey' of the story usually concerns the transformation of a central protagonist. The protagonist may begin as a normal human being, but during the journey becomes 'heroic'. This is closely linked to mythic traditions. Cocteau, for example, believed that mythic stories were initiation rites, and that confrontation with death was the necessary climax of the hero's 'trial'.

In this way movie-going achieves some of the functions previously performed by religion. A Christian film guide on the Internet, *Movies! Movies! Movies!* comments:

> Compare the experience of 'going to the movies' with that of worshipping in one of the great Gothic cathedrals of medieval Europe. Imagine what it must have been like for people in a feudal society to enter one of those cathedrals. Not only were they wonderfully impressive buildings with all the gargoyles, the flying buttresses and the soaring arches, they were also dazzling sound and light shows . . . Today in our secular world, the movie theatre functions in much the same way. People come in off the crowded highways and parking lots, to enter the semi-darkness of a theatre. And suddenly the brilliant colours and sounds appear in huge dimensions on those towering screens. Rather than being organized around the stories of the Bible or Christian tradition, however, today's movies echo the concerns and interest, the hopes and fears of people living in this post-Christian, post-industrial society.

The classic film hero has the mythic overtones of a Biblical saviour. The world is at peril and the humble, courageous man comes to the rescue. In the words of Robert Mckee: 'The bold heroes, the foolhardy people, are going to get killed. The absolute running screaming cowards are going to get killed. What you need is a balanced combination of brains, caution and courage.'[8]

Hollywood is increasingly obsessed with New Age ideas as a result of books such as Joseph Campbell's *The Hero with a Thousand Faces* and has also been strongly influenced by what one might call an 'American Renaissance' – a desire to trace America's roots to the religious belief systems of the Hopi and other native tribes that dominated the continent before the arrival of the white man.

MAKE BELIEVE

A good movie casts a spell over us, whereby we forget everything and enter into the film's universe. This requires a curious balance of dream and reality. The genius of Hollywood has been to create stories 'once upon a time, in a land far, far away' and yet give them contemporary force and reality.

The Czech director Milos Forman was attracted to Hollywood for this reason. He emphasizes that there are two essential ingredients to good story telling. The first is 'attention to detail' – which establishes authenticity and expectations. The second is 'surprise' – which produces pay-offs that are convincing and yet unexpected.

Forman was unable to use these techniques in his home country, where there was an emphasis on creating 'culture'. He expressed this frustration in his film *Amadeus* – shot in his home town of Prague – in which he portrayed Mozart as a man constrained and ultimately crucified by the cultural authorities. Forman introduces a vaudeville manager who says to Mozart, 'If you'd played Don Giovanni here you would have had a wonderful success. You belong here, not at the snobby court. You can do anything you like. The more fantastic the better! That's what people want – fantasy.'

REDSKINS

An interesting model for understanding elite and popular culture was provided by literary critic Philip Rahv, who described the two traditions as 'paleface' and 'redskin'. He identifies the former with the 'thin, solemn, semi-clerical culture of Boston and Concord' and the latter with 'the low life world of the frontier and the big cities'.9 This results in two very distinct American traditions:

> While the redskin glories in his Americanism, to the paleface it is a source of endless ambiguities. Sociologically they can be distinguished as patrician vs. plebeian, and in their aesthetic ideals one is drawn to allegory and the distillations of symbolism, whereas the other inclines to a gross riotous naturalism . . . At his highest level the paleface moves in an exquisite moral atmosphere; at his lowest he is genteel, snobbish and pedantic. In giving expression to the vitality and to the aspirations of the people, the redskin is at his best, but at his worst he is a vulgar anti-intellectual.

The 'American tradition' in the nineteenth century was very much New England 'paleface' culture, but is now solidly 'redskin', especially in Hollywood. Rahv suggests that this is because society has moved from an industrial base to a consumer base, and therefore the rugged pleasures of redskin culture are more attractive to modern society.

Hollywood has always maintained an adventuring 'frontier' atmosphere and has always been fascinated by 'redskin' culture and the frontier myth – classically represented by the western. As the frontier has closed and America has become domesticated, movies have been increasingly looking to fantasy worlds and science fiction in order to realize this frontier saga.

COMIC BOOK STORIES

William Goldman criticized Hollywood for producing an ever increasing number of mindless films for the teenage market. Director Allan Arkush (*Rock 'n' Roll High School*) went one stage further, identifying two industries in Hollywood: 'The one film industry that caters to the moviegoing public, which is the young people and which is looked down upon by everyone else, and has a certain amount of cynicism attached to it. And then there's the one that gets Academy Awards, where people have a snobbish attitude and they make a limited number of movies and those movies are the ones that are extremely dependent on stars.'[10]

Hollywood's biggest 'franchises' in recent years have been animation films and comic book adaptations such as *Batman*. These films also have huge potential for ancillary earnings in consumer products and theme parks. But unlike in Europe, many directors and stars do not feel embarrassed to make such films. Spielberg was denied an Oscar for many years because of his 'childish' movies and Oliver Stone is proud to have written *Conan the Barbarian*, emphasizing that one of the principal stages of life that interests him is the adolescent transition to adulthood.

Hollywood makes comic book films because there is a demand for them – both amongst film-makers and in the audience. Furthermore, the science fiction setting of many of these films reflects a growing need for fantasy in today's world. The fantasy allows commentaries to be made that would be impossible in a real-life context.

SOCIAL TRANSFORMATION

Hollywood has always had a fascination for 'high society', and a classic story since the days of Chaplin has been the rough diamond who gets the society girl. In Elia Kazan's opinion:

> Since many of the men who became the great producers evolved out of the very bottom of the middle class and were not blessed by birth with what might make them easily gain the favours of attractive women, and furthermore since many of them were Jews and felt in some way 'outside' the goyish upper-class society with which their films dealt, they were particularly drawn to blondes and 'proper ladies' (Grace Kelly). The unspoken, unwritten drama would consist of bringing these immaculate appearing women (Deborah Kerr) down to earth (or the sea's surf), where the rest of us wallowed and sinned.[11]

Today the role models are sometimes reversed – as in *Pretty Woman*. Now it is often the girl who comes from the gutter and seduces the high society male.

Popular culture has always placed great importance on the villain. It is the villain who establishes the force of the 'trial' for the hero. This is a recurring feature of mythic journeys including the temptation of Christ in the desert. If the tale is to have power, the temptation must be real. As the saying goes, the devil has the best parts.

In Europe, strong villains have always been accepted for children's stories but not in adult drama. The European elites have suggested that all adult film characters are 'role models' and therefore if seductive villains are portrayed this may lead to dangerous copycat behaviour.

This ties in with a general suspicion of the types of characters that are portrayed in popular culture. The Establishment prefers role models that express the virtues of the 'national character'.

ACCESSIBILITY

In the early days of cinema, the movies were one of the few friends available to the 'great unwashed'. The cinema offered a warm place where you could go and enjoy yourself – as shown brilliantly in *Cinema Paradiso*.

The characters, dialogue and narrative are all constructed in order to make people feel welcome and relaxed as they watch the film. The opposite is true of many 'paleface' films which have codes and symbols that only make them accessible to the *cognoscenti*. For instance, the majority of Europeans feel unwelcome when they go to see their 'national' films – as if they entered an exclusive club without an invitation.

LIFE-EMPOWERING

Popular culture draws on the tradition of vaudeville, popular drama and the circus. Moments of great dramatic tension are counterpoised with humour. At its best, Hollywood storytelling provides an ironic view on life that teaches us lessons and also makes us laugh.

Humour can be very 'noir'. Billy Wilder, for example, had a very negative view of humanity after the horrors of National Socialism in his native Germany, but the irony in his films strangely makes us feel good about life.

A good Hollywood film transmits a burst of energy. It makes us feel that we have the power to confront difficult challenges. Too often, European films seem to dwell on the opposite sensations and encourage despair.

CONTEMPORARY RELEVANCE

Movies are made for people today. Even if the story takes place in the past or future it will reflect the way we see those times at present. This also means that some films become quickly dated because they represent an outmoded way of seeing the universe.

To get people to want to see a film they must feel it has something to say about their lives. A successful film ripples through the world's media, sparking controversy and debate. 'It may sound corny', says Caitlin Buchman of Film Strategies, 'but the films which succeed, somehow tap into the *zeitgeist*. That's something mass-media can't do. People are going for connection – almost like a religious experience. The hit films capture the spirit of the times, and also push them forward. Movies are food for the soul.'

A famous Hollywood saying used to be 'if you want to send a message try the Western Union'. This resulted partly from the restrictions of the Hays Code, but also because the movie colony understood that moralistic or message-driven movies usually lack emotional power or dramatic truth. Today film-makers have much greater opportunity to address political themes but they try to do so in an emotive rather than cerebral manner.

DIRTY LINEN

All of us have two sides to our personalities – the public and the private. Our public 'mask' is the image we like to project for others and is conditioned by our social environment. But beneath this mask lies a private 'shadow' which is how we really are. This shadow is often revealed only in life-or-death situations.

Similarly, every country has a 'mask' and 'shadow'. The 'mask' is the image that the country's political leaders would like to project. The 'shadow' is the reality, or the 'dirty linen' that the authorities would prefer to hide.

America's commitment to freedom of speech and the First Amendment has meant that there has been a remarkable capacity to air the nation's dirty linen – from racism to political corruption.

In other countries there rarely has been such liberty. This gives enormous force to all fields of cultural expression in America, and helps people gain the confidence to express their opinions. As Woody Allen says in *Zelig*, 'You have to be your own man, and learn to speak up and say what's on your mind. Now maybe they're not free to do that in foreign countries but that's the American way.'

SHOW, DON'T TELL

An oft-repeated maxim of American screenwriting is that one should show rather than tell. This is in recognition that film is a visual medium and helps the writer concretize visual details rather than vague ideas.

In recent years this has led to an increasing emphasis on 'visceral' techniques. As Jon Boorstin comments, 'Hollywood studios, never comfortable sneaking up on an audience generally prefer to sock it to 'em . . . the way your gut twinges when you see a flashing red light in your rearview mirror, the surge in your loins a beautiful body stirs, the sickening sense that tonight your dreams will be nightmares.'[12]

Phrases such as 'high voltage', 'grab 'em by the throat', 'in your face', 'white knuckle ride' are commonplace. The danger is that such techniques turn movies into a theme park ride in constant search of the latest visceral thrill. Boorstin concludes:

> Though they can require considerable art to achieve, there is nothing artistic about the results – the passions aroused are not lofty, they're the gut reactions of the lizard brain – thrill of motion, joy of destruction, lust, blood lust, terror, disgust . . . while film catches only the shadow of a great literary character, a Rashkolnikov, it makes a bloodthirsty, insect-bodied alien more terrifyingly evocative than anything on the page.

The visceral eye becomes quickly jaded and therefore steps up its tolerance level. This forces the film-maker to look for new thrills and has perhaps contributed to the 'New Violence'. Scorsese defends this trend. 'Maybe we need the catharsis of bloodletting and decapitation', he suggests, 'like the ancient Romans needed it, as ritual but not real like the Roman circus.' Others see this as a very dangerous sign. 'What we think of now as the excess of the Roman circuses, where in the end hundreds of thousands of people died, didn't start that way', says David Puttnam. 'They started legitimately as circuses, extremely mild entertainment. But the audience demand for more and more resulted over a period of several hundred years in that form of entertainment becoming more and more bloody, more and more grotesque.' Puttnam concludes that 'movies now have an underlying nastiness in them. The thing I loathe more than anything has become fashionable – cynicism.'[13]

It is obviously true that there are examples of gratuitous sex and violence, but what is less obvious is how one should react to this. *Midnight Express*, for example, needed its visceral power to capture the barbarity of the Turkish prisons. Similarly the visceral force of *Schindler's List* was necessary to capture the true force of the Nazi concentration camps.

There are some who blame all of society's ills on screen violence. This is clearly exaggerated. We live in an increasingly violent world but this is linked to the whole cultural fabric. It is tempting to try to reverse this process through censorship and state control, but it is a very dangerous road.

4

American Indies

We are a rebellious nation. Our whole history is treason.
Our blood was contaminated before we were born.
Our creeds were infidelity to the mother church.
Our constitution is treason to our fatherland.
Theodore Parker

INDEPENDENCE IS CENTRAL TO THE AMERICAN DREAM. Even the Majors began as the Independent Motion Pictures Alliance, and everyone in Hollywood still dreams of being an Indie, from George Lucas with his Skywalker ranch, to Robert Rodriguez who made *El Mariachi* for $7,000.

The indies are the pioneers of the business. Joe Levine invented blitzkrieg marketing in the 1950s, Roger Corman laid the seeds of the American New Wave in the 1960s, Dino de Laurentiis championed new 'anti-hero' genres in the 1970s and the likes of Menahem Golan got the whole video business off the ground in the 1980s. The indies still provide the industry with its most colourful characters and also act as a vital bridge between Europe and America.

The shortage of attractive product from Europe and the drying up of independent finance in America has forced many of the leading companies into the hands of the Majors, who are now rebuilding the stranglehold over the business that they enjoyed during the Code years.

OVERVIEW

Indies include producers and distributors. In distribution, the term means everything outside the mainstream activities of the Majors. In production, it includes those who supply the indie distributors as well as producers of 'pick-ups' for the Majors who negotiate their own foreign sales. This chapter concentrates on indie distribution; foreign sales are covered in the next chapter and indie production in the succeeding chapter.

Around a third of US theatrical grosses are provided by independent productions (including pick-ups), while indie distributors have under 15% of the market. This translates into global distributor revenues (theatrical, video and TV) for indie films roughly as follows:

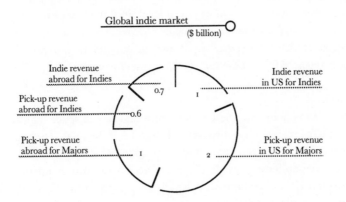

The Majors are increasingly buying world rights, even for official 'pick-ups', thus forcing the indie market to concentrate solely on 'niche' fare, worth around $1.7 billion – about 10% of the Majors' revenues.

INDIE DISTRIBUTION

During the Code years, the vast majority of theatres could only show films bearing the Seal – thereby giving the Majors an effective monopoly. The breakthrough for indie distributors was the end of the Code Seal system in 1966 and the social revolution of the 1960s which enabled them to build their market share of the US box office to nearly 30% by 1971.

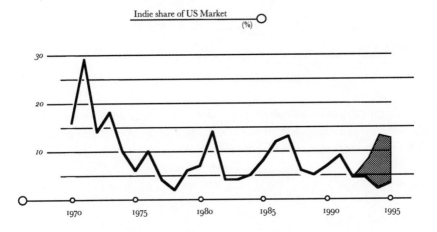

The Majors slowly clawed back their position over the 1970s, but the video boom allowed indie distributors to rise back to almost 15% by 1987 before falling once again.

The indie share seemed to grow from 1993 to 1995 but this was due to the performance of subsidiaries of larger media groups (Miramax, New Line, Gramercy and Savoy), and is represented in the previous graph by a shaded area. True indie distribution is now at its lowest level since the Code era.

An indie distributor no longer means independent ownership, but rather a company which caters for specialty product. In 1994 the mainstream divisions of the Majors released 85% of the top 100 films but only 25% of the next 300.

SOURCE OF FILMS

The Majors dominate the US box office and screen space, but in terms of number of films released they provide only a third of the total. They concentrate on 'US-made' films – in English and with recognizable stars.

The independents provide the main access for American independent films, foreign-language films and English-language films from the British Commonwealth (Britain, Canada, Australia, and New Zealand).

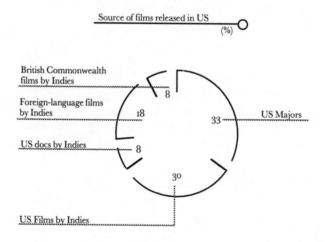

Source of films released in US (%)

British Commonwealth films by Indies — 8

Foreign-language films by Indies — 18

US Majors — 33

US docs by Indies — 8

US Films by Indies — 30

The total number of independent releases has declined since 1987 because of a slide in American independent production. The number of foreign-language films and documentaries released has remained relatively stable.

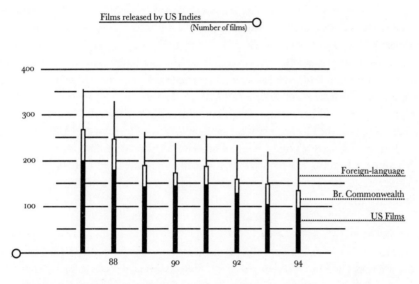

Films released by US Indies
(Number of films)

More than a hundred foreign-language films and documentaries are released each year, but most of these have minimal returns. The total gross for all foreign-language films tends to be $40–50 million a year – 0.5% of the US box office. Over half of this is earned by the top ten foreign films and most releases gross under $50,000. The full 'demand curve' for foreign-language films in 1994 was:

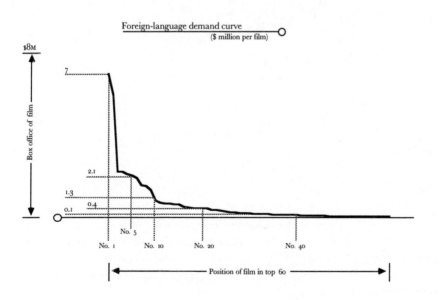

Foreign-language demand curve
($ million per film)

The best hope for a foreign-language film is to be taken up by a leading indie such as Miramax. This will guarantee a significant acquisition price and a release of up to 200 screens. In this way roughly ten foreign-language films a year gross over $1 million, with two or three higher profile films. By far the most successful foreign-language pictures in recent years were the $22 million grosses earned by both *Like Water for Chocolate* and *The Postman*.

The 'demand curve' for foreign-language films is a far cry from the heyday of the 1960s when the Majors were actively involved in releasing US films and the foreign-language share of the box office was ten times as high at 5%. One of the highest number of admissions for a foreign-language film in the US is Fellini's *La Dolce Vita*, whose US gross, if adjusted for inflation, would today be worth $60 million.

TYPES OF DISTRIBUTOR

Indie distributors can be divided into three types – mini-majors, classics and micros. The main players are all associated with larger media groups:

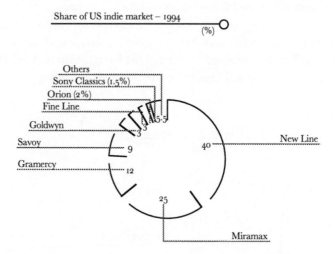

Share of US indie market – 1994 (%)

Others
Sony Classics (1.5%)
Orion (2%)
Fine Line
Goldwyn — 3
Savoy — 9
Gramercy — 12
New Line — 40
Miramax — 25
5.5

Mini-majors

Mini-majors have an eye on the mainstream and crossover market. The king of the 'mini-majors' is New Line (owned by Turner since 1993 and thus part of Time Warner since 1995). The other main players are Miramax (acquired by Disney in 1992), Gramercy (owned by PolyGram and set up as a joint venture with Universal in 1993) and until recently Savoy (set up in 1993 but which has now withdrawn from film and TV production).

Classic indies

The core of the 'art house' market is 400–500 screens in the US, 3% of the total. This market is served above all by the 'classic' distributors, all of which are now owned by bigger groups: Orion/Samuel Goldwyn (Metromedia), Sony Classics, Fine Line, and the new label Fox Searchlight.

Micro-indies

Micro-indies release films on a tiny number of screens and gross an average of $0.5 million per picture. There are around 15–20 such distributors, which are closely linked to the film festival circuit.

The micro indies tend to operate only in theatrical distribution and strike minimum guarantee deals for other media. The mini-majors and 'classics', on the other hand, have integrated foreign sales, home video and film libraries. For example, in 1992 New Line earned 18% of total revenue from US theatrical, Samuel Goldwyn 22% and Orion only 3% (most of Orion's revenue comes from library sales).

PERFORMANCE

Demand for indie distributed films is as volatile as that for the mainstream, which makes financing independent production as much a crapshoot as that for the Majors. This can be demonstrated by looking at the 'demand curve' for the main independent releases in 1994:

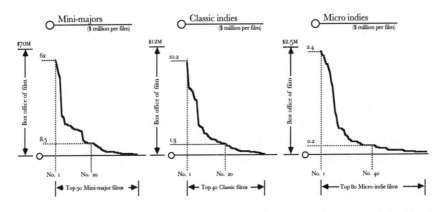

Each section of the market has its own 'demand curve'. The average grosses per film for the mini-majors nudges close to the performance of the Majors, whereas the micro-indies have to survive on very tight margins.

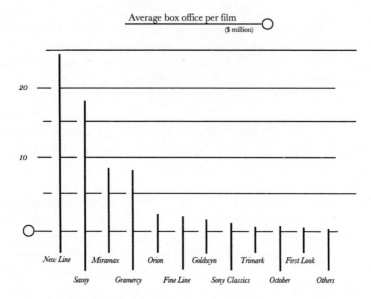

Average box office per film
($ million)

New Line is by far the strongest indie. The other 'classic' indie players have traditionally grossed an average of $2–3 million gross per picture, but a high capital injection has enabled Miramax to boost its average grosses and number of pictures released, and Gramercy has also entered the market at a comparatively high level.

COMPANY PROFILES

Just as with the Majors, each Independent has its own special atmosphere and preferred type of film. The majority of Independents have their main base in New York and this has a fundamental affect on their outlook.

Traditionally the Independents acquired finished films, rather than paying advance monies at script stage. But in the 1980s a number of Independents started providing production finance on the back of generous video deals. Many of these companies have now gone bankrupt. The influx of capital into the mini-majors in the 1990s has also allowed them to initiate production, but the verdict is still out on whether this can be profitable in the long run.

NEW LINE – PRUDENT AGGRESSION

Robert Shaye founded New Line in his Greenwich Village apartment in 1967 after attending Columbia Law School and winning a Fulbright Scholarship to Sweden. He began by distributing campy American exploitation pics such as *Reefer Madness*, and European art films to college campuses.

During the 1970s, New Line established itself as a premier art house distributor with leading Euro films like Bertrand Blier's *Get Out Your Handkerchiefs*, and American exploitation pics ranging from *The Texas Chainsaw Massacre* to John Waters' *Pink Flamingos*.

New Line began production in 1979 and started to split its energies between Hollywood and New York. The first hit film was *Nightmare on Elm Street*, which took three years to finance. The first three *Nightmare* films, 1984–87, cost under $10 million to make and grossed over $100 million. An even bigger hit was *Teenage Mutant Ninja Turtles* (1990) whose rights were acquired from Barry Diller at Fox for $3 million and went on to gross $130 million.

New Line went public in 1986 but spurned the temptation of junk bonds. In the early 1990s, the company began to establish itself as mini-major, with foreign sales, home video and television distribution, as well as a specialty wing – Fine Line. New Line also negotiated distribution rights to the film libraries of RHI Entertainment (1000 titles) and Nelson (600 titles).

In 1993 Robert Shaye sold New Line to Ted Turner for an estimated $550 million. This included the assumption of $70 million in debt and a $104 million pay-out to Shaye. The main motivation for selling according to Shaye was to achieve greater financial muscle – 'the industry going forward is going to be more of a closed shop' he predicted. The influx of capital allowed him to step up production including the Jim Carrey hits, *The Mask* and *Dumb and Dumber*.

New Line has an excellent track record. In 1994, with thirteen new releases, they had one $60 million gross and eight films grossing $15–20 million. This is far superior to any other indie. The key to New Line's success has been tight cost controls, a hands-on editorial style and a strong distribution business. Above all, it has been down to Shaye and business partner Michael Lynne.

Lynne, who has been friends with Shaye since college, describes him as 'a free spirit, a little bit of a rebel. He has always been in touch with the boyish element inside him, even today.' Peter Bart adds, '[Shaye] is an anomaly in the film business – a dreamer who is always fiercely practical, a well-read sophisticated man who has mastered the fine art of eliciting profits from Elm Street nightmares and Ninja Turtles.'

New Line's 300 staff are young and very hard working, combining 'playfulness and work ethic' according to Lynne, and typified by twenty-eight-year-old head of production Michael de Luca who joined the firm aged seventeen. Shaye has a reputation for giving young people a chance. He launched the Finnish director Renny Harlin with *Nightmare on Elm Street 4*, after which he warned 'Don't smoke the Hollywood crack pipe – the fast lane makes you phony and burns you out.'

As a result of the Time Warner–Turner merger, the company is likely to be sold, with an asking price of around $1.2 billion. Possible buyers include PolyGram and Bertelsmann.

MIRAMAX – MICKEY MOUTH

Bob and Harvey Weinstein are big men with a passion for the movies. They started in the rock concert business, which is where they began their reputation as the 'best promoters in the business'. As Harvey explains, 'The two of us wrote and produced over 1000 radio spots when we were promoting rock concerts and film series in upstate New York, prior to forming Miramax. We still come up with about 95% of the copy lines for our films.'[1]

The Weinsteins set up Miramax in their Manhattan apartment in 1980, concentrating on importing European films, which was Harvey's private passion. Their breakthrough hit was *Sex, Lies and Videotape* which won the Palme d'Or at Cannes in 1989 and went on to gross $25 million. On the back of this success Miramax was able to set up a $30 million credit line with Chase Manhattan.

Like all indies, Miramax is extremely cash conscious and has the reputation of being able to 'squeeze blood from a turnip'. They combine the chutzpah of the old movie moguls with the steely pragmatism of New York businessmen. The company has built its reputation on being able to recognize and acquire quality finished art house product and is the leading promoter of European films in the United States. 'Like diligent archaeologists', says *Variety*, 'the Weinsteins each year manage to come home from their foreign wanderings with a treasure trove of cinematic artifacts.'

Miramax is known for demanding re-cuts and re-mixes on their acquisitions, earning Harvey the reputation as 'Harvey Scissorhands'. For example, the $2.5 million Mexican film, *Like Water for Chocolate*, was cut from 144 minutes to 106 minutes and underwent three post-production overhauls. 'My favourite is the longer version' said director Arau, but 'I have been a producer and I know the pressure faced from exhibitors.' Nobody wanted to buy the original film, but it has gone on to become the biggest US foreign-language success in recent years.

Miramax began to consolidate activities in the early 1990s. The company established an international sales arm, signed an eighteen-title video and TV deal with Paramount and set up a new specialty label, Dimension Films.

But 1991–93 were troubled years for the company with costly flops such as *Map of the Human Heart, Deception, Tom and Jerry, Close to Eden* and *Little Buddha*. The company's pay-TV deal with HBO was also up for renewal in 1993 and many criticized Miramax for acquiring too much product. After arranging a $5 million advance from Rank in 1992 there were rumours that the Weinsteins were facing a cash crunch. Additional evidence was their $13 million package sale to Disney of *Sarafina* and video rights to five other films.

Their saviour was the $1.5 million acquisition of Neil Jordan's *The Crying Game* which they had turned down in script form. They were the only distributor interested in the picture when it was shown in rough cut. In a brilliant piece of marketing, they sold the film as an action thriller. The ad line read 'The movie everyone is talking about, but no one is giving away the secrets'. The film was opened on six screens and then slowly widened. Miramax bought a significant share of US rights from Channel 4 for under $2 million, and then following Oscar nominations pushed the film from 239 to 1093 screens. The film's $62 million gross proved that Miramax could organize a wide release and helped save the company, but ironically was too late to rescue its UK producer, Palace.

The Weinsteins immediately cashed in their chips and sold Miramax to Disney in May 1993, for an estimated $80 million in cash plus assumption of significant debts. At the time, Jeffrey Katzenberg said of the Weinsteins, 'They are as determined, as ambitious, as hungry and as competitive as any two people that I have ever met', adding that 'The company has survived enormous hurdles and weathered every obstacle to become a haven for independent film-makers throughout the world.'

CAA agent Robert Bookman focused on Miramax's principal motivation: 'This deal speaks to the issue of the depths of the pockets one needs to stay in the business.' Disney now organize Miramax's video distribution and make their pay-TV and free TV deals. Peter Bart wondered whether the company would change: 'Would the Weinstein brothers slow down? Would Bob stop yelling? Would Harvey stop smoking?'

The Disney deal gives Miramax complete autonomy for any acquisition or production up to $12 million. As a result, the company stepped up their acquisitions and in 1994 produced a third of their eighteen-film slate, including the $8 million *Pulp Fiction*, the $19 million *Prêt a Porter* and the $11 million *The Crossing Guard* directed by Sean Penn. The Disney muscle also made it easier to orchestrate wide releases such as the 1338 opening of *Pulp Fiction* (*Reservoir Dogs* had never played on more than 61 screens) and 2100-screen release for *The Crow*.

Many predicted that if the films bombed, Disney would withdraw their backing. But the successes of *Pulp Fiction* and *The Crow* seemed to silence the doubters. The year 1995 was relatively disappointing for Miramax. There were no mega-hits despite a continuing increase in the number of new releases (33 in 1995) and more wide releases. There were a number of costly flops, including the *Crossing Guard* which grossed under $1 million, and the $19 million *Restoration* which grossed under $4 million. Nonetheless the company announced $50 million in profits in 1995 on turnover upwards of $300 million.

In the meantime, Miramax has been recruiting top indie production talent including John Pierson and Paul Webster, and has signed talent deals with Quentin Tarantino, Woody Allen, Sean Penn, Gabriel Byrne, Kevin Gilbert, Marc and Peter Samuelson, Johnny Depp, Sharon Stone, Robert Rodriguez, and Harvey Keitel. Tarantino was also given his own specialty label, Rolling Thunder, in 1995 to release 'rougher, more jolty, visceral exploitation' films from Japan and China.

For foreign films, the company now has a subsidiary, Miramax Zoe, with a $5–6 million annual budget aimed to release up to three French films a year in dubbed version. Miramax also aims to invest in about five European films a year for a total of around $30–40 million.

The links with Disney were strained in 1995 when Miramax decided to release the gay-priest drama *Priest* on Good Friday. The Catholic League called for a nationwide boycott of Disney products. Disney backed Miramax on *Priest*, but for the more violent, NC-17 rated *Kids*, the Weinsteins were obliged to set up a new label – Shining Excalibur – outside the Disney orbit.

Harvey emphasizes that 'Miramax has always been about trying to be a Rolls Royce – a small company that makes good cars, beautiful cars. Maybe they don't sell the way GM does, but we're really proud of what we do and the quality we put into the project. There are no grand designs here to be No. 1 at the box office.'

Nonetheless, the company has proved that it is able to build market share, establish a valuable library and earn steady profits. In 1996 the brothers signed new seven-year employment contracts with Disney, quelling rumours that they might be tempted to join Jeffrey Katzenberg at Dreamworks SKG.

GRAMERCY – WEDDING BELLS

Gramercy was set up as a joint venture between PolyGram and Universal in 1993 to release specialty films on up to 1000 screens. In 1996 PolyGram bought full control of the distributor, with the intention to set up a parallel mainstream distribution arm.

Gramercy has been the cornerstone of PolyGram's ambition to become the first start-up Major since the war. The company is headed by Russell Schwartz, who was previously executive vice-president at Miramax.

PolyGram's film strategy has had mixed results. The larger budget productions have been disappointing and surprise successes released by Gramercy have been the most profitable pictures. By far the largest success has been *Four Weddings and a Funeral* which was released on five screens, but very strong word of mouth pushed the film to 1100 screens and a $53 million gross.

Out of twenty-eight releases, between 1993 and 1995 only six grossed more than $10 million, two of which were acquisitions. The future of Gramercy will ultimately depend upon PolyGram's overall strategy, which is outlined later.

SAVOY – SHADOWLANDS

Savoy was launched in 1992 by TriStar founder Victor Kaufman and financier Lewis Korman. They aimed to be the 'United Artists of the Nineties' and offered talent the chance to own a share of the film's negative. But in 1995 they withdrew from film production, and were subsequently sold to Barry Diller's Silver King Communications.

Savoy raised $165 million in capital in 1992, boosted to $400 million by the end of 1993. Equity finance was co-ordinated by top Hollywood banker Allen & Co., and shareholders came from various areas. The core team was former Columbia-TriStar staff including Kaufman and Korman, ex-Columbia chairman Frank Price, and Judd Enterprises (which included former Columbia-TriStar directors Judd and Richard Weinberg).

The investment community was represented by Allen & Co., GHK (an investment partnership managed by billionaires Jay and Tom Pritzer), plus Dan Lufkin and Mel Klein.

Other Hollywood stockholders were Cinergi's Andy Vajna and HBO (3%). Michael Fuchs at Time Warner's HBO played a crucial role in launching Savoy through a generous pay-TV deal which established a war chest enabling Savoy to finance up to 50% of their production costs.

Savoy also had important foreign investors including Cecchi Gori (5%), Berlusconi (5%), Chargeurs (10%), Mitsui and Carlton (10%). The foreign investors put up over $50 million in 1992 for these stakes and also acquired foreign rights to Savoy's films.

Savoy's business plan was originally based on distribution rather than development or production. They planned to acquire and release twelve to fifteen pictures a year for a total costs of $250–$350 million – just slightly below the MPAA average. But the lack of strong product forced them into multi-picture deals with talent and significant development spending.

Savoy was sitting on top of an equity mountain, but its initial feature film investments underperformed. Of the company's first five movies only the Paul Hogan comedy *Lightning Jack* was profitable with a $17 million US gross. *Shadowlands* ($25 million US gross) broke even and the rest all lost money, including a disastrous $13 million loss on *Exit to Eden*. While costs were comparable to the Majors, average grosses were only 50% as high.

In 1994 the company began to move towards the TV business, creating a joint venture with News Corporation, to buy up TV stations. Savoy also announced that they would begin TV production, financed by new loans worth several hundred million dollars.

The patrician Savoy seemed out of place amongst the other indies who had a low cost street-fighting attitude to the business. The company produced many small pictures, such as *Circle of Friends*, with little prospect to break into the mainstream. Stockholders began to sell out and Savoy's share price began to plummet.

In September 1995 after a series of costly flops, Savoy announced that they would reduce their feature film distribution in order to concentrate on station acquisition. In November 1995 the company was acquired by Silver King at 70% of its original share value.

ORION

Orion was created by the exodus of the highly acclaimed five senior executives at United Artists in 1978 after prolonged disagreements with parent company Transamerica (who acquired UA in 1967). The company has always had an ambiguous position between the Majors and the Independents, and for many years was a member of both the MPAA and AFMA. In the 1980s, Orion was the most important source of independent finance and distribution and also had a leading specialty division, Orion Classics. The company released five of the seven Oscars earned by Independents since 1980 – *Gandhi, Amadeus, Platoon, Dances with Wolves* and *Silence of the Lambs*.

On the basis of these films, Orion managed to build up its US theatrical rentals, with hit years in 1987 and 1991. But Orion's emphasis on 'quality' movies and failure to diversify, meant that it lived on a financial knife edge throughout the 1980s. The company was repeatedly forced to issue new equity and raise new loans. In 1984 the company sold $20 million of its library outright to Time Warner, and was on the constant look-out for buyers, including Goldcrest in 1985.

Orion was finally taken over by John Kluge's Metromedia in the late 1980s, but continued to suffer financial problems, which forced the sale of much of the upside on many of its films. As a result, Orion did not benefit from the surprise successes of *Dances with Wolves* and *Silence of the Lambs*. The company was declared bankrupt in 1991 and Kluge was estimated to have lost about $300 million. The bankruptcy created further problems for Independents such as Hemdale who had output deals with the studio.

New Line considered buying the company but later backed down, and Orion was released from bankruptcy in 1992 only through a $26 million sale of TV rights from over 200 library titles to Mitsubishi. Staff was cut from 750 to 150 and the company was forced to refocus on library sales and its Classics division. In 1992 the company had $700 million in outstanding debt, which by late 1993 had been pulled back to $289 million.

Orion was initially barred from engaging in any development, production and theatrical distribution of films not 100% financed by third-party participants, and Orion's 1994 slate was almost entirely films that had been produced two and a half years earlier. Even once the third-party ruling was relaxed, Kluge seemed unwilling to put up the $200–300 million in production financing that would be necessary to relaunch Orion as a mini-major.

In 1995 Orion looked to be getting back into the big time with a US and foreign distribution deal with Cine-Fin, but the deal fell apart after two weeks of shooting of their first feature *Divine Rapture* starring Marlon Brando. In September 1995, Chemical Bank provided Kluge with a $135 million term loan and $50 million revolving fund for new production and acquisitions. This was intended to facilitate a full merger with Metromedia, Actava Group and MCEG

Sterling. Metromedia subsequently acquired Brad Krevoy's MPCA (the creators of *Dumb and Dumber*) and Samuel Goldwyn. The ensemble could one day be the base of a new studio with the full library including 725 titles from Orion, 1200 from Goldwyn and 400 from MCEG.

In May 1996 Kluge made a new stock offering of $200 million and aimed to raise a further $200 million in debt to kick-start his studio. At the same time he announced he would start investing in Eastern European cable and telephone systems. Analysts remained sceptical of his game plan.

SAMUEL GOLDWYN

Until 1996, Goldwyn was the last of the 'true' Hollywood Independents. But after a $20 million loss in 1995 the company was sold to John Kluge's Metromedia for $42 million in equity and $77 million in assumed debt. Founded in 1980 by Samuel Goldwyn Jr. – the son of the Hollywood legend – the company has established itself as the premium distributor of 'quality' movies such as *The Madness of King George, Much Ado About Nothing* and foreign-language films such as *Eat Drink Man Woman*. Goldwyn is also heavily involved in production of syndicated TV shows, such as *American Gladiators*.

The increasing competition in the indie market forced Goldwyn to make bigger equity punts, resulting in the disastrous $10 million loss from *The Perez Family* in 1995, which cost $11 million to produce, opened on 928 screens but grossed only $3 million. Goldwyn had been looking in vain for a European 'strategic partner' and before the Metromedia buy-out, had considered selling its 126-screen Landmark Theatres as well as its library to PolyGram. Under the terms of the deal, Goldwyn lost the right to greenlight his pictures.

'I suppose the bottom line, Sam, is that you were never "street" like your father,' concluded Peter Bart at *Variety*. 'You are, in fact, "the last Hollywood Brahmin" as one British friend put it. You live the regal life of the moguls of old, replete with fabled art collection and patrician habits. Still rangy and slim, with your splendid mane of silver hair, you are an elegant anachronism, trying to cope with the tough, mean-spirited commoners of a new epoch.'

FINE LINE

The niche wing of New Line was set up in 1992 under Ira Deutschman with the remit to make 'character, story and film-maker driven' films, while New Line focuses on 'genre and high concept movies'. Deutschman put up production financing for *Death and the Maiden* and *Mrs Parker and the Vicious Circle* which underperformed at the box office. His penchant for 'dark' themes led to his replacement by Ruth Vitale in 1995. Vitale has suggested that she is looking for more commercial projects in order to provide leverage for her slate and may back films with budgets of up to $12–15 million. Fine Line has a London bureau headed by Ileen Maisel.

SONY CLASSICS

Sony Classics was set up in 1992 by the former Orion Classics team, Marcie Bloom, Tom Bernard and Michael Barker. The company has been very cautious in its acquisitions strategy. One of the biggest releases was *Howards End*. 'I don't think it's an easy time to establish what's working', says Bloom. 'I think that's one of the reasons why some of the companies are resorting to the throw-it-against-the-wall-and-see-if-it-sticks strategy.'[2]

FOX SEARCHLIGHT

Fox Searchlight is a new venture, announced at the end of 1994. It aims to release six to eight pictures a year combining in-house production and acquisitions. Originally Tom Rothman was slated to head a London branch, but he was subsequently moved to oversee the entire Fox slate. Deals have been signed with Jeremy Thomas, Bob Rafelson, Spike Lee, Gillian Armstrong, Wayne Wang, Stephen Frears and Christopher Hampton as well as two-year first-look deals with New York's Good Machine and UK producer, Sarah Radclyffe.

The first release was for micro-budget feature *The Brothers McMullen* which cost $200,000 to make and is expected to gross up to $20 million worldwide. At the end of 1995 Lindsay Law was recruited from PBS's American Playhouse to head the operation. He explained that the major attraction of his new position was the financial support provided by a Major: 'The thing I hated most in life was raising money – trying to cobble together five different distributors . . . where everybody ends up taking 25%.'[3]

MICRO-INDIES

The main micro-indies include Kino, New Yorker, October, Zeitgeist, First Run and First Look. They establish awareness for releases through the festival circuit and critics' reviews. Films are released usually on one or two specialist screens in New York, such as the Lincoln Plaza or the Angelika. The micro-indies can uncover specialist gems such as *Scent of the Green Papaya* and earn grosses of up to $3–5 million.

5
Foreign Sales

Cannes was an important international crossroads,
a great fair of cinema — joyful and alive —
where French films were exported abroad, and there
were huge transactions and co-productions . . .
Today festivals are for selling villas, ski slopes,
apartments and publicity for TV.
Alain Poiré

FOREIGN SALES ARE THE MEETING PLACE of the international film industry, where a plethora of local distributors and foreign sales agents do business. 'The truth is that most international executives, who live on jumbo jets and dine on melatonin, fall somewhere in between Willy Loman and Cary Grant', says *Variety*'s Max Alexander, 'But the expanding overseas business is attracting a younger set of aggressive players with big ideas – people who in previous eras might have been drawn into production.'

Foreign sales used to be dominated by European films, above all the giants of Italian and French cinema. Today the market is wholly orientated around American independent production, and as with the rest of the business, increasingly dominated by the Majors. Sales are conducted throughout the year, but the key periods are the main international film markets: Cannes, Mifed, and AFM.

Although foreign video and TV sales have expanded since 1980, foreign *theatrical* sales have actually shrunk in real terms over the same period, from $550 million to $400 million, and the European section of the market has almost totally disappeared.

OVERVIEW

The foreign sales business has played a pivotal role in recent years in both American independent production and the survival of local European distributors. The collapse of Europe's domestic film industry has meant that billions of investment dollars have poured into Hollywood via foreign sales.

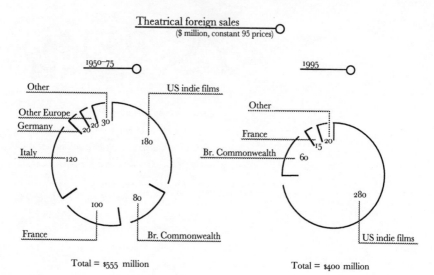

Theatrical foreign sales
($ million, constant 95 prices)

1950–75

Other
Other Europe
Germany
Italy ····120
France
100   80
US indie films
180

Br. Commonwealth

Total = $555 million

1995

Other
France
Br. Commonwealth   60
15 20
280
US indie films

Total = $400 million

EUROPEANS-IN-HOLLYWOOD

European cinema had its heyday during the era of 'Hollywood in Europe', but in the early 1970s the Majors withdrew their production presence in Europe and led to a new phenomenon – 'Europeans-in-Hollywood'. British producers such as Lew Grade and John Heyman, as well as American impresarios such as Joe Levine, refocused their attentions on Hollywood, joined by the likes of Italian producer Dino de Laurentiis and Dutch financier Frans Afman.

The players most directly linked to Hollywood include:

Britain	John Daly, John Heyman, Chris Blackwell, Lew Grade
France	Leonardo de Fuentes, Jean-Louis Rubin, Edouard Sarlui
Italy	Dino de Laurentiis, Alberto Grimaldi
Germany	Dieter Geissler, Bernd Eichinger, Willy Baer
E. Europe	Andy Vajna, Alexander and Ilya Salkind, Pierre Spengler, Zalman King
M. East	Moshé Diamant, Mario Kassar, Arnon Milchan, Menahem Golan

Europe's leading producers such as Jeremy Thomas, Steve Woolley, Nik Powell, Chris Sievernich, and Andres Vicente Gomez, also depend critically on foreign sales in order to finance their films.

Europeans working in Hollywood thereby provide popular culture through the back door for European distributors and have often used European genres and stars. A leading example is the action genre which had always been particularly popular in Europe, with super heroes such as *Hercules* and *Maciste*. Their modern equivalents are European action stars such as Arnold Schwarzenneger, Jean-Claude van Damme and Dolph Lundgren, all of whom got their breaks in the independent sector.

Another very popular tradition in Europe is the erotic genre which in its American version has produced countless direct-to-video erotic thrillers as well as bigger hits such as *9½ Weeks, Showgirls,* and *Basic Instinct,* all of which were financed, produced and directed by Europeans.

The moral ambiguities of commercial European films were also transposed to American independent cinema. For example, the Italian spaghetti western director, Corbucci, said in the 1960s: 'Our westerns are more emotional and more realistic, but let's face it, they are also more perverse. There is everything: drugs, savage cruelty. We kill babies too. Soon the Americans will understand how things are. For the time being, they remain attached to honest fights and legal duels.'

Europeans-in-Hollywood played a key role in defining post-Hays Code movies. This influence may now be coming to an end, with the collapse of the independent sector in the late 1980s and the increasing stranglehold of the Majors. Europeans risk losing one of their last lifelines to make popular films.

BOOM AND BUST IN THE 1980S

In the late 1970s and early 1980s the indies enjoyed a production boom, due to a desperate need for popular films in Europe, the investment tax credit scheme (1975–85), the bullish stock market and the video boom.

This led to a crop of new indie producers and distributors who were able to leverage significant corporate finance. One agent described these as 'Slash and dash operators. Not really film-makers but entrepreneurs. They sold the film on the basis of the poster and the "credits not contractual" talent. Most projects revolved around sex, violence and action and many never got made.'

In the 1980s the leading Hollywood Independents all had in-house sales divisions, such as Cannon who used to descend on Cannes every year with a team of track-suited marketeers. The Independent would announce a high profile project and then look for pre-sales to back it. Much of the money came from fledgling video distributors who were desperate for product. The banks, especially Credit Lyonnais, provided extensive credit lines which were used to fund production in expectation of future sales.

Several of the leading companies went public in 1985–86 in order to secure greater investment funds. Classic examples were Cannon Films and Dino de Laurentiis. 'Wall Street is partly responsible for the demise of many independent production companies', says financier Frans Afman. 'They threw money at Dino, Cannon, New World. All of these companies had very weak financial management. It was like putting a sugar pot in front of a four-year-old kid. Nobody realized it had to be repaid. If I were an investor I'd never put equity into a company. The money is used to cover overhead, development and "life-style" but not necessarily in that order.'

Many indies established theatrical distribution arms and stepped up their production slates, but the results were disastrous, which made it impossible to pay back junk bonds carrying interest of 15–17%. 'Nobody realized this debt had to be serviced' says Afman, 'and they didn't know how to. Everyone was in euphoria now they had money to play with. All of these companies went into distribution. I always said – don't go into distribution except for smaller films where you need to place them for video exploitation. Cannon, for example, made very strong video and TV but had never had a hit in the theatres other than the $36 million gross for *Breakdance*. To compete with the Majors and put up $15 million for an opening weekend you have to be out of your mind. I still think that. You have to use the Majors in the US and the Independents abroad.'

Most of the indies went bankrupt or were taken over after the stock market crash in 1987, including Cannon, De Laurentiis Entertainment Group, MCEG, New World, Vista Organisation, Atlantic, Cinema Group, Vestron, Heritage, Republic and Lorimar. The larger players such as Republic and Lorimar were taken over by the Majors. The last survivor was Carolco, which managed to carry on working through the generosity of its European and Japanese sugar daddies.

'The classic deals I invented with Dino twenty-two years ago, don't work any more', concludes Afman. 'The indie battlefield looks like a slaughterhouse. It's frightening. There's very little quality left. There are virtually no independent video distributors. The Majors have taken over the market. They're owned by huge corporations and they shake the money tree and they get what they want.'

CREDIT LYONNAIS

The French state-owned bank Credit Lyonnais was by far the most important banker for Europeans working in Hollywood. Ironically this meant that while the French state was vaunting 'culture' at home, it was often backing 'video nasties' in Hollywood.

The Credit Lyonnais connection began with Slavensberg Bank in Holland, where Dino de Laurentiis and Frans Afman had been bankrolling foreign pre-sales since the early 1970s. Credit Lyonnais took over Slavensberg in 1980 after the latter was hit by a financial scandal.

François d'Aubert later alleged in his book *Dirty Money*, that Slavensberg was rife with corruption, even though no senior executive was found guilty in court.

Credit Lyonnais had been told by the French Socialist Government that media was a priority area and as a result started providing an increasing amount of debt finance to the leading independent companies. The bank also became involved with suspect figures such as Parretti and Fiorini.

After the 1987 stock market crash, many of the Credit Lyonnais-backed Independents started to suffer severe financial problems and began to default on their loans.

Credit Lyonnais also became much less 'independent friendly' after Frans Afman left the bank in 1988, allegedly because of the Parretti connection, but perhaps in foresight of the coming storm. According to John Daly, 'I would say our problems with Credit Lyonnais really started when Frans Afman left the bank a few years ago. He was the one man there who understood us.'

The downturn in the business hit Credit Lyonnais much harder than any other player. By 1992 the bank admitted it had over 100 loans to Independents totalling $1.4 billion, of which 34 were causing problems. In 1993 it recorded an unprecedented $1.2 billion loss. (Another bank to suffer losses was Chemical Bank who had to write off $400–500 million.)

Credit Lyonnais soon found itself with a long list of belly-up Independents including Weintraub, Hemdale, Cannon, Epic, Gladden, Trans-World Entertainment, 21st Century, Carolco, Film Accord, Orion, Sovereign, Vision, Fries and Nelson/Sultan. Peter Bart commented, 'None of these companies could have made movies without the unique philanthropy of Credit Lyonnais, the bank that loves to lose.'

These Independents own a combined library of over 900 titles including *Platoon*, *The Fabulous Baker Boys*, *City Slickers* and *When Harry Met Sally*, plus a vast number of B and C titles. Some of the Independents merely suffered from a downturn in business. Many were mismanaged.

Peter Bart concentrated on the latter, when he quipped that Guy-Etienne Dufour should burn the 900 negatives: 'Think of the statement this would make, Monsieur. You would be warning all the rascals of the movie world to find some other business to loot. It's hard enough for legitimate players these days to make and market their movies, without letting all the crooks in on the action.'

Instead of a film bonfire, in 1996 the French bank suffered a fire in its Paris headquarters which destroyed important files relating to the bank's recent activities.

THE MARKET

The foreign sales market has been static since 1987 and is increasingly dependent on video and television:

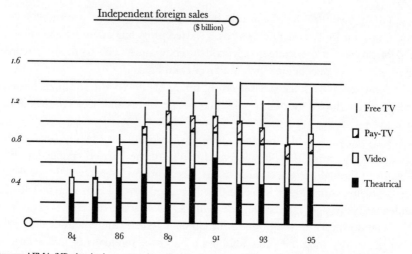

Source: AFMA (NB: the rise in revenues in early years is exaggerated by new companies joining AFMA. Data for 1987 is included in 1986 and 1988 figures).

There are five different types of films sold in the market.

- Major titles. High profile 'event' pictures with high budgets and distributed in the US by the Majors.

- Mini-major titles. Smaller $10–25 million pick-ups with the Majors or mini-majors.

- Niche. Smaller $3–10 million pictures aimed for specialty release, usually with established directors or actors.

- Foreign-language. Consigned to a niche market. Mainly with established directors and actors.

- Direct-to-video. Mainly action and erotic thrillers.

The value of the English-language sales business was $1.37 billion in 1995. To this must be added about $120 million for foreign-language sales, half of which is earned by France. The breakdown of the total market by type of film is roughly as follows:

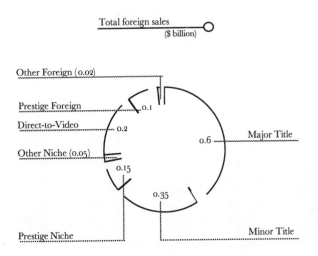

Each type of film has a different community of buyers and sellers. For example, at the 1995 Cannes Film Market there were 200 sales companies offering a total of 1300 films, about a third of which were new titles.

The largest type of film on offer (150 new titles) are direct-to-video films which are almost exclusively produced by the United States. These are low budget and have average sales of $1 million per title. The second largest category is the foreign-language market (200 new titles) but only 25% bear 'name' talent. Prestige foreign titles earn average sales of $2 million per film, the rest $0.2 million.

The most sought-after titles are English-language theatrical films. Major films (20 new titles) can earn upwards of $25 million in foreign sales. Mini-major films (45 new titles) an average of $6 million and niche titles $3 million for name talent (30 new titles), and $1 million for a good film from unknown talent (30 new titles).

America provides around 120 new theatrical films a year for foreign sales, Britain 30 films and the rest of the British Commonwealth a further 30. France provides 55 films and the other leading European countries 15–20.

THE BUYERS

The main buyers are distributors from Europe (59% of sales) and Asia (35%) who are trying to compete with the Hollywood Majors. There are also intermediary rights buyers such as the Kirch Group, Fininvest, PolyGram, BMG Video, Studio Canal+ and Lègende (TF1/Alain Goldman). The 'hot' titles tend to be the same in every country, and are often set by America which buys around 40 English-language films a year from the British Commonwealth and 75 foreign-language films.

European distributors are able to leverage a much higher share of their national box office by acquiring American independent films. In France and Italy this share is close to 45%, in Germany 27% and in the UK and Spain just under 20%.

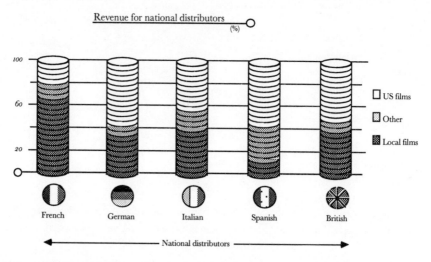

Source: London Economics (Top 200 films 1989 and 1990 combined)

The Majors were also keen buyers of foreign and independent films in the 1950s and 1960s, often grossing more money overseas from such films than from in-house product. They drastically cut back their European operations in the early 1970s, but in recent years have been hiring distribution talent from the independent sector in order to broaden their range of product. A classic example is former Palace distribution chief Daniel Battsek, who now heads Buena Vista (Disney) in the UK and releases most of Miramax's films as well as other hot independent titles.

The Majors now earn 10% of their revenues from distributing local and foreign-language product. This 'cherry picking' of the best independent films has further squeezed local distributors who have no other source of popular films.

TYPES OF BUYER

Each type of film appeals to a different buyer, and has its own range of prices. The main national buyers and their target films are as follows:

- National majors   American pick-ups from Majors and mini-majors.

- Mini-majors   Cross-over films, mainly American.

- Niche players   American indie films and prestige European.

In the main European territories these buyers include the following:

	France	Germany	Italy	Spain	UK
National major	AMLF/Pricel Gaumont/BV UGC/Fox	N. Constantin	Cecchi Gori Medusa/Berl. Filmauro	Sogepaq	Rank
Mini-major	Bac Ciby MK2 Pan-Européen	Concorde Senator Tobis	Academy Artisti Associati Life Int'l	Araba Laurenfilm Lider	Guild Entertainment
Niche	Diaphana Pyramide Haut et Court	Connexion Jugendfilm Scotia Pandora	BIM Chance Istituto Luce Mikado	Esicma M. Salvador Filmayer Surf	Mayfair Electric

Most of these distributors are critically dependent on the foreign sales market because they will earn the bulk of their revenues from imported films.

THE SALES AGENTS

The foreign sales business is organized by the sales agents, who provide the linking device between independent producers and foreign distributors. This is a small and very tight-knit community. There are many colourful characters in the business, and at the fringes a large number of cowboys.

Each sales agent will focus on one type of film and will build up a relationship of trust with their buyers. This sense of trust is particularly important for pre-sales, where the local distributors are almost buying blind.

The two main poles of the foreign sales business are Los Angeles and London. The former is the heart of talent deals and US distribution agreements. The latter is the physical base of most of the distribution activity – because of the prime importance of the European market. 'Geographically London is the place to be', explains Ralph Kamp of Icon. 'Early in the morning you can be in touch with Asia and Australia. All day long, you can talk to people from here to Russia and at the end of the day the Americans come on board. You've got to be in London to feel the pulse of the sales business.'[1]

London has been a key film exchange since the birth of cinema, when the UK market alone was worth a third of the US. In more recent years, many of the key figures in international pre-sales have been based there, starting with John Heyman and Lord Grade in the 1960s. This has led to the development of skilled back-up teams in finance and legal services.

THE STRANGLEHOLD OF THE MAJORS

The 'prestige' part of the business is now increasingly dominated by the Majors who are reluctant to cede foreign rights. In the 1980s many studios laid off foreign rights because they were desperate for capital. Now that they have established global empires they tend to keep everything in-house. Only cash-strapped studios such as MGM are willing to sell off foreign rights.

The Majors recognize that international sales is the main growth area. For example, Rupert Murdoch recently instructed his Fox executives always to acquire world rights. Entertainment lawyer Peter Dekom emphasizes, 'Today if you sell off 50% of the movie to foreign you have drastically reduced your ability to get a domestic deal.'[2]

In the late 1980s a number of US Independents were set up with complicated foreign rights deals. But the subsequent financial troughs and time consuming deal-making led them to return to the studios, including Brian Grazer and Ron Howard at Imagine, Larry Gordon who exited Largo, and James Cameron at Lightstorm.

The bankruptcy of Carolco in 1995 was a further sign that the day of the A-title Independents is over. Independent sales agents are finding it increasingly difficult to survive, unless they have privileged access to A-level talent such as Morgan Creek, Summit or Icon, or deep pockets such as Largo (JVC), Majestic (RCS), Rysher and PolyGram.

International buyers are also less willing to put up hefty pre-sales because they have been hit by flops such as *Cutthroat Island*. They now prefer output deals with indies that are backed by the Majors. The international business is being restructured with 'strategic alliances' between the leading players and local distributors. This means that over time the Majors will become global distributors catering for both mainstream and niche product.

The free-for-all of the foreign sales market is being replaced by joint ventures with the Majors, such as Gaumont/Buena Vista, UGC/Fox and Rank/Castle Rock.

The new status quo in the sales business is blamed by some commentators, such as Dutch producer Jan Verheyen, on excessive prices and a shortage of quality: 'The business of selling films has become a business of who screws who first', he claimed in 1993. 'The sales agent considers, and quite rightly so, the average distributor a lying thief who will never send you reports, let alone any overages . . . In Benelux alone, three mini-major companies went broke in less than six months time – bad management, yes, incompetence, surely, but all three companies were knowingly pillaged by sales agents who smelled an easy prey. All three companies went down because they overpaid for, at best, mediocre products.'[3] Verheyen is perhaps being overly acerbic, but he highlights the fact that the independent distribution business is increasingly short of both capital and good films.

SALES AGENTS AS PRODUCERS

As the Independents went bankrupt, they have been replaced by a new breed of sales agents who have been forced to adopt the same tactics – setting up rich parent companies and extensive credit lines. This is potentially dangerous, as recent bankruptcies have shown.

One of the first companies to move in this direction was Sovereign Pictures, set up in 1988 by Ernst Goldschmidt and Barbara Boyle, who were formerly heads of international distribution and production at Orion. They recognized that foreign distributors no longer wanted the B-pictures produced by most Independents and were looking for A-titles.

Sovereign provided production funding and also guaranteed P&A expenditure and shortfalls for local distributors in return for lower distribution fees. As a result they acted as a 'mini-studio' with output deals with Rank in the UK, Warners in Japan and Italy, Fox in Germany, Les Films Ariane in France, Lauren Film in Spain and Village Roadshow in Australia.

Sovereign also had two equity investors – Revcom/Ariane and Nordisk – plus loans from Credit Lyonnais. But the firm went bankrupt in 1993, because it could not find enough regular hits. Other bankruptcies in the early 1990s were Glinwood films and a massive restructuring in 1993 at Odyssey/Double Helix.

The 'survivors' have established financing deals with major media groups but there continues to be a shake-out in the business. There was an exceptional level of corporate restructuring in 1995 confirming the dominance of the Majors.

For the moment the only sections of the market where the Majors have shown no interest are direct-to-video, foreign-language titles and low-budget English-language films. This could be the future of the foreign sales business.

SALES COMMISSIONS

Sales agents operate either on a straight commission base or as producers. A sale typically includes a minimum guarantee (MG) payment, a minimum P&A expenditure, an agreed promotion and release plan and conditions under which overages will be paid. If the sales agent puts up its own funds, they may waive an MG payment, in return for a lower distribution fee and higher overages.

Rights are usually licensed for a specific time period (most typically 5–12 years for a new film) and then revert to the seller. The 'price' (i.e. the minimum guarantee) will depend on the type of buyer. For example, whereas a national major may pay $5 million for a prestige American film, a niche player may pay only $50,000 for a niche title.

When a sales house acts as a straightforward agent there is a 10–25% commission on sales. This fee is charged on the minimum guarantee and also on any overages paid by local distributors. Since local distributors will also charge a 30–35% distribution fee, this means that the producer may incur total commissions of 50–60%.

If the sales house also provides an up-front minimum guarantee, the commission will be higher (25–35%) but may result in lower local distributor fees. The sales agent will also charge for sales expenses, including the cost of taking the film to the main markets and sending out information to buyers.

The total value of foreign sales is over $1.3 billion, which means that total commissions (10–30% of sales) are between $200 million and $300 million. Since most sales agents are privately run, it is difficult to obtain reliable income data. UK-based sales agents which have declared earnings recently include:

Company	Year	Commissions	Profits
Majestic	1993	$6.2M	$2.4M
J&M	1994	$4.4M	$1.9M
Cori	1993	$4.1M	$0.9M
Lumière (rights)	1991	$2.1M	$0.6M
Goldcrest	1992	$5.3M	($4.2M) loss

PRE-SALES

Sales agents will attempt to 'pre-sell' higher budget films in order to raise their finance. The key pre-sale is to the US – which gives a signal to the rest of the market. The US distributor guarantees the number of screens, the P&A expenditure and a contribution to the production budget. This will create a marketing hype for the film which can then be used in the rest of the world.

The key 'elements' for selling a film are the director and the cast. These will allow the film to gain editorial attention and help 'open' the release. Both the sales companies and the talent agents are aware of who is 'hot' talent in which territory and price their deals accordingly.

The worth of each element is rated internally by each sales agent. An indication of these league tables is provided by recent surveys of leading distributors made by *The Hollywood Reporter*. The Top Ten on each list were:

Directors (1993)		*Actors (1995)*	
1.	James Cameron	1.	Tom Cruise
2.	Steven Spielberg	2.	Tom Hanks
3.	Martin Scorsese	3.	Harrison Ford
4.	Bernardo Bertolucci	4.	Mel Gibson
5.	Rob Reiner	5.	A. Schwarzenegger
6.	Oliver Stone	6.	Clint Eastwood
7.	Paul Verhoeven	7.	Jim Carrey
8.	Kevin Costner	8.	Kevin Costner
9.	Francis F. Coppola	9.	Michael Douglas
10.	Tim Burton	10.	Jodie Foster

Top talent tends to be locked into studio deals. Smaller players must focus on the 'second division'. For example, talent rated 31–40 was as follows:

Directors (1993)		*Actors (1995)*	
31.	Adrian Lyne	31.	Hugh Grant
32.	Wolfgang Petersen	32.	Warren Beatty
33.	Jean-Jacques Annaud	33.	Winona Ryder
34.	Stephen Frears	34.	J-C. Van Damme
35.	Woody Allen	35.	Anthony Hopkins
36.	Robert Altman	36.	Barbra Streisand
37.	Andrew Davis	37.	Meryl Streep
38.	John Hughes	38.	Alec Baldwin
39.	Tony Scott	39.	Geena Davis
40.	Gary Marshall	40.	Steven Seagal

The *Hollywood Reporter* survey identifies 300 directors in the world with some form of public recognition, and 800 actors. Only 140 in each category are rated as 'name' talent – with a B rating or more – necessary for a pre-sale.

	A+	A	B+	B	C
Directors	3	30	10	100	210
Actors	8	30	30	73	575

This 'name' talent includes a large number of Europeans who now work mainly in Hollywood films – 40% of the name directors and 16% of name actors.

	All Names	*UK/Ire*	*Aus/NZ*	*For.-lang.*
Directors	143	20	5	30
Actors	141	12	2	8

The leading foreign-language talent now working mainly on English-language films are as follows (with their world rank):

Directors (1993)			*Actors (1995)*		
1.	Bernardo Bertolucci	*No. 4*	1.	A. Schwarzenegger	*No. 1*
2.	Paul Verhoeven	*No. 7*	2.	J-C. Van Damme	*No. 33*
3.	Renny Harlin	*No. 18*	3.	Gérard Depardieu	*No. 46*
4.	Milos Forman	*No. 25*	4.	Antonio Banderas	*No. 70*
5.	Wolfgang Petersen	*No. 32*	5.	Dolph Lundgren	*No. 90*
6.	Jean-Jacques Annaud	*No. 33*	6.	C. Lambert	*No. 107*
7.	Wim Wenders	*No. 52*	7.	Juliette Binoche	*No. 115*

Amongst the foreign-language talent that continues to work in their native language there are only six name directors and three name actors. They are (with world rank):

Directors (1993)			*Actors (1995)*	
1.	Pedro Almodóvar	*No. 61*	1. Gérard Depardieu	*No. 46*
2.	Giuseppe Tornatore	*No. 81*	2. Juliette Binoche	*No. 115*
3.	Agniesza Holland	*No. 95*	3. Isabelle Adjani	*No. 118*
4.	Bertrand Tavernier	*No. 98*		
5.	Claude Berri	*No. 100*		
6.	Jean-Jacques Beineix	*No. 133*		

This is very different from the 'golden age' of European cinema when there was a wealth of star talent amongst directors and actors. Today many of the remaining recognizable names actually established themselves in the 1960s or early 1970s such as Alain Delon, Marcello Mastroianni, Sophia Loren, Jean-Paul Belmondo and Jeanne Moreau.

This makes the foreign sales business very Hollywood orientated. Everyone is chasing after the same talent, and the Hollywood agents place very stringent terms upon which it may be used.

THE PACKAGE

For any project, the sales agent and potential buyers will look above all at the director and the stars and will then look at the proposed budget level and the synopsis. This will give them a sense of whether the film 'feels' right or not.

The sales agent will then establish a target fee for each territory, based on the overall budget. The rough percentage guidelines are as follows:

Territory	*World share*
US	30–35%
Japan	10–12%
Germany/Austria	9–10%
France	8–9%
UK	8–9%
Italy	6–8%
Spain	4–4.5%
Benelux	2–2.5%
Scandinavia	1.5–2%
Australasia	2–3%
Rest of world	12–15%

Certain stars will command a much higher fee in specific territories. For example, Depardieu will command a bigger fee in France and so will certain US stars such as Sharon Stone.

The sales agent will pre-sell the film as widely as possible, but there will usually be a gap which must be filled either by the sales agent's funds, other sources of financing, or a budget cut. A good example of this process was the film *Four Weddings and a Funeral*. PolyGram believed that it could raise $4.5 million in world sales including $1 million from Channel 4, but this meant that the old budget had to be trimmed back by $1 million, and the production plans changed.

MARKETS AND FESTIVALS

Festivals provide awards and enable vital press coverage to be built for a film. The main festivals in the year include: Sundance (Park City, US, Jan.), Berlin (Feb.), Cannes (May), Venice (Sept.), Toronto (Sept.) Tokyo (Sept.), New York (Oct.) and London (Nov.). There are several other leading festivals and countless smaller festivals which play a vital role in promoting independent films.

The Majors rarely submit films to festivals but instead focus on the Oscar ceremonies in March which are the most important press event of the year.

Markets enable screenings and provide face to face contact between buyers and sellers. The main film markets are AFM (Los Angeles, Feb.), Cannes (May) and MIFED (Milan, Oct.) followed by IFFM (New York, Sept.). There are also key television markets in Cannes – MIP (April) and MIPCOM (Oct.) – and Las Vegas – NATPE (Jan.).

Cannes

Cannes remains a focal point of the international film business because it combines the business and social aspects, and has a very different atmosphere from the other markets. To the first-time visitor, the Festival feels like the heart of the world's film industry. As Menahem Golan used to say, 'Cannes is my Christmas.' There are film posters everywhere, crowds straining to spot a star, and the nightly ritual of ascending the Palace steps in dinner jackets and ball gowns. But like everything else in the film industry, the Festival is all smoke and mirrors and much of the hype hides a hollow facade.

Cannes is a useful place to meet people. The key sales agents are frenetically busy, but most producers and directors are relaxed and fairly accessible. The prestige locations are the Carlton, Majestic and Martinez hotels whose suites are filled with the industry's top sales agents, producers and visiting stars. The Independents are housed in two wigwam villages known as the European and American pavilions.

Cannes involves a lot of walking, talking and hype. Parties are very exciting as you try to get in, and then often a disappointment. Often the best contacts are made in late-night haunts such as the Petit Carlton and Petit Majestic.

THE MAIN SALES AGENTS

More than 200 companies are involved in foreign sales. Around ten of these are 'prestige' agents with staff of up to thirty and average sales of $40 million. Together they represent 40% of the total volume of foreign sales. A further 20% of the business is provided by around eighteen 'crossover' agents with staff of around twelve, and average sales of between $12 million and $20 million.

The main sales companies can be grouped roughly as follows:

Prestige

US	Carolco, Castle Rock, Morgan Creek, Miramax, New Line, Summit
UK	Majestic, PolyGram, Rank

Crossover

US	Alliance/MDP, August, Capella, Goldywyn, Largo, Odyssey, Overseas, Rysher, Spelling, Trans Atlantic, Trimark
UK	Capitol, Ciby, IAC, Icon, J&M, Lumiere, Mayfair
France	Pandora, UGC

Niche

Au/NZ	Beyond, NZFC, Southern Star
Benlx	Fortissimo, Brussels AVE, Flanders Image, Holland Film
E. Eur.	Sovexport film, Cinemagyar
France	Gaumont, Mercure, MK2, President, Roissy, Studio Canal+
Ger.	Atlas, Cinepool, Export-Union, Filmverlag
Italy	Cecchi Gori, Sacis, Adriana Chiesa, Filmauro
Asia	ERA, Schochiku, Golden
Scan.	Nordisk and National Film Institutes
Spain	Catalan, Esicma, Lauren, RTVE, Sogepaq
UK	BBC, BFI, Chrysalis, Cori, Ciné Electra, Film Four, Jane Balfour, Portman, Sales Company, Vine, Victor
US	Angelika, Cineville, In Pictures, Playhouse, Turner

Direct-to-Video

US	21st Century, American Video, Arrow, A. Kananack, Cinequanon, Cinetrust, Curb, Concorde, D&D, Eclipse, Full Moon, Hemdale, Image, Imperial, Live, MCEG, Moonstone, Movie Reps, New World, Pacific Shore, PM Ent., Prism, Raven, Republic, Royal Oaks, Saban, Showcase, Silver Lake, Sunset, Total, Trident, Vision

COMPANY PROFILES

The leading players are profiled below. Smaller companies are described in Appendix B.

CAROLCO

One of the highest profile indie producers, Carolco was mired in financial difficulties from 1991 onwards and finally went bankrupt in 1995. The company was established in 1976 by Lebanese-born Mario Kassar and Hungarian Andy Vajna. At the time Vajna was running a theatre chain in Hong Kong and Kassar was a Rome-based foreign sales agent. In the early 1980s they set up a US distribution deal with TriStar who shared P&A costs. Foreign sales were organized in-house, and US video rights were sold through their subsidiary Live Entertainment.

Carolco's breakthrough was *Rambo* in 1985 which grossed $250 million worldwide. The company used this success to go public and raise new loan and equity finance to produce bigger budget 'event' pictures.

Between 1986 and 1990, the company increased total revenues from $57 million to $269 million but the profit margin slid from 21% to 6%. A far larger operation was subsidiary video distributor, Live Entertainment, which in 1990 had $742 million in revenues and a 9% profit margin.

Along with the rest of the independent business, Carolco suffered a cash crisis in 1989. The flamboyant Kassar and low-key Vajna parted ways, with the latter receiving a $108 million pay-out.

Carolco was saved from bankruptcy through a massive cash injection from foreign players keen to buy into Hollywood. Studio Canal+ bought a 5% stake for $30 million and soon after doubled it. Pioneer bought a 10% stake for $60 million and Carlton and RCS each bought a 3.3% stake for $20 million. RCS later provided the same amount in convertible bonds.

Carolco used these monies to bankroll even more expensive pictures, which were also massively pre-sold. This included the $100 million *Terminator 2* which had a record $60 million in pre-sales.

The logic behind Carolco's strategy was that foreign distributors were now looking for 'event' pictures, and the only way to get the necessary top talent was to pay over the odds. The problem with the strategy was that high budget pictures are usually loss-leaders for the Majors and also that Carolco's secondary titles were flops – such as *Mountains of the Moon, The Doors, Narrow Margin, Chaplin* and *Air America*.

Immediately after the infusion of foreign cash, Carolco started haemorrhaging money, with losses of $90 million in 1991, $67 million in 1992, $63 million in 1993 and $43 million in 1994.

The company went through a restructuring in 1992 in which it sold off library rights, and received an additional $60 million from its foreign investors, sold 17.5% of the company for $60 million to MGM and signed a $90 million pay-per-view deal with TCI. Staff was cut from 220 to 83 including the exit of CEO Peter Hoffman and president Frans Afman, and the company also had to shed its private jet and luxury yacht.

The restructuring made it much more difficult for Carolco to put up equity punts. As a result, most of the rights to the $90 million *Cliffhanger* were pre-sold to TriStar who put up most of the budget and Canal+ provided the entire budget to the $55 million *Stargate*. Both films were successes but Carolco did not benefit.

In 1994 Carolco had to abandon its much-hyped *Crusades* project with Verhoeven and Schwarzenegger and also received a further $18.5 million emergency bail-out from Pioneer, RCS and Canal+. The company was forced to sell all rights to *Showgirls* and *Lolita* to Chargeurs, leaving only the $90 million *Cutthroat Island*.

Cutthroat was a massive flop, grossing $9.5 million in the US in a five-week run in early 1996. In November 1995 Carolco filed a Chapter 11 bankruptcy and provisionally accepted a $50 million offer from Fox for its library and assets, but subsequently accepted a $58 million offer from Canal+ for the library only. Mario Kassar signed a first look deal with Paramount. The foreign partners had to write off all their $300 million investment, and creditors who were owed over $100 million expected to see only 30% of their money.

CASTLE ROCK/TURNER

Castle Rock is another source of A-titles for foreign distributors, but has a far better financial record than Carolco. The Turner/Time Warner company also has a very good record in development, producing four out of every five projects developed, and has a successful TV drama arm. The company was set up in 1987, by Rob Reiner and Alan Horn, with Sony holding 34% of equity. In 1989 Westinghouse provided $50 million in production funding in return for 15% of stock. US distribution is through Columbia until 1997, when it will be replaced by an independent venture probably involving New Line. Foreign rights are sold in-house.

Between 1987 and 1992 Castle Rock supplied four of Columbia's top ten US grosses, *A Few Good Men* ($142M), *City Slickers* ($124M), *When Harry Met Sally* ($93M) and *Misery* ($61M). The company was sold to Turner in January 1994 for $100 million in equity and $260 million in assumed debt.

The injection of the capital has allowed the company to become more ambitious. In 1994 the company set up a sales division in London as a joint venture with Rank and announced distribution pacts with Rank in the UK, UGC in France, Filmayer in Spain, Concorde in Germany/Austria, Medusa (Berlusconi) in Italy and a mix of indies plus Sony for the rest of the world.

Castle Rock puts up P&A costs and controls release dates and marketing strategies. 'The ultimate goal is to control our pictures in all markets all over the world' said sales chief Martin Shafer.

In 1995 the company's production slate was eight to ten films with an average budget of $26 million. Production is planned to increase to twelve films a year by 1988, when Castle Rock may become a separate mini-studio. This depends on the track record of films, which was poor in 1994 but recovered slightly in 1995 with *Striptease, Forget Paris* and *The American President.*

In 1995 Turner wrote off $60 million in losses for Castle Rock and as a result of the Time Warner/Turner merger the company looks likely to be sold to a third party.

CIBY SALES

Ciby 2000 was set up by construction magnate Francis Bouygues in 1991 two years before his death. The company has focused on signing production deals with leading auteurs including Jane Campion, Pedro Almodóvar, David Lynch, John Boorman, Robert Altman, and Wim Wenders. 'Our strategy is to collect together the finest cinéastes, just as we would try and work with the best architects', says Christian Goullard, finance director. 'We are generalists, and leave the construction of the building to the inspiration of the architect.'

Ciby Sales was launched in 1992 under Wendy Palmer (formerly with Manifesto/PolyGram) and Fiona Mitchell. The company handles all in-house production by Ciby 2000 as well as acquisitions. Ciby 2000 has also set up a French distribution arm and has mooted plans for a pan-European structure.

Ciby 2000 has produced one major budget production, the $35 million *Little Buddha* (sold by Terry Glinwood). This was bankrolled by Ciby with pre-sales made during production. By the end of the shoot only 20–30% of the budget was covered and Ciby ultimately lost money on the venture. Christian Goullard commented that 'in retrospect it was too big a risk, but it was all part of the learning curve, due to the initial rush of enthusiasm'.

A similar hold-back strategy was used for *The Piano* but to much better effect. Miramax bought US rights for $3 million on a 50/50 gross deal which paid out considerable overages to Ciby. The film also did very well worldwide.

In 1994 the parent company provided a further $25 million in production funding, increasing the total available to $120 million. Since then, all Ciby films have gone through Ciby Sales and have been mainly niche titles including *Dead Man* by Jim Jarmusch, *Underground* from Kusturica and projects from Almodóvar.

Ciby offers attractive terms to creative talent because they often guarantee 100% financing while only taking a part share of the negative. Ciby Sales is now one of the leading players in the niche/crossover market and is looking to set up a system of global alliances with like-minded foreign distributors.

In 1995 an output deal was signed with Globe in Australasia, and Ciby also works closely with Miramax in the US, with the possibility of establishing a formal co-production and distribution partnership in the near future.

Ciby 2000 is now shifting emphasis slightly, with an entry into the French telephony market. The company wrote off $39 million in accumulated losses in 1995 and has announced that it is interested in selling equity in order to establish strategic partnerships.

J&M

J&M was set up in 1978 by Julia Palau and Michael Ryan, who previously worked with Lew Grade's ITC. The company is the only surviving founding member of AFMA in 1980 when the pre-sales clique included PSO, Osprey (Terry Glinwood), Carolco, Lorimar, Manson, Kinter Ocean and EMI.

Today the company has a 150-title library valued at over $80 million, are co-producing TV series with major broadcasters and have set up a specialist division to handle art house product.

In 1994 they signed a development deal with JVC and retained Botts & Co. to seek new investment partners. 'The days of the sales agent have gone and were gone two years ago' said Michael Ryan at the time; 'it used to be possible for smaller companies to go out and finance a film out of pre-sales, but now it's just not possible, unless you've got a Stallone, a Schwarzenegger, a Willis, a Sharon Stone, and even then it takes a long time.'[4]

J&M has a relationship with Beacon Communications, a Canadian investment fund set up in 1987 by writer-director Armyan Bernstein and Chicago financier Tom Rosenberg who helped finance Alan Parker's *The Commitments* and *The Road to Welville*.

The company is now focused on securing films in the $15–25 million budget range. A recent example is the $25 million *American Werewolf in Paris* which was formerly with PolyGram. 'We are looking at quality product with a commercial edge like Alan Parker's *The Road to Welville*' says Michael Ryan, 'as opposed to features about Asian families in Bradford.'[5]

MAJESTIC/RCS

Majestic was set up in 1988 by Guy East who had been head of sales at Goldcrest 1984–87 and then briefly held the same position at Carolco. Majestic began as a bare bones version of the old Goldcrest with the most high profile product coming from Jake Eberts's Allied Film-makers. This led to two path-breaking projects – *Driving Miss Daisy* and *Dances with Wolves* as well as a strong relationship with Kevin Costner's Tig productions.

Both films were runaway successes and catapulted Majestic into the front line of the international sales arena. A good track record and the security of a 100-title film library (including Hammer classics) facilitated a 70% sale to RCS in

1991 for a rumoured $20 million and access to a NHK/Mico $50 million revolving fund in 1992.

The new funds enabled Majestic to shift from a commission-based sales agent to a mini studio. 'The days when someone would just come in with a good film and you'd go out and sell it are long gone', explained East. 'Now we're dealing with big stars, gross points, complex financing structures, tax deals and you must have a well-financed, well-staffed, intelligent and sophisticated team to do it.'[6]

Majestic formed the cornerstone of RCS's ambitious film and television strategy which aimed to produce annually 60 hours of television programming and three to four films in the $15–30 million budget range. In order to secure A-level talent, RCS signed lucrative deals with Ridley and Tony Scott in 1993 and with Trilogy Entertainment (the writers behind *Backdraft*) in 1994. US rights were sold to Fox and MGM/UA respectively. A relationship was also established with Mel Gibson's Icon.

RCS chief Paulo Glisenti was delighted with the deals, saying 'I think that Trilogy takes RCS and Majestic above the threshold of what we were before – a major media company and an international distributor – and turns us into a really powerful developer and producer.'[7]

But films such as *Rapa Nui, 500 Nations, Into the West, Camilla,* and *Immortal Beloved* all underperformed. The final straw was when the Ridley Scott film *Crisis in the Hot Zone* fell apart at Fox at the end of 1994, and RCS had to swallow $5–7 million in development losses. Paulo Glisenti was forced to resign and RCS cut back on their commitments.

The Scotts subsequently signed deals with Largo, Trilogy set up a parallel deal with Spelling and Mel Gibson established his own sales arm at Icon. Frustration with the parent company led Guy East to leave and set up his own independent venture. He was joined by his cousin Tim Haslam, who had been head of sales, as well as business director Will Evans and press team Tristan Whalley and Sue D'Arcy.

RCS nonetheless underlined their commitment to the business and named Giovanni Toso as new chief executive. But Kevin Costner's Tig productions used its 'key man' buy back clause to reclaim rights on its films in Majestic's library, and others are likely to follow. At Cannes in 1996 Majestic had only one new film – Johnny Depp's *The Brave*, produced by Jeremy Thomas.

MIRAMAX

Miramax has built a leading position in the foreign sales business, and now dominates Cannes in the way that Golan and Globus did in the mid-1980s. 'We make a conscious effort to take advantage of what Cannes has to offer – worldwide press and a great audience', explains Harvey. 'We tend to gear our productions to be ready for Cannes.'[8]

Miramax has held the rights to three of the Palme d'Or winners in the last seven years. Sales for the first half of 1995 were $75 million, more than the 1994 total. This has been achieved by using hot titles such as *Pulp Fiction* to leverage higher prices for the entire Miramax slate.

Foreign sales are run by Rick Sands who replaced sales veteran Ian Jessel in 1995. Sales VP David Linde states that their aim is 'to do internationally what Miramax has done domestically: expand the audience for specialty films'. The company has been setting up informal partnerships with distributors throughout the world, co-ordinating trailers, posters, promotional campaigns, talent tours and press junkets as well as providing marketing seminars. Large package deals have been signed with Village Roadshow in Australia, and Cecchi Gori in Italy. In other territories, such as the UK, many Miramax titles have been released through parent company Disney.

MORGAN CREEK

Morgan Creek has a similar business plan to Castle Rock. The company was set up in 1987 by former car salesman James Robinson, originally with Joe Roth as head of production. Robinson has been very careful with his choice of projects and financial controls. 'I make sure the business side keeps its nose out of the creative side' says Robinson, 'But I will say that I pay for these films and it's my ass on the line. I give directors three cuts, but I retain the final cut.'[9] In-house staff is around thirty, and has had a relatively high turnover.

Morgan Creek originally had a distribution deal with Fox but switched to Warners in 1993. At the time, Robinson announced he wanted to own a major studio 'either through building one, buying one or merging'. In 1994 he announced plans for a $500 million production facility in the San Fernando Valley, but due to disappointing box office has trimmed back his plans.

Foreign distribution is achieved through foreign partners, but Warners is buying up an increasing proportion of foreign rights. In 1995 Morgan Creek also teamed up with Chargeurs and Warners in a bid for the MGM cinemas in the Netherlands and Denmark and was also short-listed in the final bidding for MGM, teamed with a German consortium headed by Rolf Dehyle.

NEW LINE

In 1995 New Line set up a European office in London and established output deals with Entertainment in the UK, Neue Constantin in Germany, Metropolitan in France, Village Roadshow in Australia and also deals in Italy and Spain. These are straight distribution deals without minimum guarantees (MGs). New Line also signed an MG deal with Gaga communications in Japan. 'We wanted to be closer to what our professional skills are, which is distribution, rather than being producers selling off product here and there' explained Shaye. The move was also expected to boost profits on hit pictures by 30–60%.

POLYGRAM

PolyGram is the world's largest music distributor and began its ambitious film strategy in 1989, buying stakes in Working Title and Propaganda and setting up Manifesto Film Sales. The sales company was renamed PFI in 1991 and organizes foreign sales for all PolyGram product as well as managing acquisitions for the US and other key territories. Distribution subsidiaries exist in France (Pan-Européenne), the UK, Netherlands and Australia, and the company has a distribution pact with Sogepaq in Spain. A German distribution company will be established in 1997.

Films are provided by Working Title, Propaganda, Interscope, Island and A&M as well as talent deals with Tim Robbins and Jodie Foster. The company's biggest success to date has been *Four Weddings and a Funeral* which was made for $4.5 million and grossed $250 million worldwide. Other hit titles have been acquisitions such as *Priscilla, Shallow Grave* and *The Usual Suspects*. PolyGram's bigger budget films have been less successful, particularly those produced by Interscope, which places doubts over the company's intention to step up its mainstream production and distribution activities in 1996.

SUMMIT

Summit was set up in the mid-1980s as a joint venture between Arnon Milchan's Regency, Andy Vajna's Cinergi, and Bernd Eichinger's Neue Constantin. The company was bought out by new management in 1994, led by Frenchman Patrick Wachsberger who was formerly CEO of Odyssey.

Summit has good credit lines on the back of its strong library which includes the former Sovereign library and Regency's television library. In 1996 they announced a new $50 million revolving credit line with Newmarket Capital Group, which was previously involved in single picture financing.

Summit has now set up its own development arm and aims to finance films from outside the original troika. In 1995 the company announced a deal to handle foreign distribution for Peter Guber's start-up venture Mandalay, which has signed output deals with Entertainment in the UK, Neue Constantin and Kirch in Germany and Cecchi Gori in Italy. Summit has also secured non-US rights to Jeremy Thomas's film library.

Cinergi

The Hungarian born Andy Vajna is one of the industry's most respected producers and in 1995 he was the first non-actor to receive the ShoWest Lifetime Achievement award.

After leaving Carolco, Vajna set up Cinergi in 1991 but until 1994 had produced only four films – *Medicine Man, Tombstone, Renaissance Man* and *Color of Night* – all of which underperformed. By the end of 1993, Vajna had incurred total losses of $27 million, but in 1994 managed to earn a $2.8 million profit, and used this upturn to float part of the company. In 1995 he raised a further $30 million equity in a public offering (including a 5% equity stake from Disney) and also extended his $150 million credit line with Chemical Bank.

Vajna used the finance to step up a gear in 1995 with three pictures with an average budget of $57 million: *Die Hard with a Vengeance, Judge Dredd* and *The Scarlet Letter*, as well as the $40 million *Nixon*. The disappointing results on this slate have forced the company to re-focus on medium budget films and there are rumours that the company will be sold to Regency. In the meantime Andy Vajna and Mario Kassar are both involved in Justice Department investigations into their personal tax filings.

Regency

European educated Arnon Milchan is Hollywood's most prolific foreign producer since Dino de Laurentiis. Milchan produced his first feature with Hemdale in 1977 but made his name with *Brazil* (1985) and his fortune with *Pretty Woman* (1990) after teaming up with respected Hollywood executive Steven Reuther.

Milchan then signed a massive $600 million twenty-picture deal in 1991 with Warner Brothers, Studio Canal+ and Germany's Scriba and Dehyle. The foreign partners put up a third each of the budget and Bodo Scriba (former No. 2 at the Kirch group) received 25% of Regency.

The first six films included hits such as *JFK, Under Siege* and *Sommersby* but also flops such as *The Mambo Kings* and *The Power of One*. Studio Canal+ subsequently withdrew from further equity funding, feeling that they had seen little overages on the hit pictures and excessive losses on the flops. Milchan then reorganized the financing including a rights deal to Canal+.

Milchan has a colourful past including allegations in the Israeli press that he was one of the country's largest arms dealers and tied to two international scandals. 'People always like to talk about my background', says Milchan, 'but I don't think I have any skeletons in my closet.' 'Arnon is one of those great rascals you can't help but like', said one writer. 'He is very smart, cunning and manipulative . . . one charming scoundrel, and although that charm is transparent, it's still very effective.'[10]

Milchan finances his films through his equity deal, plus credit lines with Berliner Bank and Bayer-Hypotheken-Und Wechsel Bank. In 1995 Bodo Scriba sold his 25% stake to Australian Kerry Packer who subsequently bought a further 4.5% for $150 million in cash and new credit lines. In early 1996 an additional 7.4% of the company was sold to Korea's Samsung for $60 million and in October 1996 a 7.5% stake was sold for a similar sum to Germany's Kirch Group.

6

Independent Production

I think David Puttnam made the perfect analogy for
independent film-making, with the opening scene of 'The Mission'.
You feel like Robert de Niro climbing up a waterfall with a bundle of armour.
As you struggle up the cliff face, you keep getting hit by waves of water.
It feels like people are pissing on you.
Colin Vaines

INDEPENDENT PRODUCERS ARE THE ADVENTURERS AND PIONEERS of the business who set out into uncharted waters, and make the most of their discovered territories before the Majors take over.

The Independents saved Hollywood at the end of the 1960s with films such as *The Graduate, Bonnie and Clyde* and *Easy Rider*. In the 1970s, the US Government introduced new legislation designed to encourage independent production. One of the main measures was the investment tax credit (ITC) which between 1976 and 1986 encouraged a huge flow of tax shelter investment into independent films. This was further boosted by the new video market, which led to a boom in production that peaked in the late 1980s.

Today, independent films include about 70 pick-ups at the Majors (only half of which can really be called 'independent') and 100 indie theatrical releases. Annual independent production can be broadly categorized as follows:

	No. of films	*Average Budgets*
Event pick-ups	3–5	$50+M
Major pick-ups	30	$10–15M
Indie pick-ups	30	$5–10M
Indie production	60	$1–4M
Direct-to-video	150	$1M
Micro-budget	30	$0.2M

The annual independent production investment is a little over $1 billion for theatrical features and $150 million for direct-to-video. Theatrical production has halved since 1987.

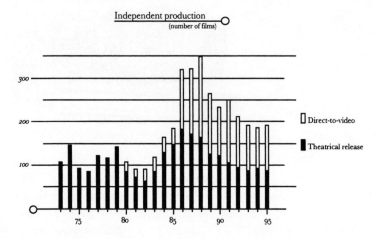

OVERVIEW

An independent film-maker is ultimately dependent on the commissioning criteria of third parties – the Majors, the indie distributors, direct-to-video and foreign sales – but tries to avoid being locked into one financing source. Independents must therefore be more inventive and single-minded than 'one-stop' shoppers. Caitlin Buchman, who advises producers, says 'they must decide who they are, what they do and then use this to articulate their vision. If you're true to your own dream and sell it with passion, you'll get there.'

It is also vital that an indie have a very tough skin. 'We work in an incredibly humbling business' says CAA agent John Ptak. 'Anybody who goes round talking about how important they are, is just waiting for the fall. Everyone gets hurt. Arrogance doesn't fly.'

Even for experienced producers, it usually takes three to five years from beginning a project before seeing it on the screen. A first film may take much longer. One producer at Cannes in 1995 explained that his film had been started by his grandfather and took fifty years to get made!

Films are giant whales that glide slowly through the water. British producer Colin Vaines (*B Monkey*) suggests that 'development is like wading through treacle. The treacle sometimes evaporates – a bit like Moses parting the waters – so you try and run quickly before it fills up again. Some days it's difficult to get out of bed. If you want to stay sane and be able to pay the bills, you have to balance film development with other activities.'

The length of time needed to get the project off the ground means that it is essential to develop several projects simultaneously and to be patient in building contacts.

'Financing a film is a bit like going fishing', says UK producer Simon Relph (*Enchanted April*). 'You have to groundbait the water and think where you're going. If you splatterblast all the fish will swim away . . . Set yourself a specific timetable for finding finance with check-points on when to tell people yes or no. This is especially important for cast and key crew. There's no point letting people hang on for ever.'

At times only a frontal assault will start the ball rolling. 'I don't like using the scattergun approach' says Colin Vaines, 'but at times you just have to.' Steve Woolley adds, 'I start making the film and let everyone else catch up.' This is much easier when a company has capital funds to invest. Otherwise it can be very risky.

THE PROJECT

When starting out as an independent producer it is not necessary to set up a production company, and for tax reasons it is usually best to set up a separate company for each film made.

A production structure can be a useful way of impressing people and getting a development deal, but it is not necessary. Even established producers try to keep their overheads to a minimum, and high overheads are usually one of the main reasons that bring a company down.

The starting point for any film is the literary 'property' on which it is based. This may be an idea, a synopsis, a script, or a novel. The film-maker must have legal proof over ownership of the 'property', and when acquired from a third party, there must be 'chain of title' proving every stage at which the property has changed hands. The more highly developed the project, the easier it is to protect, since it is virtually impossible to protect an idea or a synopsis.

Film-makers should avoid spending substantial development funds before securing a potential interest from name talent, otherwise the project will easily get lost in development hell. Potential pre-buyers or investors will look first at the talent attached to a project. Only then will they look at the script and the budget which will be used to specify the delivery requirements of the film.

The pre-eminent importance of talent makes it very difficult for newcomers to break into the business. Agents will guard their clients jealously, and in the case of leading talent will often demand an offer before their client even looks at a project. If the client commits, the agent will normally require a 'pay or play' deal which means that the talent will be paid whether the film is made or not. Agents demand such deals to avoid the practice in the 1980s of Independents selling films on the back of 'credits not contractual' talent.

Certain established players such as David Puttnam have never made 'pay or play' deals, because they started in the business before such deals became widespread and now have the contacts to avoid them. The only way round such deals is through personal contacts, or by using less well-known talent.

The decisive role of talent focuses power in the hands of the Majors and agents. 'It's the stars that everyone's looking at when they ascend the steps at Cannes', says one financier. 'Nobody trusts their judgement in this business, not even the actors. The trick is to build up as much bankable elements around a project as possible.' An actor or director may often look down on a project and only do it because of advice or pressure from the agents and studios.

Top talent can be persuaded to appear in indie product and defer or lower fees in order to do so. The problem is access, which usually depends on personal contacts and/or an established indie reputation. Whenever the system is grid-locked, which it seems to be at present, the main way to break into the business is through micro-budget features (see below).

THE BUDGET

Once the key elements of the film are identified, a production budget must be drawn up. This will depend upon the above-the-line talent fees, the shooting requirements of the script and the visual look the director is aiming for.

The producer must then pay further financing costs (detailed in Appendix C) which include a contingency (10%), insurance (3%), legal fees (0.65%), bank fees (3%), an interest reserve (10%) and a completion bond (3–6%). If the film performs well there will also be deferral payments and talent participations. The full 'negative cost' is therefore 35–60% higher than the production budget – comparable to the mark-up at the Majors.

Independent film-makers should be totally honest about the budget when putting together the financing of the project, but once the film is finished there is nothing stopping them claiming it cost more than it really did – particularly for low-budget features.

THE FINANCIAL PLAN

Having identified the negative cost, the indie must try to raise this money through a 'jigsaw puzzle' of distribution deals, tax deals, equity participations, ancillary licensing, deferrals, foreign subsidies and anything else the film-maker can think of.

'The financial engineering of a film can be as creative as the film itself'[1] says Don Ranvaud, who produced Chen Kaige's *Life on a String*. It is important, however, that time spent on financial pyrotechnics does not interfere with the overall integrity of the project. The film-maker must determine the key creative parameters of the project he or she wishes to make and then see how best that project can be sold.

The film represents a bundle of rights or 'equity' whose value can vary from zero to infinity. Rights can be either sold outright (equity) or licensed for a specific period of time (pre-sales).

The ideal option for the independent film-maker is to license a film because the rights will then revert, enabling the film to form part of a library and be licensed again and again.

The main sources of funds are as follows:

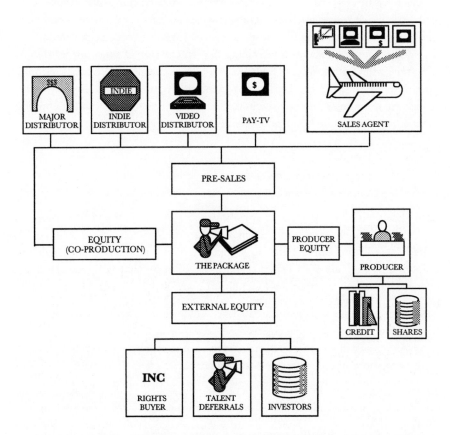

The package should be positioned to make it very clear which type of player it is considered suitable for. 'The fabric of the financing mix is key' says Simon Relph. 'The different interests must be compatible.' Financing a film is a bit like inviting guests to a dinner party. They must each be happy with their seating position and also be happy to be eating together.

Film-makers will do their best to license rights and retain equity in-house. The best way to do this is through a company structure with internal capital and the possibility of deferring fees.

It may also be possible to use tax schemes and other 'off-balance-sheet' financing in order to leverage further ownership. Certain buyers will insist on a chunk of the equity. If a substantial equity stake is demanded, the buyer becomes a co-producer.

DISCOUNTING BANKS

Having established the total pre-sale and equity contracts, all future payments must be converted into real cash. Well capitalized companies may be able to bankroll the project internally, but smaller companies need a special discounting bank to advance them the production money against promised revenues.

Discounting banks try to eliminate risk. In the case of single-project financing they will treat the loan as they would a house mortgage. The producer must demonstrate that the project has sufficient collateral to cover the loan. The banks are not interested in predictions. They want a guarantee that the film will be made (a completion bond) and sales agreements (letters of credit) covering:

- Pre-sale contracts
- Co-production contracts
- Sales agent advances

The bank will attribute a credit rating to each sales contract and also check carefully the delivery requirements and the risk of non-payment. On both counts the value of promised payments will be 'discounted'.

Further discounting will occur because of the 'cost of money'. The bank will advance less money today than it will be paid back in the future. Therefore all future payments will be discounted according to their timing, the prevailing rate of interest, and the currency risk.

As a result of all these deductions, the bank normally will be willing to lend around 75–80% of the value of future payments. This is their 'present value' and means that contractual payments must be worth up to double the production budget. For example, if the production budget is $5 million, the negative cost may will be $7 million, which means that up to $10 million is needed in pre-sales, (because their discounted present value is only $7 million).

The main discounting banks are FILMS, Guinness Mahon, ING, Paribas, Berliner, Imperial, Bankers Trust and Chemical. In the past, other major lenders were Pierson Heldring and Credit Lyonnais, but they have drastically cut back their activity. All of these banks specialize in high budget pictures and it is very difficult for them to cater for films budgeted under $5 million.

THE FINANCING GAP

Many independent productions face a financing gap between the 'present value' of contractual payments and the negative cost. This gap must be covered through:

- In-house funds (i.e. corporate finance)
- Co-production
- Ancillary revenues
- Private investors
- Insurance gap financing
- Budget cuts
- Deferrals
- Off-balance-sheet financing

During the 1980s indie boom there were high pre-sales and relatively easy access to corporate finance. Today an increasing number of Independents find it difficult to finance their films. This has led to a great interest in innovative ways to fill the gap.

CORPORATE FINANCE

The best way for an Independent to have leverage in the market-place is to have a rich corporate sugar daddy. Even if the company is only able to put up 10% of the budget this can have enormous benefits to getting projects off the ground. Corporate finance is also important to cover development and overhead costs.

To raise substantial corporate equity, an Independent must normally have private resources such as James Robinson at Morgan Creek or be backed by a larger media company such as PolyGram.

Banks also prefer corporate finance rather than single projects, because it allows risk to be spread over a portfolio of films. They will still look for collateral – in terms of library rights, physical assets, theatres and, if possible, a corporate guarantee from a strong parent company.

The main problem with corporate finance is that it is very difficult for an independent producer to recoup its equity punts. This is because pre-sales make it very difficult to earn overages. In a recent stock offering by Cinergi, one of the two underwriters, Nat West Securities, calculated that a $28 million equity punt over three pictures would need a combined US gross of $200 million to break even, a $250 million gross to produce a $11 million profit and a $350 million gross to earn a $27 million profit. On these odds, it is very easy to lose money.

CO-PRODUCTION

'At the end of 1989-90 many independents collapsed and financing hit a terrible barrier', says Chris Auty at Recorded Picture Company. 'People were running around like headless chickens trying to close the gap. The answer they came up with was often co-production which was a weird solution. Co-productions were never intended for that. It was high-tech finance bumping into a cultural dinosaur.'

Co-production enables a producer to access the corporate finance of other companies, and is very frequently the best way to access off-balance-sheet funds such as tax breaks and subsidies. Such funds are a central feature of European production and invariably require a local producer to be involved. There are several experts who provide links across the Atlantic, such as Caitlin Buchman at Film Strategies.

Many European and Asian companies are desperate to buy into the world film market and are willing to pay substantial sums in order to become co-producers. European media groups are placing an increasing emphasis on investing in English-language films, and co-production varies from event pictures with partners such as Studio Canal+ and RCS to much smaller pictures.

There are no 'official' co-productions between America and Europe since America is not signatory to any co-production treaty. There are therefore no point systems for nationality mixes or locations. The only co-productions that exist are financial co-productions, where partners share the equity risk. This makes it difficult for such co-productions to secure subsidies, but can be useful in tax breaks.

Even niche Independents can access co-production funds. A pioneer in the field is New York producer Jim Stark, who launched the career of Jim Jarmusch and has co-produced films such as Alex Rockwell's *In the Soup* with Paris-based Why Not Productions and more recently *Cold Fever* by Icelandic director Fridrik Thor Fridriksson.

Another New York indie with key foreign contacts is Good Machine, run by James Schamus and Ted Hope who have produced 'foreign films' such as *The Wedding Banquet* and *Eat Drink Man Woman*. 'As low and no-budget indie producers, we have to be as global as Time Warner', they explain. 'In our world, the director is still the star – but not because we sit around at night thumbing through old copies of Cahiers du Cinéma. It's because these simply *are* the most viable B movies being made today. Our models are not so much Godard and Truffaut as William Castle, Sam Arkoff and Val Lewton.'[2]

Hal Hartley is another leading American 'auteur' to benefit from foreign co-production. Zenith put up much of the funding for his $0.65 million *Trust* and $2 million *Simple Men* and also co-produced *Amateur* with UGC.

ANCILLARY REVENUES

Successful movies are high-profile products in today's consumer society. They can trade off this brand name for considerable ancillary earnings – from soundtracks and videogames, to theme parks and product placement. These ancillary markets can put up funds for the production budgets, and often more crucially provide advertising tie-ins which help launch the picture with much higher visibility at lower cost.

The champions in spin-off revenues are the Majors – with films such as *Batman* earning $50 million in licensing and *Jurassic Park* earning well over $100 million. Promo tie-ins have now gone global, with the ten-year $2 billion partnership deal between Disney and McDonalds and a similarly valued deal between Fox and Pepsi Co. (which includes Pizza Hut, Taco Bell and Kentucky Fried Chicken) focusing on the *Star Wars* sequels.

The Majors are the masters at cross-promotional synergies, but certain indie titles have also had high ancillary earnings such as *Nightmare on Elm Street* and *Ninja Turtles*.

The most obvious source of ancillary revenues are music soundtracks. Music rights are very expensive to acquire but can be turned to the producer's advantage if a record label can be persuaded that his music will benefit from the movie rather than the other way round. In this way, a music distributor may be willing to waive rights payments and even put up a part of the film's budget.

The problem of course is that most of the business is wrapped up in the hands of the Big Six music majors, who are not renowned for giving away freebies. But since two of the music majors – PolyGram and BMG – are interested in establishing film rights, there is considerable room for manoeuvre. The US Majors are masters in the music rights business and have perfected the art of co-ordinating their film and music releases. They often target singles for different genres of listening – from classic to rap – in order to maximize awareness for a forthcoming film. In 1995, of the Top 20 albums, three were film soundtracks.

The second most important source of ancillary income are videogames and interactive entertainment. A landmark deal was the $2 million that Warner's Steve Ross paid for videogame rights to *ET*. Independents who have struck such deals include New Line who sold the videogame rights for *Surf Ninjas* to Sega for $0.5 million.

A final source of ancillary income is product placement. A $20 million movie can easily raise over $200,000 in sponsorship. A corporate sponsor can also offer very valuable advertising tie-ins, a good recent example being BMW and the *Goldeneye* James Bond film. To set up such deals, it is best to deal with the advertising agencies or specialist players such as Entertainment Marketing Group in Los Angeles.

PRIVATE INVESTORS

Private investment in independent films was very strong in the late 1970s and early 1980s via limited partnerships. Most of this investment has now dried up. Today the main focus of private investment is micro-budget films.

High net worth individuals occasionally act as an 'angel' to a film, but this is rare and they usually lose money. As Mark Devoraugh of law firm Olswangs explains, 'Private equity *is* out there. People do come to us once in a while saying they want to invest in a film. But they're very rare birds.' One such bird was Dodi Al Fayed, the son of a Greek shipping millionaire who provided 50% of the finance for *Chariots of Fire*.

Nik Powell calls this kind of investor 'loony finance', and Jake Eberts, who has raised a considerable amount of private investor money, is even more adamant that 'private investors do not understand the film business, and there is no place for them. I can cite 200 films with private investments. Every one lost money. There are always stories of how investors can luck out, *Crocodile Dundee* being the main example. But they're so rare as to be unique.'

Wonderful schemes nonetheless continue to be invented. Venture capitalist Doug Abbott – who 100% funded *Educating Rita* – suggests that 'Producers prove continually able to secure private capital. They are very aggressive and spin wonderful stories. Investors are attracted by the glamour and the promise of the limitless upside.'

A good example is star Paul Hogan who in 1994 offered public shares on the Australian stock exchange for his new film *Lightning Jack*, and the backers will probably make a profit.

INSURANCE GAP FINANCING

If there are still foreign territories unsold ('blue sky'), money can also be sought from boutique firms providing 'insurance gap' finance. One of the main firms is Screen Partners in the UK, which was set up in the early 1990s and has provided 20% completion financing for a range of British films including *The Hawk, Shopping* and *Nostradamus*.

Insurance gap financing has existed since the 1970s. The gap financier has corporate backing from an insurance company and works in tandem with a sales agent on sales estimates for unsold territories. Other revenue sources such as subsidies may also be considered.

The gap financier will look for as strong a guarantee as possible that sales will be made. In return for monies advanced, the gap financier will demand an arrangement fee of 20–25%, a privileged recoupment position and a share of the film's equity – usually 50% of the sum advanced.

BUDGET CUTS

A financing gap may also be covered by trimming the budget, but there are limits to which this can be achieved. Production can be relocated to cheaper sites and cast and crew can be offered cut rates in order to make the production financially viable.

In this way up to 20–25% of the budget can be cut. If more substantial cuts are required the whole film must be redesigned with different cast and crew and the process of financing must be started again.

DEFERRALS

Leading talent may be willing to defer all or some of up-front fees in return for equity and net profits. An even better solution is to get them to work for cut-price or minimum ('scale') payments. For example, the star-studded cast of the \$9 million *Pulp Fiction* worked mainly for scale because they believed in the project.

Talent will usually be open to salary negotiations. Their agents will not. The agents depend on 10% fees and also do not want their clients to lower their asking price in the market-place.

OFF-BALANCE-SHEET FINANCING

Off-balance-sheet financing needs an expert to set up, who will charge a fee for his services. The film-maker does not need to understand all the details, but it is useful to be aware of their possibilities.

Recognized off-balance-sheet experts include John Heyman (World Films), Lewis Korman (Savoy), Graham Bradstreet (Bradstreet Media), Roger Gewolb (Alliance Equicorp) and top entertainment lawyers. Heyman alone is believed to have generated \$2.4 billion in off-balance-sheet financing for the studios.

These experts have attracted a certain mystique, but in Heyman's opinion they should never get in the way of the true objective which is making a good film.

'We all look for new and exciting ways to finance films,' declares Heyman. 'But if one is looking only to avoid tax by investing in films, this is the wrong reason for doing it . . . A producer who comes to you and says invest with me because I'll get you a tax break is really saying "in orgasm one procreates and if you masturbate enough you'll have babies".'

Financial wizards use worldwide tax and subsidy legislation to provide a public contribution to the cost of the film. Since these depend on the state, they are subject to the changing political climate.

The main forms of off-balance-sheet financing are:

- Taxation
- Subsidies
- Blocked currency and debt swaps

These are complex but vital tools for the independent producer and are explained in Appendix A.

The effect of such financing will be to provide an additional percentage of the budget, but is dependent on the other funding sources already being in place. It is a 're-financing' rather than a financing technique.

An expert will quote what extra percentage of the budget can be generated through 're-financing'. In the early 1980s it stood at 20% which meant that the producer only needed to cover 80% of the budget through traditional means. Today it is rare for more than a 5% benefit to be generated by off-balance-sheet techniques and, because of the paperwork, few producers bother.

Tax and subsidy legislation can have a critical effect on the film industry. The growth of the Independents and the re-capitalization of the Majors in the 1970s and 1980s was the fruit of 'small business administration' and 'investment tax credit' legislation. Similarly, the burst of film-making activity in Australia, Canada and Britain in the early 1980s was also due to generous tax and subsidy breaks. But tax breaks only have real long-term effect if they can be used by a substantial distribution infrastructure. Otherwise tax breaks lead to ephemeral production booms such as UK's Goldcrest in the early 1980s, and then die away.

CASE STUDIES

The world of independent film finance can be properly understood only through concrete examples. Films financed by a US distributor and a foreign sales agent are usually a simple split of rights between US and the world, with the US providing 35–50% of the budget. Co-productions tend to be far more complex. Below are the financing models for four films: *Cutthroat Island, Until the End of the World, The Crying Game*, and *Four Weddings and a Funeral*.

CUTTHROAT ISLAND (1996)

Carolco hoped to find buried treasure with their pirate picture but instead were shipwrecked. They raised over $60 million in pre-sales and also made an estimated equity investment of $46 million drawn from internal funds provided by Pioneer, Canal+ and RCS.

The equity investment was entirely written off, and even pre-buyers are likely to have lost money on the film. This can be shown by matching pre-sale minimum guarantees against estimated box office (which is a broad indicator of the distributor's ultimate revenues):

Territory	Buyer	MG	Distrib. rev.
US	MGM (\$18M P&A only)	–	\$4M
	Live video, TCI pay-TV	\$14M	\$8M
			Box Office
France	Canal+	\$8M	\$1M
UK	Guild	\$6M	\$1M
Germany	Neue Constantin, VCL	\$5M	\$1.5M
Italy	RCS	\$3M	\$0.75M
Spain	U Films	\$2.5M	\$0.75M
Benelux	Filmlux/Concorde	\$1.2M	\$0.3M
Scandinavia	Nordisk	\$1.2M	\$0.3M
Other Europe	Rigi, Lusomundo	\$0.3M	\$0.2M
Japan	Pioneer (Toho-Towa)	\$10M	\$3.5M
Korea	Samsung	\$4.5M	\$1.5M
Taiwan	Jih-Sun	\$2M	\$0.75M
Australia/NZ	Village Roadshow	\$1.5M	\$0.75M
Hong Kong	Intercontinental	\$0.3M	\$0.3M
Middle East	Jaguar Films	\$0.2M	\$0.2M

Source: *Variety*

In America the film performed disastrously. It was released by MGM/UA on 1619 screens but with a \$4.4 million first week gross, did not even get into the Top Ten. The film lasted only five weeks and grossed a total of \$9.6 million, equivalent to around \$4 million in rentals. MGM will have lost \$14 million on the release, and in video and pay-TV it is unlikely to earn distributor revenues of more than \$8 million, which also represents a loss. In most foreign territories the film had a wide release, but went in at number 8 or 9 and disappeared from the Top Ten after one week.

The film's total worldwide gross is under \$20 million. Carolco will also have lost virtually its entire \$46 million equity stake. This forced the company into bankruptcy and represented a major loss for Pioneer, Canal+ and RCS.

UNTIL THE END OF THE WORLD (1991)

The film had several pre-sellable elements: Wim Wenders (ranked No. 52 of world directors), William Hurt (ranked No. 87 of world actors), Sam Neill (No. 153), Max von Sydow (No. 250) and Jeanne Moreau (No. 350).

The film was a co-production between Argos Films (Anatole Dauman) in France, Road Movies (Wim Wenders) in Germany and Village Roadshow in Australia. US investment was from Transpacific (Jonathan Taplin) with sales co-ordinated by Majestic Films. Argos also brokered a pre-sale to Penta in Italy.

Transpacific was backed by three Japanese investors (Dentsu, Central Kousan and Mitsubishi) with bank finance from Pierson Heldring. Overall bank discounting for the film was provided by Pierson Heldring and Guinness Mahon.

The budget contribution and share of rights was as follows:

Argos Films	$7M	France and Francophone territories
Road Movies	$2.5M	Germany/Austria
Village Roadshow	$3.5M	Australasia
Transpacific	$7.2M	US and rest of world
Italian pre-sale	$1.8M	Italy
Total	$22M	

Source: *Ciné Finances* (exchange rate $1 = 5FF).

Each partner had full right to net revenues in their territory until they had recouped their advance. After this break-even point, 50% of revenues would be returned to a pool to be shared as follows:

Argos	30%
Road Movies	12%
Village Roadshow	8%
Transpacific	50%

Argos provided a completion guarantee for French production and Film Garantie Finance for the German and American side. The production eventually went $5.5 million over budget with FGF providing $3 million and Argos $2.5 million.

The film was expensive at $27.5 million and flopped. Box office was $0.8 million in the US, under $0.5 million in Australasia and the UK, slightly over $2 million in France, $2 million in Germany and $3 million in Italy.

Because of promotion costs, there would have been theatrical surplus revenue only in France, Germany and Italy.

We can estimate the film's production revenue (minus P&A and distribution fees) and net break-even as follows (NB: these are estimates, not official figures):

Territories	Investment	Theat.	Video	TV	Net
France/Franco.	9.5	0.5	1.0	3.0	-5.0
Ger./Austria	2.5	0.5	1.0	1.0	0.0
Italy	1.8	1.0	1.0	1.0	1.2
Australia/NZ	3.5	0.0	0.5	1.0	-2.0
US/world*	7.2	0.0	1.2	2.5	-3.5

* Majestic/Trans-pacific earnings may have been higher because of pre-sales.

The only territory with profits was Italy, but since this was a pre-sale the co-producers are unlikely to have seen overages. Transpacific/Majestic were protected by pre-sales, but probably lost money. Village Roadshow were probably insulated from funds from the state AFFC. The biggest loss was suffered by Argos Films, which may have lost up to $5 million on the film. Wenders subsequently severed his production relationship with Dauman.

THE CRYING GAME (1991)

The Crying Game was financed entirely in Europe and is therefore not typical of an American independent production. It is a good example, however, of the complexities of film finance.

The film had recognizable talent – Neil Jordan and Forest Whitaker – who did not have 'name' status, but were enough to reassure Palace's partners. The film became the first and only film under fledgling European rights buyer Eurotrustees – made up of Palace, Iberoamericana (Spain), Academy (Italy), Bac (France) and Senator (Germany). The gap in the budget was filled by a Japanese tax deal with Nippon Film Development. Palace's direct investment was mainly provided by deferred fees.

The cash cost was £2.2 million, with a further £0.2 million in financing fees and £0.4 million in deferrals (a total of £2.8 million, about $4.8 million at the time). The budget contribution and rights were as follows (NB: estimates):

Palace	$0.8M	UK video and equity
Channel 4	$1.2M	UK TV rights ($0.6M) plus equity
British Screen	$0.9M	Loan against UK rights
Eurotrustees	$1.2M	European rights in Fr/Ger/It/Sp
Nippon Film Devlt	$0.7M	Japan and equity
Total	$4.8M	

Bank discounting was provided by Berliner/Sodete for Palace and by both Pierson Heldring and Banque Worms for Eurotrustees. A completion bond was provided by Film Finances. International sales were made through The Sales Company, but there were no pre-sales.

The film grossed over $76 million worldwide, but $62 million of this was in the US, where Miramax bought initial rights for $1.5 million (40% of the film's cost) and then bought out most other rights for $2 million before widening the release.

The returns to the investors can be broadly estimated as follows (NB: not official figures):

Territories	Investment	Theat.	Video	TV	Net
France	0.5	0.8	1.0	1.0	2.3
Ger./Austria	0.5	0.1	0.5	1.0	1.1
Italy	0.3	1.0	1.0	0.8	2.5
Spain	0.2	0.4	0.5	0.8	1.5
Japan	0.5	0.3	0.5	0.8	1.1
UK/world	2.0	3.0	2.0	4.0	7.0
US	–	———	3.5	———	3.5

The film probably provided over a 300% return for investors and demonstrates the very high profits that can be earned by a low-budget film which goes on to become a big hit.

FOUR WEDDINGS AND A FUNERAL (1994)

Four Weddings had a relatively simple financing structure. PolyGram put up advance funding against expected foreign sales. With Andie McDowell and Mike Newell attached, the investment was considered fairly secure.

Channel 4	$1M	UK TV rights and equity
PolyGram Int'l	$3.5M	Rest of world

Four Weddings shows how to promote a hit independent film. The film was written by Richard Curtis, one of Britain's top TV writers (*Blackadder* and *Mr Bean*), and produced by Duncan Kenworthy, in-house producer at Jim Henson Productions where he had produced *The Storyteller* TV series.

Kenworthy is British but studied film in the US and worked there for several years, which taught him the dynamics of the international market. Curtis had approached him with several scripts but none had clicked until then. Kenworthy agreed to work on the project under two conditions – the right to appoint the director and to demand a substantial rewrite. The script was subsequently fine tuned across seventeen drafts.

With Mike Newell attached – hot from his success on *Enchanted April* – the project was taken to Working Title who felt nervous about it. According to Stewart Till, 'the production company wasn't sure about it, but the script was so funny and with Andie McDowell and an established director we could cover the film with sales estimates'. The budget nonetheless had to be trimmed from $5.5 million to $4.5 million.

The film was released first in the US – on five screens and then slowly widened. It maintained high screen averages and by week seven, was booked into 721 screens and ranked number one at the US box office, ahead of two 1800-screen new releases that week. The film stayed in the US Top Ten for the subsequent eight weeks, proving its extremely long legs.

The performance abroad was even better – vindicating PolyGram's international distribution network and proving the hunger in the foreign market for original titles.

	UK	France	Ger.	It.	Spain	Austral.	Jap
Four Weddings	45	35	34	8	8.5	16	5
Crying Game	3	1.5	0.5	2.7	1	3	1

Note: These are estimates, not official figures. They are based on *Variety*'s international box office data.

Four Weddings' high US performance enabled wide releases to be made in other foreign territories – which is unheard of for a small British film. The film was also further boosted by a $600,000 P&A loan from EFDO for nine territories.

In Britain, the film is the best-selling domestic film of all time. The closest recent British film is *The Fish Called Wanda* in 1988 with $11 million box office. This outstanding success is reminiscent of other huge national blockbusters in recent years, such as *Les Visiteurs* in France ($81M). The difference is that *Four Weddings* travelled. The film earned four times as much abroad as in the US, and almost fifteen times the foreign earnings of *The Crying Game* ($15M foreign).

Even assuming considerable P&A spends and a 30–40% overhead deduction, the $4.5 million film should have provided a considerable boost to PolyGram's bottom line (NB: these are estimates):

US performance			International			Net
Rental	*P&A*	*Vid, TV*	*Rental*	*P&A*	*Vid, TV*	
23.5	15	35	75	10	65	67

Because of the spectacular foreign performance, *Four Weddings* is one of the most successful independent films of all time.

MICRO-BUDGET FILMS

The mainstream and independent system is based on limiting risks and working with recognized talent. The majority of new talent therefore breaks through in micro-budget films.

Roger Corman perfected these techniques in the 1950s and 1960s and produced classic films such as the Edgar Allen Poe adaptations and the *Little Shop of Horrors*. Corman's high-paced low-budget film-making gave a vital training ground to new talent. He launched the careers of Martin Scorsese, Francis Ford Coppola, Peter Bogdanovich, Jonathan Demme, Jonathan Kaplan, Joe Dante, James Cameron, Denis Hopper, Peter Fonda, Robert Towne, William Shatner, Sylvester Stallone and many others.

Corman also produced two key counter-culture hits of the 1960s – *The Wild Angels* and *The Trip* in 1966 which paved the way towards Columbia financing *Easy Rider* in 1969. The 'pope of pop cinema' as the French called him, was the midwife of the New Hollywood which grew out of European influences and American exploitation films. Martin Scorsese recalls 'Every morning at NYU you had to light a candle to Ingmar Bergman. They had little shrines to Bergman all over the place. I love Bergman pictures but it was Corman's movies that we studied in those strange dives all over New York.'[3]

Other film-makers who came up via the micro-budget route include Steven Spielberg – who was making full-length Super 8 features at the age of sixteen – and Woody Allen, whose first film was *What's Up Tiger Lily*, a comic dubbed version of an obscure Chinese film.

The punk-style atmosphere of micro-budget films continues to pump oxygen into the American film industry. In Corman's heyday there was a captive market because the studios were straitjacketed by the Hays Code. When the Code was dropped in 1966 the Majors shifted their commissioning strategy and started producing many of the former exploitation genres.

Today's low-budget film-makers try to catch the cusp of a new wave such as Spike Lee who launched black film-making with *She's Gotta Have It* or Richard Linklater who made the first Generation X picture with *Slacker*.

Micro-budget films are usually made by everyone deferring their fees. All technical equipment is hired at rock bottom prices and the film is shot as quickly as possible, usually with one or two takes per shot. Many films are shot on 16mm which is grainier but also much cheaper than 35mm, and then blown up.

Perhaps the all-time lowest budget was *El Mariachi* which had a two-man crew and spent $2,300 on buying stock, $1,300 in developing the negative and $2,800 on transferring to video. The camera was borrowed for free and the film was edited on video.

Most micro-budget films disappear without trace. But the best can launch a new career and pay back handsome dividends to investors. A list of some of the leading micro-budget films is provided below with their budget and US rentals. About a third of rentals would trickle through to the producer (after deduction of the distribution fee and P&A costs), but this would be considerably boosted by earnings in foreign sales, and in TV/video. The rentals figure is therefore a very conservative estimate of the total commercial performance of the film, and demonstrates the potential windfalls a micro-budget film can provide.

Director	Film	Year	Budget ($K)	Rentals ($M)
Francis F. Coppola	Dementia 13	1963	22	<1
Peter Bogdanovich	Targets	1968	150	<1
George Romero	Night/Living Dead	1968	114	3
Martin Scorsese	Boxcar Bertha	1972	100	<1
John Waters	Pink Flamingos	1972	60	1.9
Jonathan Demme	Caged Heat	1974	180	<1
Tobe Hooper	Texas Chainsaw	1974	200	14.4
David Lynch	Eraserhead	1977	80	3
John Carpenter	Halloween	1978	300	18.5
John Sayles	R. of Secaucus 7	1980	60	2.5
Sam Raimi	Evil Dead	1982	150	1.2
Jim Jarmusch	Stranger/Paradise	1984	120	1.25
Joel & Ethan Coen	Blood Simple	1985	1500	3.3
Spike Lee	She's Gotta Have It	1986	122	3.1
Lizzie Borden	Working Girls	1986	300	1.5
Robert Townsend	Hollywood Shuffle	1987	100	2.4
Steven Soderbergh	Sex Lies & Video	1989	1100	11
Hal Hartley	Unbelievable Truth	1990	75	<1
Richard Linklater	Slacker	1991	40	<1
Nick Gomez	Laws of Gravity	1991	38	<1
Robert Rodriguez	El Mariachi	1992	7	2
Edward Burns	Brothers McMullen	1995	200	10

HOW MICRO-BUDGET FILMS ARE MADE

Alongside the film-makers who made their debut with Corman (including *Dementia 13*, *Targets*, *Boxcar Bertha* and *Caged Heat*) a key breakthrough film was *Night of the Living Dead*, by George Romero.

Romero started his career with a $2,000 loan from his uncle to buy a Bolex camera and with a group of friends started making wedding pictures. The Romero team then expanded into commercials with a $30,000 bank loan co-signed by his uncle.

With the revenues earned, they began shooting *Night of the Living Dead* on 35mm, with additional loans from friends who also served as zombies. The producer John Russo even volunteered to be set on fire with gasoline because they couldn't afford an asbestos suit. George Romero later commented, 'The film was shot over a period of about nine months, with great breaks in between to come back and do a pickle commercial or something, which was distressing. After we got some footage in the can, people started coming around and saying, 'Hey, that looks like a movie!' and we said, 'Well, that's what it is!'[4] The film quickly became a classic and its total world earnings are believed to have exceeded $50 million.

Night of the Living Dead was a revelation to Tobe Hooper who had begun his career making over sixty documentaries and an art house film about the end of hippiedom. After seeing *Night,* he got the idea for the *Texas Chainsaw Massacre* and shot it on 16mm on a micro-budget.

Night and *Texas* then inspired Sam Raimi, who had begun his career by making Super 8 films. In 1979 along with his brother and two friends, he set up a limited partnership called Renaissance Motion Pictures. They did a variety of odd jobs to pool together $1,600 and then shot thirty minutes of the *Evil Dead* on Super 8 as a selling tool. Wearing suits and ties and with a detailed prospectus, they hit the road and raised $150,000 from dentists, doctors and lawyers. They also got some up-front money for foreign sales, and it was foreign sales that ultimately enabled them to pay back their investors.

The assistant editor on *Evil Dead* was Joel Coen. He and his brother Ethan had made Super 8 films as children and they managed to raise over $1 million from local businessmen in Minneapolis to make *Blood Simple.*

Other micro-budget film-makers include Spike Lee, Robert Townsend, Hal Hartley, Nick Gomez and Robert Rodriguez.

Spike Lee and Monte Ross made a feature length Super 8 film and then Lee's NYU graduation 16mm film *Joe's Bed-Study Barber Shop,* which won the Oscar for best student film in 1982. Spike used the award plus a friend's life savings to put together $22,000 and shoot for twelve days. He and Ross then used the rushes to appeal for more money from friends and also win the support of producer's rep John Pierson at Island Pictures. Pierson put in the final $10,000 in return for distribution rights and helped promote *She's Gotta Have It* in festivals.

Robert Townsend used the money he earned in acting in *American Flyers* and *A Soldier's Story* to begin shooting *Hollywood Shuffle.* But he needed an extra $40,000 to finish the film and didn't know where to look. By chance he received several credit card applications in the mail, each with a $1,000 spending limit. He took out all the cards he could and ran up $40,000 in credit card debt. Fortunately he managed to sell the picture to Samuel Goldwyn, otherwise he would have gone to prison.

Hal Hartley worked with his father in the construction business as an apprentice iron worker and then took a job answering phones for a company making public service announcements. He had already made two shorts, when the PSA company agreed to fund his $75,000 feature *The Unbelievable Truth,* which was shot in twelve days.

Nick Gomez is a central figure in New York's Shooting Gallery which is at the heart of the low-budget scene, and *Laws of Gravity* was their first feature after funding many short films. Gomez raised $35,000 from 'uncles and friends from college' and the Shooting Gallery raised $3,000 for post-production. The film was shot in twelve days and got a free sound mix from The Power Station in return for a prominent credit.

Finally, Robert Rodriguez had made many no-budget video shorts and an award-winning short, *Bedhead.* He tried to raise $12,000 from friends and family but came up with only $9,000, partly from his own funds and the sale of land by his friend Carlos Gallardo, who played the lead role. Rodriguez then checked into a drug testing facility and earned the final $3,000. Everything on the film was done by Rodriguez and Gallardo. 'Before I wrote the script, Carlos and I sat down and listed our assets,' says Rodriguez. 'We had access to a school bus, two bars, a jail, a motorcycle, a ranch, and a pit bull. So I wrote the film around these elements.' They shot the film in two weeks on non-sync sound. When Columbia saw the rough-cut they paid the expensive mix and 35mm blow-up.

Several independent films began as micro-budget features but were finally backed by independent producers on the strength of their script. This allowed them to access a superior cast.

Steven Soderbergh aimed to make *Sex, Lies and Videotape* with money from friends for $60,000, but RCA/Columbia and UK's Virgin Vision were hooked by the script and put in $1.2 million.

Quentin Tarantino spent three years trying to raise $1.2 million in a limited partnership in order to make *True Romance.* He then wrote *Natural Born Killers* with the intention to make it for $0.5 million, but still to no avail. He managed to sell both scripts and wrote *Reservoir Dogs* aiming to then shoot the film guerrilla style on a $50,000 budget, inspired by Nick Gomez's *Laws of Gravity.* But his acting teacher showed the script to Harvey Keitel who liked it and helped secure a $5 million production deal.

MICRO-BUDGET COMMUNITY

Micro-budget films need to draw on many favours. The support system is therefore essential to making things happen. New York is the centre of the micro-budget world, with specialist production companies such as the Shooting Gallery, facilities such as the Tribeca Film Center, and producer reps such as John Pierson at Miramax (who previously launched Spike Lee, Michael Moore and Richard Linklater at Island Pictures) and Jamie Ader Brown and Suzanne Fedok at In Pictures.

The Shooting Gallery was founded in 1991 with $7,000 and has established a pool of 1800 investors willing to subscribe to limited partnerships designed for micro-budget films. In 1996 the Gallery also signed a two-year first look production deal with New Line, which provides backing on films budgeted up to $8 million. The company also continues to groom zero-budget films.

Once micro-budget films are made, the festival circuit is key for generating word of mouth about the film. Festivals are looking for films with 'edge', and there are also a growing number of 'underground' film festivals which are dedicated to micro-budget features.

For the more mainstream festivals it can be an advantage to have a film on 35mm rather than 16mm because it provides a glossier entry for the festival. It is also helpful to establish contacts with festival selectors because if they know you, they are more likely to look favourably on your film. An excellent way to build contacts is through making a short, but with the knowledge that shorts are expensive and are very hard to sell.

Certain workshops have played a big part in boosting micro-budget films. One of the most prominent is by Dov S-S Simens, who began his career with Roger Corman. Both Tarantino and Spike Lee claim that the workshop inspired them to 'go out and do it'. Scriptwriting and producer workshops are also provided by the Sundance Film Institute, which helped develop *Reservoir Dogs*.

These support-systems help a lot, but ultimately the film-maker has to do his or her own running. It is a hard and often lonely struggle and it is important to not risk everything and to try to keep a perspective on things. Some film-makers will do anything – sell their house, take out loans – to make a film. Sometimes the money just goes down the drain.

SELLING THE MICRO-BUDGET FILM

Micro-budget films make people think very quickly about the need to repay their investors, particularly since the film-maker often has personal money on the line. The reality is that despite certain spectacular successes, many films fail to sell at all. It is a question of the quality of the film and the ability of the producer to promote it.

Again there are support systems. Festivals such as Sundance and Hampton are invaded by buyers and agents looking for the latest talent. Another key sales event is the Independent Feature Film Market (IFFM) founded in New York in 1978. Around 80 to 100 films are shown a year, but only about 10% get any sales deals. The best are selected to be taken to Cannes under the banner of the Independents Showcase. One third of the IFFM films go on to Sundance.

Distributors do release independent films. Columbia bought the rights to *El Mariachi,* but this is almost the only example of a Major buying such a film. The best bet are the mini-majors and classics, followed by the micro-indies and sales agents.

A new venture specifically designed for micro-budget films has been set up by In Pictures with the backing of Bertelsmann. In Pictures has already overseen the release of films such as *Claire de la Lune* and *Federal Hill* and now aim to cater for more of these cutting edge indie films.

The terms of a distribution deal for a micro-budget film are the same as any other film. The producer should look for an MG (often needed to cover final post-production costs) and a P&A commitment. The distribution deal should lock off the value of distribution expenses so that they do not eat into overages. On average the producer should aim for a third of theatrical rentals.

The producer should be wary of selling all rights to a single distributor and should negotiate separate deals for US and world rights. It is also important to recognize the market muscle of an established distributor. The producer should keep close tabs on the distributor and make sure that the film does not disappear behind other titles. If nobody wants to buy the film, it is always possible to opt for 'self publishing' – booking a theatre and doing your own publicity.

Micro-budget films require a lot of time and money. Some micro-budget film-makers are rich kids who have the privilege to try their hand at film. Others scrape together funds by any way possible. There is no formula, just a golden rule: make something different, that people want to see.

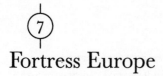

Fortress Europe

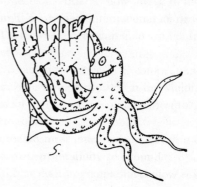

*In France there are five people who decide which films get made
and always the same fifteen directors. There is plenty of other talent.
We must rescue the underdog and not hang up a sign – as in
the beginning of 'Citizen Kane' – saying 'Do Not Enter'.*

Gilles Jacob

EVER SINCE LENIN DESCRIBED CINEMA as the 'most important art', the European state has been preoccupied with controlling all forms of cinematic expression. Today the state is intensely involved in European cinema, officially to protect European artists from the American aggressor. Anything veering away from this official line is immediately dubbed 'polemical'.

The fact that cinema is a 'politically sensitive' area in Europe means that it is subject to smoke and confusion and is defined under 'party lines'. There is also considerable risk in discussing such matters for anyone working within the European system. If you speak up against the system you may quickly find that you never eat lunch in town again.

In a recent conference, French director Jacques Fansten challenged what he saw as complacency on the part of Gaetano Adinolfi, the President of the Council of Europe: 'When you say that you've never heard a word of criticism from producers about Eurimages, I immediately thought of the story of the Chinese emperor who insisted that he be criticized and then immediately executed anyone who did so. Perhaps Eurimages is perfect, perhaps there are also some producers who don't dare to speak up.'[1]

The crisis of European cinema cannot be understood without placing it in the wider context of cultural and political crisis in Europe, including war in Bosnia, terrorism and the Clean Hands campaign. As Hungarian director Istvan Szabo commented recently, 'It's not just a problem with film-making, it's a problem with Europe's way of thinking, and the current European way of life. How can we be thinking positively when we are killing or arguing with one another? The current confusion within Europe is terrible: to accept each other or not, to be a member of Europe or not, which minority can survive, which minority can have a state and which cannot, and which group of people have to be killed or not? That's a terrible set of questions that makes today's Europe seem more like the Middle Ages than anything else.'[2]

One might expect at a moment of such turmoil that the cinema would be enriched with stories that captured the flavour of contemporary life. Instead there is silence, especially when it comes to mainstream cinema. This silence has been furthered by the Union's MEDIA Programme which has claimed to be 'shaping the audiovisual arena' but has been doing so in such a way that makes it very difficult for mainstream voices to appear.

At a recent MEDIA seminar, German producer Wieland Schulz-Kiel (*The Innocent, The Dead*) complained that 'money with a cultural mission' is detrimental to telling a story: 'A good story should have an element of transgression and these funds seem designed to stamp this out. By the time you've got the money you've told the story so many times you've been forced to shed light on the story's dark areas – that in itself is bad.' Others at the same conference blamed Europe's 'international gang' or 'cultural mafia' who hold the purse strings.

There is a sharp division between 'us' and 'them' in Europe, with a strong bias against anything that is not elite culture. Therefore it is no surprise that the European public does not rush in droves to see 'national films'. The majority of people who try to make films in Europe are made to feel unwelcome – as if they are not worthy to carry the name of their nation. British director Mike Figgis (*Stormy Monday, Internal Affairs*) summed this up in relation to Britain:

> It's so inundated with class and snobbery and nepotism that all the talent that is there waiting to be used, waiting to be involved, waiting to be creative – and I have no doubt it is there, it's there in spades – is not welcome, is not brought in. No one's really looking for new talent, real new talent, they just hop off to Cambridge or Oxford and find some bright young thing who might make a film or two because it's a fairly interesting thing to do. It's fucked up. It's the problem of Britain [and it won't change] until they can separate talent from class, which I have to say in America they can – they really do not give a toss unless you can make a film which a) will sell and b) will be interesting, and they're often the same thing.

Europe is an amalgam of very different cultures and peoples. That's what makes her interesting. At the same time there are enormous parallels between the political and cultural systems of each country, and in the case of cinema very similar state control mechanisms. Today the films that are made are increasingly provincial. There has been an almost total destruction of the cultural fabric of the film industry and this has coincided with massive intervention by the state under the guise of defending the cinema.

Europe this century has revealed a Jekyll and Hyde personality. On one side, she is urbane, sophisticated and civilized with the finest in wit, wisdom and culture. On the other she is prejudiced, barbaric and corrupt.

Modern-day Europe is the consequence of centuries of historical development which has built up massive 'nation-state' structures, now slowly cementing into a European super-state. All shades of the political spectrum have been allied this century to the idea that the state should have a dominant role over society.

Alongside an increasing powerful state, there is a *de facto* equilibrium whereby power and wealth are concentrated in a small number of private hands which have a monopoly over the national market. The state has tended to reinforce this monopoly position, and power is concentrated around political lobbies rather than open competition in the market-place.

Europe now represents a series of national fortresses which are united at the top by the national power elite. This system is now extending to a pan-European level.

Cinema has a very ambiguous role within this fortress structure. Although an industrial process, cinema has shown from its beginning that it can only truly flourish when given total freedom for personal expression.

This is the issue at the heart of the debate about European cinema. It is not about comparing the artistic merits of Hollywood and European cinema. It is a question of how a flourishing film industry that guarantees personal expression can be maintained.

Many of Europe's film-makers continue to be convinced that the only way that Europe can maintain her cinema is through state support. This fits perfectly into the corporatist vision of Fortress Europe, but it is by no means obvious that it is the best way forward.

THE STATE AND EUROPEAN CINEMA

Since its birth, European cinema has been declared to be in 'crisis', and this has usually been used to justify state intervention. In recent years, the crisis is not that films are not made, it is that very few can attract an audience.

In America, Hollywood releases around 150 films a year and a further 100 independent films are released. The total production cost is around $5 billion. In the European Union almost twice as many theatrical films are produced and released (499 in 1992), but the official production cost ($1.4 billion) is 30% of that in America.

The main difference between America and Europe is that while the former is paid for by private corporations who sell to the public, the latter is paid for by the state and the state organizes the main means of exhibition.

The average global gross for a Hollywood film is approximately $200 million, of which half is earned by the distributor. For a two-hour film the effective price (including advertising) and audience per window is as follows:

Average results per film

		Cinema	Video	Pay-TV	Free TV
Hollywood	Price	$5.5	$3	$0.7	$0.15
	Audience	10.5M	34M	24M	147M
	Gross	$58M	$103M	$17M	$22M

The total audience for the average Hollywood film in the United States, Europe and Japan is 220 million viewers, one third in 'premium media' and two thirds in 'mass media'.

For European films over 80% of commercial revenue comes from television, but most of this is a state subsidy because audience levels (average 1–2 million) do not justify the acquisition and co-production prices paid. Television in effect 'overpays' because it is part of the state's cultural policy and forms part of the channel remit, as in the case of Channel 4, or because of blanket legislation as in France (where TV channels must invest 3% of their total income in film production).

The true 'market revenues' for the average European film is $2 million of which the distributor earns $1 million. The overall audience is as follows:

Average results per film

		Cinema	Video	Pay-TV	Free TV
Europe	Price	$5.5	$3	$0.7	$0.15
	Audience	0.15M	0.25M	0.3M	1.5M
	Gross	$0.8M	$0.75M	$0.2M	$0.22M

Averages are higher for the larger countries where theatrical admissions for national films are 200,000. For smaller countries the average theatrical audience is 75,000. The typical European film has 1% of the audience of the average Hollywood film and this crushing disparity is continuing to grow.

Hollywood has maintained healthy average audience figures throughout the post-war period. In the United States and the five largest European territories the average combined audience for US and UK films is as follows:

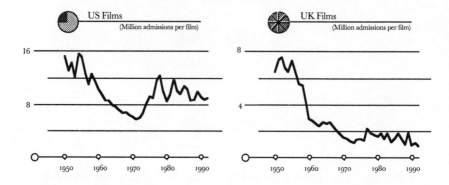

The statistics demonstrate that the average audience per American film halved between 1960 and 1970. This was the result of changing audience habits due to television and migration to the suburbs and also the result of poor management and the straitjacket of the Hays Code. The New Hollywood succeeded in cutting back production levels and increasing popularity per film both in America and Europe.

The decline in performance of British films has been far more severe. The main periods of collapse were 1955–60 and then a further fall between 1965–73. It is easy to blame this entirely on television but there were also significant changes in commissioning policy at this time.

British films were traditionally very parochial in outlook but enjoyed a burst of activity in the war years and immediately thereafter. After Rank's disastrous attempt to corner the American market in the late 1940s there was a significant retrenchment in the scale and type of films made.

The second retrenchment was at the end of the 1960s as a result of withdrawal of Hollywood financing from London and a much greater dependence on national funding mechanisms, which has resulted in the present average of 1 million admissions per film (most of which come from outside the UK).

The figure for British films is further distorted by 'pick-ups' with American distributors which still qualify as British films. If one excludes these figures then the audience for British films is around 200,000 – comparable to other European countries.

The decline in average popularity of continental European films is even more devastating:

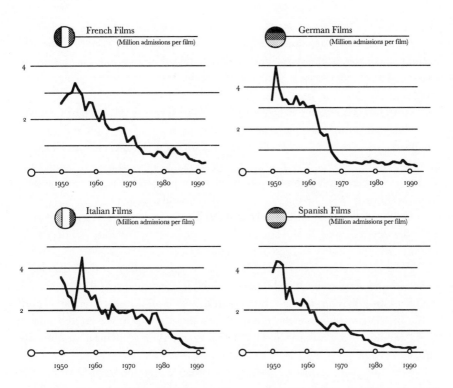

The first industry to collapse was Germany in the 1960s. Again, television played a role, but far more significant was a huge shift in commissioning strategies away from commercial genres and towards state-funded 'autorenfilm'.

The Italian industry, once the heart of European cinema, collapsed at the end of the 1970s as the country nose-dived into political chaos and corruption scandals.

Spanish cinema had its heyday during the war years and immediately after. The Fascist government was keen to support comedies and allowed considerable leeway in the range of topics which could be expressed. Tighter controls were introduced at the beginning of the 1950s and the popularity of films progressively decreased. Once Spain was liberated from Fascism, the cinema continued to be dependent on state patronage and the commissioning policy focused on small cultural films.

France is the last bastion of continental European cinema. But she too has been shedding audiences throughout the post-war era, as she has progressively shifted from commercial genres, co-produced with Italy and Hollywood, and solidly focused on culture films. French films are now only marginally more popular than her continental counterparts. The average audience is 330,000 compared to 200,000 in Germany, Italy and Spain. The main reason why France is so important to the shape of European cinema is the extent of French taxpayer money which flows into the industry.

THE TRADITION OF STATE PATRONAGE

One cannot understand European society without appreciating the all-encompassing role of the state. The 'nation-state' is Europe's main achievement since the late Middle Ages. The first 'state-builders' included Machiavelli in Italy and Louis XIV in France.

In the feudal era, the centrifugal force of society was the Roman Church. The Church's power was undermined by the invention of the Gutenberg press, which played a crucial role in the Reformation and Renaissance and helped launch the process whereby Europe began to be divided up into nation-states. These states were built around centralized control of the language and culture, which were used to define the essence of the 'national heritage'.

Culture is the 'holy of the holies' of the European power systems, and ever since the days of Louis XIV, subsidies have been used by the state to encourage certain national authors and discourage others.

After the French Revolution, Europe was split between two tendencies – humanist and corporatist. The humanist tradition advocated that Europe should shed her elitist divisions and embrace equal rights for all citizens. The corporatist tradition tried to preserve the monarchical idea that society is united into a single 'family' led by a patrician elite acting as guardian of civilization and culture.

State intervention in culture was forbidden in the nineteenth century in most countries except at times of war, but this was changed in the 1930s as Nazi Germany and Soviet Russia pioneered state control mechanisms. One of the last countries to resist this new trend was France, who finally capitulated with the German Occupation in 1940.

European cinema has been dominated by the state ever since, although there was a relapse in the immediate post-war era as Hollywood co-produced European films and there was a general call for a reduction in state censorship.

State cinema is based on defining the film industry as a 'corporation' which revolves around a National Cinema Centre. The latter organizes the financial and administrative structure of the film industry, including financing, cultural subsidies, film education and film festivals.

Although those involved in the state subsidy system are often driven by very idealistic principles, the inevitable result seems to be bureaucratic decision-making and insider lobbying that severely undermines both creative and commercial vitality.

In effect, the system establishes 'positive censorship'. There is no messy 'negative censorship' involving bans and cuts in films that are already made. Instead the film-making process is controlled at source by selecting which individuals are to be trusted as 'national authors'.

Today the vast majority of funding for European films comes from the state. The average market revenues that would be earned by producers under a commercial system in each territory are as follows (excluding Hollywood pick-ups):

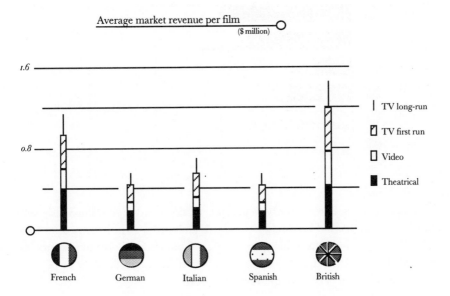

The value of market revenues is far below average budgets. The difference is made up by the state, through subsidies and overpayment by television channels.

The state now provides 70% of the funding for the average continental film, and 50% of the average British film. The state's contribution is further amplified in most continental countries because the state provides completion bond and discounting services, thus boosting the state's effective contribution to over 80% of negative cost. The state also spends a large amount of money on supporting distribution, exhibition, short films and festivals.

The dominance of the state over the European film industry has built up progressively since the early 1960s, when state funding represented under 20% of the total financing mix and was granted through automatic 'industrial' subsidies.

The central role of state patronage was sealed in the 1980s as a massive influx of state subsidy and television subsidy money caused hyper-inflation in production budgets. For example, French national films alone have tripled in budget since 1980, shifting their state dependence from 25% to 70%.

Today total market revenues for European films are under $300 million a year, whereas state subsidies are worth over $800 million and rising. For the main countries this breaks down as follows:

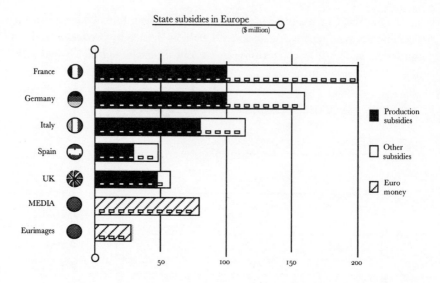

State subsidies in Europe
($ million)

Britain is the latest country to join the subsidy bandwagon. Previously subsidies stood at around $12 million a year, mainly from British Screen and the BFI. With the new $22 million a year Arts Council fund, Britain is moving towards harmonization with her European partners, which is likely to be soon supplemented by a version of the French Soficas.

HARE AND THE TORTOISE

Europe is run by what is known as a 'mixed economy' – a constant overlap of private and public interests, particularly in the fields of education, culture and communication. The state brings with it a heavy baggage of bureaucracy and lobbying which tends to freeze up development in certain areas. This has been most evident in all areas of the information revolution where Europe has been dragging her feet.

The collapse of European cinema is only one example of the continent's lethargy. In 1970 Europe had a talent network capable of making popular films, and produced around 150–200 popular films a year, most of which were co-productions and earned average audiences of 6–7 million. Hollywood produced a similar number of films with only slightly higher audiences.

Then something changed. The New Hollywood emerged and took advantage of new ideas, marketing techniques and special effects, and over time has forged links with Silicon Valley and the cyber revolution.

In Europe the state took charge of the cinema and the sector has been reduced to a marginal existence – a world unto itself with few connections to contemporary events.

This gap is also mirrored in other information sectors such as the CD-ROM and the Internet. In 1994 while there were 10 million CD-ROM drives in use in America, mainly by consumers, in Europe the market was still virtually non-existent. As *Variety* commented, 'The new interactive medium requires a whole new way of creative thinking, which is in its infancy in the US but barely out of the womb in Europe . . . The American telephone, computer, entertainment and publishing companies are thundering headlong toward the new frontier while Europe is still catching its breath.'[3]

The world is undergoing an information revolution which is likely to be as significant as the industrial revolution and yet Europe seems to be at a standstill – gridlocked by bureaucracy and corruption scandals. Whereas in America there are scaremongers who talk about the transfer of power from the old elite to a new cyber elite, in Europe this discussion is irrelevant.

Whenever this issue is raised, the immediate explanation for Europe's backwardness is unfair competition from America. The proposed solution is yet more intervention from the state. And then nothing happens. A classic example is the $250 million already spent by the Union's MEDIA programme to no demonstrable success.

The politicians have also suggested that any new media channels should be overseen by a Union agency. French culture minister Jacques Toubon has said 'We have to favour the development of a European multi-media industry, just as we do with the European industry of audiovisual programmes.'

Many people in Europe recognize that the problem is the over-reaching powers of politicians and state bureaucracy. Politicians such as Lady Thatcher and Silvio Berlusconi were elected with promises to 'roll back the frontiers of the state', and yet what has happened throughout Europe is an increase in interference by the state in education, culture and information – the core areas in the transition from a manufacturing to a communications based economy.

There are some who would argue that Europe's tortoise-like pace will allow her to win in the long run. It is clear that America, while sprinting ahead to a new future, is racked with doubts and uncertainties. Perhaps Europe can learn from America's failures and do even better. But to do so, at some time she has to join the race.

PRIVATE MONOPOLIES

Alongside massive state intervention in the information sector, there is also a very high degree of concentration of media ownership in a small number of hands. This is often in violation of EU anti-trust legislation, but the companies concerned usually have very strong political connections and in practice it is difficult to do much about them.

In 1993 the Union produced a Green Paper on pluralism and media concentration which focused on these monopolies. Although many criticisms were aired it was recognized that no government had the power to do anything about it. A source within the Commission said 'it's a problem that's been around for years . . . Since 1990 the parliament has called for urgent regulations on this issue. But it also considers it a very complex and sensitive matter on which all shades of opinion should be considered.' UK media lawyer William Field of S. J. Berwin commented, 'If national governments cannot control the moguls – who have proven very quick to manoeuvre around domestic anti-trust laws – then where does that leave the EC?' The fact that Europe's main media companies are privately owned also means that there is a lack of transparency in the accounting systems and operational structure.

The willingness of politicians to turn a blind eye to anti-trust legislation makes it very difficult for newcomers to break into the market. This has been particularly frustrating to the Americans who in recent years have been attempting to break into Europe, especially the German market. *Variety* described Germany as 'Europe's largest territory, generally perceived as a sleeping giant quietly controlled by a few private players . . . The big publishing houses are all still attached like feudal estates to prominent German families: Holtzbrinck, Bauer, Burda.'

European groups also suffer from monopolistic practices. For example, former RCS film chief Paolo Glisenti explained:

> It will take a long time to rebuild Italian cinema back to what it once was. It must escape from the disastrous period when it has been nurtured by state subsidies and domestic television. The golden age was when there was an open market and Italy was intellectually and culturally alive. This ended over fifteen years ago. Today the presence of monopolistic TV capable of overbidding makes it impossible to nurture films outside this system. Anti-trust laws make it very difficult for us to expand into Italian television. It is an absurd situation, and one can only hope that the crumbling of Berlin walls within the system will open up new opportunities.

Criticism of private monopolies is usually deflected by the argument that the real menace is America. Media is given a 'cultural exception' from the Union's competition rules, and private monopolies are considered necessary to combat the Americans. In recent years this has meant that anti-trust legislation has actually been relaxed – despite the fact that in the case of film, national monopolies have expressed a very limited interest in domestic production and their first objective is often to sign distribution pacts with the Americans. French producer Marin Karmitz comments, 'We don't have the protections that exist in America of anti-trust laws and separation between production and distribution. Our legislative arsenal is unable to defend independent companies from powerhouses such as Canal+, Bouygues or alliances such as Gaumont-Pathé.'[4]

European cinematic exhibition is held almost entirely in national hands, and yet constant reference is made to Hollywood's 'unfair monopoly position'.

The reality is that the main European media groups choose to ally with the Americans rather than try to nurture domestic production.

A classic example is Britain, where the exhibition business is dominated by Rank and the MGM chain. Rank has expressed little interest in producing British films from 1980 until very recently, and it is often considered easier to release a British film abroad than at home. This issue was confronted in a report by the Monopolies and Mergers Commission in 1993, but the report ultimately concentrated on the question of whether the American Majors used unfair business practices. It did not confront the more thorny question of why many British media groups are not interested in British film.

In Portugal there was a long battle 1990–93 between Antonio Pedro Vasconcelos, then national secretary for audiovisual affairs, and the leading cinema chain, Lusomondo. Vasconcelos insisted that Lusomundo – which is believed to control 60–70% of the exhibition business – is in violation of EC anti-trust regulations in the Treaty of Rome. 'With Lusomundo we are talking a clear monopoly' he commented. 'That is something that Americans, above all, should understand. They have had anti-trust laws longer than anyone. The point is not to block out the Americans. We simply need to regulate our market with laws that allow for fair distribution.'

Lusomundo, run by Colonel Luis Silva, also owns two leading newspapers, real estate and radio stations and has considerable political clout. When Vasconcelos resigned in 1993, many believed it was due to pressure from the group. Vasconcelos explained that 'two and a half years is too long to fight for something that you see will not work. The government hired me to design new legislation, but in the end I was only fighting a no-win battle.'[5]

Lusomundo argued in their defence that they did not give Portuguese films a wide enough release, simply because they weren't popular enough. To prove the point they invested in a Portuguese film *Adão e Eva* in 1995 on the basis of the script alone, and the film went on to become the biggest local hit in recent years.

Vasconcelos nonetheless took his campaign wider by attacking Hollywood distributor, UIP (the foreign sales arm of Universal, Paramount and MGM) . He emphasized that the real issue was not Hollywood but rather European monopolies. 'Speaking personally, I see it not about UIP *per se* but about fair competition. In some territories UIP has too strong a dominance – such as in Portugal, where the UIP representative also handles Buena Vista and Touchstone and represents 60% of the market. In other countries it is national groups which hold too much power.'

Anti-trust watchdogs have also been barking at the trusts of Gaumont-Pathé in France, Kirch in Germany and Berlusconi in Italy. But the issue is complicated by the fact that Europe does genuinely need powerful media groups, and those groups have proved willing to invest in popular projects when they become available.

CORRUPTION SCANDALS

Europe has been devastated by corruption scandals in recent years. Only a few media players have been touched by these scandals, but they nonetheless provide the context from which Europe's media industry can be understood.

Television and cinema have traditionally been owned by the state in Europe, so a new government leads to a reshuffle amongst the heads of public television and cinema agencies. Top jobs within public television, particularly in Southern Europe, are distributed according to political affiliation. In Italy this is known as *Lottizzazzione*. For example, the three RAI channels have traditionally been identified as RAI-1 for the Christian Democrats, RAI-2 for the Socialists and RAI-3 for the Communists.

In the 1980s there was an explosion of private television companies in Europe, but the new owners had overt political connections. A classic example was Germany where Kirch has close ties to the ruling CDU-CSU coalition and Bertelsmann is linked to the centre-left SPD.

Although Europe now operates under a 'commercial' framework, there continue to be very tight political controls. For example, after the election of the Right in France in 1993 there was a reshuffle in the heads of France Television, Canal+, the CNC and Unifrance. In Britain, the shake-up in broadcasting has also been used to extend the power of government patronage and the appointment of commissioning editors is now more political than ever.

The pre-eminent role of political patronage means that commissioning editors, particularly for cinema, are often appointed because of political connections rather than from any prior expertise. Many heads of the national cinema centres do not have time to familiarize themselves with the medium. One film tsar, when attacked by the press for knowing nothing about cinema, used the defence that the previous head knew nothing about cinema either!

The all-encompassing role of political parties leads to amateurism and bureaucracy, to which anyone who lives in Europe is very familiar. Bureaucracy freezes new initiatives and gives power to those with 'connections' who can cut through red tape. Bureaucracy is also a well-known breeding ground for corruption and conspiracy.

Every new government claims that they will make a break with the past. For example, when the Socialist Party was elected in Portugal in 1995 the new Minister of Culture, Manuel Maria Carrilho, said that the previous regime was 'the opposite of transparency, it was jobs for the boys, nepotism, incompetence, nomination of people who didn't know anything about the sector they were in charge of – in theatre, music and other areas'.

Each new government claims to be different but cultural appointments always 'round up the usual suspects'. As a result, Europe's culture is decided by the 'great and the good', a small group of elite 'experts' who are omni-present in cultural debates, and whose criterion of success is approval by their peers.

THE NEW MEDIA ENVIRONMENT IN EUROPE

Europe's media groups are caught in a paradoxical situation. Several owe their existence to political patronage, but the new 'de-regulated' environment means that the most dynamically managed groups will reap the highest dividends. In the case of the film industry, the leading media groups are conscious of the critical importance, and yet are also aware that the state has defined cinema as part of its 'territory'.

The most ambitious media groups have so far avoided potential conflict with the state, by concentrating on trying to produce Hollywood films, usually with substantial financial losses. Their only long-term solution is to try to revive the commercial performance of Europe's domestic film industries, but this will require a shift in commissioning strategy and a challenge of the monopoly of the state.

It is clear that the principal reason for the decline of European cinema as well as many other areas of European cultural life is the consequence of the over-reaching power of the political sphere. If Europe manages to break free from this benign 'paternalistic' influence then she may begin to rejuvenate her culture.

Europe's Media Barons

*In a few years you'll see a couple of foreign companies,
like a Bertelsmann and a Philips, and a few American companies
running the whole business.*

Jerry Katzman

THE FUTURE OF EUROPEAN CINEMA depends critically upon Europe's media groups and their capacity to compete in the open market. Alain Lévy of Poly-Gram predicts that 'At the end of the century there will be five to ten major broadcasters worldwide. I don't know how it will pan out, but in the next few years there will be tremendous jockeying to link up with them or risk being cut out of the picture.'[1]

PolyGram is one of the most dynamic European companies, but the commercial necessity of developing a strong film strategy is becoming increasingly pressing for many players.

Unless Europe's media groups develop strength in film software it will be increasingly difficult to hold back the advances of the American Majors. The new multi-media environment will enable the Majors to set up their own pay-TV, digital and CD-i networks and European players risk being left on the sidelines. Quotas are a stop-gap solution but will be useless in the long run.

OVERVIEW

European cinema has excelled when strong vertically integrated film publishers have been combined with autonomous creative workshops headed by a producer/film-maker.

In the pioneer days, the two main film empires were Pathé and Gaumont, and the workshops included those of Ferdinand Zecca, Max Linder, Alice Guy, and Louis Feuillade.

During the Great War, Germany recognized the superiority of Allied propaganda, and under instructions from General Ludendorff (Germany's 'power behind the throne') a state-backed consortium, Ufa, was established.

At the end of the war there were revolutions in Russia, Germany and much of Eastern Europe. This led to the emergence of new talent such as Alexander Korda in Hungary, the workshops of Ernst Lubitsch, Fritz Lang, F. W. Murnau in Germany, and Dziga Vertov and Lev Kuleshov in Russia.

Many of these film-makers were inspired by modernist and American influences, and helped build up very successful film industries in their native countries.

In the late 1920s and 1930s this flowering of talent was attacked, and new authoritarian regimes were established in Central and Eastern Europe. Totalitarianism made cinema 'the most important art' and strong infrastructures were developed and the basic framework of 'national cinema' and European co-production was established.

The advent of sound stepped up the movement towards state control of the industry, because the use of the 'national language' provided justification for 'national control'. The large expenses entailed by sound equipment also forced many of the leading film companies into bankruptcy and thereby into the arms of the state.

In Germany the state began to take over the industry via the front man of Max Winkler. In Italy the state set up a vertically integrated industry led by Luigi Freddi and Vittorio Mussolini (son of Il Duce). In France the state bailed out the leading companies, and state ad agency Havas took over Gaumont. In Britain, J. Arthur Rank began to emerge as the authorities' candidate for running the industry.

During the war, all of European cinema was under control of the state, and the need to produce rousing popular propaganda provided a great stimulus to the cinematic infrastructure and led to some surprising cinematic gems – even amongst the most despicable regimes.

After the war, the talent pools that had been built up by the authoritarian regimes started to work in tandem with the Hollywood Majors.

The memory of Fascism made it illegal for the state to influence the content of films, and thereby provided sufficient creative freedom for European auteurs to make interesting and controversial films. They were aided by the Hollywood distributors who played a very significant role in financing and distributing European films.

In the late 1940s, Rank had ambitions to become a world Major and stepped up their production plans, only to shut down because of huge losses by 1949. This was the first of several spectacular management failures in Europe that have severely undermined the industry.

In Italy, the legacy of Luigi Freddi and Vittorio Mussolini meant that there were strong producers and distributors, which forged a powerful industry based around companies such as Lux, Universalcine, Rizzoli, Ponti/de Laurentiis and Titanus.

In France, Gaumont resumed a major production role under the guidance of Alain Poiré. Pathé and the state-owned UGC were also active until the late 1950s. Entrepreneurial producers such as Pierre Braunberger, Georges Beauregard and Anatole Dauman laid the seeds for what would become the Nouvelle Vague.

In 1957 several leading European producers met with the idea to establish European Majors. The producers included Poiré, Fresnay, Durand and Deutschmeister from France, Kurt Shore and Rieze from Germany and Eitel Monaco, Goffredo Lombardo, Ricardo Gualino and Angelo Rizzoli from Italy. Nothing came of their plans.

During the 1960s, there was a fundamental change in the world film industry. Hollywood suffered a severe cash crisis, partly as a result of declining audiences in Europe and also because its movies seemed to be out of touch with the times.

The Hays Code was abandoned in 1966 and major multinationals took over the studios, ushering in a management and talent revolution which has created the juggernaut of today. Charles Bluhdorn of Gulf and Western predicted with foresight in 1970, 'There is a tremendous future in the leisure field. Movies in cassettes for home viewing will open a tremendous market. Satellite someday will relay first-run movies into millions of homes. It's a great challenge.'

In Europe, the opposite occurred. National cinema centres were set up throughout Europe, and the state began actively influencing film commissioning through selective subsidies and investments by state television. Most leading film companies were taken over by new media groups who introduced 'technocratic' management styles that either cut back production entirely or shifted it onto a higher 'cultural' plane.

In the 1970s, the most ambitious player was Gaumont who suffered huge losses by expanding into Italy. Under the weight of terrorism, political instability and corruption, the Italian film industry also collapsed and leading producers such as Carlo Ponti, Dino de Laurentiis and Alberto Grimaldi fled the country.

State-funded films were increasingly channelled via art house circuits, and the main media groups began to focus on securing independent Hollywood productions.

During the 1980s, the media groups further consolidated their control over European cinema and mooted plans to revive local production. They have so far invested more resources in Hollywood production.

Europe's leading twenty-one media companies earned combined revenues of $77 billion in 1995, far more than the $65 billion combined income of the seven US Majors. But very little of this revenue was earned in film production or distribution.

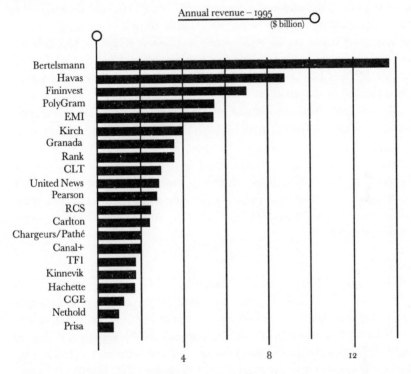

Annual revenue – 1995 ($ billion)

Bertelsmann
Havas
Fininvest
PolyGram
EMI
Kirch
Granada
Rank
CLT
United News
Pearson
RCS
Carlton
Chargeurs/Pathé
Canal+
TF1
Kinnevik
Hachette
CGE
Nethold
Prisa

4   8   12

Other important media companies in Europe include Reed/Elsevier, Axel Springer, Richemont, the newspaper groups and the state television companies. The 'missing' company on the list is Maxwell Communications which fell apart after the mysterious death of its owner Robert Maxwell, who had been a lifelong supporter of the Socialist cause. His media interests spanned the press (the Mirror Group), book publishing and television (including 12.5% ownership of TF1).

Most of Europe's leading media groups are run by media barons with strong political connections. They have a critical hold over European media, with many international links established in recent years. The full 'media map' of Europe is a jigsaw puzzle of cross-ownership. Majority control of the 'hardware' delivery systems is in the hands of the leading European players. But these companies are very weak in software, and as a consequence the Majors dominate film distribution.

Europe's media groups have so far been able to reap important revenues from premium media outlets such as film exhibition and pay-TV. But their total dependence on Hollywood software makes them extremely vulnerable.

This issue is coming to a head as Europe moves towards digital TV channels which involve a fresh set of rights negotiations. As *Variety* put it, 'The digital revolution is giving the studios a second chance to catch the boat they missed so lucratively first time around, when they failed to grab an equity stake in European pay-TV and saw such companies as Canal+, BSkyB and Nethold get a vice-like grip on the business.' The first battleground is likely to be Germany which Jim McNamara, head of MCA TV, described as 'the laboratory for the digital revolution in the rest of the world.'

The software incapacities of Europe's media groups are now forcing them into a series of mega-alliances to try to protect their markets.

FAMILY GROUPS

There are five leading 'family groups' within the European industry, followed by smaller but important players such as Bouygues, RCS, Carlton, Rank, Cecchi Gori, Prisa, Granada, Hachette, Pearson, Virgin and Cerezo who are profiled in Appendix B.

Havas/CGE

Havas and CGE are the leading elements of the consortium that now runs Canal+. Havas is also a lead shareholder in CLT (now merged with Bertelsmann), along with Albert Frère's Groupe Bruxelles Lambert, and CGE is 32% owner of UGC/Lumière with the ambition to increase this stake. CGE also has several joint ventures with Hachette Premiere. This puts Havas and CGE at the centre of a film and television empire which includes UGC, Lumiere, Canal+ Nethold, CLT, and Berlin-Babelsberg. It also provides a series of strong links with Bertelsmann through the latter three entities.

Bertelsmann

Bertelsmann is an empire in its own right, and in 1996 merged its film and television arm with CLT, thereby establishing Europe's largest media company. Bertelsmann is also at the heart of an alliance for digital broadcasting which includes CLT, Canal+ and Havas and is now allied to Kirch and News Corp.

Berlusconi/Kirch

Silvio and Leo are old friends and partners. They have dominant positions over the German and Italian markets and also strategic stakes in France and Spain. Family friends include Swiss billionaire Otto Beisheim, Johann Rupert of South Africa (Richemont), and Saudi Prince al-Waleed ben Talal. Berlusconi has private wealth of $1.5 billion, Kirch $2.5 billion and Beisheim $2.8 billion.

The Seydoux Brothers

Jerome, Nicolas and Michel Seydoux have a dominant control over the French film industry, and through Jerome have strategic interests throughout Europe. The list of associated companies is impressive: Pathé, AMLF, Allied, Renn, Guild, Tobis, Gaumont, Pyramide and stakes in BSkyB, Savoy and CGE. The Seydoux brothers' combined private wealth is $2.9 billion.

PolyGram

PolyGram, which is 75% owned by Philips, is the furthest down the road towards the ambition of becoming a European major with direct distribution in the United States, Britain, France, Spain, Netherlands and Australia. Of all Europe's media groups, they seem the most ambitious in relation to securing a strong supply of film and television software.

COMPANY PROFILES

European media companies are much more introverted and discrete than their American counterparts. They nonetheless have very distinct corporate philosophies and working styles, which can be best understood by describing the breadths of their interests.

HAVAS/CGE

The leading French media 'family group' has a long tradition of close ties with the French state. Its component parts are very well placed to take advantage of new media developments and over time may converge into a single media empire.

Havas

Havas is the largest media company in France. During the war it was owned jointly by the French and German governments, and for most of the post-war period was 50% owned by the French state. This gave the state influence over new private ventures such as Canal+.

Havas was privatized by Chirac in 1987, while he was briefly French prime minister, and the company retains strong political connections.

The single most important source of Havas's revenue is international media buying (Havas sells all of CLT's air-time). The company also owns 73% of C.E.P. Communication – Europe's sixth largest book and magazine publisher (including *L'Express* and *Le Point*) – and 39% of Havas Advertising which includes EURO RSCG.

The company's main film and television interests are as follows:

- Pay television   Canal+ (24%)

- Free television   CLT (20%)

- Film distrib./production   MK2 (20%)

- Television production   Télé Images (44%)

After the election of the Right in France in 1993, media ownership laws were relaxed and Havas won managerial control of Canal+ by combining with CGE and Société Générale (the consortium owns 48.7%). This led to the resignation of André Rousselet.

Havas is now a key shareholder in both Canal+ and Bertelsmann/CLT. Key associates are represented on the Board of Directors, including CGE, Canal+, Alcatel Alsthom, Caisse des Dépôts, Société Générale and Albert Frère.

Canal+

Canal+ was the invention of French Socialists and the success story of French television in the 1980s. The company was launched in 1984 with a monopoly over the pay television business in France. The company president was André Rousselet, friend and golfing partner to François Mitterand.

Canal+ got off to a slow start and many believed that it would not have its licence renewed. This was because Hollywood was reluctant to sell product, and French films were not attractive enough to boost subscriptions. The saviour was when the channel began broadcasting hard-core pornography, which led to a major increase in the subscriber base and provided the market muscle to negotiate sports rights and better terms with Hollywood.

By the late 1980s the channel was spewing out profits and began to expand internationally. Canal+ now has joint pay-TV ventures in Germany, Spain, Belgium, Poland, Tunisia and Senegal and has several co-ventures with Bertelsmann.

Canal+'s impressive track record hides considerable vulnerability. This is because of the severe dependence on Hollywood films in order to attract subscribers. Canal+ is required by law to show a minimum 60% European films, of which 40% must be French-language. This means that Canal+ needs over 100 new French films a year, but the channel has struggled to find films of sufficient quality. André Rousselet complained that only two thirds of French films met the minimum standards needed for screening, and another Canal+ executive has complained that most French feature films actually score lower ratings than TV movies.

Canal+ nonetheless has faced considerable lobbying both from political overseers and within the industry not to interfere in the type of French films made.

The channel is not allowed to be involved directly in production, but has important stakes in Studio Canal+ (60%), Alain Sarde (49.9%), Cerito (Jean Paul Belmondo) (99.9%), Chrysalide (35.3%) and TV producer Ellipse (61%). The national films produced have been fairly typical 'Franco-Français' films, and seem to have been designed to appease the French film industry, while significant funds are poured into Hollywood.

After massive losses from its Hollywood investments, the channel has been refocusing its attentions and adopting a more selective approach to backing French films.

In December 1994 the company established a rights arm, Canal+ DA (25% owned by Havas). This division has been building up an important film library, with acquisition of the Paravision library, over 300 titles from Dino de Laurentiis's DEG, Nelson and Embassy, and French rights to the Korda film library. In early 1996 Canal+ DA bought the Carolco film library for $58 million and later sealed a $541 million share swap with UGC DA whereby they gained control of the 5000-title UGC library.

With the election of the Right, there has been a significant shake-up in senior management, with Rousselet resigning in 1993, Marc Tessier leaving in mid-1995 and René Bonnell exiting in early 1996. There have also been rumours of pressures on Pierre Lescure, although many believe he has a fairly good relationship with Chirac.

Canal+'s next main priorities are digital broadcasting and the German market, which is believed to represent 50% of the total European digital market. Canal+ is allied with Bertelsmann and have together inked $500 million to corner the new market. This relationship is strained by a separate CLT alliance with TF1, France Television and M6.

Studio Canal+

Studio Canal+ was launched in December 1990 in order to guarantee access to Hollywood product. The company was originally 60% directly owned by Canal+ and 25% by Havas, but is now a wholly-owned subsidiary. The first president was René Bonnell – 'Mr Cinema' – formerly a university professor, distribution chief for Gaumont and Canal+'s film rights buyer.

The two main elements of the Studio's initial strategy were equity stakes in Carolco and a $600 million multi-picture deal involving Arnon Milchan's Regency, Warner Brothers, and Scriba/Dehyle in Germany. But these deals led to significant losses and resulted in a decrease of powers for Bonnell in 1991 and his return to film buying in 1993. Bonnell seemed to irritate several Hollywood producers, who claimed he was sending out the 'wrong signals'.

The Hollywood investments were made at a critical time. The channel felt that it could afford to lose a certain amount of money, because high profile deals would secure product and help keep down acquisition prices. Losses were seen as part of an inevitable learning curve.

But the cost of learning about the movie business was considered to be excessive by many observers. As one US agent explained, 'If anybody from Hollywood went into the European market and started pouring in millions of dollars without doing any prior research or hiring any experienced talent, you'd think they were crazy.'

The Milchan-Warners deal was fundamentally restructured in 1993 and the channel subsequently had to write off its entire Carolco investment (as well as putting up a further $58 million to acquire the library).

In the meantime, Canal+ is several years down the line, and still highly dependent on Hollywood. To change this, the channel has started to be more selective in its support of French films, and in 1995 signed a co-venture with Sony to develop English-language films based in Europe.

The link-up with Sony began with the scriptwriting workshop Equinoxe, founded by the two companies in 1993 with additional money from the CNC, British Screen and the European Script Fund.

Kenneth Lemberger of Sony commented on the venture, 'Canal+ has an incredible network of relationships with talent all over Europe, primarily in France. We bring to the table a more commercial, more institutional sensibility and a development process that is really lacking in Europe.'[2]

Nethold

Nethold was set up in May 1995 as a 50/50 holding company between Johann Rupert and South Africa's M-Net. In September 1996 the company merged with Canal+, thereby making Canal+ the undisputed champion of pay-TV in Europe.

Nethold owns the Filmnet pay-TV channels with 2.7 million subscribers in Scandinavia, Benelux and Africa.

CLT – Compagnie Luxembourgeoise de la Télédiffusion
See Bertelsmann.

CGE – Compagnie Générale des Eaux (audiovisual division)

The French 'water company' earns $32 billion a year, $1.1 billion of which is earned from audiovisual. The company is a major investor in French and UK cable where they have made major losses (over $120 million in 1994). Media investments are made through the subsidiary Générale d'Images (GI) which is 90% owned by CGE. CGE also owns 2.6% of Havas.

CGE's main media interests include:

- Pay television   Canal+ (20.3%, part of the Havas consortium)

- Cable television   Canal Jimmy, Planète, Ciné Cinémas,
  Canal J, MCM Euromusique, TV Sport

- Film   UGC/Lumière (33.6%)
  Paradis/Bac (25%)
  Ellipse (15%)
  Berlin-Babelsberg studio (75%)
  Boulogne Studios
  Christian Fechner film library ($80 million)

UGC

UGC has a colourful history, originally having been established during the Nazi occupation of France via the acquisition of the Siritzky chain and other Jewish cinemas. After the Liberation, the theatre chain was taken over by the state and renamed UGC. It was then privatized in 1972 and sold to a group of independent exhibitors led by Guy Verecchia.

UGC succeeded in building up one of the strongest libraries in Europe (including the CGE titles) by merging with Cyril de Rouvre's Robur in 1992 (660 titles estimated to be worth $160 million), buying United Communication for $75 million in 1993 (extensive French rights to US films) and acquiring Lumière for $140 million in 1996. The full library now represents 5000 film titles and 2000 hours of TV programming, evenly divided between English language and French language titles.

In June 1996 UGC signed a $541 million share swap deal with Canal+, whereby the pay-TV channel gained control of the library, in return for giving UGC DA shareholders 10% of the company. This deal is important in that it cements the two companies within the Havas/CGE group and also will be a key element in the digital alliance of Canal+ and Bertelsmann. Guy Verecchia said after the deal, 'With this deal we are not talking about an acquisition of the library but a coming together of the two companies.'

The weak link in the UGC strategy has been production. They have equity stakes in several French producers – including Gérard Mital and Christian Bourgeois and co-ventures with Ariel Zeitoun. Since 1980 there has also been an agreement with Hachette Première (René Cleitman) in which Hachette puts up a third of the production funding of UGC's films.

A shortage of popular French and American films has meant that UGC's theatrical earnings in France have fallen well behind AMLF and Gaumont. To change this, UGC signed a co-distribution agreement with Fox in 1995.

Lumière

After acquisition in 1996, UGC confirmed that they would back Lumière's production strategy for another five years. The production outfit, Lumière International, will be 50% owned by UGC and the rest by Jean and Lila Cazès.

Cazès (b. 1955) went to UCLA film school and was formerly head of international co-production at French state broadcaster Antenne 2, and then adviser to Minister of Culture, Jack Lang. In 1984, Cazès used his excellent connections to attract state institutions Caisse des Dépots and France Telecom as well as Time Warner to set up a production outfit, Initiale Groupe, run with his wife, Lila. In 1987, Cazès used the same shareholders to set up a rights library entitled IDA, to buy cartoon producer France Animation and establish a stake in French distributor AFMD.

Jean Cazès explains that his original strategy was based above all on building up a catalogue and working in both film and TV. 'From the beginning' he says, 'I realized production needed to be a slim operation with good creative contacts, whereas a catalogue was based on volume and business contacts. I was stronger in the latter and so concentrated my energies on building a catalogue.'

Cazès started buying up the libraries of smaller French producers and in 1991 bought the former Weintraub/Thorn EMI catalogue. In May 1993 Initial and IDA merged to form Lumière, with ambitions to step up English and French-language production in order to fuel higher library sales.

In 1990 Cazès also bought a stake in Spanish rights library Esicma which is linked to producer Elias Querejeta.

Lumière has US development deals with Barry Spikings and Eric Pleskow and also with IRS Media. The company has so far concentrated on indie product, and US films to date include *Fresh*, *Somebody to Love* and *Leaving Las Vegas*. French films include *La Vengeance du Blonde* and *The City of Lost Children* (helmed by Jeunet and Caro).

Lumière has suffered a high level of management turnover. In 1993 chief executive Alisdair Waddell left the company and the following year the state owned Caisse des Depots announced its desire to sell its majority stake. In 1995 there was major exodus of staff, with head of sales, Ralph Kamp, head of UK production, James Graham, and finance director, David Adair, all leaving. Following the UGC acquisition, there will be further rationalization.

Paradis/Bac

Set up in 1986 by Eric Heumann and Jean Labadie, the company has a profile similar to the former Palace Pictures in the UK, beginning in distribution and then expanding into production.

The association with CGE via Générale d'Images has allowed more ambitious projects such as the $24 million *Indochine*, which was backed 50/50 by Paradis and CGE, with additional support from the Club des Investisseurs.

The Babelsberg Studios

In 1992 CGE paid $86 million for the former Defa studios at Berlin-Brandenberg with Bertelsmann as a non-equity partner. The two companies originally agreed to invest $43 million in film and TV production over four years.

Skeptics believed that the deal had as much to do with real estate as any commitment to film production, and in 1993 operating losses were covered by the sale of land.

In 1993 the studios signed a production deal with Island World (John Heyman and Chris Blackwell), aiming to produce five films a year with budgets of $15–30 million. The project fell apart when Heyman and Blackwell dissolved their company the following year.

Babelsberg has a cash fund enabling it to invest cash and facilities in return for equity. Production has so far been limited, the most recent big shoots being Schloendorff's *The Ogre* and Regis Warnier's *Une Femme Française.*

Hachette Première

The Hachette group publishes national newspapers and magazines including 29 editions of *Elle* magazine around the world and owns a major stake in radio channel Europa 1.

Hachette became the lead shareholder (25%) in La 5 in 1990, which led to losses of over $640 million two years later when the channel went bankrupt. Hachette's bankers (which include Credit Lyonnais) subsequently encouraged a merger with the defence, automobiles and telecommunications giant, Matra.

Hachette Première – the company's film division – has been operating since 1980, and is run by René Cleitman. There is a co-production agreement with UGC whereby Hachette puts up one third of the budget. Hachette also owns 26% of the holding company Audiopar, which in turn owns 63% of the UGC rights library.

BERTELSMANN

Bertelsmann is the largest media group in Europe and also one of the most international. The company was founded by Carl Bertelsmann in the 1830s and passed to his maternal great-great-grandson, Reinhard Mohn, in 1947. Ownership remains in private hands, split 68.8% to the Bertelsmann foundation and 20.5% to the Mohn family.

The company is one of the Big Six music majors, a major player in German newspapers and international magazines (*Vogue, Marie Claire, Prima*) and also owns Bantam Doubleday Dell books.

In 1996 Bertelsmann announced that its film and television interests would merge with CLT, establishing a single media group. Bertelsmann also invested an extra $1.1 billion in the new company to compensate for the difference in values between CLT and Ufa.

The split of business by area and region in 1993 was as follows:

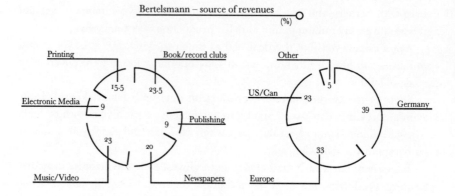

The company's film and television interests before the CLT merger were under a separate Ufa banner and include:

- Pay-TV   Premiere (37.5%)

- Free television   RTL Plus (38.9%)
                RTL 2 (7.8%)
                Vox (24.9%)
                CLT (5%)

- Film exhibition   Ufa

- Film production   Ufa

Bertelsmann is linked to the centre-left political interests of the SPD, whereas Kirch is tied to the centre-right CSU. In 1994 the two companies tried to set up a digital alliance along with state-owned German Telecom but the venture was disallowed by the EU Commission. Kirch instead decided to set up a solo service and Bertelsmann established an alliance with Canal+, Havas and News Corp. The EU Commission were also unhappy with Murdoch's presence, so he shifted his alliance to the Kirch group. In the summer of 1996 the two German media giants announced a renewed peace pact which included Kirch and News Corp on one side and Bertelsmann and Canal+ on the other. The EU has still to rule on the pact.

Bertelsmann has been making very tentative moves towards the film business. The Ufa production division is involved in two or three co-productions a year, and very active in the production of TV films, mini-series and soaps. In

1996 Ufa announced a joint venture with Paramount and Procter and Gamble to spend up to $90 million to produce and distribute 36 English-language TV movies.

In 1994 Bertelsmann acquired New York headquarters and appointed former 20th Century Fox CEO Strauss Zelnick as head of BMG Entertainment with responsibilities for music, film and new technology. In 1995 the company announced it was interested in buying video rights to feature films.

Bertelsmann is still waiting in the wings in terms of its film strategy, but its joint venture with CLT, its huge international business and a worldwide video network makes it one of the most likely players to succeed.

CLT – Compagnie Luxembourgeoise de la Télédiffusion

CLT was set up as a radio company in Luxembourg in 1931 and merged with Bertelsmann's Ufa division in 1996. The company is owned by a complex group of shareholders including Albert Frère's Groupe Bruxelles Lambert (20%), Havas (16%), Paribas (20%), Bertelsmann (5%) and CGE (1%). Havas controls the lion's share of the company's income because of its monopoly over ad sales.

CLT has key ownership stakes in 10 TV channels across Europe as well as interests in radio, production, press and publishing; 70% of revenue is earned in television, the vast majority in Germany.

The company has played a pivotal role in the development of commercial television in the heart of Europe, which has exposed it to power players between its French, German and Benelux shareholders. CLT began its international expansion in 1973, first in Benelux and then in France. In the 1990s the main success story has been RTL and RTL 2 in Germany, which was the motive behind the Bertelsmann merger.

KIRCH/BERLUSCONI

The Kirch and Berlusconi empires have both been in the spotlight in recent years because of their political connections. Both are privately owned but Berlusconi's media interests are slowly being privatized (one of the main buyers being Kirch). Berlusconi was for many years a supporter of the Italian Socialists, but after the revelation of corruption associated with his old friend Bettino Craxi shifted to the right. Kirch is much more low profile, but has close ties to Chancellor Kohl.

Fininvest

Silvio Berlusconi is a very controversial figure. Some see him as the force of the future – Milanese, efficient and disciplined – while others believe he is tainted by political connections and kickbacks.

One of the blackest marks in his past is proof that he held membership of a secret masonic network, Propaganda Due (P2) that had tried to undermine

Italy's democratic system, and had been involved in terrorist activities. But Berlusconi denies that he was ever an active member of the lodge, and suggests that his membership card was the result of Communist attempts to incriminate him.

'Il Cavaliere' began working as a cruise ship entertainer and in the early 1970s shifted into the construction business. He was able to build Milano 2 because the Milan city government (with the aid of Bettino Craxi) waived zoning regulations.

From 1974, Berlusconi also began developing three commercial television stations which were technically illegal, but gave Berlusconi a virtual monopoly of the private television market and earned him huge revenues through his advertising division Publi-Italia.

With the implicit support of the government, massive debt finance from the banks, and an excellent management team, Berlusconi built up a family-owned business empire, whose revenues grew from $2 billion in 1986 to over $10 billion by the early 1990s. In 1991 turnover broke down as follows:

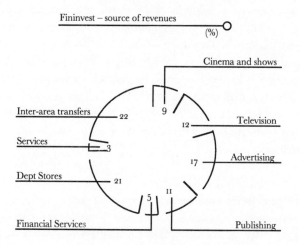

The Fininvest holding company is now a giant force in Italian life, including cinema chains, advertising, book publishing, insurance and the football team A. C. Milan. In 1995 Berlusconi's film and television interests were formed into a separate company, Mediaset, over 30% of which has already been sold to outside groups.

In 1996 the new Olive Tree government announced its intention to force Berlusconi to shed one of his three television channels and also placed him on trial for corruption.

Mediaset's film and television interests in Italy include:

•	Advertising	Publi-Italia
•	Pay-TV	Tele+ (10%)
•	Free television	Rete 4, Canale 5, Italia Uno
•	Television production	Rete Italia, SBC and Video Time
•	Film and TV library	63,000 programming hours ($1 billion)
•	Film exhibition	Cinema 5 (51%), Mondialcine (49%)
•	Film distribution	Medusa

In the 1980s Berlusconi tried to build a web of Fifth Channels across Europe, but was frustrated by local regulation, particularly in France where La 5 went bankrupt. Present interests include 25% of Tele-5 in Spain and 33.5% of DSF (formerly Tele-5) in Germany, but in both cases there are rumours that Fininvest wishes to sell its stake.

Berlusconi's strongest foreign ally is Germany's Leo Kirch. Together they have co-produced many television programmes including *Scarlett*, and traded shares in broadcast companies. Kirch is an equity partner in DSF and owns 45% of Italian pay-TV channel Tele+.

Cinema activities represents 1% of Fininvest's total turnover, but the group nonetheless has a dominant hold over film exhibition and distribution. This film empire has been built up in the early 1990s, after the acquisition of Italy's largest theatre chain from Pathé/MGM in 1990.

This position was even stronger between 1989 and 1993 when Berlusconi was allied with veteran Italian film producer Mario Cecchi Gori and his son Vittorio, under the banner Penta. Together the partnership owned 75% of the screens in Rome.

Penta declared that their ambition was to become the first European Major and set up a series of output deals across Europe. They plunged into expensive Hollywood production, with a three-picture slate worth over $60 million of *Folks*, *Man Trouble* and *House of Cards*. The films were all greenlighted without a US distributor and all flopped. Several of the domestic quickie comedies also flopped and in 1993 the partners declared that they would not be renewing their pact.

Fininvest now concentrates on exhibition, distribution and buying US rights through Medusa, with distribution pacts signed with Morgan Creek, Castle Rock and Turner.

Television is much more central to the Fininvest empire and is the main focus of the Berlusconi saga. For two decades Berlusconi's three channels were technically illegal, but were finally given official status in 1992 by the so-called 'Mammi law'.

The new law attracted many critics. Mass media expert Carlo Sartori commented at the time, 'If new resources and players are forever hindered from finding space, Berlusconi is going to find himself emperor of a minor-league colony, dominator of a market that is still rich but on the road to being obsolete in terms of technology, production and programming.'[3]

Soon after, the Socialist leader Bettino Craxi was investigated for kickbacks and corruption and fled justice to Tunisia. Berlusconi immediately began to distance himself from his former ally and reiterated, 'We've already got our TV licences.'

But the growing Tangentopolis scandal meant that Berlusconi desperately needed a new political ally, particularly as the Clean Hands investigators in Italy who had discovered massive kickbacks in the state broadcaster RAI, now began to switch their attention to Fininvest.

The former right-hand man to Oscar Mammi, David Giacolone, who had helped draw up the commercial licences for Berlusconi, was jailed on three counts of corruption. He had been hired as a $300,000-a-year consultant by Fininvest and was accused of receiving several million dollars of kickbacks in order to grant Berlusconi the licences.

Berlusconi decided to move into the public arena, to defend himself against what he considered to be unjust charges. He set up a new party, Forza Italia, using the slogan chanted on the terraces of the national football team, and made allies with the neo-Fascist National Alliance and the right-wing Lombard League led by Umberto Bossi whose slogan was 'ours is the party with a hard on'.

Opinion polls showed that Italians were fed up with the old political parties and 40% would vote for the Left. They also showed that the charismatic newcomer Berlusconi was growing in popularity. Berlusconi's candidacy divided the nation between those who saw him as a white knight entrepreneur and others who feared for an electronic dictatorship.

In order to pursue his political campaign Berlusconi needed to distance himself from his business empire. In 1993 he announced that he would be floating 40–50% of his $650 million a year publishing division on the stock exchange. But at the same time, Berlusconi began to step up the use of his media megaphone.

In January 1994 one of Italy's most respected journalists, Indro Montanelli, resigned after twenty years as editor-in-chief of the *Il Giornale* newspaper, owned by Berlusconi's brother Paolo. He claimed that he was being pressured to support the political ambitions of Silvio, who had paid a visit to the newsroom and pleaded to journalists to 'join in the fight against the left coming to power'.

Berlusconi also began to use his television channels in direct support of his campaign, which created editorial dissent within Fininvest. Free commercials gave Berlusconi considerable power over his rivals who had to pay for their ads. Peter Bart of *Variety* called the campaign Fellini-esque:

> Where else but in Italy would an entrepreneur run on a ticket of fiscal probity, when his own company, Fininvest is staggering under a $2.2 billion debt load? In what other nation would a candidate give speeches against corruption when his own brother and top business associates bounce in and out of jail under charges of fiscal malfeasance. If Ronald Reagan was the Teflon candidate, Silvio Berlusconi must have commissioned Armani to design a new protective coating that puts Teflon to shame. How else could he promise at one moment to put Italy on a new path . . . and at the same time admit to having once belonged to one of those murky Masonic lodges that keep popping up amid scandal and conspiracy.4

Berlusconi won enough votes in the March election to form a coalition government in May 1994. He claimed he would distance himself from his business empire, and at the same time, the heads of Publi-Italia, Tele+ and a third key management figure were arrested for massive falsification of invoices and accounts to create an illicit cash pool. Berlusconi insisted that these were 'fireworks' intended to discredit him. In particular, he blamed foreign journalists who he claimed were Communist conspirators.

Berlusconi immediately began to attack the debt-ridden and bloated RAI. In July he forced the management board to resign and replaced it by a friendlier group of inexperienced directors. 'RAI is becoming a unit of Fininvest' said Giuseppe Giulietti, chief of the RAI journalists union. 'We will have a single national broadcaster, like during the [1930s] Fascist regime.' A similar campaign was mounted to replace unfriendly editors at the national newspapers.

Those under attack came back fighting. 'We are now run by a consumer-oriented television and advertising-driven corporation that attacks freedom and culture with a strength never before seen', wrote Eugenio Scalfari, editor of *La Repubblica*. Indro Montanelli, who had been forced to resign from *Il Giornale* went even further, 'We are very close to a dictatorial regime, perhaps we have already arrived.' A national opinion poll declared that 40% of Italians feared for democracy.

Berlusconi also began to attack the Clean Hands campaign, accusing it of being politically motivated, with links to the Communists. He freed over two thousand corruption-accused politicians and businessmen and introduced an emergency measure forbidding judges to jail bribery and corruption suspects. As a consequence leading Clean Hands investigator Antonio di Pietro announced he would resign.

The next target was programming. Berlusconi took particular offence to RAI's *Octopus* series, Italy's most popular TV series ever, which suggests links between the criminal organization in the South, the political nucleus in Rome and banking circles in Milan. 'Let's hope that no more of these things are made' he said. 'This is a disaster that we are all responsible for all over the world. These works, from *The Octopus* on down have given an extremely negative image of our country . . . The reality of the Mafia in Italy is nothing compared to the industrious reality of the good people. It must be one ten-thousandth or a millionth of 56 million Italians, and do we want a hundred or so people giving a negative image to the whole world?'

Rather than decreasing his media business interests, Berlusconi used monies from the stock exchange flotation of a minority stake in his publishing division to acquire the prestigious leftist publishing house Giulio Einaudi in November 1994, after which several writers left.

Two weeks later Berlusconi was told that he was being investigated for corruption and he reiterated his promise to float some of Fininvest. In December he suffered the further blow that the Constitutional Court threw out the 1993 Mammi law, saying that the law allowed 'the creation of dominant positions which not only hinder competition but can also lead to a situation of oligopoly that threatens pluralism and freedom of expression and thought'. Fininvest declared that this went 'against the basic rules of the free market' and added that 'our efficient organization is a reason for pride for Italy as well as a creator of wealth for all the nation'.

Berlusconi stepped down as prime minister in 1995 and announced he would stand for re-election. He also announced the sale of his electronic media interests which were grouped under a Mediaset holding company.

On 11 June there was a national referendum as to whether Berlusconi should have to sell off two of his channels. His former ally Vittorio Cecchi Gori announced that he would cease selling films to Fininvest. 'The idea of supplying more fuel to the bombardier that's bombarding Italy doesn't sit well with me', he said. 'I'm tired of giving my films to groups that are running Italy, that exploit the audience for cinema or sport to pursue their own particular personal goals, which are against the general interests of the country.'[5]

Fininvest pumped out commercials to vote 'No' to the changes, accompanied by plugs by television celebrities. The changes were defeated by 57% to 43%. Immediately after, 20% of Mediaset was sold for an estimated $1.1 billion to old allies Leo Kirch (10%), Johann Rupert of South Africa (Richemont) (5.7%) and Saudi Prince al-Waleed ben Talal (4.1%). Kirch said that it bought its stake 'to compete against US media giants and to protect Europe's culture and its film and TV industry'. A further 5.5% stake was sold in December 1995 for $230 million to a group of Italian banks. In March 1996, 2.3% was sold for $100 million to two US funds controlled by Capital Research & Management (which owns 11%

of Time Warner) and 2.4% was sold to British Telecom and BNL in May 1996. A further 20% is scheduled to be floated publicly in late 1996.

Berlusconi now officially maintains an arms-length relationship from Fininvest and his future remains uncertain after the defeat in the 1996 elections. He now stands trial on several charges of corruption including allegations that he channelled $6.5 million in illegal funds to Bettino Craxi and that he bribed auditors in order to falsify his tax statements.

The Kirch Group

In recent years, Leo Kirch has been the subject of almost as much political attention as his long-time ally Silvio Berlusconi, but he is notoriously press shy and has only ever granted two press interviews in his life.

Kirch became a billionaire by selling US films to German state television, establishing a virtual monopoly on the buying of German TV rights. When Germany embraced private TV in the 1980s, Kirch was one of the main beneficiaries. German TV is now split between Kirch and Bertelsmann/CLT.

Kirch's film and television interests include:

•	Pay-TV	Premiere (25%)
		Tele+ (Italy) (45%)
•	Free television	SAT-1 (43%)
		DSF (24.5%)
•	TV prod./distrib.	Beta, Taurus, Unitel
•	Film and TV library	15,000 feature films
		50,000 hours of programmes
		(worth $2 billion)
•	Film distrib./exhibition	Neue Constantin (46.5%)
•	Film exhibition	Studio Film Theatre

Kirch also owns over 35% of print media giant Axel Springer and 49% of Swiss-based Ringier Holding. Axel Springer controls 22.8% of the German daily newspaper market, is a major magazine publisher and owns 25% of DSF and 20% of SAT-1.

Kirch's son, Thomas, owns 24.5% of Pro 7 which in turn owns 45% of KabelKanal. Until 1993 the latter two channels lay under a common management unit with DSF (formerly Tele-5).

Kirch also owns a myriad of stakes in TV production companies, post-production facilities, merchandising, and music publishing. The main film activity is through Bernd Eichinger's Neue Constantin of which Kirch holds 46.5% (see below).

The focus of Kirch's business is Germany, where a key associate has been Swiss billionaire Otto Beisheim, who helped Kirch out of a liquidity crisis in the mid-1980s by buying 2500 films for $250 million. Since then Beisheim and Kirch have been partners and reinforced Kirch's ties to Germany's other key media players, including Bodo Scriba, Rolf Dehyle and Willi Baer (see below).

Some of the fiercest critics of Kirch have been the German Socialists whose representative, Peter Glotz, demands greater transparency in media ownership saying 'It's not important to know who owns a marmalade factory, but media is different.' RTL's chief executive, Helmut Thoma, is also a strong opponent of Kirch and in 1992 was prevented by a German high-court from comparing Kirch to Alfred Hugenberg, the Nazi press baron.

Other vocal critics of Kirch have been the Americans, who are irritated by Kirch's buying monopoly and problems they face in cornering some of the lucrative German audiovisual market. *Variety* asserted in 1995 that 'A reticent old German, half-blind and in ill health, is holding the world's biggest media powers hostage in Germany . . . The Kirch group remains as German – perhaps as provincial – as *lederhosen*. It is certainly as thick skinned.'[6]

For years there was an unwritten rule that Germany was Kirch's market, but in the new digital era, the Americans have been trying to use competition between Kirch and Bertelsmann/CLT in order to leverage more lucrative deals. Disney and Warners both signed deals with CLT in 1994 and 1995 respectively, and Warners also signed a ten-year strategic pay-TV alliance with Kirch. MCA followed suit, by signing a $1.5 million free TV deal with CLT and a $1 million pay-TV deal with Kirch.

In 1996 Kirch responded by signing a five-year $1.1 billion output deal with Sony for all film and TV product, a ten-year $1.8 billion strategic alliance with Viacom/Paramount and a $650 million digital alliance with News Corp./Fox. Under the latter deal News Corporation agrees to fund up to half the start-up costs of Kirch's digital TV service DF1 in return for up to 49% equity. In October 1996, Kirch bought a 7.5% stake in Arnon Milchan's New Regency Productions for an estimated $60 million.

Neue Constantin

Neue Constantin is a vertically integrated company with a theatre chain, film and video distribution and music publishing. Eichinger produces a major English-language film about every eighteen months and also makes German films up to a $5 million budget, most notably the $2.4 million *Der Bewegte Mann*, based on a famous comic-strip, which grossed over $48 million in Germany.

Eichinger is a graduate of the Munich Film School and began his career as a writer and producer on various films before buying the Constantin Group in 1979. He has been one of the few 'commercial' producers in Germany, with hits such as *Christiane F, The Never Ending Story, Name of the Rose, Last Exit to Brooklyn* and *Werner Beinhart.*

Scriba/Dehyle/Baer

Bodo Scriba was formerly second in command at the Kirch group. In the late 1980s he put together a 2000-title film library and set up a joint venture with construction magnate Rolf Dehyle and his partner Willi Baer. Together they were part of the $600 million deal involving Arnon Milchan's Regency, Canal+ and Warners. Scriba and Dehyle have subsequently separated their business interests but remain broadly within the Kirch/Beisheim universe.

Scriba, Dehyle and Baer established their film library with equity support from Axel Springer, who later sold their stake. In 1991 they sold a package of 1000 films to the Kirch group for an estimated $212 million. In the same year, Beisheim paid an estimated $250 million for rights to a thousand films and in 1995 he bought a further 100 films from Baer, establishing a privileged partnership deal extending to 1997.

Scriba, Dehyle and Baer have between them key holdings in Tobis, Connexion, Flebbe Theatres, Capitol films, Alcor Films, Senator, and Capella. In 1996 Rolf Dehyle teamed up with Morgan Creek in an unsuccessful bid for MGM.

Johann Rupert (Richemont)

Richemont is the Swiss holding company of South African entrepreneur Johann Rupert with annual revenues in 1995 of $6 billion and profits of $1.1 billion. His brands include Dunhill, Cartier, Karl Lagerfeld, Baume and Mercier, Piaget and Montblanc. Johann Rupert also owns Remgro, which is known as the 'Vatican of South African business'.

Johann Rupert owns 45% of Italian pay-TV channel Tele+ alongside Kirch, and also owns 5.5% of Berlusconi's Mediaset. In May 1995 he launched Nethold, a 50/50 joint venture with South Africa's M-Net. Nethold was taken over by Canal+ in September, 1996.

THE SEYDOUX BROTHERS

Jerome, Nicolas and Michel are members of the Schlumberger family, one of the oldest and richest families in France whose ancestors include François Guizot, prime minister under Louis Philippe. Their father, René Seydoux Fornier de Clauzonne was an old friend of François Mitterand and their eldest sister, Véronique married one of Charles de Gaulle's official advisers. Overall, the Schlumberger family are renowned as generous supporters of the non-

Communist Left which led Mitterand's cabinet secretary, Jean-Claude Colliara to once comment, 'There are only two groups we can completely count on: Maxwell and Seydoux.'

The Schlumberger group was run until recently by the late Jean Riboud, whose family friends included Henri Langlois, Roberto Rossellini and François Mitterand.

The youngest brother, 'babyboomer' Michel (b. 1947), was the first to be seized by a passion for the cinema. He set up his own production company, Camera One, in 1971 while Jerome and Nicolas were immersed in investment banking. He later commented in frustration, 'I launch myself in the world of cinema and Nicolas buys Gaumont. I make an investment in Air Martinique and Jerome takes control of UTA'.7

In 1970, the Schlumberger group acquired the Compteurs de Montrouge which was the principal shareholder of Gaumont. French producer Jean-Pierre Rassam (brother-in-law of Claude Berri) was a close friend of Nicolas Seydoux (b. 1939) and persuaded him to use the Schlumberger fortunes to take control of Gaumont in 1975.

In the same year, elder brother Jerome (b. 1934) was made president of the Schlumberger group, but was fired by Jean Riboud five months later. He then took over the reins of the shipping company, Chargeurs, which he subsequently moved out of shipping, in and out of the airline business, into textiles and in the mid-1980s into the media business, finally acquiring Pathé in 1990.

Despite the fact that one of Jack Lang's first measures in 1982 had been to dissolve a Gaumont-Pathé holding company, the Socialist government gave its blessing to Jerome's acquisition of Pathé (with behind-the-scenes support from André Rousselet). Jack Lang declared that it was 'happy news for our national cinema' which would 'return vitality to Pathé and tenacity to European cinema'.

Jerome defended the takeover by saying, 'French cinema is described as three monsters – UGC, Gaumont and Pathé when we are only Lilliputians and Tom Thumbs next to the large American companies.' Gaumont and Pathé subsequently arranged a screen swap in 1992, giving Pathé control of key regional towns and Gaumont dominance in Paris. The Schlumberger group also owns 5% of CGE, thus giving the brothers a stake in UGC and Canal+.

Chargeurs/Pathé International

The eldest son, Jerome, is the thirteenth wealthiest man in France and a lifelong Socialist. He began his interest in film and TV in 1985 when he became CEO of the new French television channel La 5, partnered with Silvio Berlusconi, Christophe Riboud (son of Jean Riboud) and his brother Michel. In the same year Seydoux, Berlusconi, Robert Maxwell and Leo Kirch created the European Consortium for Commercial Television.

Between 1986 and 1988 Jerome Seydoux bought 50% of AMLF and Renn Productions (boosted to 100% in 1996) and in 1990 he sold his interests in La 5 and acquired Pathé France from Giancarlo Parretti for $220 million.

In 1996 Chargeurs' media interests became a separate entity called Pathé International. Jerome Seydoux is now CEO of Pathé while his right-hand man Eduardo Malone takes responsibility for the textile group now known as Chargeurs International. (Seydoux personally owns 29% of both.)

Pathé International ranks just behind PolyGram in developing a significant film strategy in Europe. Its media interests include:

- TV channels   BSkyB (17%)
      Canal+ (5%)

- Film exhibition   Pathé France (98%)
      MGM Netherlands
      Dutch joint venture with Morgan Creek/Warners

- Film distribution   US – Savoy (13%)
      France – AMLF (100%)
      UK – Guild (95%)
      Germany – Tobis (Bodo Scriba) (20%)

- Film production   Renn (Claude Berri) – 100%
      Allied (Jake Eberts) – 75%
      Pricel (Paul Rassam) – 100%
      Films 7 (Claude Zidi) – 100%

Jerome's strategy is long-term. In 1994 there were losses in film and TV, including Guild losing $12.5 million, French film production and distribution losing $2 million and a further $3 million lost in cable. This was balanced by a $14.5 million contribution to net profits from the stake in BSkyB. In 1995 the company lost $37 million on film production alone.

The heart of the company's strategy revolves around brothers-in-law Claude Berri and Paul Rassam, plus old friend Jake Eberts. UK projects are developed through Timothy Burrill.

Berri divides his activities between English-language films including *Tess, Valmont, The Bear* and *The Lover* and high profile French projects, such as *Jean de Florette* which was co-produced with Nicolas Seydoux's Gaumont. In 1993 he directed and produced the massive $29 million film *Germinal* which made a small profit, and the following year he produced the $21 million *La Reine Margot* which lost money.

Rassam is an astute buyer of foreign films and was one of the first to invest in *Dances with Wolves,* which secured the link with Jake Eberts in 1991. The Hollywood projects backed by the group in recent years have had mixed results, the worst being *Super Mario Brothers* which is believed to have lost $19 million.

Gaumont

Gaumont was founded in 1895 and is France's most prestigious Major. The company has had four main phases.

1895–1918. Léon Gaumont built up a vertically integrated Major, with in-house producers including Alice Guy and Louis Feuillade.

1918–38. The Great War devastated French cinema and all the main producers slashed production. Gaumont was progressively taken over by state banks. Léon Gaumont resigned in 1932 and after investing in sound equipment the company was declared bankrupt in 1935.

1938–70. State ad agency Havas bought majority control. New secretary-general was Alain Poiré, grandson of Havas president, Léon Renier. In 1941 after the Nazi occupation, Jean Le Duc bought a significant stake through Les Compteurs du Montrouge and became Gaumont's president. Le Duc and Poiré maintained a low profile during the Occupation and then become the leading popular film producers in the immediate post-war era.

1970 onwards. The Schlumberger family bought control of Les Compteurs in 1970 and two years later a joint holding company was established with Pathé. In 1974 Le Duc died and Jerome Seydoux ceded control of Les Compteurs to his brother Nicolas. Nicolas took control of Gaumont, with the aid of two old friends from the elite school Sciences Po – Jean-Pierre Rassam and Savoy aristocrat, Daniel Toscan du Plantier.

Toscan, who was a former senior advertising director, was then appointed managing director and declared that 'the new tendency of French cinema' should be quality production and grandiose opera movies. The company established major interests in Italy, run by Roberto Rossellini's son Renzo, and minor interests in the US and Brazil. By 1983, losses had reached $98 million and Nicolas Seydoux had to start using his private wealth to bail out the company. Gaumont began a total withdrawal from foreign expansion, and in 1985 Nicolas had to take the unhappy step of firing Toscan. This management failure cast a shadow over French cinema.

Gaumont now produces seven or eight films a year, benefiting from Sofica tax-shelters and automatic subsidies. The company fully funds its pictures, sometimes pre-selling French TV rights. The company is very loyal to its talent via two production arms, one headed by Alain Poiré for classic comedy film-makers such as Yves Robert, Francis Veber, Christian Fechner, Alain Terzian and his son Jean-Marie Poiré, the other headed by Patrice Ledoux which concentrates on younger talent such as Jean-Jacques Beineix and Luc Besson.

The company is increasingly interested in English-language production and also has a high-profile development deal with Alain Goldman.

In 1993 Gaumont established a theatrical joint venture with Disney – the first of its kind since MGM-Gaumont between 1920–35. For video, Gaumont has a joint venture with Columbia-TriStar.

Michel Seydoux – Camera One / Pyramide

Michel Seydoux has been producing since 1971 and also owns 82% of distributor Pyramide (2% French market share). Most of his films have had mixed results, but he hit the big time in 1990 with the $20 million *Cyrano de Bergerac* co-produced with René Cleitman. In the early 1990s he suffered a major flop with *Toxic Affair* starring Isabelle Adjani.

POLYGRAM

PolyGram is 75% owned by Dutch consumer electronics giant Philips, and has had the most ambitious film strategy of any European media group in recent years. The company has enjoyed strong growth since the mid-1980s from its music business and in 1988 declared its intention to tap into the growing film market.

The main advantage that PolyGram has over other start-up film ventures is its worldwide music video distribution network. This huge 'hidden asset' has been adapted to film at little extra cost.

PolyGram has a very down-to-earth business attitude, summarized by PFE president Michael Kuhn: 'If you mix up culture and business, you get yourself in a big mess. Nobody talks about French penicillin. You have to say there's a huge worldwide industry – in the movie business, whether you like it or not, the business is the Hollywood movie industry, a $60 billion worldwide industry. The big question for France – for Europe – is how can we get our share?'[8]

PolyGram decided from the beginning that the key target was to penetrate the US market, a maxim learned from 25 years' experience of selling music into the US. The main focus of the company has been to produce American and British films intended to open first in the US market and then be sold abroad. But PolyGram also makes four or five French films a year and two or three Dutch films, using the traditional financing mix of private and public money. These films provide useful leverage in the local markets and in the long run could be big money spinners.

PolyGram has had a major impact on the British film industry with hits such as *Four Weddings*, *Shallow Grave* and *Trainspotting* and is now spreading this 'commercial' attitude to the rest of Europe. Recent local language hits include Dutch films *Little Sister* and *Little Film* which both grossed over $8 million, and Jaco van Dormael's *The Eighth Day* which grossed over $22 million in France and Belgium.

PolyGram already has direct distribution in the US, UK, France, Netherlands, Spain and Australia and will launch a German distributor in 1997. Foreign sales and acquisitions are made through PolyGram Films International.

The future of PolyGram's 'natural move' is still uncertain. The company's film division has lost $20–40 million in every year since starting but this is compensated by the growing value of the film library and is part of the inevitable learning curve.

The main question mark over PolyGram's strategy is whether they can provide a consistent flow of successful big budget films. As Michael Kuhn says, 'Most of all I want a string of hit movies', adding: 'It's a judgement call. We've got the necessary quantity of films – we're now making nearly 20 a year – but we must be sure that the quality is right. If it isn't, I'll be out of Hollywood and back in London driving a number 19 bus.'9

1996 results (by October 1996) have been promising. In the US, *Mr. Holland's Opus* (Buena Vista) grossed $83 million, *Dead Man Walking* $40 million and *Fargo* $24 million. Danny Boyle's second feature *Trainspotting* has grossed over $55 million worldwide, and in Spain *Two Much* grossed over $5 million. But there were also disappointments, most notably the $18 million *Barb Wire* starring Pamela Anderson which grossed only $3.7 million in the US and was pulled from release after five weeks.

In 1996 Michael Kuhn announced that the company will set up a mainstream US distribution arm in the fourth quarter of 1997. This will add to the risk exposure but is also a critical step towards becoming a fully fledged Major. PolyGram lost out in the bidding for MGM/UA, and are believed to be interested in acquiring New Line if it is put up for sale by Time Warner.

EUROPEAN MAJORS

The Hollywood Majors have substantial interests in European film and television and want to use their programming strength to buy up delivery outlets.

One of the strongest developments has been in multiplexes, which began in Britain and is now spreading throughout Europe. The Majors recognized that Europe's cinemas had been left in a state of decay for decades and this was one of the main reasons for low attendances. In Britain alone the multiplex drive has doubled national audiences since 1985, giving the Majors an estimated 30% of UK box office.

On the continent there have been co-ventures such as UCI and Alfredo Matas in Spain, but such projects have not always been harmonious. A joint venture was established between Warners and the Kirch Group's Neue Constantin but later fell apart.

Warners and UIP are actively involved in distributing European films and the Majors also have substantial interests in television including the following:

Disney/ABC	TeleMunchen (50%), TM3, Super RTL, RTL 2, GMTV (25%), Hamster (33%)
News Corp/Fox	BSkyB (50%), Pearson (9.9%), Antena 3 (25%)
Sony	Co-venture with Canal+

News Corporation has by far the strongest presence in Europe. They own 40% of BSkyB with 5 million subscribers and now look set to own 25% of the German digital and pay-TV business and possibly the same in Italy.

THE ABSENCE OF EUROPEAN MAJORS

The competition between European cinema and Hollywood is often portrayed as David vs. Goliath, but in fact Europe's media groups are just as powerful and wealthy as their American counterparts. The problem has been their consistent inability to produce popular entertainment.

Just as Hollywood has seen a massive level of concentration and integration within the communications industry since the 1960s, the same phenomenon has occurred within Europe, but on a national level. In both cases this has been heavily influenced by public policy, which controls media regulation and the tax regime.

In America the government has allowed a high level of concentration, but under a system of oligopoly rather than monopoly. There are six or seven giant media companies, which are kept very much at arm's length, in order to ensure fierce competition between them.

The US Government also gave US media a huge boost in the 1970s and early 1980s through extensive tax breaks, which was in effect a government subsidy for the industry. These subsidies were provided with few strings attached. There was no state control of media content.

In Europe, governments also allowed a high level of media ownership in film and television from the 1960s onwards, but with the opposite effects. Groups such as Gaumont, UGC, Bertelsmann, Pathé and Rank were allowed to acquire a dominant position within film exhibition.

These groups were vertically integrated national majors, including exhibition, distribution, production, foreign sales and film libraries. They enjoyed a far greater level of media concentration than their Hollywood counterparts and were also given generous tax breaks, particularly the Bertelsmann group when it bought Ufa in 1962.

European governments also stepped up their level of subsidy support for film and television, but unlike the American model, they used this funding to gain a control over the cultural agenda.

State control was accentuated by massive rationalization programmes by the national majors. Instead of using their privileged position as a base from which to develop new and innovative film and television programming, Europe's media groups seem much more concerned with cut-backs – closing down screens and cutting back production investment.

There have been some expansion attempts in Europe. Gaumont tried to set up an Italian base in the 1970s and many players have invested heavily in Hollywood in the early 1990s. But the results have been disastrous.

State policy is now focusing on the need for an 'official' pan-European distribution network. This debate dates from the 1960s, when several high-level conferences concentrated on the need for pan-European distributors to fill the gap left by the Hollywood Majors.

At the time, analyst Jean-Claude Batz suggested that 'Distribution has been either forgotten or misunderstood by national authorities. Distribution is the "black hole" in the systems of state support for the cinema. But this omission is not as surprising as it first seems. It is due to the fact that distribution only has sense when structured on an international level, or at least across several territories, which means that governments realise that they would be unable to control such companies, because their activities go beyond the state's narrow frontiers.'[10] It is only today, as the European super-state emerges that it makes sense to make distribution an official priority.

In the late 1980s a group of European niche distributors tried to set up a pan-European consortium backed by the Dutch Bank Pierson Heldring. Euro-trustees was founded by Palace in the UK, Bac Films in Spain, Iberoamericana in Spain, Concorde in Germany and Erre (Angelo Rizzoli) in Italy. The aim was to decide jointly on projects and each put up a minimum guarantee which would represent an equity stake on the entire global revenues, rather than a stake in a specific territory. After considerable time spent trying to come to agreement on a project, the first film backed was *The Crying Game*. The venture then collapsed when Palace went bankrupt.

The overall management failure of Europe's media groups has been one of the main reasons for the decline of European cinema. But this failure must also be understood within the context of the close links between the political sphere and the media in Europe.

Although a powerful film industry is very desirable in the abstract, it is recognized as being very dangerous when concretized. Whenever Europe has shown signs of having a popular film industry, there have been howls of outrage from the political sphere.

The prime concern of the political sphere is to have control over all means of expression within society. The best means of achieving this is to grant media concentration to groups who are known to be 'trustworthy'. The groups are thereby able to earn a generous living, as long as they do not 'rock the boat'. As a consequence media groups have concentrated on the retail end of the business, only dabbling in production. Inevitably this requires output deals and alliances with Hollywood because they are the only providers of popular entertainment.

The dominance of Hollywood entertainment in Europe cannot be explained through unfair monopoly power, because all the strongholds of European media are owned by European media groups and are regulated by national governments. Europe's key media groups have actually been increasing ownership concentration in recent years and expanding this to a pan-European scale. There are some new players such as Canal+ and PolyGram which have already created a stir in the business, but up to now their main emphasis has been the American market.

The most dynamic players are united in the European Film Companies Alliance – PolyGram, Chargeurs, Bertelsmann, Ciby 2000, RCS, Sogepaq and Rank. Several of these companies aim to become European Majors.

At the end of 1995 the European Commission proposed a $265 million guarantee fund which would further the development of European Majors as proposed in the 1994 Green Paper. However, the political reaction, especially in Britain and Germany, was negative. This serves as a reminder that although some European media companies may continue to move towards becoming European Majors it will always be within a very tight political straitjacket.

TALENT RELATIONSHIPS

Europe's media groups are the only significant sources of production financing on the continent and therefore most of Europe's leading producers are linked to these networks. The latest example is Marin Karmitz's MK2 which has its own exhibition chain and foreign sales arms, but sold a 20% stake to Havas. Finally there are some producers such as David Puttnam and Dieter Geissler who have deals with the US Majors.

Producers linked to larger media groups have access to more substantial production funding and can invest in more ambitious projects. A classic example is Claude Berri who after the success of *Jean de Florette*, sold 50% of his company to Chargeurs and then used the influx of capital to finance even more ambitious pictures such as *The Lover, Germinal* and *La Reine Margot.*

A lot of attention has been paid in recent years to the lack of good producers in Europe, but in fact there is a far greater shortage of acting and directing talent. A few directors and actors are tied to groups, but most European talent that does emerge tends to migrate to Hollywood because of the lack of infrastructure and energy in Europe.

The main talent relationships in Europe include the following:

Havas/CGE	*Bertelsmann*	*Seydoux Brothers*
Alain Sarde	V. Schloendorff	Claude Berri
J-F. Le Petit	Strauss Zelnick	Jake Eberts
Jean Labadie	Jamie Ader Brown	Paul Rassam
Jean Cazès		Timothy Burrill
E. Querejeta	*Kirch/Berlusconi*	Jean-Louis Livi
Marin Karmitz	Bernd Eichinger	Roland Joffé
René Cleitman	Bodo Scriba	Alain Poiré
GuyVerecchia	Dehyle/Baer	Luc Besson
Yves Marmion	Martin Bregman	J-J. Beineix
Jeremy Thomas	Silvio Berlusconi	J-C. Fleury
Alain Rocca	Ettore Barnabei	Alain Goldman
E. Goldschmidt		Alain Terzian

PolyGram	*Bouygues*	*Independents*
Michael Kuhn	Almodovar	Anatole Dauman
Tim Bevan	D. Lynch	Paulo Branco
Eric Fellner	W. Wenders	Tino Navarro
Jodie Foster	Toscan du Plantier	Artur Brauner
Tim Robbins	E. Kusturica	François Duplat
Ted Field	G. de Verges	Silvio Clementelli
Steve Golin	Alain Goldman	Leo Pescarolo,
Philip Carcassone		A. de Laurentiis
		Pedro Pérez
		Pere Fages,
		G. Herrero
		Antonio Llorens

This list is very producer-heavy, suggesting that there are many more Chiefs than Indians. Other key talent relationships in Europe are with the Majors, including producers such as David Puttnam, Dieter Geissler, Sarah Radclyffe, Simon Relph, Stephen Evans, Nik Powell and Steve Woolley.

TALENT SHORTAGE

Europe's media groups suffer from a dramatic shortage of talent – composers, story editors, creative producers and commissioning editors. This is in marked contrast to the situation thirty years ago when Europe's creative community was thriving and throwing up new talent every year.

The main talent 'names' that still exist in Europe were discovered in the 1960s or early 1970s before the media groups established their hold over the industry. For example, amongst Europe's top 100 directors over 90 were born before 1945.

This is despite a massive commitment to 'first films' from the state funding mechanisms. A third of the films produced in Europe are from first-time directors – over 150 a year – and yet virtually none achieve any significant critical or commercial acclaim. In the last twenty-five years Europe has funded over 3500 first-time directors, yet only a handful have proven to have any long-term appeal. This is a staggering inability to spot genuine talent amongst Europe's commissioning editors.

The talent shortage is likely to increase in the near future. For example, in France, which is one of the few countries to have maintained a workable film infrastructure, there is a huge dependence on talent born before the end of the war. This includes Annaud (b. 1943), Berri (1934), Blier (1939) Chabrol (1930), Corneau (1943), Costa-Gavras (1933), Enrico (1931), Godard (1930), Lautner (1926), Lelouch (1937), Miller (1942), Mocky (1932), Molinaro (1928), Pialat (1925), Rappeneau (1932), Resnais (1922), Rivette (1928), Rohmer (1920), Sautet (1924), Tacchella (1925), Tavernier (1941), Techiné (1943) and Varda (1928). The average age of French directors has increased from twenty-eight in 1960 to fifty-five in 1993 and 85% of registered directors are now over fifty. The above list represents a wealth of film-making talent, but is not immortal, as confirmed by the death of Louis Malle (b. 1932) in 1995.

The inability in Europe to nurture new film-making talent means that as the established directors retire or die, there will be no one to replace them. This talent loss has already destroyed the Italian cinema and is likely to do the same to French cinema in the near future.

The talent shortage is even more striking amongst actors, where there are few actors with any name recognition. Again this represents an inability of the 'system' to discover fresh faces. The few names that have appeared in recent years – Bohringer, Béart, Birkin, Mastroianni, Rassam – are the children of established talent. Once again, many of the biggest names were discovered in the 'golden age': Alain Delon, Marcello Mastroianni, Sophia Loren, Jean-Paul Belmondo, Max von Sydow, Jeanne Moreau, Liv Ullman, Jean-Claude Trintignant, Hanna Schygulla, Richard Bohringer. Even more recent stars such as Gérard Depardieu, Isabelle Adjani, Roberto Benigni, Isabelle Huppert and Nanni Moretti made their first films in the early 1970s.

Most new talent in Europe eventually migrates to Hollywood: 40% of Hollywood's name directors come from Europe and 16% of name actors. Many live in effective 'exile' because their domestic industries are not interested in using their talent.

As Alan Parker said to the UK National Heritage Select Committee in 1994: ' I don't want to *have* to go to the United States. We don't go there because we're actually so desperate to sit around swimming pools and make American films. I went because I couldn't make them here. And that's what your job is. It's to say – you're pretty good at what you do, film is really important. This committee for once could be different from all the other committees and all the other advisory boards. You could actually do something really exciting and wonderful.' The government's answer was to give money to the Arts Council.

PRODUCTION

Europe's media groups have been traditionally conservative in production, preferring to concentrate on the less risky aspects of the business – exhibition, library sales and television.

However, these groups are the only 'bankable' names in the business and they are therefore the heart of Europe's 'commercial' production. Recent production levels have been as follows:

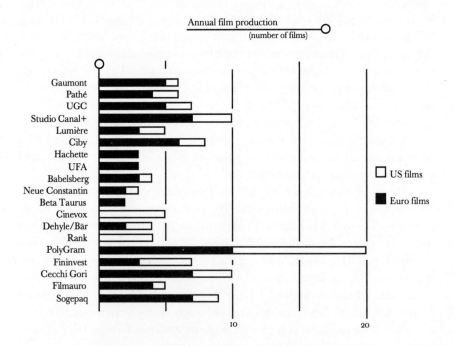

Europe's main media groups produce around 70 European films a year at an average budget of $4–5 million – over 50% higher than the European average. They are also equity partners in around 40 American films a year with an average budget of $20–25 million.

In total, Europe's media groups invest about $120–150 million a year in European films, $250-350 million in American films, and a further $200–250 million in pre-sales to Hollywood. The high level of investment in Hollywood films is considered to be necessary because of the shortage of commercial talent in Europe.

LIBRARIES

Since the 1980s, Europe's main media groups have been establishing huge media libraries. The main libraries in 1996 were:

Canal+	French films, DEG library, 800 hrs of programming ($60 million)
	Carolco library ($53 million)
UGC/Lumiere	2500 French films, 1500 English films, 2000 hrs of programming (estimated value $400–600 million)
Gaumont	400–500 French films
Pathé/Berri	250–300 films
Pandora	100 films
Kirch	15,000 films, 50,000 hours of programming (German and US) (estimated value $2 billion)
Bertelsmann	films and programming
Transit	650 titles
Atlas	450 titles
Rank	over 1000 titles
PolyGram	450–500 films, 10,000 hours of programming ($250–300 million)
Majestic	168 titles
J&M	150 titles (worth $80 million)
Fininvest	63000 programming hours – Italian and US ($1 billion)
Movietime	900 titles
RCS	150 titles
Sogepaq	1400 titles
Cerezo	1500 titles
Svensk	1100 titles

These libraries combine American and European titles. Their value depends on being replenished by new product, which has been a major cause of concern for the media groups. The older European titles were very popular in their day, but Europe now concentrates on producing niche films with very narrow appeal. As a consequence, many old European films are virtually worthless and never played by European TV channels.

Media groups have been investing in Hollywood films to gain 'locomotive' titles for their catalogues, but this has proved extremely costly.

DEVELOPMENT

Unlike the American Majors, most of Europe's media groups have traditionally proved very reluctant to invest development funds, or even take the concept of script development very seriously. This is now changing slowly.

PolyGram spends the most on development – around $5 million a year, which is spread across PolyGram's different labels. Smaller players such as Cinevox, Neue Constantin and Filmauro also have hefty annual development budgets of around $1 million, $2 million and $0.5 million respectively.

Canal+ has also started putting up development money in tandem with Equinoxe, its screenwriting joint venture with Sony. Sogepaq has also stepped up its development spending and acquires rights to best-selling books.

The total level of development expenditure by Europe's media groups is around $12–15 million a year – 3% of the Hollywood total. Most of these funds are for Hollywood projects.

Traditionally the film division of most media groups has been run by a tiny management staff – a head of production, an assistant and two secretaries. This small staff is usually burdened by a high level of immediate responsibilities and unable to establish any longer-term strategy. The more commercial players are now slowly building stronger infrastructures.

FOCUS ON HOLLYWOOD

The inability to produce a high number of popular domestic films creates a tremendous dependence on Hollywood. This is the reason why Europe's media groups invest far more in American production than domestic production. But at the same time they are only accentuating their dependence. It is the Majors which mainly benefit from European investments and use them to cement their staggering superiority in film software.

Hollywood now controls immensely valuable libraries and new production which is critical to the success of Europe's delivery systems. This is a huge strategic advantage in the control of pay-TV and all forms of new media.

The overriding imperative for Europe's media groups is to rejuvenate domestic production which was once hugely popular in Europe, but the main players continue to be focused on Hollywood and in the process have lost over a billion dollars.

Europe has been unable to nurture substantial production or managerial talent at home, whereas Hollywood, ironically, has proved much more adept at giving Europeans a chance to work in the industry.

The only conclusion to be drawn from this inertia is that there is no real desire to stimulate domestic production. Since there is a close connection between media and the political sphere this is ultimately a political issue.

9

The Cultural Ghetto

*The core of the problem is the extraordinarily divergent paths taken by
the Hollywood and European film industries over the past generation.
In Hollywood an array of multi-national corporations have honed the
studio system into an extravagantly quirky but hugely productive
assembly line of mass entertainment for the world markets.
In Europe, by contrast, the economic structure of film-making
seems to be retreating into a sort of medieval guild system.*

Peter Bart (Editor of *Variety*)

WHILE HOLLYWOOD HAS BEEN GROWING at 25% per year for two decades, European films have experienced a nose-dive in revenues and admissions.

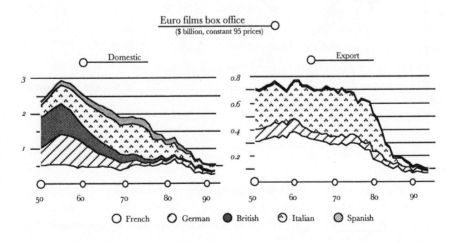

Source: Michel Gyory (British exports are excluded because they are distorted by US pick-ups.)

Over the post-war period a $4.5 billion industry (adjusted for inflation and including Scandinavia and the rest of Europe) has declined to a $0.5 billion industry. European cinema now lives in a world unto itself, financed by the state.

If European cinema had been able to maintain its popular appeal, then on top of box office returns there would today be hefty video, pay-TV, free TV and other ancillary earnings, as well as synergy with developing multi-media. Europe has thereby missed out on a $15–20 billion film industry, plus a similar amount in lost synergy with multi-media. This is equivalent in value to the size of the entire European television industry.

OVERVIEW

European cinema used to be extremely popular at the box office. This included domestic films, but also glossy co-productions which mixed talent from different countries. Today the majority of European films have virtually zero box office appeal. For example, the demand curve for the top 100 films in France in the early 1990s was as follows:

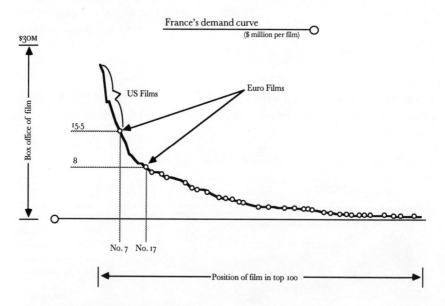

Only a handful of 'foreign-language' films fall within the top 100 every year. The rest are English-language.

European films have progressively lost their popularity in the 'charts'. For example, in Germany, local films represented on average seven of the top ten films during the 1950s, 5.5 during the 1960s, 1.5 during the 1970s and two during the 1980s.

This trend is found throughout Europe and is usually explained by the European public 'deserting' her cinema. In fact there was a sea change in commissioning policies, particularly after 1968.

In the 'golden age' of European cinema, the most popular films were local films, but many of these were co-productions linking together talent from across the continent.

The high point of co-production was 1965 when 45% of European films were co-produced. Co-productions formed the nexus of an emerging true 'European' cinema, but this trend was reversed as the state took over the commissioning process and shifted films to a more parochial outlook.

The destruction of popular European cinema has meant that the 'demand curve' for European films has shifted significantly downwards. The local-film-only demand curve for French, German and Italian films in 1990 was as follows:

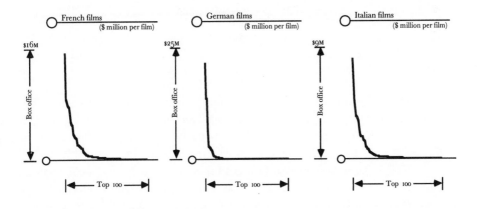

Source: London Economics

This shows that a handful of European films have a genuine audience appeal, despite the fact that in the main territories, 100–150 new European films are released every year.

Only 23 films in France, 18 in Italy and 10 in Germany achieved theatrical admissions in excess of 200,000 in 1990, which is 1% of the average audience for a Hollywood film and justifies a budget level in a commercial system of under $1 million. If the threshold is raised to 500,000 admissions ($2.5–3 million at the box office), only 15 films in France, 8 in Italy and 5 in Germany qualify.

The demand curve is dramatically different from Europe's 'golden age'. The following graph compares the inflation-adjusted demand curve for non-English language films in France in 1960 and 1990.

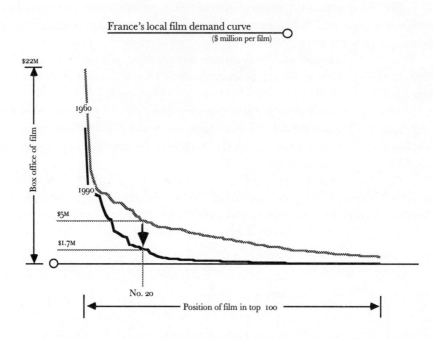

France's local film demand curve
($ million per film)

$22M

1960

Box office of film

1990

$5M

$1.7M

No. 20

Position of film in top 100

In the past many of the popular films were co-productions (especially French-Italian) which meant that they enjoyed high returns across Europe. Average budgets were also lower, which meant that over 50% of films achieved break-even.

Today there are under 50 European films a year with any public recognition. Most of these are niche films produced by auteurs who established their careers in the 1960s and early 1970s, and are financed by Europe's media groups.

This leaves over 300 films a year with virtually no theatrical or video career and low ratings on television. Some of these films are showcased in festivals, some disappear without trace. No other part of the world produces so many films which are immediately forgotten. They are reminiscent of the wine lakes and food lakes produced by the Common Agricultural Policy.

In its heyday Europe produced many popular genres – comedies, adventure stories, police thrillers. For example, the top 20 in France in 1960 included European films *The War of the Buttons, La Belle Americaine, Divorce – Italian Style, Crime Doesn't Pay, La Fayette, Amours Célèbres, Vie Privée, The Count of Monte Cristo, Seven Deadly Sins, Jules and Jim* and *Tintin*. Five of the top 20 films were French, nine were French-Italian, four were American, one was Italian-American and one was British.

At this time the state had virtually no role in the content of European films. There was an automatic industrial subsidy in most countries, but there were no politically appointed authorities who had any influence over the type of film that should be made. Films were financed jointly by distributors and producers with a single objective – to make money.

But this avowedly commercial system also created great works of art. Producers such as Dino de Laurentiis and Carlo Ponti combined super-productions with the pioneering work of Italy's leading auteurs. French producers such as Anatole Dauman, Georges Beauregard and Pierre Braunberger were classic entrepreneurs and yet were patrons to the Nouvelle Vague.

The majority of Europe's classic 'art films' were also commercial successes. Truffaut explained that he was investing in Godard's *2 or 3 things I know about her* (1967) because 'everyone who has invested in Godard's previous films has made money'.

Today the situation is very different. French producer Anatole Dauman claims that 'the reason for cinema's crisis is because there isn't enough capitalism – there's only capitalism at its most savage – monopoly – which is the denial of capitalism. We're run by a conspiracy of mediocrity.' The European film industry is no longer run by adventurers but by a mixture of private monopoly and state control which seems incapable of producing popular films.

European audiences are eager for fresh faces. A recent poll of Italian moviegoers showed that over 40% preferred Italian films to American films and yet only 15% go to see Italian films because of their disappointing quality. A French poll demonstrated a desire for more great comedies, more films about young people, and more imaginative flights of fantasy. The same poll criticized the over-intellectual nature of many French films and the lack of competent young actors.

When a good popular film does appear it can generate blockbuster results – most spectacularly the $80 million gross for *Les Visiteurs* in France. But even this handful of blockbuster successes does not address the underlying problem of a 'critical mass' of popular films.

An industry can only be built once there is a regular supply of popular films. For example, in France in 1960 close to fifty films had admissions of 500,000. This 'critical mass' helps all sections of the cinema – mainstream, niche, avant-garde.

EXPORTS

Very few European films 'travel', that is, achieve a theatrical release in a foreign territory. The most successful exporters are the UK and France which both succeed in selling 15–25 of their films (around 35% and 20% of their national production respectively) to the main foreign territories.

Five to ten of the official UK films are actually US pick-ups and ride on the English-language coat-tails of Hollywood. As a result they can secure much higher foreign MGs than French films.

French film exports concentrate around the auteurs who established their careers in the 1960s and early 1970s, plus a small number of new names such as Besson, Beineix, Carax and Jeunet/Caro.

Amongst the other European countries, Italy and Germany export under ten films each, and Spain and the rest of Europe exports two to six films each. In each case this represents about 10% of national production.

Overall there are about twenty English films and fifty other European titles which succeed in exporting every year. But very few films earn sufficient box office revenues to cover their release costs.

A small number of local hits – such as *Cyrano*, *Nikita*, *Delicatessen* or *Cinema Paradiso* do go on to earn greater box office revenues at home than abroad, whereas most national blockbusters – such as *Germinal* or *Der Bewegte Mann* – earn minimal results abroad.

If there were more 'break-out' films then it might be possible to build enough 'critical mass' to establish a European Major. At present, most European films are only given a niche release when exported. For example, *Nikita* and *Cyrano* had wide releases of over 250 prints with heavy marketing campaigns in France, but were released on under ten screens abroad. This lack of distribution muscle effectively condemns European films to an art house ghetto.

The only way to reverse this trend is if Europe's media groups begin to invest more seriously in European production and distribution. The best example to date is PolyGram, who through its global distribution network was able to make *Four Weddings* such a spectacular success.

The 'problem' has been the disintegration of popular European cinema. As recently as 1980, the main European countries imported over double the present number of films and many of the films achieved a 'break-out' audience. The two main powerhouses of European exports were France and Italy who used to export over 50% of their local production.

Commissioning strategies have progressively moved away from popular cinema, and have left a 'rump' of name directors who continue to export. Some of these have a more specialized audience such as Wenders, Greenaway or Kieslowski. Others have a much wider popular audience, such as Jean-Jacques Annaud or Pedro Almodóvar.

The main constraint for European exports is the fact that the 'talent pool' across all genres of film has not been replenished.

THE ROLE OF TELEVISION

Most European films earn close to zero earnings in theatrical release and earn over 80% of their revenue from television (most of which is an implicit subsidy). In effect, the 'theatrical' film industry has almost completely disappeared.

Fifteen years ago there were over 500 'foreign-language' films which earned significant theatrical revenues within Europe. Today there are under fifty, and most are niche releases.

Television is now the main source of financing for European films, but the television channels rarely commission films which earn high ratings. This is particularly evident in the secondary market, where the number of 'resellable' films is growing smaller every year.

A certain number of European films are shown on television abroad. Over 500 French films are broadcast in Germany every year, and over 200 in Spain and Italy. But more than 50% of these films were produced before 1980. The main reason for channels to buy 'foreign-language' films today is as 'cheap fillers' for the small hours which thereby help satisfy European quotas.

Nonetheless, foreign buyers of a European film will usually base their minimum guarantee payment on the expected television sale. This reinforces the 'cultural ghetto' for European cinema because television tends to equate Hollywood with popular entertainment and Europe with 'culture'.

THE DECLINE AND FALL OF EUROPEAN CINEMA

Europe traditionally was even more film crazy than America. This has changed dramatically over the last thirty-five years.

In 1960 the annual cinema admissions in what is now the European Union were 3 billion, compared to 1.2 billion in the US. The average European bought nine tickets a year compared to five tickets in America.

A significant difference between Europe and America at that time was the penetration of television, which had already hit America, Germany and Britain but had only begun to be successful in France and Southern Europe. In Britain, for example, average attendances had dropped from 25 times a year in 1955 to 10 times a year by 1960.

But television was only one factor in the decline in film-going. In the US, the total number of admissions dropped from 4 billion in 1945 to 1 billion in 1962. But this fall was influenced by several other factors.

First, attendances were artificially high during the war and it was inevitable that they would drop back to their pre-war level which was around 2 billion. Second, ticket prices had risen by 50% in real terms, which further reduced audiences. Third, migration to the suburbs meant there was a lack of screens for many customers.

Immediate post-war film attendances in Europe were similar to America – around 4 billion – and it was quite probable that her audiences would eventually fall to around 1.5 billion. In fact the fall was far more staggering, especially in the countries where film was most popular – Italy, Britain and Germany:

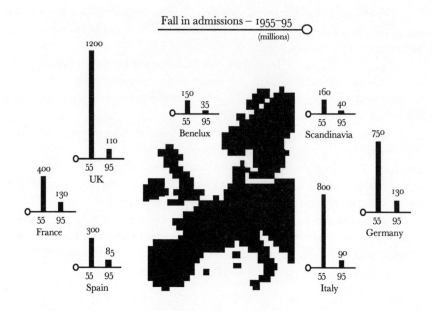

Fall in admissions – 1955–95
(millions)

By 1995 0.7 billion cinema tickets were sold in the Union compared to 1.2 billion in the US. Other factors than television need to be considered to explain the extent of this fall.

PRICE

A significant cause in the fall of admissions in Europe was the increase in prices, which more than doubled in real terms between 1955 and 1995. The increase in prices was strongest in Europe and average prices are now considerably higher than in the US.

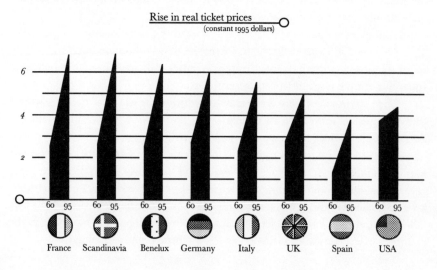

Rise in real ticket prices
(constant 1995 dollars)

One of the main reasons for higher prices in Europe is the high level of sales taxes (VAT) and also in many countries a supplementary film tax to pay for subsidies. Ironically these higher taxes make it even more difficult for local films to compete.

Negligence in exhibition

Another critical factor in the decline of admissions has been the massive rationalization programme of European cinemas. In the United States the number of screens has actually increased, from around 18,000 in 1960 to almost 26,000 in 1995, but the types of cinema are very different.

Average seating per screen in the US is now 200 (compared to 600 per screen in 1960), and most cinemas are multiplexes. The total seat capacity in America has reduced from 11 million in 1960 to 5 million in 1995.

In Europe the number of screens has been slashed, from 40,000 in 1960 to 18,000 in 1995. The seat capacity has been cut even further from 18 million seats in 1960 to 4 million in 1995.

Negligence in the exhibition business has been one of the main factors in the decline of film-going. Massive rationalization plans were implemented in a very short period of time without any strategic planning as to the future of the film business.

The cinemas that remained were often left to decay as 'flea pits', turning film-going into a 'slum activity watched in slum conditions'.

The country that paid the greatest attention to its exhibition business was France, and it is no surprise that she has the strongest film industry in Europe today.

The greatest negligence has been in Britain, and after the Majors started to build multiplexes in 1985, attendances doubled. Multiplexes are now being built throughout Europe, which is likely to further boost European attendances.

Shortage of Popular European Films

The 'golden age' of European cinema was driven by local films and stars. The love affair between countries such as Italy and the cinema was stimulated by the richness of local talent.

Today European cinema has turned its back on its popular traditions, and decided to focus on 'culture'. The state-subsidized cinema seems to have neither the capacity, nor the desire, to provide more popular films.

American films have maintained a constant box office in Europe ($2.5 billion in real terms) since 1960, while box office for European films in the same period has fallen from over $4 billion to $0.5 billion.

THE PROBLEM OF LANGUAGE

It is often suggested that European cinema is inevitably condemned to a niche status because of the dominance of the American idiom. While it is true that English-language films have a larger potential market, 'foreign-language' films can also have a wide potential market – particularly within Europe.

In the immediate post-war period, European films travelled extremely well within Europe. Most films were post-synchronized and many co-productions featured actors of different languages that were then dubbed into multiple language versions.

The main stumbling block for European exports in the 'golden age' was the American market, but even in America there was considerable success for dubbing. Most of the Bardot films, and several other popular films, were dubbed into English, especially by the Hollywood Majors who were committed to wide releases for the European films they invested in.

Dubbing was recognized to be so successful that the Catholic League only granted *La Dolce Vita* a US export licence in 1960 on condition that it be released in a subtitled version. This was intended to restrict the potential market. The film was re-released as a dubbed version in 1967 and made handsome returns.

European films in the 'golden age' were able to enjoy extensive earnings outside their native language territory and blockbusters did exist. *La Dolce Vita*, for example, earned a worldwide box office which at today's prices would be close to $150 million.

The problem of dubbing and exports is not so much one of language, as idiom. The idiom of Hollywood films is popular cinema, whereas that for European films has become niche cultural films. The audience for the latter tend to prefer to hear the film in its original language with subtitles. Studies have demonstrated time and again that in the US the audience most likely to see foreign films prefers a subtitled version, and in previews, the subtitled version scores better. There is a preconceived image of European films, which puts off the mainstream audience. This was not the case with the films starring Brigitte Bardot. Audiences did not care whether she was in lip-sync or not.

The French continue to believe that the main obstacle to penetrating the US market is dubbing. A recent example was Luc Besson's action thriller *Nikita*. The French believed that this could achieve mainstream success and invested in an expensive dub, but previews showed that the subtitled version was preferred by audiences.

Miramax has a co-venture with France, starting with a dubbed version of the French smash hit, *Les Visiteurs*, overseen by Mel Brooks. Despite using state of the art techniques, audiences still seem to prefer the subtitled version.

Language will continue to be a problem, as long as the 'grammar' of the European film is the 'art film'. Without a critical mass of popular European films, exports will always be limited to a niche market which prefers subtitles.

EUROPEAN PRODUCTION

The level of European production has been dropping dramatically in recent years because of cut-backs at the national cinema centres and in public television. In 1995 around 360 films were produced in the countries of the European Union, compared to over 500 in 1992 and over 600 in 1980. Around one third of the current films are co-productions.

PRODUCTION BY COUNTRY

France is the most important producer with over 60 national productions and a similar level of co-productions (half of which are majority French, the other half being recorded under the production of other countries):

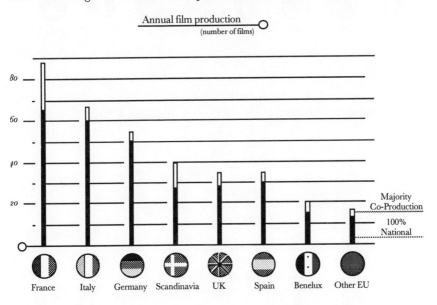

In addition to these films, Europe also co-produces about forty American films a year via Europe's media groups.

BUDGETS

France also has the highest average budget levels, because of the extensive state subsidies available.

Overall, Europe's 'official' budgets must be discounted for 'padding' by producers. Most producers claim that the 'official' budget is 20–30% higher than the real budget in order to gain higher subsidies and TV prices. In France this tendency was further accentuated by a legal requirement for producers to put up 15% of the budget, which was abolished in 1994 in order to reduce padding.

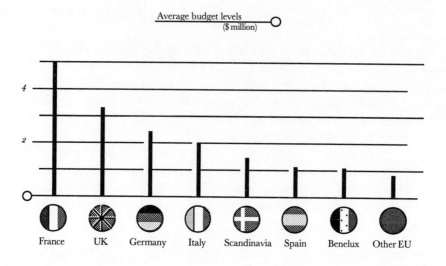

FUNDING SOURCES

The main sources of funds for European films are state subsidies and the state broadcasters. The average contribution to production budgets by funding source is as follows:

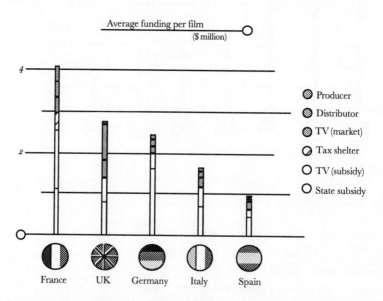

The state thereby provides 70% of finance in most of Europe and 50% in Britain. Further state support is provided in most countries through state film credits and discounting, bringing effective state funding up to 80%.

ABSENCE OF FILM PUBLISHERS

The American system is based on the central role of the distributor as film publisher. The Majors, the indie distributors and the foreign sales companies are all 'publishers'.

In Europe the distributor used to be at the heart of the film-making process. Films were traditionally financed with 25–30% of the budget coming from the local distributor and a further 10–20% derived from foreign distributors.

Today this role has been taken over by the state. As a consequence films are no longer decided by the 'interest of the public' but rather by the 'public interest'. The majority are financed through bureaucratic committees who do not decide on the demand for the film, but rather whether it is 'worthy' to be made.

The state has taken over the role of film publisher and uses subsidies to determine the manner in which European films are shown. The state has helped establish a parallel exhibition circuit for European films and also organizes film festivals and overseas promotion through a state export agency.

The only films which escape what has become a 'cultural ghetto' are those backed by the large media groups. Films from companies such as Gaumont, Neue Constantin, PolyGram or Renn/AMLF are able to secure a wide release in mainstream theatres. Occasionally a smaller culture film will be picked up for these circuits, but only very rarely.

LIQUIDITY CRISIS

The continuing decline in performance of European films has created a major liquidity crisis. This has been the main cause of the reduction in the number of films produced.

In France, an official report by Jean-Paul Cluzel and Guillaume Cerruti (Cluzel Report, 1992) demonstrated that whereas 99% of total production budgets were covered in advance by subsidies and pre-sales in 1981, this had fallen to 69% by 1991.

The Cluzel report concluded, 'Since over half of French films have zero value on the secondary television market – having been rejected in theatrical and/or on first television broadcast- and the average price for a repeat broadcast is below $400,000, this raises serious doubts on the possibility of recoupment of the 1992 "vintage" (and those of the previous two or three years), and suggests that there will be a liquidity crisis for French producers in the near future.'

This crisis is the result in the decline of popularity of French films and also hyper-inflation in production budgets. The Cluzel Report demonstrated that whereas in 1981 theatrical rentals covered 85% of production finance, this had fallen to 30% by 1991.

The same phenomenon has occurred throughout Europe, creating a dependency on the state, and a production crisis whenever the state freezes public funding. In Britain, producers have been more dependent on market revenues, but this may now be changing as lottery funds pour into the industry.

TYPES OF FILM

Most European films are in the $1–2 million budget range, with a few more ambitious projects. For example, the 1992 Cluzel Report divided French production into four types, which in 1991 broke down as follows:

- Big-budget   10 films
- Safe bets   24 films
- Parisian appeal   38 films
- Low-budget   30 films

Big-budget films had on average a budget of $16 million, a 200+ screen national release and $7.6 million box office. Safe bets had on average a $6 million budget, a 100+ screen release and $4.4 million box office. Parisian films had on average a $4 million budget, a 12-screen release in Paris and $0.7 million box office. Low-budget films had on average a $2.1 million budget, a 6-screen release in Paris and $0.3 million box office.

Only the top 30 films had a significant theatrical career, and few broke even on market revenues alone. Without state support, the system would grind to a halt. Most films are financed through the 'golden triangle' of the state, state television and the producer, and as a general rule, the higher the dependence on the state, the lower the audience.

Only a handful of European films have a significant financing contribution from market sources (theatrical distributors, foreign sales and media groups). This can be demonstrated by an interpretative analysis of the figures provided in the Cluzel Report for the financing for French films in 1991:

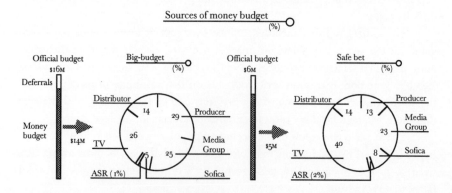

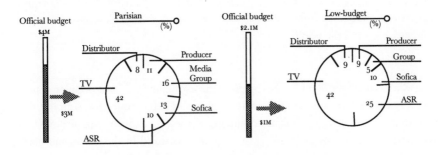

Source: Cluzel Report 1992. ASR = avance sur recettes (selective subsidy).
Analysis of money budget is based on assumption that the producer's true money investment matches the value of the automatic subsidy.

French films are 90% financed within France. All films involve a certain level of deferrals, but for low-budget films this is as high as 50% (including deferrals and 'padding' by producers). TV is the decisive source of income, and for the majority of films the main TV sale is Canal+ which is almost an 'automatic purchase'. For low-budget films, the other main source of financing is *avance sur recettes* (70% of such films).

The collapse of the French film industry has been above all in 'Parisian' and 'low-budget' films. These were traditionally the source of new talent for the French film industry, but have been spectacularly unsuccessful in recent years.

The financing of smaller French films is the typical model for all European films, where the two main ports of call are television and the state selective funds. This is also true in Britain, where the main funding sources are British Screen/ Arts Council and Channel 4 (with its public service remit). The commissioning remit of these selective funds is usually to avoid making 'commercial' or popular films, and as a result very little popular talent has emerged in recent years.

RELEASE STRATEGY

Most European films are released in a parallel exhibition circuit that corresponds to 'art house' or *art et essai*. A small number of national films achieve a wider release – particularly in France where the leading titles are opened on over 200 screens.

The 'major' releases have advertising budgets comparable to the American Majors. For example, *Cyrano de Bergerac* had a $2.4 million P&A spend in France – double that of *Terminator 2*. But the majority of releases are made on far lower P&A budgets. The average film supported by EFDO – which is the 'cream' of European cinema – has a total P&A spend per country of under $100,000.

Most European films achieve promotion through 'free advertising' from the local TV channels and press. The TV and press critics have consistently shown that they will do their best to undermine most attempts at popular film-making in Europe, but will give a generous boost to 'culture'. This has perhaps further encouraged Europe's film tsars to commission films which please the film critics rather than the public.

GENRES

The crucial problem for European films has been the loss of popular genres and a switch in commissioning towards 'culture'. Each country has suffered this transition as the state has taken command of the film industry. In Britain and Germany the move away from popular genres occurred in the 1960s and early 1970s. In Italy the switch was in the late 1970s and early 1980s.

The last of the great European film communities to collapse is the French. New talent and stories were discovered throughout the 1970s which helped French cinema maintain a wide popular appeal. The dominant genres were comedies and police thrillers which represented 55% of production and 75% of the audience.

During the 1980s under the guidance of the ruling Socialist party, film commissioning switched progressively towards 'culture'. Police thrillers virtually disappeared and comedies fell to 27% of production. Very little new popular talent emerged and admissions for French films fell from 81 million in 1983 to 25 million in 1992 while American films remained constant in popularity. The government blamed this collapse entirely on Hollywood.

The 1992 Cluzel Report emphasized the inability of French films to adapt to the demands of the public: 'French cinema offers neither the themes, nor some would say, the faces that correspond to the desires of an ever younger film-going public (almost 50% of filmgoers are under twenty-five). Adventure films, comedies, police thrillers, science fiction, animation are the most popular genres, especially for younger people, and yet are increasingly rare in French film production.'

Young people have always been the core audience of the cinema and the healthiest period of French cinema was the explosion of young talent in the early 1960s. In debates about the cinema there is constant reference to the need to make more films that appeal to young people.

At the ARP conference in 1995 Léon Schwartzenberg (ex-president of the cinema group at the European parliament) commented, 'If anyone is conscious of what Europe is today, it's the young. The young people in every European country have a keen awareness of what it means to be European. They are wracked by anxiety. They have no future. They're afraid of unemployment. They're afraid of mortal illnesses. They have no objectives. And worst of all, they're bored. Young people in Europe and the rest of the population are menaced by boredom . . . there must be a revolutionary change, a new breeze that floats through Europe.'[1]

The need for more films is constantly reiterated and yet change seems to be occurring at a snail's pace. The main motors of change have been certain media groups, particularly PolyGram, who with films such as *Trainspotting* has at last begun to make films that can win the respect of young people.

The Subsidy System

*Wenders, Lars von Trier, Kieslowski, Almodóvar, Kusturica, Moretti
have all been more or less financed by the French system of production
which urgently needs to be installed throughout Europe.*
Daniel Toscan du Plantier

THE IDEA THAT THE FRENCH SUBSIDY SYSTEM is the only 'solution' for the European film industry is fairly widespread in Europe. Even US-orientated producers such as Jake Eberts agree: 'The French system for all its warts, provides France with an industry. I think Europe should dupe the French system -- it would create lots of jobs, enthusiasm and business.'

The campaign in favour of subsidies reached its peak in the GATT negotiations in 1993 and resulted in a 'cultural exemption' for subsidies and quotas. But the cultural debate was conducted in the most primitive terms, focusing on whether Europe needs subsidies or not. This is a bit like having a debate about whether we should wear clothes or not.

All industries are enveloped in government regulation and any form of tax legislation has an implicit 'subsidy' effect. The choice is not between nudity or clothing, it is what type of clothing is most suitable. 'The cultural exemption from GATT is another example of intellectual posturing' says financier John Heyman. 'It is a ruse to justify the commercial failure of the non-American film industry.'

Many believe that subsidies were introduced during the 1960s as a defence against the rising Hollywood giant. In fact the basic elements of the system were designed in the 1930s in Germany and Russia, in order to promote National Socialism and 'Socialism in One Country'. The objective of these systems is to place all forms of cultural expression under 'culture chambers' which ultimately respond to the Minister of Culture.

The subsidy system is therefore more accurately described as the 'German model'. The Germans invented the system in the early 1930s and then exported it to like-minded regimes and occupied territories. The French were one of the last countries to adopt this system, as a result of the Occupation.

The key aspect of cultural subsidies, as in any form of fiscal incentive, is that they allow the state to shape the cultural and commercial environment. Since the 1960s the state has been disbursing selective cultural subsidies which have encouraged European cinema towards the margins of society and also confirmed its economic dependence. The state now decides the cultural agenda of the nation and appoints the key commissioning editors whose editorial remits make it very difficult for them to make popular films.

At best, commissioners are excellent film professionals who do their best to make good films within the limits that have been placed on them. At worst, commissioning is the result of bribery and corruption and the films that are made are mediocre.

NATIONAL SYSTEMS

Each national subsidy system is designed to create a village-style film corporation which revolves around the state-controlled 'centre'. The key elements include:

- National cinema centre
- State film taxes
- Approval of national films
- Approval of official co-productions
- Quotas and other regulation
- State film subsidies
- State film prizes
- Authors' rights
- State credit bank
- Film investment by television companies
- Film taxation
- State film education

NATIONAL CINEMA CENTRES

In the immediate post-war era the role of 'national cinema centres' was limited to 'industrial' aid. In Germany it was illegal to have either a single national centre, or to have state cultural subsidies. During the 1960s, state cultural subsides were revived – pioneered by France and Germany – and 'national film institutes' were set up across Europe which took increasing control of domestic film industries.

The only countries in Europe without unified national film centres are Britain and Germany. In Britain there are a series of overlapping public bodies – the British Film Institute, British Screen and the Arts Council. In Germany there are a panoply of regional funds, which in the near future may well be unified into a single Ministry of Culture.

The national cinema centre is responsible for administering the rest of the state subsidy system. The head of the centre is a political appointment and is immediately responsible to the Minister of Culture.

STATE FILM TAXES

When cinema was invented at the end of the nineteenth century, it was generally considered by European authorities to be dangerous to moral health. It was subjected to high taxation rates intended to discourage film-going. The highest rates were in France, where film taxation was 30–35% (compared to 8% for the theatre) and as a result film-going per head in France was the lowest in Europe.

When the new authoritarian regimes appeared in the 1930s, they promised to ensure that domestic film production would be more 'wholesome'. As a result it was proposed that domestic films be 'detaxed' and receive this taxation money instead as an 'automatic subsidy'. Further selective incentives were offered to steer domestic production towards the types of production favoured by the state.

The principle of special film taxes has been maintained in many European countries. Anybody wishing to see an American film must effectively pay a surcharge which will then be invested in 'culturally superior' local production. The highest film levy is in France, where there is a 12% surcharge on film-goers, a 5.5% tax on the TV channels and a 2.5% surcharge on video cassettes.

State film funds are supplemented through income taxes, VAT, taxes on pornographic films and surcharges on state gambling. Ironically, many of these taxes are levied on 'social vices' and then used to promote 'culture'.

In addition to film levies, VAT is charged on film admissions in most countries. VAT is typically 18–22% (compared to 5–7% sales tax in the US) but often carries a 50% reduction for the cinema. VAT is used for national government funding and also pays for European ventures such as the MEDIA programme.

APPROVAL OF NATIONAL FILMS

In order to qualify for national subsidies and quotas, a film must be an 'official' national film. This means that it must satisfy minimum requirements in terms of the nationality of the producer, director and finance (see Appendix C). A co-production must satisfy the terms of official co-production treaties.

The definition of a 'national film' has been progressively tightened since the 1960s. In the immediate post-war years companies with links to the Holly-wood Majors could apply for subsidy funds as long as they were willing to use local talent and the local language. This was essential to the phenomenon of 'Hollywood in Europe'. Today under the EU rules, a producer such as David Puttnam (who finances his films through Warners) is not technically making a European film. Similarly, directors such as Luc Besson who made *Léon – The Professional*, in English (financed by Gaumont), did not make a European film.

A major restriction in many countries, is the insistence that a national film be filmed in the national language. In France there was an expansion in co-productions during the 1980s which was halted as new regulations insisted that all French films be shot in French. This was paralleled in the César film awards which excluded films such as *The Lover* because they were shot in English.

The clamp-down on the language issue has been the result of EU directives which insist that the only way that subsidies can be exempted from free trade laws is if they are linked to the defence of the local language. Marc Nicolas, assistant to the former Minister of Culture, Jack Lang, explained that the French would like to have a more 'supple' regulation concerning language but that the EU prevents it.

Ironically the country which has enjoyed the greatest flexibility on this issue is Germany, which is also the most powerful country within the Union. Several German films are originated in English and yet still qualify as official German films, because they benefit from 'industrial' subsidies.

APPROVAL OF CO-PRODUCTIONS

Co-production legislation was initiated in the 1930s as a means by which the national cinema centres could co-operate on pan-European productions. Several German-Italian co-productions were pioneered during the 1930s, and during the Occupation years this was extended to French-Italian and Franco-German co-production

In the immediate post-war era co-production legislation was liberally applied and provided the basis for a genuine European film industry, which was in the spirit of the Treaty of Rome and US initiatives such as the Marshall Plan.

Once the state began to re-establish its dominance over the cinema in the early 1970s, co-productions declined dramatically and have only revived in recent years under the aegis of the MEDIA programme and Eurimages. Co-productions now represent around 20% of total European production, and their main attraction is that they can be used to pool together the subsidy money from several countries.

Co-productions are governed by a panoply of bilateral treaties. Where no treaty has been signed, or in the case of tripartite co-productions, the more general European co-production treaty of the Council of Europe is usually applied. Each co-production treaty is different, and no producer should try to draw up a co-production without consulting a lawyer (see Appendix C).

QUOTAS

Quotas have often been used to stimulate local production, but have fallen out of favour because they result in 'quota quickies' and cannot easily be controlled. Exhibition quotas for film still exist in Italy and Spain, where cinemas must show:

- Italian/EU films at least 25 days a quarter.
- Spanish/EU films on a minimum 1:3 ratio to other films, or 2:3 ratio if other films are shown in a dubbed version.

These quotas are hard to enforce in practice, and there are plans to scrap them in Spain. Much more important quotas exist for television under the 1989 Télévision sans Frontières decree of the European Union which specifies that every European television channel must broadcast at least 60% of European programming in each strand area. National legislation establishes a national minimum (usually 40–50% in the larger countries) to be included within this blanket 60%. Observance of television quotas is the responsibility of a separate national television authority which normally reports to the Minister of Culture.

SUBSIDIES

At the heart of the European system are the financial grants provided by the state. The state allocates subsidies to all levels of the film chain: development, production, distribution, exhibition, festivals, and education. Production subsidies can be divided into two main types: automatic and selective. Automatic subsidies are 'industrial' aid, designed to ensure that 'official' national films trade on a more favourable basis to other films from the rest of the EU or from the US. Selective subsidies are designed to promote a particular type of production, and in general are used by the state to shift the film industry towards 'culture'.

There is a growing recognition that 'cultural subsidies' have undermined the performance of European cinema. In 1995 Europe's cultural ministers agreed to redirect support towards more automatic measures and 'commercial' projects. This is slowly changing both national and European subsidy systems.

FRENCH SUBSIDIES

France has the highest level of state subsidy and regulation in Europe. The French system was born after the Nazi occupation in 1940, with the creation of COIC, which became the CNC in 1946.

The CNC receives $330 million a year from special taxes which is split 55:45 between support for film and television. The key areas of annual film support are automatic aid ($65 million), *avances sur recettes* ($21 million), festivals ($25 million) and exhibition ($55 million). The CNC also provides guarantees to the state film credit bank – IFCIC – which cash-flows French production.

Automatic aid

The bedrock of French production is automatic aid, which is in effect a form of 'de-taxation'. The producer must be registered with the CNC, and the aid is only available for 'official' French films or co-productions, with approvals registered both before and after shooting. To qualify, the film must satisfy a minimum number of 'points' (14 out of 18) based on the nationality of the actors, director, screenplay, studio, laboratory, etc.

The value of the subsidy is based on theatrical and television earnings. In theatrical, the producer is returned the special film tax that was charged on his film, plus a 20% top-up. This is equivalent to 14% of the film's box office. In television, the producer receives 16% of the amount of any broadcast fee up to 1.5 million francs ($300,000) and 8% of the excess if the fee is higher.

The CNC sets up a special account for the producer, into which the 'detaxed' funds are deposited. The funds can be used only to pay secured debts (deferrals etc.) or to invest in a new 'official' production.

This system offers an in-built advantage for French films against American and other EU competition. By creating a direct corridor of payment from box office to the producer, the system also encourages a producer-based system rather than strong distributors.

Avance sur recettes

After the ascent to power of General de Gaulle in 1958, a new *avance sur recettes* (ASR) scheme was introduced. The scheme became a key funding scheme over the 1960s and progressively shifted French production towards 'culture'.

In the early 1960s, 40–50% of the advances were repaid but after 1968 the commissioning strategy shifted rapidly to cultural niche films, with only 10–15% of funds repaid. ASR is only available for French-language films (and not minority co-productions). Subsidies are decided on the basis of two colleges, one for first films, one for other films. The process takes about 6–8 months for first films and 3–4 months for other films.

Applicants may be either directors or scriptwriters and they must submit a script and key creative elements. Each script is then read by two readers and summaries are provided to a series of 'reading committees' before the projects go to the final 'college'.

Each college has eight members and includes representatives of the film industry, the Ministry of Culture and 'cultural figures' such as authors, painters and film critics. The final allocation of subsidies must be approved by the Minister of Culture.

In principle, subsidies are granted to those projects with the greatest 'cultural merit' and funds are allocated directly to the director or scriptwriter. This gives the 'auteur' a significant bargaining tool in negotiating with producers and distributors.

In practice, most allocations are the result of lobbying. A successful project needs at least one member of the college to back the project and act as a 'piston' to push it through. French producer Alain Terzian (*Les Visiteurs*) suggests that 'The Avance sur Recettes is the kingdom of lobbying and jobs for the boys. We give subsidies of 2 million francs to films where the producer's salary is 10 million francs. There has been a decline in morality and there will be a scandal!'[1]

Club des Investisseurs

There was a brief experiment in France using a mixture of private and public capital, known as 'Club des Investisseurs'. The Club was set up at the beginning of 1990 and invested 81 million francs ($15M) in ten films over two years. The venture capital for the club was provided by seven French banks and all investments were guaranteed up to 75% by the state finance guarantee system IFCIC. Investment decisions were decided by two panels – one with representatives from the investing banks, the other with nine leading producers.

The Club was the initiative of George Prost, the head of IFCIC, and was based on the logic that the higher budget French films (over $8M) were the most commercially successful. But the experience of the club was generally considered by industry experts to have been a 'disaster'. Most of the funds were allocated to the producers of the selection committee and the only two films which enjoyed a strong success – *Cyrano* and *Indochine* – had very stringent repayment terms. The profits in no way repaid the losses on some of the other films.

Other subsidies

The Ministry of Culture provides both automatic and selective aids to distributors, but this is restricted to films with 'cultural merit'. There are also other cultural subsidies for screenwriting and music and also for co-productions with Eastern Europe and developing countries.

Regional subsidies

The Ministry of Culture has regional directorates known as DRACs which provide a small amount of production funds and also help subsidize the very large number of film festivals that take place in France. Regional councils also have their own culture budgets and often co-ordinate their activities with the DRACs. Two of the most active Regional Councils are those of Aquitaine and Languedoc-Roussillon. Production subsidies vary between $80,000 and $200,000 and are supplemented by logistic and technical support.

The most active of all regional funding bodies is the CEC-Rhône Alpes which was set up in 1991 as a joint initiative with the CNC with annual funds of $4 million. To be eligible, the majority of the shooting must take place in the region (minimum of 25%) and a maximum of 75% of the budget may be provided by the scheme.

The German subsidy system is the second richest in Europe (over $120 million in production grants), but unlike the French system is highly decentralized.

This is the result of conditions imposed by the Allies at the end of the Second World War. Following unification, Germany may well now establish a centralized Minister of Culture. State involvement in the German film industry is regulated by the Film Assistance Law and complemented by a Film/Television Agreement.

The main funding sources include the following (1993 data, DM 1.5 = $1):

•	Federal film agency	$40 million
•	Cultural film assistance	$10 million
•	Berlin-Brandenburg	$25 million
•	Hamburg	$13.5 million
•	Bavaria	$17.5 million
•	North-Rhine Westphalia	$33 million

Federal Film Agency (FFA)

The FFA is Germany's 'national cinema centre' but has far less power than the French CNC. The FFA board of directors is composed of seven government representatives, two delegates from the Catholic and Evangelist Churches and eighteen members nominated from the German film industry. As in France, two types of subsidy are awarded: automatic and selective.

To apply for automatic aid, a film must achieve over 100,000 admissions, or 50,000 if it has a state 'quality' label. Funds are collected by state film taxes and then allocated to all those films which pass the admissions threshold. The typical 'detaxation' grant is between $0.3 million and $0.8 million, but discretionary cultural bonuses can shift this to $2.4 million. Automatic funds must be used for future productions.

Selective or 'Projekt' aid is an 'advance on receipts' scheme for 'cultural' projects which first began in 1974. The standard grant is $300,000 but in exceptional cases may be as high as $1.2 million. Projects are submitted in script form and are assessed by an eleven-member 'college' selected by the FFA board. The rate of repayment is 7%.

Other selective aids include script development, intended for 'cultural films'. As in the rest of Europe, subsidies are being shifted away from selective cultural aid and towards automatic support. Rolf Baer the head of the FFA said in 1995, 'We are seeing far more acceptable results in the last year or two. There is suddenly talent everywhere.'

Cultural Film Assistance (BMI)

The cultural film assistance programme provides 'quality' prizes and subsidies and also funds the Berlin Film Festival, the German Film & Television Academy and the Kinemathek.

The German Film Prize has up to ten nominations, decided by a commission of cultural luminaries appointed by the Ministry of Interior. It thereby gives an indication of what the German state considers to be 'quality' production. Each nominated film receives $200,000, with two $400,000 Silver Prizes and a $635,000 Gold Prize.

Production grants of up to $300,000, development grants and a script development fund are also available for 'cultural films'. Until very recently, the nominations for the film prize were for niche films rarely heard of by the general public.

Since 1994 there has been an increasing emphasis on popular films, and the awards ceremony has received extensive television coverage. In 1996 the best film award was for *The Deathmaker*, which grossed $2 million in Germany, and the best actress was Katja Riemann, star of the hit film *Talk of the Town* which grossed $11 million.

Curatorium of Young German Film

Established in 1964, indirectly as the result of the 1962 'Oberhausen Manifesto' in favour of a 'new German cinema', the Curatorium re-established the principle of federal cultural subsidies.

In 1968 the Curatorium's funding was shifted to a communal fund provided by the German Länder. In 1992 the Curatorium had a total budget of $1.5 million used to support 15–20 films a year, with a maximum grant per film of $100,000.

In its early years the selection committee included mainly independent film-makers, critics and distributors, and was decisive in supporting the new generation of German film-makers – Herzog, Kluge, Wenders and Fassbinder. But in 1977 the statutes were changed, giving much more direct control by bureaucrats appointed by the German regional governments.

Regional funds

Germany's panoply of regional aid systems offers a mix of 'industrial' and 'cultural' schemes, with an average rate of repayment of 10%. Most German films are funded by combining grants from a 'jigsaw puzzle' or regional and federal funds.

The prime importance of the regional funds to the German funding system has created a series of 'film villages', including Berlin, Hamburg, Munich and more recently North-Rhine Westphalia.

In 1994, a new Berlin-Brandenberg fund was established, headed by Klaus Keil, former president of the Munich Film Academy. The fund gives Keil full autonomy in his decisions, and is intended for 'commercial' projects.

To qualify for subsidies, a production company must have an office in the Berlin-Brandenberg area, invest at least 30% of its own resources, and spend 100% of the subsidy in the region (including the former DEFA studios).

Funds are provided as soft loans repayable from 50% of receipts. The rate of repayment is 25%. The film does not have to be in the German language, and theoretically is available to any production (including Hollywood films) located in Berlin.

Loans are provided for every stage of production. Production loans of up to a maximum of $1.2 million or 30% of production costs are available for feature films costing more than $1 million. An amount equal to 1.5 times the loan amount must be used in Berlin.

In 1995 Klaus Keil announced plans to set up a more ambitious $75 million fund with support from private and public funds.

Hamburg

Traditionally there were two film funds in Hamburg – the 'culturally orientated' Hamburg Film Office and the 'economic assistance' of Film Fund Hamburg. In both cases funds were provided as conditional loans, with average repayment 20–25%. The two funds often backed the same projects and also jointly ran a distribution subsidy scheme. In 1994 the state government cut funding to 15% of their former level, but then reinstated it under a new film fund, with a similar structure to the old system.

The management board is appointed by the Senate of the Hamburg Länder and is composed of state officials responsible for taxation, trade and industry, transport and agriculture, plus two persons from the film industry.

Bavaria

The Film Assistance Programme is located in Munich and covers script development, film and TV production, distribution and investments in film companies.

The loan subsidy must be spent in Bavaria, and if there is studio filming it must take place in Bavaria. The applicant has to prove that he will also invest in the project.

Loans of up to 50% of the budget may be provided with a ceiling of $650,000. The awarding committee is composed of one member each from the Film Fund, the Ministry of Finance, the local state broadcaster and the Film Information Bureau, plus three representatives from the local film industry. These are appointed by the Senate of the Bavarian Länder.

North-Rhine Westphalia (NRW)

The 'Filmstiftung NRW Gmbh' scheme, based in Cologne, is the richest regional fund in Germany, and was set up in 1991 as a joint venture between the local state broadcaster (WDR) and the local state government. The scheme is run by Dieter Koslick who is also head of EFDO, the former distribution wing of the MEDIA programme.

Subsidies are available for pre-production and production (80%), distribution and exhibition (15%), and script-development and training (5%). Funds are provided as a conditional loan, a financial grant or a mixture of the two. The fund is designed for 'low-budget' films.

To be eligible for production funding, most of the shooting, and post-production must be located in the NRW area, and 150% of the full amount of the subsidy must be spent in the region. Up to 50% of the budget (maximum $0.7 million) may be provided by the scheme, with the producer putting up at least 5% of the budget. As part of the funding agreement, the television rights for most films will be acquired by WDR.

The awarding committee is composed of three members appointed by the local state government and three by the local state broadcaster (WDR). Senior management of WDR is in turn appointed by the local state government.

Only projects pre-selected by Dieter Koslick may be considered by the committee. Funding decisions are then made on a simple majority on the basis of industrial and cultural merit. Around 20–25 films are supported each year. Films backed to date include: *Baby of Macon, The Innocent, Farinelli* and *Je m'appelle Victor*.

Other regional funds

Most regional Länder have small film funds, including funds based in Potsdam, Hanover, Frankfurt, Saarbrücken, Lübeck and Stuttgart. The largest is the Baden-Würtemberg scheme, whose budget was boosted from $1 million to $7 million in 1994.

UK SUBSIDIES

Britain has been far more reluctant to embrace cultural subsidies, or create a Ministry of Culture, than other European countries, but nonetheless has a very strong 'public service' tradition exemplified by institutions such as the BBC.

Under the Conservative Government there has been an increasing desire to achieve centralized political control over key areas of 'culture', and the creation of a Department of National Heritage in 1992 is perhaps the prototype for a Ministry of Culture, bringing Britain into harmony with the rest of Europe.

During most of the post-war period, UK film subsidies were based around the Eady levy (automatic and cultural subsidies), the National Film Development Fund and the 'film bank' – the National Film Finance Corporation.

Under the Conservative Government, film funding has been restructured around a very strong 'cultural remit', with funds provided by British Screen, the European Co-Production Fund, the Arts Council, the British Film Institute and television funding from Channel 4 and the BBC. Regional schemes include the Scottish Film Production Fund (SFPF), the Glasgow Film Fund and regional arts boards managed by the Arts Council. There are also special trusts such as the Children's Film and Television Foundation and the First Film Foundation.

The annual production funding by the main subsidy schemes is as follows:

•	BFI	$2 million
•	British Screen	$7.5 million
•	ECF	$3 million
•	Arts Council	$30 million

In addition to these schemes the government also set up the British Film Commission in 1991 to co-ordinate regional screen commissions and provide support services designed to attract overseas productions to Britain.

British Film Institute

The BFI is the heart of Britain's public funding systems and represents a limited form of 'national cinema centre'. It receives £15 million a year from the Department of National Heritage, £450,000 from Channel 4 and £50,000 from the ITVA.

Key disbursements include production funding (£1 million) the National Film and Television School (£1.8 million), the National Film Theatre, the Film Archive, the library, distribution and exhibition aid for niche cinemas, grants to Regional Art Boards, and co-ordination of film activities throughout Britain.

The BFI is set up under a Royal Charter which ties it to a strong public service remit. The Production Board supports low-budget films, feature-length documentaries and scripts, all of which must display 'significant artistic quality'.

The BFI also runs a New Directors Scheme designed to produce six to eight short films a year in order to nurture new talent. The senior management of the BFI is appointed by the Minister of National Heritage.

British Screen

A public trust was established in 1986 and is funded through government grants, plus subscriptions from its private shareholders, which are Rank, Granada, Channel 4 and MGM Cinemas. British Screen also has significant revenue from returns from prior loans and those inherited from the NFFC.

In 1991 the fund's existence seemed precarious, but it finally won renewed support from the government. Simon Perry commented at the time, 'We are a real sore thumb. The fact that the DTI gives us a grant at all is completely inconsistent with Tory ideology. And when you can't make the ideology stick you put a bandage over it – give them a grant but make it difficult for them to get it.'[2]

In 1994, British Screen signed a three-year co-financing deal with BSkyB, providing a securer source of revenues and providing the satellite channel with pay-TV rights to a minimum of ten films a year.

The Conservative Government has also expressed greater interest in British cinema, as long as it concentrates on 'quality' entertainment. In 1995 British Screen announced that it will receive an extra $8 million as a Greenlight Fund, from the Arts Council lottery monies, designed to be invested in bigger budget pictures.

To be eligible for support from British Screen, the film-maker must be British or an EC resident and the bulk of production must take place in a Commonwealth country or the Republic of Ireland. A completion bond is normally required. British Screen funds 10–12 films a year and normally puts up around 20% of the budget with a ceiling of £500,000.

The final decision on projects is entirely the responsibility of the chief executive, originally Simon Relph and currently Simon Perry. The chief executive is appointed by the UK government. The selection criteria for production support are:

- *Additionality*. Money can only be granted if the film otherwise would not be made. A 'multiplier effect' of private investment should be generated.

- *Cultural merit*. 'British Screen will consider material from any genre or any style although it is unlikely to invest in pure exploitation where there is no *redeeming* creative content.'

- *Britishness*. The film should explore and reflect British cultural themes and have cultural origins which link back to Britain. New British talent should also be developed.

- *Commerciality*. The projects chosen should be those with strong enough commercial potential to have a good chance of repayment.

This remit obliges British Screen to concentrate on niche films, but to do so in a way that is commercially viable. Conditional loans are provided on a 'last-in, first-out' basis, which means that they will be granted only when all other funds are secured, and then have priority in recoupment. The rate of repayment is 50%, which is the highest of all European subsidy schemes.

British Screen also runs a short film programme with Channel 4, 'Short and Curlies', designed to nurture new film-making talent.

The European Co-Production Fund

This was established in 1991 and is also run by the chief executive of British Screen. The ECF is designed to encourage co-production between Britain and other EU member states.

The scheme has a much tighter commercial remit than British Screen, and the same film may be supported by both schemes. According to Simon Perry, 'The ECF was deliberately devised so that if you tick the right boxes, you get the money. As long as the project is a bona-fide co-production, has the requisite number of pre-sales and gives the ECF a decent chance of recouping, then the applicant stands a strong chance of success.'[3]

To be eligible, a film must be likely to achieve commercial success, be capable of international distribution, and involve co-producers from at least two EU member states. The total contribution from direct public subsidies in the project supported cannot exceed 30%.

The ECF has helped considerably to boost the share of British film finance sourced from the continent – from 2% in 1987 to 40% in 1993, which has helped 'harmonize' British films with their European counterparts.

This trend may now be dampened as a result of a government decision at the end of 1995 for the UK to withdraw from Eurimages (the UK joined in 1993).

The Arts Council

The Arts Council is part of the state infrastructure for influencing artistic expression within Britain. Traditionally the Arts Council provided a limited amount of production funding both nationally and through Regional Art Boards for avant-garde and innovative film and video. The government decided that this made it the perfect vehicle to revitalize the UK film industry.

In 1994 the government launched a state gambling scheme known as the UK Lottery which generates $7 billion profits a year, 25% of which is used to help certain charities and 'the arts' (especially the Royal Opera House).

Over $23 million a year has been committed to film production and a further $3 million a year for film distribution. As in the rest of Europe, projects are decided by a committee of 'cultural worthies'.

The main film representative is Sir David Puttnam; the other committee members include a jazz singer, an architect and a museum curator. Other advice boards include the BFI, and members of the regional arts councils. Simon Perry of British Screen warned, 'They're releasing pure heroin on the streets rather than the diluted methadone that everyone's used to. So they had best be sure they get it right.'[4]

Projects must have at least 50% of their funding in place, and the Arts Council aims to invest in around twenty films a year (providing 10–15% of the budget).

Projects are evaluated on the following criteria:

- Quality of artistic activity
- Benefit to the public (the project must 'promote the public good')
- Quality of design and construction (commercial viability)
- Regional relevance
- Partnership funding (with BFI, British Screen, BBC or C4)

The first disbursements emphasized 'quality' and 'heritage' films, with adaptations of Thomas Hardy, William Golding and Shakespeare. One member of the selection board called the selection criteria 'a horribly fudgy mixture' and a senior adviser to the Arts Council warned that 'the whole thing is evolving into a classic British shambles of the highest order'.

Jeremy Thomas, chairman of the BFI, commented, 'It is difficult to see precisely what this first policy statement since 1984 is going to achieve in real terms. I suspect that if the British car industry and UK defence manufacturers were told that their future depended on applying to the Arts Council for a share of the National Lottery, and on the establishment of a committee to examine their financing needs, they would be rather concerned.'[5]

In response to these criticisms the Arts Council commissioned a report from media consultancy Spectrum, which suggested that alongside the selective grants, there should be the creation of 'mini-studio' investment funds. A separate report was provided to the government by an advisory committee chaired by Peter Middleton, which also concluded in favour of a UK-studio structure.

Arts Council film funding is expected to rise to $45 million a year and up to half of this will be granted to mini-studios, linked to media groups with distribution capabilities. This is comparable to the French Sofica system where media groups guarantee private investment with the state offering a 50% tax break. The new investment funds will be confirmed at the end of 1996.

Britain's leading producers all announced they were interested in a share of the pie, and Rank and the ITV companies relaunched their film activities in order to be eligible. The crucial question remains as to who decides which companies are to receive the 'freebie', and on what criteria.

Scottish Funds

The two main Scottish funds are the Scottish Film Council (SFC) and the Scottish Film Production Fund (SCPF). Both have limited resources and receive grants from the Arts Council. The SCPF also receives money from the BBC and Channel 4.

The SFC co-ordinates film activities in Scotland and provides very small production grants as well as a First Reels scheme designed to nurture local talent.

The SFPF runs a production scheme and also administers the Glasgow Film Fund (GFF) with additional funding from the European Regional Development Fund, the Glasgow Development Agency, the Glasgow City Council and Strathclyde Regional Council.

Both schemes aim to support one or two films a year with an investment up to £150,000 or 20% of the film's budget. The SFPF also has a short film scheme with BBC Scotland aimed to nurture local talent.

Foundations

Foundations concentrate on nurturing new talent and providing development assistance and contact with producers.

Children's Film and Television Foundation provides development funding of between £16,000 and £20,000 to help develop feature films designed for children between the ages of five and twelve.

First Film Foundation helps new directors and has been one of the most dynamic schemes in recent years. It is funded by industry sponsors and has strong links with the industry. The FFF has also pioneered low-budget short films in order to prove the talent of the directors they are supporting, and has arranged trips to Hollywood in order to gain American interest.

ITALIAN SUBSIDIES

The Italian subsidy system has been revolutionized in recent years, as the country has been rocked by political and corruption scandals. The key elements of the Italian system were established under Mussolini, and then modified in the post-war era. The state has a number of key holdings in the film industry controlled by the state holding company 'Ente Autonomo di Gestione per il Cinema'. These include Cinecitta (soon to be privatized) and Istituto Luce.

Italian subsidies were traditionally administered by a series of committees within the Ministry of Tourism and Entertainment. The Ministry decided which films should receive status as 'official' Italian films and on that basis which should be eligible for a maze of funding sources, including the following:

- Automatic 'detaxation' subsidies equal to 13% of box office
- Cheap loans from the state bank, BNL
- 'Article 28' loans designed for first films and films with 'cultural merit'
- Quality prizes for films with special 'cultural merit'

In practice, subsidies – like everything else in Italy – tended to be allocated to those producers with good political connections.

The whole Italian subsidy system ground to a halt in 1992 as the Tangentopolis scandal broke. The Article 28 selection board failed to meet for over a year, and film budgets had to be cut by 25%.

In 1993 the Italian public voted by a huge 81.6% to dissolve the Ministry of Tourism and Entertainment which had been providing over $650 million in cultural subsidies, spread over opera (47%), cinema (8%), theatre (16%) and music (14%). The Ministry was notorious for its bureaucracy, corruption and political connections.

In February 1994 a new film subsidy scheme, known as Article 8, was announced using the same funds as before, administered by the same state bank, BNL, and with an even greater focus on films with 'cultural interest'. State loans could cover up to 70% of the budget, and 90% if above-the-line talent deferred 30% of their fees.

The Italian administrators vowed that the new fund would be untainted by corruption. The new regulations also aimed to produce fewer films with higher budgets and a greater opportunity to find a wider market. But in April 1994 the activities of the new board were suspended under a general corruption probe of film funding. This focused on the activities of the previous Article 28 funds which had backed projects such as the sex comedy *Bad Girls*, directed by the wife of then minister Carlo Ripa di Meana. Accusations against the fund included failure to submit projects to the required assessment process, financing in excess of legal limit, and misjudgement of commercial potential. Overall repayment rates were believed to be under 5%.

By 1995 Italian production had slumped to 75 titles – the first time since 1950 that fewer than a hundred films were produced – and a corruption probe ordered $66 million in subsidies to be repaid.

The new 'Olive Tree' coalition elected in 1996 has been warmly greeted by the Italian film community. It promises to create a new Ministry of Culture and to improve the fair policing of the system including new anti-trust measures, a crackdown on video piracy and a fairer system of allocating exhibition licences.

The deputy prime minister, Walter Veltroni, has affirmed his commitment to the film industry and has helped create a French-Italian Cinema Association, which aims to stimulate co-production and official co-operation between France and Italy.

SPANISH SUBSIDIES

Spain has been heavily marked by forty years of Fascism under which the state had the right to control all areas of cultural expression. In 1975 General Franco approved Spain's transition to a democracy, but the tradition of cultural intervention was maintained by the 1978 Spanish Constitution which specified that the state had the 'obligation to promote and protect access to culture'.

The national film centre is the Institute of Cinematography and Audio-visual Arts (ICAA), which is a division of the Ministry of Culture. Spain also has important regional state aids, the largest of which is Catalonia, administered by the Generalitat.

The basic funding schemes were designed under Franco in the 1960s and, as in the rest of Europe, are based on two principal measures – automatic and selective.

For many years the most important of the two systems were selective cultural subsidies, but as a result of a government decision in October 1994 there has been a progressive switch towards automatic subsidies, confirmed by the new centre-right government elected in 1996.

Once a film has been accepted as an 'official' Spanish film, then producers must decide whether to seek subsidies before or after production. If they wait, they receive a higher level of automatic subsidy.

Automatic subsidies are provided as 15% of the box office, and if the film grosses over $385,000 it will receive an additional amount equal to a third of its budget. The total sum paid out cannot exceed $850,000.

There are also a series of 'exceptional' selective funds including an extra subsidy of up to $1.7 million for very high-budget films, and up to ten additional grants of $0.25 million for projects of special cultural merit.

Selective subsidies have traditionally been granted to films with 'cultural merit', but since 1993 the Ministry of Culture has tried to back more 'commercial' films, matching selective funds to outside private investment and trying to encourage automatic over selective subsidies. Only first-time and second-time film-makers may now apply for advance subsidy funding.

The ICAA also provides development funding, distribution and exhibition aids and funding for film education and festivals.

SCANDINAVIAN SUBSIDIES

The five Scandinavian countries – Denmark, Sweden, Norway, Finland and Iceland – each have their own film institute which operates as a national cinema centre. The head of each institute is appointed by the respective national government.

The bulk of production subsidies are allocated with the aid of consultants who assess the cultural merit of projects. All selective subsidies are provided as conditional loans.

There are also automatic systems in Denmark and Sweden. In Denmark this operates as a 50/50 model, with subsidies available up to $0.6 million as long as these are matched by private investment. In Sweden there is a 'performance subsidy' based on the number of tickets sold.

In addition to the national schemes there is also the Nordic Film and TV Foundation which was established in 1990 by the state TV networks and state film institutes of the five countries. The Foundation provides support for co-productions involving at least two Scandinavian countries.

STATE FILM PRIZES

Amongst the first measures introduced by totalitarian regimes in order to control the cultural agenda were state 'quality awards'. These are the flip side of censorship. Just as censorship indicates what the state does not want to be produced, prizes demonstrate the type of films they would like to produce.

Official state prizes and state funding for film festivals also establish an essential link with the film critics. In Europe the practice of film criticism is far more 'politicized' than in America. The tradition of European journalism is that everything should follow a specific political line. Each newspaper is identified with a clear political standpoint and all editorial comment within the newspaper follows this 'leader'. As a result, film criticism is less to do with 'appreciation' of the film and much more about delivering a political verdict.

The official 'critics' in Europe are selected on political grounds, and form part of the 'cultural establishment'. State control over the cinema further enhances the power of the critics. The state decides which critics should preside over subsidy selection boards and the judging panels of the leading film festivals and state film prizes.

Official state film prizes are awarded in Germany, Italy and Spain. In addition, all film festivals are state sponsored and the state is involved in the selection of the festival organizers, the juries and also the process by which national films are submitted for official selection.

AUTHOR RIGHTS

The legal system in most European countries is based on the Napoleonic code. This means that most of the continent operates under 'author rights' rather than 'copyright'. The main difference between the two systems is that 'author rights' locates ownership of intellectual property with a physical person, whereas under copyright, ownership can be held by a company.

Over time, author rights have been supplemented by 'inalienable moral rights', which allow the author to veto commercial exploitation of his work. This has led to the belief that the continental system protects the individual whereas copyright protects capitalist corporations. According to Jean-Claude Carrière:

> The Anglo-Saxon tradition . . . allowed publishers and printers to buy a work from an author and do what they wanted with it . . . A contrary tradition, born in late eighteenth-century France with Beaumarchais holds that the author of the work remains its owner, with financial and moral rights to the work . . . This fundamental contradiction between the two traditions explains why American film, never considered an art, has for so long been the work of producers. In Europe, on the other hand (and particularly in France) the idea that film is a form of artistic expression (and even an art in its own right) has taken root and matured.[6]

The alleged contrast between the two legal systems is highly misleading. In both systems the film-maker has the right to negotiate 'final cut' and also control of commercial exploitation. Furthermore, the cinema is officially recognized in the US as an 'art form' by a 1952 Supreme Court ruling, which means that the state cannot interfere in film content. In Europe there is no equivalent protection.

The real differences between the two legal systems is far more subtle. For example, although an author theoretically has the right to veto the use of his or her work, in practice if they did so they would soon find it difficult to carry on working.

Furthermore, during the immediate post-war period several European countries, including Italy, Austria and Holland, considered the effective 'author' of a film to be the producer. Moral rights for film were first introduced in France in 1928, despite fierce opposition from producers. Modifications were introduced in 1957 and 1985 which further undermined the position of the producer. Moral rights did not exist in any EU country (except Portugal) in the immediate post-war years. Germany adopted the French system in 1955, and via the European Community the system has slowly been extended to the rest of Europe. In Britain copyright legislation continues to be in force, but attempts to harmonize European legislation may force Britain to adopt the author rights system. This would require a massive legal overhaul and a complete reassessment of royalty payments and ownership structures of the UK's film libraries.

This shift in the legal systems parallels the state's emphasis on the director as the sole author. Previously, even in France, authorship was split between the 'creative authors' – director, screenwriter, dialogue writer, music composer – and the 'technical authors' – the crew. The overriding emphasis on the director undermines the role of the producer and creates two extremes within the film industry – the centralized state and the atomized community of authors.

The state decides which films should be made and provides the funding for their production and distribution. As such, the film-maker is wholly dependent on the state, which is no greater a freedom than being dependent on a capitalist corporation.

STATE CREDIT BANK

The film industry is highly dependent on the credit system because of the high one-off cost in expectation of future revenues. This has made the industry particularly dependent on intelligent management by financial institutions.

In most continental countries, it is the state which provides the bulk of production financing and also cash-flows production. Producers are obliged to use the low-interest state system, because other banks are reluctant to provide loans and if they do so, it is at very high interest rates.

The state credit system implicitly includes a completion bond. If the film goes over budget, the state credit bank often ensures completion. As a consequence the independent completion bond business is virtually non-existent on the continent.

State credit is also very 'supply' granted in expectation of future revenues. In certain countries such as Italy, the credit itself thereby becomes a subsidy, with only a fraction of loans being repaid – the rest being met by the state.

France

The most sophisticated state credit system is in France and is co-ordinated by IFCIC, which cash-flows many areas of cultural expression. The French credit system was established in 1941 under Nazi Occupation with guarantees provided by the state bank, Credit National.

The importance of the Credit National declined during the 1950s and was replaced by a new state guarantee system – Pool Exportation and Pool Production backed by state banks BNP, Credit Lyonnais and BFCE and overseen by the CNC.

These funds were administered by a series of specialist financing institutions created by the state – UFIC, SOFET, SOFIDI – which later merged with SOCODEC and SODETE to form a single entity Sodete/UFCA, which had a near monopoly of film finance by the early 1980s.

This monopoly was eroded during the 1980s by two other specialist companies: Coficine (formed by Rouvre in 1947) and Cofiloisirs (formed by UGC in 1972).

In 1983 Pool Production and Pool Exportation were unified under a wider state credit system for all areas of culture, known as IFCIC, run by George Prost, former president of UFCA.

IFCIC is a private limited company, 20% held directly by the state, 20% by the state-owned Credit National, 20% by the state-owned CEPME and 40% by thirteen private banking institutions.

The state provides a fund of $20 million which is then used by IFCIC to guarantee over $100 million in loans provided by specialist financiers. The three financing institutions – Sodete/UFCA, Coficine and Cofiloisirs – provide 90% of loans, the rest provided by commercial banks.

As for independent discount financing, the producer must present a dossier to the specialist financier – with the budget, financial plan and expected sales. But because French cinema is a 'village', not all pre-sales have to be cut and dried on paper. Often only a simple phone call will be needed to confirm whether a film will be sold or not. There is a much greater reliance on trust.

The specialist financier will assess the risk involved and decide what proportion of the loan to cover himself, and what proportion is to be covered by the

IFCIC guarantee (between 30% and 75%). IFCIC will analyse the dossier and keep close tabs on what is happening in the industry. According to Hugues de Chastellux at IFCIC, 'French cinema is a small world, and you have to know everything about what's going on, even to the extent of who's sleeping with who.'

If a loan is granted, IFCIC will charge a 0.8% fee, and the specialist financier will charge a small fee and interest at between 3% and 3.5% over the market rate. The system is very effective. The state loses $2–4 million a year but guarantees over $100 million in loans.

IFCIC also provides guarantees for medium-term loans made to production companies on the basis of their film libraries and has a 20% stake in venture capital fund, Capital Images, which makes strategic investments in the cultural sector.

IFCIC also runs the Soficas – Investimage and Sofi-arp – and has a stake in the new completion bond firm Film Garantie Finance (linked to Film Finances in London).

Germany

The subsidy systems in Germany are usually co-ordinated through regional Kredietbank institutions. Producers must provide a detailed financing plan as part of their subsidy allocation and the subsidy loans are provided in tranches during the production.

United Kingdom

The UK traditionally had a film bank in the form of the NFFC, but its role diminished over the 1970s and was finally dissolved in 1985. This leaves a significant 'gap' for UK producers, especially for low-budget films.

For higher budget films financed through international pre-sales, discounted finance can be provided by specialist institutions such as FILMS and Guinness Mahon. For smaller films, cash flow is provided by the main funding institutions – British Screen, Channel 4, the Arts Council and media groups such as PolyGram.

Italy

State subsidies are agreed before production but often only paid afterwards. The state bank, Banco Nazionale de Lavore, has a specialist film division which advances monies against promised state subsidies and other expected revenues.

BNL is able to advance up to 80% of the 'official' cost. In practice this has meant that state loans are often a disguised form of subsidy and most easily secured by those with good connections.

Spain

An agreement between the national cinema centre (ICAA) and Banco Exterior de España in 1992 provides for soft loans at low interest rates of around 6–7%. BEX thereby provides a total value of loans up to $30 million, any one loan covering up to 90% of a film's budget.

In 1995 a new $240 million bridging loan facility was established under the Instituto de Credito Oficial (ICO), designed to provide guarantees for more 'commercial projects'.

Scandinavia

The film institutes provide the bulk of production finance and also cash-flow most productions.

FILM INVESTMENT BY TELEVISION COMPANIES

The advent of television terrified many European film-makers because it would erode their audience, and also because state television was considered to be run by politically-appointed bureaucrats and therefore likely to extend state control over free expression.

Today television has become almost the *raison d'être* of the European film industry. The television channels are required by domestic quota legislation to broadcast a minimum percentage of national and European films – typically 40% and 60% for the main European countries.

These quotas oblige television to pre-buy a large number of national films, and domestic legislation often specifies minimum levels of investment by the channels.

The most important investors in film are the state television channels, who also have a very strict 'public service' remit as to the appropriate type of film they should support.

France

French television channels are obliged to invest at least 3% of their net annual turnover in French-language films. This investment may be divided between equity stakes and broadcast licence fees.

Investments must be made through a separate subsidiary which cannot be a majority co-producer. The total television investment cannot exceed 50% of the budget.

Canal+ is required to pre-buy pay-TV rights to the vast majority of French films but is not allowed to be an equity investor. The channel must invest 9% of annual revenues on French-language films and a further 3% on European films. Equity investments are allowed through the subsidiary Le Studio Canal+.

All television channels are expected to follow a 'cultural remit' and back films which are considered appropriate to France's cinematic heritage.

The two state television networks – ARD and ZDF – are obliged to invest directly in the German film industry and also provide money to the state film fund, the FFA. Investments are made in line with these channels' overall 'public service' remit.

Private TV channels in Germany – owned by Kirch and Bertelsmann/ CLT – have been far more reluctant to invest in cinema, but recently agreed to commit funds to the FFA.

With the creation of Channel 4 in 1981, there was an implicit understanding that the channel would be the new 'home' of the British film industry. Channel 4 is financed through advertising but has a strict public service remit, which makes it comparable to state television channels in other countries.

Channel 4's remit is to avoid straightforward popular genres and concentrate on films with 'artistic quality'. The channel also provides annual grants to the BFI, British Screen, the Arts Council, the SFPF and a number of independent film and video workshops.

The BBC has also had several flirtations with the film industry, and at present has a film unit headed by Mark Shivas, as well as producing other in-house feature length films which occasionally achieve theatrical release. In line with the BBC's overall public service remit, investments concentrate on 'quality' films.

The ITV companies have no state obligation to invest in feature films, but in response to the potential Arts Council mini-studio system the ITV system announced in 1996 a £100 million commitment to back 'commercial' feature films.

There are no legal obligations on free TV broadcasters to invest in feature films, but there is a broad understanding that the state broadcaster, RAI, should be a significant supporter of Italian cinema.

The privileged monopoly position that has been granted to Berlusconi's web of film and television interests also gives him a vested interest to invest in a small number of Italian films. Tele+ is also obliged to invest 10% of its revenues in film production.

There are quota obligations on Spanish television stations and also a general understanding that the state broadcaster, RTVE, should invest in Spanish films. Most Spanish films are funded through combining state subsidies and state television money. The state broadcaster and the national cinema centre consult with each other as to which films are worthy of funding.

Scandinavia

There is a general understanding that the state broadcasters should be the main 'private' investors in Scandinavian films.

FILM TAXATION

Taxation is one of the principal fiscal instruments through which the state can shape society. All film activities are subject to taxation and this is regulated in such a way as to be consistent with the overall state policy for film.

The principal objective of taxation regulation in most countries is that any tax benefits granted to film should be controlled by the national cinema centre. The most typical form of aid is 'detaxation' through automatic subsidies.

Other areas of taxation which affect film are withholding taxes on film revenues and artists' earnings, capital allowances and tax shelter schemes. The most important tax shelter schemes are the French Soficas, Ireland's Schedule 35 and the Luxembourg tax credits. These are explained in Appendix A.

STATE FILM EDUCATION

In today's multi-media world, film education is increasingly important to help the coming generations become more aware of the possibilities offered by communications media. America and Europe have chosen different paths, the former increasingly practical, the latter more and more academic.

In America, film and communications is the most popular subject after business school, and the top film schools – NYU, Columbia, UCLA and USC – are seen as an entry ticket to the industry. As CAA agent John Ptak explains:

> When I went to UCLA film school in the Sixties, my parents thought I'd gone crazy. Film schools in those days were like art schools. Now they're like business schools. In the 1980s, people began to see that you could leave film school and earn lots of money. Studying film and communications is no longer seen as irresponsible, particularly now that America is caught up in the whole media thing. Film education teaches you about cinema, television and commercials. Students often make shorts – like Tim Burton did – which they can use as calling cards. Film schools are now a key source of talent.

In Europe there is no equivalent phenomenon. Film education is almost entirely in the hands of the state and is dominated by a critical consensus which denigrates mainstream cinema and the traditional production crafts. Theoretical courses emphasize semiotics and New Left analysis. Practical courses encourage the idea that the director should do everything and pay little attention to the professions of producer, screenwriter, production designer or any of the basic skills necessary to build a popular film industry. This is the result of a shift in state policy in the 1960s.

Many national film schools were established in the 1930s and at first were tailored to producing popular films. The famous names of VGIK in Moscow, FAMU in Prague, Lódz in Poland, CSC in Rome and IDHEC in France played a vital role in developing powerful new talent.

In the 1960s the outlook of these schools, along with the whole apparatus of state film education, was transformed by the 'new orthodoxy' and film education moved from being a business school to an art education with a peripheral role in society.

Things are now slowly changing in the 1990s as the state recognizes the need to develop a more commercially successful industry, but for the moment there is still a terrifying lack of momentum in state film education.

EUROPEAN SYSTEMS

The European Community began as a free trade area, the fruit of the Marshall Plan and crystallized by the 1956 Treaty of Rome. Europe had recently emerged from an attempt by Germany to establish a super-state over Europe which would control all areas of personal expression. The Treaty of Rome made it very clear that the state should act as a guardian of free competition and not be involved in cultural censorship.

The free trade outlook of the immediate post-war period gradually transformed into the idea that 'Europe is a cultural entity or nothing', which now means that the pre-eminent role of the state is to control cultural expression.

The Europe of Maastricht is very different from that of Rome. A corporatist 'union' rather than a federalist 'community' now increasingly revolves around a common cultural, industrial, defence and agricultural policy and in the near future a single currency.

Europe has been built upon the 'marriage' between France and Germany who together produce 50% of Europe's gross domestic product. This marriage took two centuries to cement and was fundamentally influenced by the Franco-German military conflicts initiated by Napoleon, Bismarck and Hitler.

Many people have commented that the heart of the new Europe is a revival of the empire of Charlemagne – France, Northern Italy and Germany – and forged around the same Germanic tribes – the Franks, the Lombards and the Alemanni.

Germany is the heart of the new Europe, as political scientist Werner Weidenfeld explained in 1990: 'We have always said German and European unification were two sides of the same coin. We now have the opportunity of confirming the correctness of this position . . . "Integration" thus becomes the key concept of the new epoch in Germany, as in Europe.'

The old empire of Charlemagne broke down with the Reformation and Renaissance which led to the emergence of new nation-states. But the techniques of these nation-states – above all the hallowed role of 'culture' – is now being transposed to the new Europe.

The Union nonetheless continues to have a fundamental problem, in that the majority of its citizens have no enthusiasm whatsoever for its creation. Most people see the Union as a bureaucratic entity which imposes absurd laws and has in general undermined the cultural and social traditions of the individual nation-states.

Perhaps the worst example of EU absurdity is the Common Agricultural Policy, which has industrialized European agriculture and is blamed by some for the destruction of many European rural communities as well as introducing techniques which have led to breakdowns in the food chain such as salmonella and 'mad cows' disease.

It is true that the Union has unfairly become the 'scapegoat' upon which all evils can be blamed. But it is also true that Brussels is a 'control-freak' bureaucratic nightmare, which it is very difficult to admire.

The British have been the most outspoken critics of the new Europe, with some people even claiming that it represents a 'Fourth Reich'. These criticisms are motivated above all by a recognition that Britain spent two centuries trying to 'divide and rule' the continent and now stands outside the key power centres. Britain still claims that she is 'different' from the rest of Europe, but in fact, despite her lower taxation burden, she has in recent years 'harmonized' her cultural control mechanisms with the rest of Europe.

There is now a surprising harmony and 'monotony' amongst Europe's nation-states. Billions of dollars of taxpayers' money are poured into 'culture' every year, but the general recognition is that European culture is dormant, if not dead.

Europe is united under a flag of golden stars, but there are no real stars in her firmament. Instead of film stars there are super-models. Instead of a film industry there is advertising and television-driven mass media. Europe risks becoming what German director Bo Syberberg described as 'a society without joy'. State control over free expression has been a key factor in bringing the continent to this stage.

THE MEDIA PROGRAMME

The MEDIA programme was launched as a pilot phase in 1987 and then as the fully fledged Media 1 from 1990–95 with a budget of $225 million over five years. A new $400 million Media 2 began in 1996 to extend to the new millennium.

'Mamma Media' is co-ordinated within DG X of the Union, which is responsible for 'Information, Communication and Culture' and is overseen by the EU's Ministers of Culture.

The programme is managed by a Media Unit, but real power lies with the Media Committee which includes political representatives from the member states and keeps constant tabs on the projects. The Committee is a minefield of political lobbying. One source at the European Commission said that 'The real problems of collaboration . . . stem from inter-country rivalries, which manifest themselves within the powerful Media Committee. The worst offenders are the French, Germans and Italians.'[7]

The Commission technically does not have the right to interfere in the cultural agenda of the Union, so the MEDIA programme is justified as an economic and structural initiative which will lead to a rebirth of the European film and television industries. It is also the justification for the 1989 Télévision sans Frontières Directive which requires European television channels to move towards more than 50% of European programming.

Media 1 was divided into three priority areas: training, development and distribution, with equal concern for film and television. The programme began as seven 'projects', but in true bureaucratic tradition subdivided over time into smaller and smaller units with little co-ordination between them. By 1995, there were nineteen projects and over twice as many mini-projects.

The programme was officially appraised in 1993 by German auditing firm Roland Berger, which described most projects as 'excellent' or 'very good'. A further progress report was published by the Commission in 1996, fronted by a picture of a hot-air balloon heading for mist-enshrouded cliffs. Commissioner for DG X, Marcelino Oreja, announced that Media 1 has 'undeniably played a non-negligible role' and the report concluded that results have been 'encouraging'.

Outside MEDIA's hallowed walls, many point out that the first eight years of the programme have actually failed miserably in the target goal of improving the commercial performance of the European film industry. Admissions for European films have continued to slide, and the rare examples of local blockbusters that have occurred in recent years have been produced outside MEDIA's orbit.

Critics of the programme include those who have been intimately involved with its development. Rudi Barnet, the founder of Euro-Aim, said in 1994, 'It is time to admit that MEDIA 95 has had far more failures, generally hidden, than successes, and that the state of national production in the various countries of Europe, is just as critical now as it was in 1988 – if not worse . . . For the past two years, Media 95 has run exorbitant advertising campaigns obviously designed more to impress the authorities than to develop efficacious action.'[8]

Pascal Volle, who drew up the original draft document that led to the creation of the Script Fund, added, 'MEDIA has become like any public institution –

its only goal is to re-create itself from one year to the next. It's got to the stage where it carries such weight and is filled with such inertia that nobody there in a position of real power is able to look at it objectively.'9 The UK talent agent Julian Friedmann, who set up the Pilots, commented in 1995 that 'MEDIA has given the European film industry a massive blood transfusion. The problem is that they've put back the old blood.'10

At the end of 1994, French budget minister Nicolas Sarkozy made a severe attack on MEDIA's performance, saying 'sometimes in trying to do too much you end up doing nothing'. This criticism led directly to the re-drafting of Media 2 around fewer action lines.

The programme has become increasingly bureaucratic. A media consultant suggested that an analogy might be drawn from William Burroughs' *Naked Lunch* where he writes: 'Democracy is cancerous and bureaus are its cancer. A bureau takes root anywhere in the state, turns malignant like the Narcotics Bureau, and grows and grows, always reproducing more of its own kind, until it chokes the host.'

It is perhaps unfair to describe MEDIA as a 'virus' but it is true that it is establishing increasing dominance over European cinema. Many people interviewed for this book commented about 'a whiff of amateurism and corruption' in the selection procedures and were irritated by the endless conferences with MEDIA 'experts' talking about how to save European cinema.

The Commission also recognizes that there have been tremendous inefficiencies within the organization of the programme and this has been one of the main reasons for it being restructured. One member of the MEDIA Unit claimed that administrative expenses were eating up close to a third of the funds, through high salaries, expensive media junkets and meetings booked into luxurious surroundings.11

According to Pascal Volle, 'it is scandalously badly run in private management terms . . . probably as much as 50% of what has gone into it could have been used in a far more effective way'. At the same time Volle places MEDIA within the overall EU context: 'If you look at the EC's farming subsidies, oil refinery subsidies, mining subsidies, in fact anything distributed by the EC, the MEDIA Programme is one of the best-run shows around.'12

STRATEGY

The official line of the MEDIA programme is that it is a ladder intended to be kicked away. The seed money provided by the programme is hoped to result in a flourishing commercial industry which will no longer need Union aid.

A more accurate picture of the MEDIA programme is that it is a co-ordinating structure designed to link together the cultural control mechanisms of the member states. The first head of the programme, Holde Lhoest, confirmed this in a conference in 1991 where she said 'We are the first European Major.'13

Amongst the key personnel of the MEDIA projects there is virtually no one with a track record in making popular films, and key figures such as EFDO president Dieter Koslick, have carved their reputations as supporters of low-budget niche films.

The MEDIA programme has provided a lifeline to some smaller European films, but its contribution towards building a popular European film industry is almost zero. This is inevitable given the structure of the vast majority of the projects, which are deliberately designed to help low-budget 'cultural films'.

The creation of the MEDIA programme led to a series of studies culminating in the 1994 Green Paper which made the obvious point that the only way Europe can have a stronger film industry is if she has strong film publishers or 'European Majors'. But the creation of powerful independent film publishers would undermine the ability of national states and the European super-state to control cultural expression.

Since the Commission needs the Council of Culture Ministers to endorse any new initiative, the MEDIA programme is effectively hamstrung unless there is a concerted political consensus in favour of developing a popular film industry.

A leading official at the DG X think-tank explained to me that the only way a stronger film industry can be built is through positive action by the larger member states. Without that, the Commission is restricted to its general remit which is to help smaller regions and small and medium sized enterprises. The official admitted that the present structures are unlikely to make any significant change in the situation of the European film industry, but that this will not change unless there is a change in strategy at the national level.

Since the member states are committed to state control of the national film industry, it is inevitable that the MEDIA programme becomes a co-ordinating structure linking together these control mechanisms. Instead of a series of commercially competing major companies as in America, over time there will be a single entity – the European super-state.

MEDIA 2

The new Media 2 promised to be simpler and more effective than the old Media 1, but by the end of 1996 many European film-makers were still confused at how the new structures are supposed to operate.

In place of the relatively user-friendly application forms, there are now bureaucratic tender documents and more stringent eligibility conditions, which have significantly reduced the number of applications. In the first six months of Media 2, all applicants were advised to send their documentation to Jacques Delmoly at the European Commission. As a result, the Commission was deluged by funding applications which remained stacked in a corridor for weeks as a lone secretary sorted them into separate rooms.

Media 2 is divided into three action lines – distribution, development and training – each co-ordinated by an Intermediary Organization (IO). Almost half of the funds will be spent on distribution, a further 20% on development, and 15% on training. The final 20% of the budget will be spent on administrative costs and public relations (to be co-ordinated by a separate IO).

The new action lines are claimed to be 'totally distinct' from the projects of Media 1, but despite important differences in the funding objectives, there is a high level of continuity in personnel. It is thus important to review the performance of Media 1, in order to understand how the new programme is likely to operate.

Media Distribution is headed by John Dick in Brussels, who previously ran EVE. The objectives of the initiative encompass the activities of the former EFDO, EVE and Greco, but with three times the funding and important changes in emphasis.

Media Development is run by David Kavanagh and Christian Routh in London, who were previously in charge of the European Script Fund.

Media Training is run by Fernando Labrada in Madrid, former chief of the Media Business School.

There are also three 'industrial platforms' which are a continuation of the old programmes – MAP-TV, Cartoon and Multi-Media Investments. The main projects to have disappeared are Sources, Scale and Documentary.

The rough breakdown of the old Media 1 budget per project was as follows:

Distribution

EFDO	Film distribution	20%
EVE	Video distribution	5%
Babel	Dubbing/subtitling	5%
Cartoon	Animation	12%
MAP/Lumière	Archives, secondary market	5%

Development

Script	Development	12%
Scale	Small countries	7.5%
Investment Club	New technologies	10%
EMG...	Stimulate investment	4%

Training/Management

MBS	Training	4%
EAVE	Training of young producers	3%
Euro-Aim	Independent producers	12.5%

Most projects received their principal funding from the Commission, but had co-ventures with local public authorities to cover some of the administrative costs.

Media Training is run by Fernando Labrada in Madrid, who formerly ran the Media Business School. Many of the old mini-projects such as Pilots and EAVE continue to exist and have received funding from Media Training. Other initiatives such as the Media Business School also exist and are expected to apply for further funding.

In addition to existing mini-projects, Media Training aims to encourage groupings of media education institutions across Europe. The main focus of the latter initiative will be training in media management, new technologies and script-writing.

The overall direction of the training initiatives will draw upon the lines previously established by the Media Business School and EAVE.

The experience of the Media Business School

The MBS was the 'think-tank' for training and strategy within Media 1, and was the only part of the programme which went outside the general orbit of low-budget 'cultural films'.

The 'school' covered both training and development, and organized publications into the structural problems of the industry, seminars, Master Classes and mini-projects such as the Film Business School, ACE (European Film Studio), Television Business School and Pilots, most of which will continue to operate.

The MBS was based in Madrid but was heavily Anglo-orientated with research studies commissioned from *Screen Digest* and the media consultancy London Economics, and most mini-projects were run by Brits.

The research reports published by the MBS concentrated on the technocratic problems of the industry – the lack of training, distribution and marketing expertise. Some of the publications were very useful – particularly those by Neil Watson, Terry Ilott and London Economics – but there was often a lack of historical dimension, explaining how the industry arrived at its present crisis. The solutions offered seem so simple, it was difficult to understand why they have not already been adopted.

The 'blind spot' for the MBS and for the MEDIA programme overall, was that they are in fact part of the problem rather than a 'solution'. Like the view of Paris from the Eiffel tower, the only thing they could not see was themselves.

The MBS reports were based on a 'public service' remit which made it impossible for them to grapple thorny issues, and some writers who tried a more hard-hitting approach were fired. For example, when one writer tried to refer to the fact that most European producers inflate their budgets in order to secure a higher subsidy, he was censored by an MBS official saying 'everyone knows that it's a common practice amongst European producers but I hardly think we can use public money to say so'.

As a consequence, several publications offered technocratic analyses, filled with 'nuggets of detail' about financing formulae and legal rules, but missed the real issues. Certain editors of MBS documents were also hired because of their political contacts rather than any prior editorial expertise. Like European films, many documents were produced for the state, rather than for the public.

The main thrust of the MBS approach was that European talent should get on the plane for Hollywood as soon as possible. As Jonathan Olsberg, head of the FBS, explains, 'As far as I'm concerned the way that European films are financed is wrong. The way forward is English-language films financed through international pre-sales.'[14] David Puttnam, adds, 'Europe must adapt to making English-language films, just as Britain must learn to drive on the right side of the road. It's the way of the future.'[15]

The problem with this approach is that most of Europe's talent is not fluent in English and the English-language market is increasingly tied up by Hollywood talent agents and companies. In effect, the advice reflects the fact that there is no European film industry, and is no different from the trend of the last twenty years – a talent drain to Hollywood.

The MBS pinned its hopes on the emergence of European Majors. Colin Young at ACE comments, 'Most European producers are used to satisfying subsidy committees, but the real judge should be the public. There are countless examples of films and television series approved by committees which have flopped miserably. We are trying to develop more commercial antennae, but we are permanently frustrated because the national funding systems don't think that way.'[16]

In the absence of a commercial system the MBS tried to deify the 'creative producer' in order to try to replicate success stories such as David Puttnam. But in order to build such producers the main emphasis was technocratic rather than creative.

The European film studio, ACE, has been building up a database of budgets, sales revenues, marketing costs and box office results. They then intend to 'bombard producers with questions about the precise shape of those markets, how they break down, their different revenue recoupment figures, the range of marketing strategies, and ways of reaching windows on a medium-by-medium basis'.[17]

ACE even hints that such technocratic techniques can be used to judge whether a film will be popular or not: 'Detailed case studies will examine the release strategy for selected films in Europe, and a map of the European film economy will be drawn up, against which ACE will evaluate the commercial and cultural prospects of the producers' projects.'[18]

The MEDIA programme seems to believe that the strength of Hollywood is its statistical databases and market research, when in fact these are only really relevant at the distribution stage, not in commissioning or production.

Jonathan Olsberg suggests that 'In this age of computer assisted solutions, the science of market research has become widely accepted as an invaluable tool, particularly in consumer led businesses . . . Through research our industry can learn how to encourage consumers to attend the cinema more often, as well as to learn how films will succeed or fail. This is not a backward looking science, but a predictive one. By "asking the audience" we can improve our competitive position on a macro-economic and a micro-economic scale.'[19]

The problem with this approach is that it is likely to breed an elite of technocrats who understand the quantum physics of film finance but have been removed from the creative lifeblood of cinema.

Many ACE and FBS participants have criticized the number-crunching approach. For example, Katrina Bayonas, the Spanish producer of *Tango Feroz* and a veteran talent manager in Madrid, says that the FBS showed her that she should shift gears and move to directing: 'I went in paddling and I came out swimming', she commented, 'although in a different direction.'[20]

Hollywood producers are not required to amass such detailed technocratic knowledge. That is left to the studios, who offer 'one-stop shopping'.

In the absence of a vibrant creative and commercial industry within Europe, the emphasis on 'creative producers' has little meaning, because the real void in Europe is not good producers but good commissioning editors.

However, some welcome initiatives such as ACE because they do at least help producers feel that they are not alone. Colin Vaines likens MEDIA producer meetings, like the Script fund gathering at Sitges, to sessions of Alcoholics Anonymous – 'Hi, I'm Colin, I'm a producer.' But Vaines believes that these junkets are valuable because they help people see that there are other people out there. He particularly praises the sense of motivation provided by ACE.

The main problem with MEDIA's development initiatives has been a lack of co-ordination. For example, projects that have received glowing reports at the FBS have failed even to get a first interview at Script, and projects short-listed and then rejected by Script, have later re-emerged in a similar form but with a different producer at the FBS.

MEDIA claims to provide a professional disciplined structure capable of competing with Hollywood but far too often seems to collapse into bureaucratic amateurism.

MEDIA DEVELOPMENT

Media Development builds on the experience of the European Script Fund with two main initiatives – project funding and company support. There is now a far greater emphasis on production potential and incentives for groupings of production companies across Europe.

Project funding provides a loan of up to 35,000 ECU ($44,000) per project, with a maximum of 100,000 ECU per company. There is strong emphasis on projects with proof of co-production partners, and which are aimed at a young audience.

Company support provides a loan of between 50,000 and 150,000 ECU to cover up to 50% of management and development costs. Applicants must be the lead partner in at least two international co-productions.

The core personnel of Media Development is drawn from the European Script Fund, and many of the old structures apply.

The experience of the European Script Fund

The Roland Berger audit ranked Script as one of the strongest projects and Script itself boasted in 1993 that 'the indications are that 25% of the funded projects which are developed and delivered to Script will go into production. A statistic that is more than double the Hollywood major studio's average.'

Despite this 'statistic', out of over 800 projects funded to date as single projects, fewer than 80 (1 in 10) have gone into production, and of these only 20 (1 in 40) have achieved any significant critical or commercial acclaim. The best-known titles are *Rob Roy*, *Toto le Héros*, *Breaking the Waves*, *Accion Mutante*, *The Cement Garden*, *Backbeat*, *Daens*, *Farinelli*, *The Flemish Board*, *Je m'appelle Victor*, *Jeanne la Pucelle*, *The Englishman who went up a hill . . .* , *The Long Day Closes*, *Naked*, *Orlando*, and *Young Americans*. There are of course other films in the pipeline.

Single Projects

Single Project funding was for individual screenwriters (up to $6,000) and teams involving a producer (up to $43,000 and an average of $30,000). Selected projects were given back-up support and could apply for second-stage funding.

Development loans were subject to 5% interest and were expected to be repaid on the first day of principal photography. In certain instances where Script really believed in a project, such as *Orlando*, repayment was deferred.

The selection procedure involved an initial summary of story and structure by a freelance reader. These summaries were then shown to a script editor who drew up a short-list. The short-list was then shown to national advisers who gave an indication of whether the project was likely to be considered to be 'worthy' of support by the national funding mechanisms. Bo Christensen, former head of Script, emphasized that this was very important, especially for new producers.

A final short-list was then drawn up and interviews were arranged with the head of funding recommendations, Christian Routh. The national advisers met and discussed the final allocations, with the ultimate decision resting with Christian Routh. The key criteria were the story, the 'European potential' and above all the likelihood of national funding.

Support from national cinema centres usually reflected the 'cultural merit' of projects. As Antonio Saura, the Spanish representative commented, 'We can't take risks, we have to be seen to be out there winning prizes at festivals like Cannes.' Another senior Script employee confirmed 'The MEDIA programme is all about winning prizes in festivals.'

The cultural remit meant that more ambitious 'mainstream' projects found it very difficult to receive funding. Christian Routh explained that 'although we are generally focused on smaller projects we will occasionally a consider a more ambitious film but we need much more stringent requirements, e.g. a name Hollywood director'.

It was also a disadvantage for ambitious projects to be submitted from countries outside Britain, France or Germany because the 'economic climate' in the rest of Europe was considered too difficult for anything other than small niche films to be produced.

Sean Dromgoole, head of Incentive Funding, suggested that 'production finance in Europe is painfully director led and looking for safe bets. That's what we have to go for. The best strategy for a newcomer is to pick a two-hander with a beautiful story, like the Italian/Australian film *Epsilon*. Two characters in a single location are much easier for new talent to get financed and thus is more likely to get our support.'

This pragmatic emphasis on 'sure values' and small films was perhaps inevitable, but according to Bettina Kozlowski who made a detailed study of Script in 1992, it resulted in 'mediocrity, safe genre values, and few new ideas'. Dimitri Balakoff of the European Academy for Film and TV agrees: '[Script] has become, in my eyes, a genuine trap for creators, yet another hell paved with the best intentions. Seduced by the siren song of juries whose erudite members support one another in mutual gratification, the author ends up forgetting the basics: to move the man in the street, to make him laugh or to enchant him.'[21]

Script nonetheless prided itself on injecting 'fresh blood into the market-place', and it is true that if a young producer did manage to secure Script funding, it was a very useful foot in the door. Many of the next generation of European producers secured one or more loans (plus in certain cases Incentive Funding) including: Luc Roeg, Stefan Schwartz, Andreas Habermeyer, Paul Trybits, Enrique Posner, Jeremy Bolt, Marc Samuelson, Colin Vaines, Andrew Bendel, Peter Bloore, Judy Counihan, Joaquim Pinto, Emjay Rechsteiner, Saskia Sutton and Kenneth Madsen.

Incentive Funding

This scheme supported companies with a strong track record and a slate of three or more projects in development. Companies specialized either in film or television. Script paid up to 30% of development costs, with a maximum of $150,000 per company. The projects that received support were decided in association between Script and the funded company.

Occasionally Script turned down winners such as *Four Weddings and a Funeral*, but overall, Incentive Funding was considered to be the most effective part of Script.

The producers which were backed included: Alain Rocca, Sarah Radclyffe, Stephen Evans, Steve Woolley/Nik Powell, Tim Bevan, Ann Scott, Ann Skinner/Simon Relph, Jeremy Thomas, Linda James, Per Holst, Simone Harari, Wim Wenders, Gerardo Herrero, Andres Vicente Gomez, Antoine de Clermont Tonnere, Volker Schloendorff, Andy Paterson, Chris Sievernich, Claudie Ossard, Antonio da Cunha Telles, Guy East, Ken Loach and Regina Ziegler.

Overall

According to Bo Christensen, 'the main achievement of Script is to have made the national cinema centres aware of the importance of development. We still have a long way to go but we are on the right track.'

The Script team built up a linking network between the state control mechanisms which helped them judge the 'cultural merits' of films. Several broadcasters used Script readers' advice in order to assess projects. Media Development will aim to build upon these foundations.

MEDIA DISTRIBUTION

Distribution is the biggest concern of Media 2. The Intermediate Organization is D & S Media Service Gmbh (John Dick and Robert Strasser).

Media Distribution is divided into three main types of funding, each run from a different base and co-ordinated by Brussels: Cinema (Brussels), Video (Ireland) and TV (Munich). The annual $40 million budget breaks down as follows:

Cinema Distribution	$15 million
Cinema Exhibition	$5 million
Television	$11 million
Video	$5 million
Promotion	$4.2 million

The initiatives of greatest direct concern to film-makers are cinema distribution, exhibition and promotion.

Cinema distribution

The Cinema initiative takes the place of EFDO, and now places its main emphasis on trans-national groupings of distributors. At least three distributors from three different countries must join together in the application, with a plan to release one or more European film(s).

As with EFDO, there is a requirement that the distributors be committed to low-budget films, with at least half of the films proposed during one year with a budget below $6 million and 10% below $3.75 million. There is nonetheless considerable room for supporting bigger budget pictures, with up to half of the $15 million theatrical budget available for such pictures.

In 1997 an automatic distribution aid initiative will be introduced, which will tend to encourage the distribution of mainstream popular films.

Applications will be judged on the basis of the:

* Number of European films proposed for trans-national distribution
* Distribution and marketing strategies
* Number of distributors and extent of co-operation
* Number of distributors from small countries
* Contribution of films to Europe's cultural diversity.

A successful application will receive $125,000 per distributor for the first film distributed by all members of the grouping, $150,000 per distributor for the second film, and $162,000 per distributor for all subsequent films.

Between 15% and 30% of funds granted should be spent on promotion and all funds should be matched privately. Funds are provided as repayable loans, to be repaid after the distributor has recouped its own costs and a 15% overhead.

The cinema distribution initiative will aim to avoid some of the controversy which engulfed EFDO.

The experience of EFDO

EFDO was designed to support the distribution of low-budget films which represent 'independent movies and intelligent entertainment'. There were originally three categories of budget eligible for support – up to $0.85 million (20% of funds), $0.85–2.5 million (60%) and $2.5–5 million (20%). In 1994 the maximum budget was increased to $5.6 million.

EFDO still exists and has old Media 1 funding still to allocate. It has also received Media 2 money for EFDO Abroad. The president of EFDO is Dieter Koslick, a champion of low-budget art movies and the vice-president is Maria João Seixas, an expert for the Portuguese state TV culture channel. The EFDO association is made up of representatives of the national cinema centres and niche film distributors.

Although the MEDIA programme overall is justified as a means of improving the economic performance of the European film industry, this was only a secondary objective of EFDO. The secretary-general Ute Schneider explained that 'if you look at it purely in economic terms, support is not justified. But if you see film as an expression of cultural identity, EFDO is worth it.'

EFDO generally focused on films that otherwise would not get a theatrical release, but also occasionally provided support for more 'commercial' projects such as *Four Weddings and a Funeral* and *The Snapper*.

The eligibility and funding conditions were similar to Media Development, but were decided on a film-by-film basis. EFDO also worked closely in conjunction with Eurimages in indicating 'appropriate' European films. The overall repayment rate for EFDO was 20–25%.

The modest level of P&A support and the cap on production budgets meant that EFDO played a key role in linking together niche distributors of 'cultural films'. These groupings will provide the basis of Media Distribution. But the emphasis on low-budget films made it difficult to have an impact on the wider problem of the lack of pan-European distribution structures for mainstream European films.

The low-budget emphasis of EFDO meant that the initiative felt severely challenged by the 1994 Green Paper which suggested support for commercial distribution companies. 'We were delighted that both the EU Green Paper and the Think Tank placed such an emphasis on distribution', said Dieter Koslick. 'I'm not convinced by the idea of setting up one or two supra-national European Majors, however. Smaller distribution companies would go bust . . . Europe already has a pan-European distribution network – EFDO.'[22]

Koslick was also opposed to suggestions by the CNC for an automatic system. Instead he proposed a scheme known as EFDO Plus offering loans up to $1 million to be shared between five or more distributors.

In its early years, EFDO granted loans to European films distributed by the US Majors, but in 1994 declined to grant funds to UIP to distribute *Nostradamus* in Scandinavia, despite the fact that the film's other European distributors had been given support. UIP were also turned down for *Maniaci Sentimentali*, despite a promise to release it in nine European territories. This decision was influenced by political factors, after the Commission's attack on UIP's legal status.

EFDO subsequently decided not to give loans to any distributor whose ultimate shareholders were not at least 51% European. This is despite the long history of American Majors playing a key role in distributing European films. Ricky Tognazzi, who produced and starred in *Maniaci Sentimentali* commented, 'The audiovisual directorate of the European Commission, which should be helping European films, is working against them. They are indulging in gesture politics which can damage the future chances of our industry.'[23]

Cinema promotion

In Media 1, promotion activities were co-ordinated by Euro-Aim, an initiative which suffered from considerable controversy including a court case with the Commission over 1994 funding disbursements. Under Media 2, promotion at the TV festivals MIP and MIP-COM is now co-ordinated by a company called The Marketplace, whose personnel are drawn from the former promotion team at Euro-Aim. Euro-Aim still exists and organizes an annual Rendezvous meeting designed to bring projects together with financing partners.

Cinema exhibition

The main exhibition initiative is Europa Cinemas, with Media Salles also in existence for promoting special European cinema events.

Europa Cinemas supports a series of 'flagship theatres' across Europe which programme over 50% of European films. These cinemas are designed for niche cultural films and provide a parallel circuit to the mainstream cinemas owned by Europe's major media groups which mainly programme American films.

OVERALL

The MEDIA programme has created a vast superstructure of public funding, almost as comprehensive as the national funding systems. Despite the lack of production funding, the MEDIA programme has played a key role in 'shaping the audiovisual arena'. Far from establishing 'seed money' that would produce a self-supporting industry, European cinema is now more dependent than ever.

The 'experts' employed by the MEDIA programme now play a critical role in deciding which films should be developed and exported, and have helped consolid-ate the idea that European cinema is uniquely about niche films which represent 'intelligent' entertainment. There may be a slow movement towards more popular mainstream films under Media 2, but this remains a very sensitive issue.

The MEDIA programme has established a collection of industry 'insiders' and formed bridging links between the cultural establishments of the member states. These insiders include not only the permanent employees, but also select-ed members of the national film industries. This has created an 'inside' network within the European film industry, which benefits those on the 'inside' but excludes others.

A classic example of 'blurred lines' within MEDIA commissioning is that numerous funding grants have been given to industry figures who themselves serve as 'experts' on MEDIA judging panels. In certain cases the head of a funding body has given grants to direct family members.

Equally damaging, projects have been short-listed and rejected by one arm of the programme and then a very similar project with a different producer has re-appeared in another arm of the programme. This is of grave concern since the film industry is notorious for plagiarism and theft of ideas, but is inevitable when there are blurred lines between commissioners and producers.

If these practices occurred within a Hollywood studio, a film-maker could sue, but in the case of public subsidy funds, which are considered to be the 'people's friend', there is no such protection. This makes the programme the perfect grapevine for 'insider trading'.

There is nonetheless a genuine commitment to try and help the European film industry, amongst the project leaders of Media 2. It remains to be seen whether the next five years will be any more productive than the last.

OTHER EUROPEAN INITIATIVES

The MEDIA Programme is the most important European initiative, with direct backing from the European Commission. There are additional programmes which benefit from other sources of European funding and have links with MEDIA.

EURIMAGES

President Mitterand had originally proposed that there be a production support system within the auspices of the MEDIA programme. This was eventually rejected out of fear of loss of sovereignty over production decisions. Instead a European Support Fund was established in 1988 under the Council of Europe. One insider described it as 'very laudable, very French and not very practical'.

The Council of Europe (whose membership is wider than the Union) has also pioneered a series of legal initiatives intended to harmonize Europe's author rights system and provide a model co-production treaty.

Eurimages is an 'advance on receipts' for feature films, documentaries and distribution aid. To be eligible, projects must involve three independent producers from three of the Fund's member states. The government of each member state must contribute to the fund (Britain was a member from 1993 to 1995).

Films should have 70% of finance in place before applying. The majority co-producer may not contribute more than 60% of the budget, the minority co-producer not less than 10%, and at least 70% of the budget must come from the fund's member states. The film must be an official co-production, although the third minority partner (with a 10–25% contribution) may be a financing partner only and not contribute to the artistic or technical team. The language of the film must be that of the majority co-producer and all co-productions must be approved by the national authorities.

Eurimages has an annual budget of over \$25 million and may support up to \$850,000 or 20% of a film's production budget (the average is 12.5%). Fifty to seventy films are supported a year – around half of all European co-productions.

To apply for the scheme, producers must submit thirty-five copies of full details of the budget, financing plan, script and artistic details, and the decision process takes about three months. Payment is made 40% at the start of shooting, 40% at the end, 10% with the answer print and 10% on release.

Projects are decided by a committee of twenty-four representatives, one from each member state. To be selected a film must have two-thirds of votes. The committee must consider the 'cultural merit' of the project, 'whether it is likely to reflect and promote the contribution of diverse national components to Europe's cultural identity'. Preference is given to projects from smaller countries. Of all the European funding schemes, Eurimages generally receives the strongest praise, but within the overall context of Europe's cultural ghetto. French producer René Cleitman said in 1995, 'Even Eurimages, which at one stage appeared to be useful, has in the long term turned out to be relatively inefficient . . . it is a system condemned to fail.'

AUDIOVISUAL EUREKA

AVE was set up in 1989 as part of the general initiatives to 'revitalize' the European film industry. It is signed by twenty-six Member States and also by the EU Commission and the Council of Europe. There is a separate 'technological' initiative for HDTV and other new technologies.

Projects supported by the scheme include EMG (with MEDIA), the European Observatory, support for training schemes throughout Europe and the GEECT which links together twenty European film schools.

EURO-MEDIA GUARANTEES

EMG was created in 1991 as a joint initiative of the Commission and Audiovisual Eureka and three state credit banks – IFCIC in France, BNL in Italy and BEX in Spain. It now also includes Germany's Deutsche Bank and the Dutch BNP.

In broad terms, EMG aims to transpose the IFCIC system to the European level and guarantees up to 70% of a loan. It played a key role in cash-flowing Ridley Scott's film *1492, Conquest of Paradise*.

In November 1995, the Commission proposed a \$265 million guarantee fund to underwrite bank loans for European film and TV productions. The Council of Ministers looks unlikely to accept the proposal in its present form, but if adopted, it is likely to be administered by the European Investment Bank, in consultation with EMG.

EUROPEAN FILM ACADEMY

The Berlin-based Academy was set up in 1988 as the European Film Society with the grandiose aim to rival Hollywood's Academy of Motion Picture Arts and Sciences. The Felix Awards (which did not have MEDIA funding) were designed to be Europe's equivalent to the Oscars.

Wim Wenders was the first chairman of the Academy, but he was succeeded in 1996 by British producer Nik Powell. Powell's early objectives including widening membership to the younger generation (the average age of members in 1996 was sixty-two) and to raise the profile of the Felix Awards.

The Academy mainly concentrates on giving Master Classes in various aspects of film-making, publishing the Felix magazine and sponsoring publications about European cinema such as Angus Finney's excellent *A Dose of Reality* which was co-published with *Screen International*.[24]

11

Euro Production

Europe has never had a film industry,
only a collection of isolated producers.
David Puttnam

EUROPEAN FILM-MAKERS are not that different from those in America. Some want to make popular mainstream films, others are more attracted to quirky independent fare. What separates the two film industries is that one is run as a business, the other as a charity.

Most European producers work within a 'subsidy trap' mentality. They are dependent on the state and secure funding through connections and lobbying. Any producer who wishes to break out of this trap faces an uphill battle. Like Sisyphus, they will roll their stone many times up the mountain, only to see it slip through their fingers just as they reach the top.

Many European producers actually have a more sophisticated understanding of the intricacies of the business than those working in America. This is because Hollywood producers can plug into a system, whose forward momentum compensates the deficiencies of any individual player. In Europe, each film-maker is an island and must do everything himself – from development through to promotion.

One of the most remarkable examples of such 'self-made' producers is David Puttnam. He succeeded in building popular British films despite the indifference of key players such as Rank, and also established a vital dialogue with Hollywood. This required a special mixture of nervous energy and humility. As Alan Parker recalls, 'It was never easy for him in those early days; in Britain it was a depressed industry and the people who were running it were pretty pathetic. It was mostly run by narrow-minded chartered accountants and Wardour Street bookies in Burton suits and dandruff, who *knew* absolutely nothing, but couldn't be *told* anything, even though the industry was a disaster. In David's trips to America, it was even more humiliating for him. He was treated like a carpet salesman coming from nowhere and no one knowing who he was . . . They were very hard times for him and they left a mark . . . He was always thought of as a sort of swift-of-foot spiv, an energetic loonie, and no one would ever acknowledge that he might actually be any good, let alone brilliant.'[1]

European cinema was once run by 'Titans' like Alexander Korda and Carlo Ponti who had celluloid in their blood. They were then succeeded by contemporary producers, such as Puttnam or Claude Berri who emerged in the 1960s and often won their spurs in other areas of pop culture. The new generation of film-makers, such as Luc Besson and Pedro Almodóvar, have been forced to launch their careers punk style, outside the traditional system.

The biggest challenge for European producers is how to pay the rent while they chase their dreams. For example, David Puttnam in 1978, despite having produced nine films, had run up a bank overdraft of £68,000 and lost a further £30,000 in personal savings – a total debt of over $300,000 at today's prices. 'At a certain point', says Simon Perry of British Screen, 'being broke begins to erode the quality of the work.'

'While the producers are making their deals,' Fellini once said, 'I hang there like a diver on a high board, constantly poised for the jump, hands pointed in front of me, waiting for them to build the pool, fill it with water and arrange the spectators.' In today's climate, the wait may be for ever. The poverty of European cinema means that most talent either leaves to work in other areas, or goes to Hollywood. An increasing number of Europe's young film-makers are targeting Hollywood for film funding.

There are two main types of European film – small-scale subsidy-driven films (75%) and more ambitious market-driven films (25%) backed by Europe's media groups.

For subsidy-driven films, which are crucial for the discovery of new talent, most film-makers have to prove that their project isn't 'commercial' in order to secure funding, and as a consequence they usually find it impossible to achieve any market impact.

As New York-based German producer Chris Sievernich explains, 'The funding in Hollywood depends on the ability to put people in cinema seats, but in Europe it's based on a jigsaw puzzle of how to spend the money. It's difficult to have a partnership in that system, because governmental bodies and subsidized companies have a gulf of expectations with commercial companies, which is difficult to bridge.'[2]

Even Europe's media groups, who have a vested interest in securing software to drive their retail empires, are 'reactive' rather than 'pro-active' when it comes to investing in domestic films. They are far more concerned with securing 'safe' local bets, and the best of American independent cinema.

HOW EUROPEAN FILMS ARE FINANCED

Europe's funding model, unlike that of Hollywood, is based on the producer rather than the distributor as the focal point of the industry. The producer is expected to put up a portion of the budget and organize commercial exploitation. In effect, the producer is a mini-publisher.

This 'independence' is, however, misleading. Unless a producer has an integrated exhibition and distribution structure, he is almost entirely dependent on the decisions of third parties – essentially those of the state and the major media groups. In both cases this means negotiating a series of bureaucratic obstacles and being able to put together an alliance of various different players.

In practice, commissioning power within Europe lies in the hands of a handful of 'film tsars' whose connections can be used to bring together the necessary partners to the table.

The main power players have traditionally been the subsidy kingpins and television commissioning editors, but as the media groups increase in power, they also begin to take on a key commissioning role.

The 'film tsars' must be courted by any aspiring film-maker. They are often extremely busy and understaffed, and often a personal introduction is the only way to attract their attention.

For subsidy-driven films, the producer relies on his contacts with the state committees and television stations, and acts as a middle man between the director and the state funding bodies.

At this level, producers earn their living from the production fee and tend to pay little attention to the market-place or release strategy. 'In the old days the budget was the final consideration' says Italian lawyer Luigi Ferrara, 'now it's the first stop. Art is the last consideration.' But this is slowly beginning to change as state funding bodies demand knowledge of script, marketing and distribution.

Market-driven films have a genuine risk investment from a media group and are usually secured against in-house distribution capabilities. At this level, in-house producers are much more important and can set the ball rolling even if there is negligible interest from the cultural subsidy system. It is these films which tend to have the highest budgets and promotional spending and the best performance in the market-place.

Finally, there is always the option for European producers to operate as if they were American Independents and make English-language films backed by Hollywood name talent and financed through pre-sales. This is also an attractive option because many of Europe's media groups place their greatest emphasis on investing in Hollywood films.

To play this game involves the same rules as those already described for American Independents.

THE JIGSAW PUZZLE

European producers are often compared to American Independents, because they are required to put together complex financial packages and work within a more quirky auteur tradition. But the similarities are only fleeting, because American independent films are funded entirely by market revenues, whereas the majority of European films are funded by the state (via subsidies and state television).

However, it is true that European producers must know how to link together a wide variety of different funding sources. Locking down these monies is time-consuming and frustrating and, as in the case of *Orlando*, can easily take over five years. This lethargy in itself acts as a form of 'barbed wire' which puts off many would-be film-makers. The best way through the maze is a 'godfather' figure who supports the project and will help secure development funds and financing contacts.

There are three main sources of finance – pre-sales, equity and subsidies. In the immediate post-war era, 80% of finance came from market sources – pre-sales (domestic distribution and foreign sales) and internal equity. Today, these sources have largely withered away and been replaced by two key power players – the major media groups and the state. The full jigsaw puzzle is as follows:

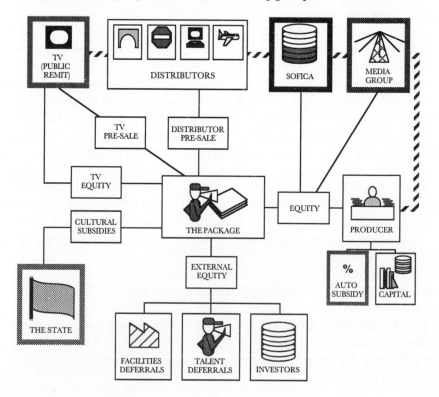

The state has interests throughout the film industry including automatic and selective subsidies, tax shelter funds (in France), television regulation and state credit banks. The media groups also have a variety of interests including controlling stakes in television channels, distribution pipelines, tax-shelter funds and equity stakes in leading producers. The 'privileges' of the main media groups are also dependent in many cases on a close relationship with the state.

The above 'jigsaw puzzle' is the funding map for national productions. In order to achieve higher budget levels, and combine the subsidy funding from several states, it is necessary to enter into a co-production. A co-production must be approved by the respective state authorities and satisfy a 'points system' concerning funding levels, key talent and shooting locations. The co-producers typically secure the rights to their 'language area' and then split all other world rights according to their budget contribution.

THE PACKAGE

The 'package' must be designed according to its potential 'buyers'. Most European films are funded through state television and selective subsidies which means that funds are allocated according to 'cultural merit'. Subsidy committee members do not have either the time or the skills to properly evaluate scripts and therefore depend above all on direct acquaintance with the applicant or personal recommendations. The judges are mainly concerned to know that the project has the right 'cultural' feel to it, and is not likely to ruffle any important feathers.

The major media groups have a slightly different outlook. For years, they have backed either 'quality' films or safe local comedies, but they are now becoming more adventurous. This is particularly true of PolyGram which has backed successful European films such as Jaco van Dormael's *The Eighth Day* and Dutch films *Little Film* and *Little Sister*.

THE ROLE OF AGENTS

Europe does not have agents along the Hollywood model, because the principal 'clients' in the business are not commercial entities, but the state. There are nonetheless a few examples of powerful local agents and the Hollywood agencies also represent European talent – particularly ICM which has an office in every European territory.

The British agents are closest to the American model, although they focus mainly on television as their core business. The main agencies include ICM/ Duncan Heath, Peters Fraser and Dunlop, Curtis Brown, Judy Daish, Blake Friedmann and William Morris. The UK agencies have a strong hold over acting and literary talent and can play an invaluable role in helping put together a UK project. A good example is Steve Kenis who heads WMA in London and helped launch the careers of Mandie Fletcher, Gary Sinyor, Danny Cannon and John Madden.

The French agency scene is dominated by Art-Média, followed by smaller players such as Les Agents Associés. Art-Média began as Lebovici-Méritz, with Claude Berri as one of its four founder members. For many years, Gérard Lebovici was its head, and extended its activities to producing, distribution (AAA), foreign sales (Roissy), and a 50% stake in Les Films Ariane (Alexandre Mnouchkine). In 1981 Lebovici passed leadership over to Jean-Louis Livi and the agency returned to its core activities. Livi subsequently expanded into production in 1991 and Bertrand de Labbey became the new head. Between 1992 and 1995 Art-Média was allied with ICM in France.

In Germany there were strict laws limiting the number of official talent agents from 1945 to 1994. In the new environment a clutch of dynamic agencies is growing up, including Sigrid Narjes, Marlis Happeler, Mechtild Holter, Carola Studlar and Bernhard Hoestermann. These bright young agents are helping nurture a revival of German cinema through acting clients such as Til Schweiger and Maria Schrader and directing clients such as Soenke Wortmann and Katja von Garnier.

In the rest of Europe, talent agents continue to be shoestring operations, but this is likely to evolve over the coming years.

CO-PRODUCTIONS

Sooner or later, European producers must get used to 'co-production', which can be achieved nationally – by linking together several national production companies – or internationally within the terms of official co-production treaties.

Certain co-productions are achieved via 'paper' companies and channelling sales income into countries which are desired as a 'partner'. If the authorities look favourably on the project they will normally turn a blind eye to such practices.

The crossroads of international co-production is France, which is involved in half of all European co-productions and is also the location of Eurimages. This means that European producers must become familiar with the French funding system, French media groups and special French structures such as the Sofica tax-shelter funds.

Film-makers who focus on the European system will therefore establish contacts and funding techniques which are very distinct from those in America. As Jonathan Olsberg of the Film Business School points out, 'It can be a real disadvantage to producers who have a solid understanding of how the European system works. It provides a mental block for them to understand how to finance films through international pre-sales, which I think is the way forward.' Young producers, especially in Britain, have to decide whether their outlook is better suited to the American or European system.

PRODUCER'S EQUITY

Even when a film is made as a co-production, there will be a lead producer responsible for the line management of the film and co-ordinating distribution. Most funding bodies expect the producer to be able to put up part of the budget.

Official statistics continue to show producers putting up 30–40% of the budget, but this is very misleading. In practice, most producer investments are achieved through automatic state subsidies, 'padding' of the budget and a 'rolling debt mountain' of technical credits and deferred fees.

The biggest obstacle for a first-time film-maker is how to pay the rent while trying to get his or her project off the ground. Development funds are scarce in Europe, so many companies draw their cash flow from parallel activities such as television and commercials production, or technical facilities.

Europe has a wealth of government grants available for development, including the world's largest development agency – Media Development. These grants are highly advantageous because they establish a formal expression of interest from government funding bodies, which substantially increases the chances of later production monies. The problem is that such funds are subject to a tight cultural remit and severe lobbying.

Europe's media groups also have limited development budgets, but these are usually reserved for established talent and projects destined for Hollywood.

Most first-time producers seek parallel areas of work, in order to subsidize their development activity, or to try to find a group of private sponsors willing to back a film project. The ideal option is to have a wealthy and well connected financial backer. For example, David Puttnam started up his film company with the backing of Evelyn de Rothschild, and Jeremy Thomas established a co-venture with music mogul Chris Blackwell.

STATE CULTURAL SUBSIDIES

The state underpins all levels of European cinema, and therefore the 'echo' of the state through subsidy commissions, television commissions, film festivals and film education is vital to the career of any European film-maker.

At least half of the battle in securing funding for a European film is to convince the local cultural mandarins that the film is worthy of support. The classic examples of this process are selective cultural subsidies which are decided by state-appointed committees and represent over a third of European films. These committees are the true 'battlefield' of European cinematic culture.

State commissioning editors and committee judges are rarely given any clear performance criteria through which they will be evaluated. In particular, they are not expected to achieve theatrical successes, and will be judged mainly by the word of mouth that they evoke within the cultural establishment. Even commissioners within the major media groups have been given tremendous leeway in terms of their commercial performance.

Similarly, film-makers who receive subsidy funding are not expected to achieve public success in return. They must come back with a solid piece of cultural cinema and general approval from the critics. It is always a bonus if state films earn prizes in film festivals, but these are selected and judged by the same people who sit as committee judges, which means that prizes tend to be carved up amongst the 'usual suspects'.

High-level discussions within the European body politic has meant that there is now a higher concern to achieve theatrical success with state films. Ironically this is described as if it were a change in the creative community – that film-makers are now more interested in finding a public. In fact the real change is in state policy.

The new 'commercial reality' is a bit like the winds of change that have swept through the BBC in recent years. It does not mean that European cinema has suddenly 'gone Hollywood'. There are still 'public service' criteria and taboos, and projects continue to be allocated because of connections and lobbying. However, there is now greater attention to the needs of a well structured script, good marketing, a well thought out financial plan and a greater willingness to accept comedies.

Lobbying and intrigue

European cinema likes to pride itself on its friendly atmosphere, in contrast to cut-throat Hollywood. But there is a lot of behind the scenes intrigue, and at times someone who pats you on the back is only looking for the soft place to put the knife in.

Europeans are often guilty of hypocrisy and double-speak, which comes from the tradition of 'civilized reserve'. As Michael Grade, who has worked in both systems, comments, 'Hollywood toughened me up. It taught me to adopt a more direct management style. English managers are so anal retentive – you can sit through an entire meeting with your boss and leave the room without realizing you've been fired.'

The arts world is particularly notorious for its back-biting, and the film community, like any other area of the 'arts', tends to be divided into lobby groups who defend their offspring. This fundamentally 'political' atmosphere extends to critics, committee judges and film-makers.

Each national film 'industry' is more like a medieval village, with its own family feuds and rivalries, and as in any village, family members take preference and it takes years before an outsider will be accepted.

There is a limited amount of taxpayer money available, and a large number of applicants. Funds therefore tend to be allocated to those individuals with greatest lobbying strength because of their village contacts. Alain Terzian (*Les Visiteurs*) claims that 'The CNC spends more time defending lobbies than its own long forgotten rules.'[3]

Like any other aspect of European society, the cinema is intimately connected to the social and political elite. It helps enormously to have been born into a 'well connected' family, or to develop social links with the leading circles.

These connections are important in gaining selective state grants, and even more so in integrating within the media groups that control the industry. 'The world of French cinema is a caste', says French critic Jean-Michel Frodon, 'not hermetically sealed . . . but one where you must follow certain rules of conduct in order to be fully accepted.'

When Europe had a vibrant popular cinema, there was greater access for actors, directors and writers who came from outside the social elite. But now that public policy emphasizes cinema as 'culture', it is very difficult to break in from the outside.

Many of Europe's most renowned auteurs had excellent family pedigrees, such as Visconti, Rossellini, Bertolucci, Tarkovsky, Malle, and Godard. There were also a few outsiders who were 'adopted' such as Fellini and Truffaut. This was influenced by the general climate of left-wing humanism. Today, it is very difficult for someone outside the elite to appear to possess sufficient 'culture' to make films. Jean-Claude Carrière concludes that one 'still can become a great artist through film, without the help of university degrees or a private fortune. But it's getting harder.'

The importance of a good piston

The key for people to break into the industry is to find a 'piston' from within the state system who is willing to push forward the project. The 'piston' is particularly important for co-productions, because he or she will help smooth the way through a maze of funding sources.

The need for a 'piston' means that new film-makers tend to be those with excellent connections. Otherwise they must wear their cultural credentials clearly on their sleeve, backed if possible by support from a state film school or a track record in another area of the arts.

The key role of the 'piston' opens the system to corruption abuses including favours, the casting couch and occasionally bribery kickbacks. In Italy there was a standard 10–12% surcharge paid into the coffers of the political party who arranged the subsidy.

More typically, it is a question of 'I'll scratch your back, if you'll scratch mine' because the committee judges are critics and film-makers who will later need to call on favours.

Subsidy bodies provide broad guidelines for the type of films they are looking for, including 'excellence of artistic expression', 'exploration of cultural difference and identity' and 'concern for important political, economic and social issues'. But in practice funds are committed to projects with the strongest lobby behind them.

The key to the business is understanding the politics, as UK co-production lawyer and producer, Cameron McCracken emphasizes, 'It's not really about pieces of paper, because the realities of what you can and cannot do are never publicized. The politics behind the business is the area co-producers need to get grips with . . . If the authorities really like a project, they'll push it through.'

This comes down to who you know, and whether your tastes mesh with those of the 'film tsars'. McCracken adds, 'It's a tired cliché that it's a people's business, but that's what it is. It's all about people's tastes or who you can trust. People come to me with their ideas. They get to know my taste. They don't come to me if it's a cop story or a thriller unless it's got a twist. They know that if it's a straight down the line commercial film that's not what I'm interested in. It's not about snobbism or elitism, it's just that's what I prefer. For funding bodies it's the same thing – you have to find out what they're looking for.'

TELEVISION INVESTMENTS

Television began investing in European cinema in the late 1960s and has been increasingly supported by the state as the natural 'home' of European cinema. The main television investors are state channels or channels with a tight public service remit such as Channel 4. In France, all channels are required by law to invest in cinema, but the types of investment are closely monitored.

For Hollywood films, television is the least important stage in the value chain. Films are sold by the distributor in bulk packages which vary between ten and a hundred films. In Europe, the producer must establish a direct relationship with the television channels and is dependent on their decisions.

The value of television investments in European films is vastly in excess of their market rate, making them a form of 'disguised subsidy', which reflects the overall cultural policy of the state. This close connection with the political sphere is reinforced by the fact that the appointment of commissioning editors – particularly within state television – is directly influenced by the government.

Television channels usually make two types of investment – a pre-sale of broadcast rights and an equity stake in the film. The television channel is thus a 'sleeping partner' with the lead producer. Most European channels operate within the broad terms of 'cultural cinema', but there is a distinct atmosphere within each broadcaster, which can be indicated by a few profiles.

Channel 4

Channel 4 is paid for by advertising, but has a strict 'public service' remit to 'experiment and innovate and cater for audiences not previously addressed'.

The first head of films was David Rose, a veteran BBC documentary and drama producer, and early films included *The Draughtsman's Contract, A Letter to Brezhnev, My Beautiful Laundrette* and an investment in *Paris, Texas*. Channel 4 also supported independent film and video workshops.

In 1988 Michael Grade took over from Jeremy Isaacs and the channel began to shift its emphasis – taking charge of the sale of its own advertising, reducing its support of workshops and adopting a slightly more 'commercial' outlook. The new film chief was David Aukin, formerly director of the National Theatre.

Aukin has maintained the channel's commitment to unconventional topics but has backed some key successes such as *The Crying Game, Four Weddings and a Funeral* and *Shallow Grave.* 'There is real energy out there' he commented in 1995. 'People are not just interested in the traditional heritage movie. The success of films like *Shallow Grave* has provided an enormous fillip to the British film-making community, especially the younger generation. Suddenly they see themselves enfranchised for a certain kind of film that wasn't being made ten years ago.'[4]

Channel 4 funds around fifteen theatrical films a year and develops thirty, spending $1 million a year on development and $27 million on production. The channel also backs the 'short and curlies' short film scheme and 50% of new features are shot by new directors, many of whom previously made a short. The channel's typical budget contribution is $0.5–0.6 million for broadcast rights plus the same amount in equity. The channel also fully funds three or four films a year with an average budget of $1.5 million which may stretch up to $2.5 million.

The film department is run by Aukin, his deputy and a couple of readers. Between 1991 and 1994 the deputy was Jack Lechner, an American who previously worked at Columbia under David Puttnam. Lechner explained that he was attracted to Channel 4 because he could make films there that the Majors would not normally consider. 'Our first commitment is to the film, and not its commercial success', he said at the time. 'Many of our films cannot be justified from a purely market point of view, but they deserve to be made. It's the same kind of philosophy that David Puttnam introduced at Columbia . . . What we like to hear is that no one else will back this film.' Aukin confirms this idea: 'One Hollywood executive said to me, "*Four Weddings and a Funeral* breaks all the rules. If it passed my desk, I would've had to reject it." That is what we should be doing in Britain: making films Hollywood wouldn't touch.'[5]

Aukin and Lechner nonetheless succeeded in backing 'alternative' films which attract an audience. 'The problem' declared Lechner in 1992, 'is that there was a certain kind of movie which they made which was neither fish nor fowl – neither cinema nor television. We want to make films that are cinematic and accessible.'[6] The eclectic range of films backed by the channel in recent years includes: Ken Loach's *Ladybird, Ladybird,* Paul Anderson's *Shopping,* Roman Polanski's *Death and the Maiden,* Terence Davies' *The Neon Bible,* and Nicholas Hytner's *The Madness of King George.*

Channel 4 has its own foreign sales arm, Film Four International, and in 1995 also established a UK theatrical distribution division. The commercial success of the channel's films has been used by Michael Grade as a bargaining tool to receive the full share of the channel's advertising sales (at present C4 donates around $80 million in ad sales to ITV). He has promised to spend $150 million on film production over the next four years if he can keep full revenues.

With competition from players such as PolyGram and the need to prove commercial success, the channel is likely to remain one of the strongest film investors in Europe in the near future.

France Television

The two French state channels France 2 and 3 maintain an overall public service remit in their investments. Unlike TF1, they do not aim to break even on their investments and tend to back more niche projects. Recent more commercial films in which they made a small investment include *1492* (France 2), *Les Visiteurs* (France 3) and the *City of Lost Children* (France 3). Of the 15–20 pictures backed by the two channels every year, only three score significant television audiences. Even successful theatrical releases such as *Tous les Matins du Monde* have performed poorly on television.

In the 1990s the television ratings for all French films have declined significantly. Jean-Pierre Elkabbach, while president of France Television, stated that this was because 'French cinema is too far removed from the realities and psycho-sociological state of the public. We must do our best to reduce the lag between the content of our films and the spirit of the times.'

Elkabbach underlined the emphasis on cultural cinema. 'Our two channels operate on common principles, each with their own style. They aim to support quality films of different genres . . . films with a strong cultural content, directed by artists of great discrimination.' He denies allegations of cultural elitism and also believes that the channel is able to resist lobbying. 'Certain film professionals have developed the habit of going directly to the Ministry of Culture', he said, 'in order to secure co-production funds which are often a misuse of public money. We are able to avoid such pressures.'

Canal+

Canal+ is required by law to invest 9% of its annual revenues on French-language films and a further 3% on European films. This has meant that the channel has backed over 90% of French production, with little input over content. The typical broadcast fee for a European film is $0.4–1 million and for a big-budget French film may go as high as $2.5 million.

The typical pay-TV deal includes a bonus if the film has admissions over 800,000. This is calculated by matching the broadcast fee against a reference price and then adding 4 FF for every ticket sold over 800,000. There is now a cap on the maximum pay-out.

The subsidiary, Le Studio Canal+ is able to make equity investments in films. In its start-up period, the Studio's French investments were for veteran talent such as Georges Lautner and Alain Delon, but the production outfit has become increasingly adventurous and is now linked into the joint venture with Sony for English-language pictures.

TF1 was formerly owned by the state, but was privatized in 1987 and quickly became the dominant force in French television. The film arm initially concentrated on 'Franco-Français' popular comedies but since 1992 has been widening its remit to more diverse films. The main producing partners include Gaumont, Jean-Claude Fleury, Claude Lelouch, and Claude Zidi. The average investment is $1 million with film, upon which the channel aims to break even.

TF1 also has a rights deal with Alain Goldman to invest in American production aiming to produce up to six American features a year (including $13 million in Martin Scorsese's *Casino* and a co-venture with Disney on the $46 million remake of *Un Indien dans la Ville*).

EUROPE'S MEDIA GROUPS

Europe's media groups have vast retail empires which are dependent on securing attractive product for customers. Their main emphasis is on acquiring American films, but there is a growing recognition that they must pay greater attention to nurturing popular local fare.

Europe's media groups have a number of ways in which they may invest in European cinema. The simplest is to provide a distributor advance. For example, companies such as Gaumont and PolyGram regularly provide the bulk of financing for their films. Another common alternative is 'equity partnership' between the media group and the lead producer. This can be achieved through an investment division such as Générale d'Images or Le Studio Canal+ or through an equity stake or first-look deal with a producer. Finally, in the French system, the main media groups have controlling interests in the Sofica tax-shelter funds whereby their investments are effectively 50% backed by state funds.

Different units from within the same 'family' group often combine their support – for example, Hachette Première and UGC both backed *Delicatessen*. In rare cases two 'family groups' will both back the same project, such as *Cyrano de Bergerac*, which was backed by both Havas/CGE and the Seydoux Brothers.

Europe's media groups have been given increasing powers in recent years, which has forced most Independents into their hands. In 1996 even Marin Karmitz – with an integrated distribution, exhibition and foreign sales organization – sold a 20% stake in his company to Havas.

The production chiefs and in-house producers within the media groups are overworked and understaffed. There are no development departments or executive structures as in the American Majors. Instead a single individual has a huge level of responsibility and is usually defended by one or two secretaries.

In practice, a first-time film-maker has no chance of gaining the support of a media group, unless he or she is backed by a producer with privileged access. Usually media groups will only back talent which has already proved itself through one or two films, and therefore has come up either through the subsidy system or micro-budget film-making.

The dominant position established by the media groups over European cinema nonetheless means that their editorial management skills will be the key to the future of the sector. If European cinema is to recover her vitality, then Europe's major companies must throw off the jinx that has haunted media management and led to debacles such as the Rank collapse in the late 1940s, the Gaumont collapse in the late 1970s and the disastrous Hollywood investments in the early 1990s.

By far the most 'talent friendly' and international of Europe's groups is PolyGram, but there are also pockets of local success such as Neue Constantin/Kirch in Germany.

Over time it seems inevitable that European media groups will adopt some of the management structures used by the Hollywood Majors, but it will take a long time for this system to evolve.

TAX-SHELTER FUNDS

Any film-maker wishing to work with the French funding system must become familiar with the Sofica investment funds. These were set up in 1985 ostensibly to fill the gap left by the withdrawal of distribution minimum guarantees.

In their initial years of operation, Soficas were designed to target independent production, but a legislation change in 1991 means that they now basically serve the interests of the main media groups.

The media groups now provide investors with a buy-back guarantee which eliminates their risk and means that the 50% tax break can be split between the investor and the media group. This enables media groups to increase their investment in the sector while offsetting some of the risk onto the state. The main Soficas and their lead backers are:

BNP Images	Gaumont
Bymage	Ciby 2000 (Bouygues)
Cofimage	Caisse des Depots (former owner of Lumière)
Investimage	IFCIC
Jaguar Invest	SFP
Sofiarp	ARP (president Claude Berri) and IFCIC
Sofilmka	MK2
Sofinergie	CGE and UGC
Studio Images	Le Studio Canal+

The Soficas are effectively run by their lead investor and anyone wishing to access Sofica funds should go via the respective media group (or in the case of Investimage, should contact IFCIC). In the early years Soficas could invest only in French-language productions, but from 1993 20% of investments may be for foreign-language films.

The Sofica investment has a high repayment rate until recoupment but then only a small share of the producer's subsequent income. This share is not equity, but functions in the same way, and may be sold to third parties.

For very successful films there is a 'bonus' pay-out, and overall the investment terms are fairly generous to the producer. The main source of revenue for the Soficas are second and third television transmissions.

The success of the Sofica system has led to plans to copy the system in other countries. The recent proposal in Britain for 'mini-studio' investment funds backed by Arts Council money would establish Sofica-style bodies.

COMPLETION BONDS

Completion bonds have traditionally been rare in contintental Europe (under 5% of films) but are now growing in number. Production companies have traditionally guaranteed completion internally, backed up by the state credit bank. This has led some producers to incur huge losses – such as Luc Besson on *Subway* and Andres Vicente Gomez on *Eldorado*. The major media groups usually guarantee completion from internal funds.

English-language films almost always have a completion bond and use the same facilities as those of American indies. On the continent, several bond companies are linked to Film Finances in the UK. The most important is Film Garantie Finance in France (set up in association with IFCIC in 1990) which also has close relations with Film Garantie Gesellschaft (FGG) in Germany (set up in association with Nordstein in 1991). A longer established company is Assurances Continentales in France run by Jean-Claude Beineix.

DISTRIBUTION AND MARKETING

The European funding system is often described as the tail wagging the dog, because distribution is the last consideration rather than the first. This is because distribution is a fundamentally commercial and international operation, whereas state policy is concerned above all with shaping national production. In the immediate post-war period, European and American distributors played a major role in the financing of European films, but since the 1970s this role has largely disappeared.

The main form of distribution finance today comes from the media groups who own distribution activities. This is the best way for a producer to ensure a wide release for his film and a reasonable promotional spend. Otherwise filmmakers are forced to rely on niche distributors who struggle to find screen space.

As a result of this situation, around 20% of European production has a prominent release in its home territory and a niche release abroad. A further 40–50% achieves a token national release, and 30–40% of films secure no release at all.

A conscientious producer should do his utmost to ensure that he gets the widest release and promotional spend possible. Even if the film has no distribution finance, the producer should cultivate connections with distributors and aim to get a contract signed before starting production, with a guaranteed minimum level of P&A spending.

As the film moves towards release, it is down to the producer to make the most of the promotional spend and also to seek as many ways to hype the film as possible. Many producers are dependent on favourable press and television coverage for their film, which is strictly national and tends to be biased towards 'cultural' films. Other ways of generating publicity are through the talent involved in the film and tie-ins such as a music soundtrack.

In order to generate international recognition for the film there are two main strategies. The first is to try to achieve a successful US release, which thereby sends a signal to the rest of the world. This is particularly important for British films, and can also help foreign-language films such as *Il Postino, Cinema Paradiso* and *Like Water for Chocolate*. The second strategy is to be selected in important film festivals, which can help build a niche following in the main territories.

FOREIGN SALES

In the 'golden age' of European cinema there was a genuine star system of actors and directors and many films were either co-produced or pre-sold. Today there is very little European talent, and that which there is tends to drift towards Hollywood. As a consequence it is very difficult to pre-sell most European films. A few name auteurs can be pre-sold, such as Tavernier, Kieslowski, Kusturica or Dormael and pre-sales can provide a small proportion of the budget of their films.

Foreign sales can also be a source of limited revenue once the film is completed, and producers should try to build close contacts with at least one leading foreign sales agent.

The sales agents are desperate for attractive product, since their business is being squeezed by the Majors, but they are extremely reluctant to put up any funding, unless there is bankable name talent attached to the project. Producers should nonetheless aim to establish a partnership with a foreign sales agent who is willing to bear the promotional costs of taking the film to the major film markets. The producer should also try to help any foreign distributors in their local release, but given the limited funds available in Europe, this is very much an uphill struggle.

The easiest way to generate foreign sales is if the film is in English and involves name talent recognized in Hollywood, but this forces the producer to compete with other American independent producers in a very aggressive market.

THE FINANCING GAP

As for American Independents, even if all of the above funding sources are tapped, there will often be a funding gap. The same techniques can be used to fill the gap, including deferrals, off-balance-sheet financing such as Ireland's Section 35 (see Appendix A) and insurance gap financing such as that offered by Screen Partners.

A producer should also explore ancillary rights, in particular music soundtracks. Product placement may also generate limited revenue (although this is limited by law in some countries such as Germany). Recent examples of product placement include Almodóvar's *High Heels* for which Chanel donated clothes, and Claude Lelouch's *La Belle Histoire* which had sponsorship from Renault, France Telecom, Champagne Piper-Heidsiech and Air France. Even for Wim Wender's *Until the End of the World* $20,000 was raised from Evian.

DISCOUNT FINANCE

In most European countries, production finance is discounted by the state credit system. This brings the added advantage that since each film community is like a small village, contracts do not have to be tied down to precise details. In Britain, for films budgeted over $5 million, discount finance is provided by specialist players such as FILMS or Guinness Mahon. Smaller films are effectively cash-flowed by the main funding bodies – Channel 4, British Screen and the Arts Council.

THE NEW CLIMATE IN EUROPE

European cinema has been locked into a 'public-service' mould since 1968, but there are small signs of change, riding on the back of growing interest from the media groups in attracting popular titles. The most important trans-national player has been PolyGram which has made a major contribution to the recent revival of British cinema and also made powerful and successful films in France, Spain and the Benelux.

At the national level, the biggest turnaround has been in Germany, where the state committees and film prizes have placed increasing emphasis on popular comedies, and Bernd Eichinger's Neue Constantin (50% owned by the Kirch Group) has released a string of successful local language films including *Der Bewegte Mann* ($45 million gross), *The Super Wife* ($17 million) and *Werner – That's*

Hot (over $35 million). Another recent hit is *Jailbirds/Maennerpension* which was released by Delphi and grossed over $23 million.

The German revival has also benefited from creative and organizational links with America. The Majors have targeted the huge German market as the key battleground in the new multi-media universe. In 1995 Warner Brothers put up 20% of the $3 million *Only for Love* starring comedy actress Katja Riemann (50% of the budget came from regional subsidies), which grossed a modest $3 million. In 1996 Buena Vista (Disney) released *Regular Guys*, which grossed $2 million in its first two weeks. Hollywood marketing techniques have forced German distributors to adopt similar high profile strategies.

American screenwriters have also played an important role in the new crop of popular films, most notably thirty-five-year-old Ben Taylor who wrote *Talk of the Town* (distributed by Disney) which grossed over $11 million in 1995, making it the No. 1 German film of the year.

These successes, however, should be kept in context. They represent a handful of films a year, while the majority of German films continue to fail to even secure a theatrical release. The share of German films in the national market was 10.4% in 1994, 9,5% in 1995 and is expected to be 15–18% in 1996.

The blips of commercial success in Germany, Britain and France are to be applauded, but are far from establishing the critical mass which is needed to revive Europe's film industry and her prowess in premium media.

TEAMING UP WITH AMERICA

The final and often most interesting alternative for European producers is to sidestep the European funding system altogether and to link into the Majors or American independent production. Most of Europe's leading producers pursue this strategy, and it was also the option recommended by the Union's Media Business School.

A small number of European producers have output deals with the Majors, such as David Puttnam and Dieter Geissler with Warners. They deliver English-language product for the international market. Other producers such as Jeremy Thomas, Steve Woolley and Nik Powell, Jake Eberts, Stephen Evans and Bernd Eichinger finance their films through international pre-sales, with additional backing from Europe's media groups and, where possible, subsidies.

Tapping the American market is particularly attractive to British film-makers, and several have first-look deals – including Simon Relph with Fine Line, Sarah Radclyffe with Fox Searchlight, Duncan Kenworthy with Jim Henson Pictures and Mike Newell with Touchstone. Many of Europe's younger producers are also targeting the American market, such as Colin Vaines, Alain Goldman, Ricky Posner, Jeremy Bolt and Domenico Procacci.

The main obstacle with this strategy is that European producers operate 8,000 miles from Hollywood. Unless they have privileged talent relationships, it is very difficult for them to access top scripts and name talent. The capital risks involved are also very considerable, which normally requires a link-up with a European media group or an American first-look deal.

In order to crack the American market, it is often very useful for producers to spend some time working within the Hollywood system to establish contacts and understand its editorial agenda. This is particularly true for younger film-makers, who in the present climate are much better advised to gain their film training and first work experience in America rather than Europe.

MICRO-BUDGET FILMS

Many of Europe's well known film-makers started their careers outside the state system, mainly through micro-budget films, and such films have always been a weapon against industry sclerosis.

At the end of the 1950s, guerrilla film-making techniques were advocated in Italy and led to the discovery of talent such as Bertolucci, Risi and Pasolini. The key figures of the French New Wave, such as Resnais, Godard and Truffaut, also began with micro-budget films.

Recent 'guerrilla' film-makers include Pedro Almodóvar, Luc Besson, Gary Sinyor and the Belgian trio who made *Man Bites Dog*. There are also strange pockets of micro-budget films such as Iceland where recent films include the $100,000 *Wallpaper* and the $150,000 *Sodoma*.

There are nonetheless far fewer micro-budget films made in Europe than in America. This is mainly because of the lack of a vibrant industry in other areas, which means that there are fewer actors, crew and technical facilities able to offer 'freebies'. The 'ghettoized' image of European films also means that fewer investors are willing to back unknown talent.

Micro-budget techniques are more common in short films, which can sometimes be used as a calling card for a bigger project. For example, short films such as techno-pop *Vibroboy* by French director Jan Kounen, and *The Debt*, by Portuguese director Bruno de Almeida, have helped them put together funding for a feature.

The most active area of guerrilla cinema is in Britain, where a new young generation of film-makers wants to produce more mainstream cinema. Their masthead is the New Producers' Alliance (NPA) which was set up in 1992 by Jeremy Bolt, Alex Usborne, Sue Richards and Laurie Borg in frustration with existing funding mechanisms. Britain's young Turks also took advantage of the BES tax-shelter legislation for small companies (which was abolished at the end of 1993) and succeeded in raising capital from City investors.

The final stimulus was from American gurus such as Robert McKee and Dov S-S. Simens. The latter goaded, 'In Britain you've got the talent, the know-how, the creativity . . . but you're slightly constipated, you're not entrepreneurial. You don't know about marketing.'

The new generation have been called multiplexers, 'tech-noirs' and cyber-punks, and even films like *Shopping* and *Shallow Grave* which have been funded by more traditional methods, draw their oxygen from the micro-budget boom.

Britain's punk films have been made in the £0.3–0.4 million range, designed to cash in on the worldwide video demand for edgy English-language titles. The basic technique of fund-raising – like all tax-break schemes – is to try to lock off the investor's risk through a foreign rights deal. The investor thus effectively provides 'bridging finance' in return for which he receives up to a 40% tax break. One of the main centres of BES fund-raising was City solicitors Gouldens, which organized the offerings for *Leon the Pig Farmer* and *Henry V*.

There are several examples of micro-budget films. Noel Cronin's company, String of Pearls, raised over £350,000 in a BES offering in 1991 and made *Double X*. Cronin had previously made several micro-budget features including *Mirage* (1989), *Home for Christmas* (1990) and *Midnight Fear* (1991) and had established a worldwide video distribution deal with New World International. This video deal provided the security against which private equity could be raised. With String of Pearls, Cronin made two further £0.5 million BES offerings to make *Little Devils* and *To Catch a Yeti* (which also benefited from Canadian tax breaks).

Property developer Andrew Johnson and his brother Simon set up State-screen in 1990 as part of their unsuccessful bid to buy the State Cinema in Grays, Essex. They began making promotional videos under the title of Naked Films and then produced *Tale of a Vampire* directed by Japanese Shimako Sato and starring Julian Sands, which cost 'well under £1 million'. It was principally financed by Japanese low-budget video producer Tsuburaya who took Japanese rights and 50% of all revenues outside the UK. Statescreen kept UK rights and arranged a do-it-yourself release across more than twenty independent cinemas. Their P&A spend was under £10,000 and total gross was around £50,000. The producers hoped to earn much more money in UK video with Columbia Tri-Star shipping around 5000 units. For foreign sales, the film was sold to American video distributor Trimark, who produced a glossy brochure and helped recoup the budget. Statescreen then secured a £2 million investment fund from Tsuburaya aiming to invest in a series of £0.3–0.4 million films.

The Gruber brothers (producer Richard Holmes and director Stefan Schwartz) started working together as a comedy double act. They then produced two £12,000 shorts – *Bonded* and *The Lake* – which won them support from the First Film Foundation. After a BAFTA screening of *The Lake*, a single private investor offered to back their £250,000 feature, *Soft Top, Hard Shoulder* written by actor Peter Capaldi (*Local Hero*). The budget was supplemented by other small equity stakes and deferrals and the film's cast including Frances Barber, Simon Callow and Phyllis Logan, deferred most of their fees. The duo then developed their next feature, *The Lake*, in association with ACE (European Film Studio).

Videodrome financed the £200,000 *The Punk* through an acquaintance of director Mike Sarne who took out a £500,000 mortgage on his house. The film was extensively hyped at Cannes and earned modest foreign sales.

Living Spirit's £140,000 *The Runner* was made by Chris Jones and Genevieve Joliffe – two graduates at the Bournemouth Film Schoool who had been inspired by Sam Raimi's technique for financing *Evil Dead*. They completed a two-minute trailer and then got backing from Welsh sales agent EGM, plus private investors. The film failed to get a UK theatrical release, but they used work on corporate videos to begin financing a second feature, the £500,000 *White Angel* (1992) starring Peter Firth and Don Henderson.

CASE STUDIES

The best way to make sense of the European system is by looking at the financing structure of specific films, from small-scale to big-budget productions.

Traditional European films are far less dependent on the market-place than the case studies provided earlier for Independent Production. Equity funding is provided by the producer, media groups and tax shelters and in each case the state covers about half the risk. The rest of the budget is made up through selective state subsidies and television pre-sales.

A visual overview of the financing plans of the films profiled in the case studies is provided below and overleaf:

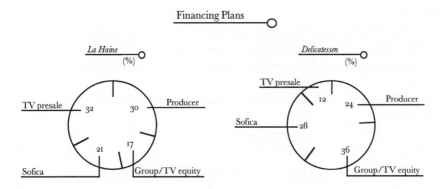

Financing Plans

La Haine (%)
TV presale 32
Producer 30
Sofica 21
Group/TV equity 17

Delicatessen (%)
TV presale 12
Producer 24
Sofica 28
Group/TV equity 36

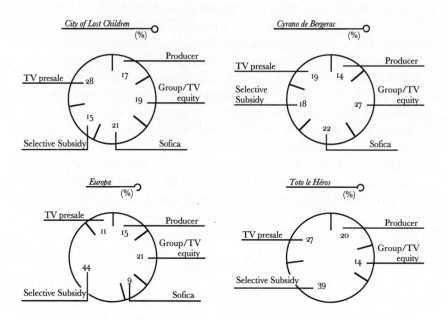

The lead production company typically puts up 20–25% of the budget, much of this coming from automatic subsidies, deferrals and in certain cases 'padding'.

This investment is then leveraged to give a much greater ownership of the film negative. The rest of the negative is owned by the media groups and tax-shelter funds which invest in the film.

The following case studies explain how the films were financed, how they performed and the broad terms of their deal structures.

LA HAINE/HATRED (1995)

Matthieu Kassowitz's $3.3 million second feature was a 100% French film produced by Alain Rocca's Lazennec. The director's company Kasso Inc. also invested a token $24,000 in return for which he received 20% of Lazennec's revenues.

Lazennec's $1 million investment includes monies from the Fonds de Soutien and also deferred fees.

The main outside funding came from television-linked companies – La Sept and Canal+, who took 26% of the producer's share of revenues.

Additional backing was provided by Cofimage and Studio Image tax-shelter funds.

Equity

Lazennec/Kasso Inc	$1M	All remaining rights
Studio Canal+	$0.07M	6% of producer's share
La Sept Cinema	$0.5M	20% of producer's share

Tax shelter

Cofimage (Lumière)	$0.2M	40–44% until recoupment, then 7.5%
Studio Image (Studio C+)	$0.5M	29% of producer's share

Pre-sales

Studio C+ (video)	$0.01M	right to distribute in video
Studio C+ (foreign)	$0.02M	right to sell abroad (for commission)
Canal+	$0.9M	pay-TV rights
La Sept	$0.18M	free TV for Arte (La Sept/ARD)

The film was included in the Official Selection at Cannes in 1995 and was released in France in June 1995 by MKL (a joint venture between Marin Karmitz and Lazennec). The film opened on 118 screens and went straight in at 'number one'. It spent eleven weeks in the Top Ten and finally grossed close to $15 million.

Abroad, the film had a good critical reception which will help boost TV sales, but had only a small niche success in the box office. Foreign MG sales were probably in the region of $1.5–2 million. Total market revenues to the producer were therefore in excess of $7 million and the film will also have generated close to $2.5 million in automatic subsidies.

DELICATESSEN (1991)

Delicatessen was the first film by young directing duo Jean-Pierre Jeunet and Marc Caro, who had previously worked mainly in commercials. The producer was Claudie Ossard, whose debut was Jean-Jacques Beineix's *Betty Blue* and who had a significant *fonds de soutien* available. 'This was a difficult film to finance', commented Ossard, 'because it didn't have either Avance sur Recettes or support from free TV.'

To finance the $3.8 million film, Ossard established a two-year 50/50 production joint venture with UGC (other films included *Arizona Dream*). Additional investors were from the Havas/CGE family group – Hachette Première and Canal+ – as well as $0.45 million of deferred facilities fees and a small grant from the Fondation Gan.

Equity

C. Ossard (*fonds de soutien*)	$0.9M	30% of producer's share
UGC	$0.6M	33.5% of producer's share
Hachette Première	$0.3M	16.5% of producer's share
Deferred facilities	$0.45M	
Fondation Gan	$0.04M	

Tax shelter

Sofinergie 1/2 (UGC)	$0.8M	16% of producer's share after recoupment
Investimage 2/3 (IFCIC)	$0.25M	4% of producer's share after recoupment

Pre-sales

UGC	$0M	Theatrical distribution (15% fee)
Canal+	$0.44M	French pay-TV

Delicatessen proved to be a cult hit, with a narrow release in France but an extremely long run. The film enjoyed a late boost after winning prizes in the César awards. The French box office for the film was close to $9 million with only a $0.5 million P&A spend.

The producer's share of theatrical revenues was therefore around $3 million, to which should be added video and free TV earnings of over $1 million. The film therefore turned a small profit in France alone.

Unusually for a French film, foreign gross was even higher – around $15 million. Foreign MG sales were over $2 million. The film therefore had close to a 100% profit. It also will have earned close to $1.5 million in French automatic subsidies.

THE CITY OF LOST CHILDREN (1995)

The $18 million production was the second film by *Delicatessen* duo Marc Caro and Jean-Pierre Jeunet and was produced by Claudie Ossard for Lumière. The film was produced within the CGE/Havas orbit, with strong backing from UGC and Canal+.

The City of Lost Children also involved Lumière's Spanish associate Elias Querejeta/Esicma and had a German pre-sale which qualified it as an official co-production, thus winning a small Eurimages loan. The film had unusually high pre-sales ($7.5 million including Germany) and also had special aid from the CNC totalling $1.5 million.

Equity

C. Ossard (*fonds de soutien*)	$0.3M	producer's share
Lumière	$0.3M	10% of producer's share
Générale d'Images (CGE)	$0.15M	5% of producer's share
Studio Canal+	$0.8M	20% of producer's share
France 3 Cinema	$0.6M	9% of producer's share
German pre-sale	$2.7 M	Germanophone rights + producer's share
Querejeta/Lumière	$2.7 M	Sp. rights + producer's share

Tax shelter

Cofimage 4 (Lumière)	$1M	4.5% of producer's share
Cofimage 5 (Lumière)	$2.25M	10.5% of producer's share
Studio Image (Studio C+)	$0.6M	11% of producer's share

Subsidies

Avance sur Recettes	$0.75M	repayable loan
CNC (experimental prod.)	$0.4M	grant
CNC (studios)	$0.4M	grant
Eurimages	$0.2M	repayable loan

Pre-sales

UGC	$1.5M	Theatrical distribution (30% fee)
Canal+	$2.8 M	French pay-TV
France 3	$0.8 M	French free TV

The film was released in France by UGC on 175 screens during Cannes 1995 where it was in Official Selection. It widened to 312 screens and stayed five weeks in the Top Ten.

The total promotional spend was over $1.5 million, but the final French gross was only around $9 million – similar to that of the far lower budgeted *Delicatessen*.

The film's foreign performance was very disappointing, with $0.4 million in the US and under $5 million worldwide. Total pre-sales (including TV) were around $10 million.

There will have been no market overages above this amount, but the film will have earned over $1.5 million in French automatic subsidies to be shared between the French producers. Overall the film will almost certainly have lost money.

CYRANO DE BERGERAC (1991)

Cyrano was one of the most successful European films in recent years – a classic case of a 'quality film', helmed by veteran director Jean-Paul Rappeneau and adapted by Jean-Claude Carrière. The $18 million film was a 100% French production between two family groups – Hachette/UGC and the Seydoux brothers (Michel Seydoux's Camera One and Renn Productions). It also benefited from Avance sur Recettes and from the Club des Investisseurs. The financing was as follows (breakdown of producer's share is unavailable):

Equity

Hachette Première	$2.5M	
UGC	$1M	includes distribution rights
M. Seydoux (Camera 1)	$2.5M	
France 2	$1M	
DD Productions	$0.4M	

Tax shelter

Sofinergie 1	$1.2M
Sofinergie 2	$2.8M

Subsidies

Avances sur Recettes	$0.9M	repayable loan
Club des Investisseurs	$2.4M	repayable loan

Pre-sales

Renn (MG Video)	$1M	French video rights
Canal +	$1.5M	French pay-TV
France 2	$1M	French free TV

Cyrano was awarded Best Film at the César Awards and the European Felix Awards, and Dépardieu won Best Actor at Cannes. The film was released on 390 screens in France with an exceptional $2.3 million P&A spend. It grossed $23 million at the French box office, and earned $11 million in rentals. From this UGC earned a 20% distribution fee and also had to recoup P&A, leaving a producer's share of $6.5 million.

In video, around 500,000 units were sold at $25, producing gross revenues of $12.5 million. The producer's share of this was around $5 million. For television, first broadcast rights were pre-sold for $2.5 million and second broadcast on free TV probably generated $0.8 million.

Thus the producer's share of total market revenues was in the region of $15 million – representing a $3 million loss on the French market alone. But the film also earned close to $4 million in automatic subsidies which covered this 'loss'.

Cyrano also performed strongly abroad – very rare for a French film – and grossed over $30 million (see Appendix C). Foreign sales were probably in the region of $4–5 million. The film earned a modest profit in market terms, but around a 40% profit once automatic subsidies are included.

EUROPA (1991)

The $4.7 million *Europa* (released as *Zentropa* in the US) was Lars von Trier's first major international feature, and completed a trilogy begun with two smaller Danish films *The Element of Crime* (1984) and *Epidemic* (1987). The script was funded by the Danish Film Institute. After the third draft they approached Bo Christensen at Nordisk, who set up an international co-production, later commenting, 'I went running around half a year just to get the systems to work together when we made *Europa* and that was a hellish loss and waste of time.'

The film was an official Franco-Danish-German co-production, with half of the budget provided by France. The film was shot in German and English, and the lead roles were played by Jean-Marc Barr and Barbara Sukowa. The French partners were from the CGE/Havas family group, combining UGC producers Gérard Mital and Patrick Godeau (PCC) plus Canal+ and the Sofinergie tax-shelter fund (of which UGC holds 30%). The French producers were able to invest automatic subsidies and the film also benefited from subsidies from the Danish and Swedish Film Institutes, the French Avance sur Recettes, and a loan from Eurimages.

Equity

G. Mital/PCC/UGC	$0.4M	France and 39% rest of world
Nordisk	$0.4M	Danish rights and 29% rest of world
Svensk	$0.15M	Swedish rights and 12% rest of world
Telefilm/NEF (Ger)	$0.75M	German rights and 20% rest of world

Tax shelter

Sofinergie 1 and 2	$0.45M	50% producer share until recoupment

Subsidies

Avance sur Recettes (Fr)	$0.6M	repayable loan
Danish Film Inst.	$0.5M	repayable loan
Swedish Film Inst.	$0.2M	repayable loan
Eurimages	$0.75M	repayable loan

Pre-sales

Canal+	$0.5M	French pay-TV

France and Denmark were jointly responsible for world sales. French theatrical distribution was co-ordinated through UGC with a 20% distribution fee.

The film was launched in Cannes 1991 where it won the Special Jury Prize. It then opened on 23 screens in France, with a $0.3 million ad spend. Despite significant critical acclaim, the film had limited box office, earning under $4 million box office worldwide (see breakdown in Appendix C). Video sales were minimal and television sales were hampered by the fact that much of the film was in black and white.

In a purely market-based system the film would have lost money, but because of the large amount of subsidy and tax-shelter investment involved, it made a profit for its German and Scandinavian backers, although it lost money in France.

TOTO LE HÉROS (1991)

Toto was the flagship of European aid programmes, having secured support from the Script fund, EFDO and Eurimages. The director, Jaco Van Dormael (b. 1957) a former circus clown, is the son of a theatre director and was a student of Czech script guru Frank Daniel. He had directed a short, *É pericoloso spoggersi* which was produced by Danys Geys and Pierre Drout of Iblis Films. For Toto he wrote a thousand-page script with which he approached producers. He then went through an extensive rewriting process (aided by script doctor Pascal Lonhay).

The $4 million film was financed as an official Belgian-Franco-German co-production and had support from Eurimages. The producers were Iblis Films, Les Productions Dussart and Metropolis Films, each with substantial subsidy and state TV monies.

Iblis's contribution was made possible by a special arrangement set up by the Belgian government, whereby a discount bank could advance monies against the automatic subsidy (based on 25% of Belgian box office) and any losses made by the bank could be written off against taxes as a form of sponsoring.

The financing plan was as follows (the figures for producer's share are estimates):

Equity

Iblis Films (Bel)	$0.3M	30% Francophone, 25% rest of world
Productions Dussart (Fr)	$0.5M	30% Francophone, 25% rest of world
Metropolis (Ger)	$0.1M	50% Germanophone, 10% rest of world
RTBF (Bel)	$0.3M	30% Francophone, 25% rest of world
FR3 (Fr)	$0.12M	10% Francophone, 5% rest of world
ZDF (Ger)	$0.2M	50% Germanophone, 10% rest of world

Subsidies

Cultural aid Belgium	$1.1M	repayable loan
CNC (Franco-Belgian)	$0.1M	grant
Eurimages	$0.5M	repayable loan

Pre-sales

RTBF/Canal+ Bel	$0.05M	Belgian pay-TV and free TV
UGC Video	$0.05M	right to distribute on video
Canal+	$0.44M	French pay-TV
FR3	$0.3M	French free TV
ZDF	$0.2M	German free TV
NEF2	$0.1M	German theatrical distribution

Toto won the Camera d'Or at Cannes in 1991 and Best Foreign Film at the César awards. The film performed well for a niche title, grossing $0.57 million in Belgium and $4 million in France. In France the release went as wide as 100 screens with a $0.5 million P&A spend. It also sold 1300 video rental cassettes in France at $139 a cassette and 5000 sell-through units at $25.

Outside France, the film benefited from an EFDO award of $0.22 million and went on to gross over $7 million worldwide. The sales agent Mainstream earned over $2.5 million in minimum guarantees.

For the French co-producers, the film's market revenues were around $4 million, which means that even without subsidies the film would have just about achieved break-even. The film will also have generated over $1 million in automatic subsidies in France and Belgium.

Dormael's second film, *The Eighth Day*, was backed by PolyGram and has grossed over $22 million in France and Belgium alone.

IL POSTINO (THE POSTMAN) (1995)

Il Postino has been one of Italy's biggest critical and commercial successes in recent years. The film was based on Antonio Skarnetta's novel and was written by Massimo Troisi and Furio Scarpelli. Troisi was one of Italy's best-known comedy actors and was also aware that because of cancer this film was likely to be his last. He chose Michael Radford to direct the film and his co-star was French actor Philippe Noiret who had starred in *Cinema Paradiso*.

The lead producer for the film was Gaetano Daniele's Esterno Mediterraneo – one of Italy's top comedy producers. Daniele set up the company with Troisi in 1987 and has a first-look deal with the Cecchi Gori group, who have so far backed all their films. The track record of Daniele and the financial strength of Cecchi Gori (via the Penta alliance) enabled them to jointly finance the $2.4 million film.

Equity

Esterno Mediterraneo	$1.2M	50% of world rights
Penta	$1.2M	50% of world rights

Il Postino was released by Penta in Italy in September 1994 on 56 screens and quickly built to 100 screens. It lasted eight weeks in the Top Ten and ultimately grossed $14 million in Italy. The international breakthrough came when American and other key foreign rights were sold to Miramax, thereby giving access to Disney's worldwide network.

Miramax opened the film in the US in June 1995 on 10 screens. The film quickly built tremendous word of mouth and after five weeks was playing on an exceptional 100 screens. Over the next 30 weeks the film grossed $10 million. Miramax had wanted the film to be nominated for Best Foreign Language Oscar by the Italian authorities, but it was refused because of Radford's UK nationality. Instead Miramax succeeded in getting a nomination for Best Picture Oscar and immediately widened the release from 23 screens to 250. The film spent another 20 weeks in release, eventually grossing a US total of $22 million.

The US success helped the film reach a wide audience throughout the world, with a total world gross in excess of $80 million – one of the most popular Italian films since *La Dolce Vita*. The low-budgeted film will probably earn overages well over 500% its cost.

Man Bites Dog (C'est Arrivé Pres de Chez Vous) (1992)

André Bonzel, Rémy Belvaux and Benoit Poelvoorde were students at the Belgian state film school and received subsidy monies to make a short film and also a commission to make an anti-cholestorol public service announcement. On the $10,000 proceeds they decided to make a feature film, covering the extra costs through donations by friends and family. The film was shot in 16mm as a mock documentary. Equipment and crew came mainly from film school, and they sought favours all the way down the production and post-production chain. The final money cost was $100,000, including a $30,000 subsidy from the Belgian Community to blow up the film to 35mm for the Cannes Film Festival.

The film enjoyed a good reception from both the public and the critics. It was awarded several prizes at Cannes, was screened at the Sundance Film Festival and received favourable write-ups in *Newsweek* and *Time*. The film grossed $0.55 million in Belgium, close to $3 million in France and achieved wide international release, with a particularly strong performance on video.

Man Bites Dog was an interesting example of a popular film which would not have received funding through traditional methods. The film buyer at Belgian state broadcaster RTBF turned down the film at first screening and only bought it because of its spectacular success at the box office.

The film-makers used the film as a launching pad. Poelvoorde opened a one-man comedy show which played to packed houses for months and Belvaux and Bonzel have moved towards directing new projects. The trio subsequently became embroiled in a court case with sales agent Claude Nouchi of World Marketing Film because they claimed that they were seeing minimal revenues from the film's success.

LEON THE PIG FARMER (1993)

Probably the best-known of Britain's recent micro-budget films, *Pig Farmer* was co-directed by Gary Sinyor (b. 1963) and Vadim Jean (b. 1965) and produced by Paul Brooks (b. 1959). Gary Sinyor is a National Film School graduate and his seventeen-minute short *The Unkindest Cut* won a Bafta award and was shown on BBC 2. After the television screening he got a call from Eric Idle at Prominent Features who then commissioned the original *Pig Farmer* script from him, aiming to make a £3 million film. They spent fifteen months trying to raise finance, after which Prominent put the script into turnaround.

Sinyor met Vadim Jean, a history major who began his career on Mike Figgis's *Stormy Monday* (1987). They decided to fund the picture themselves, together with Paul Brooks who had previously been working in the property business.

The cast of Mark Frankel, Maryam d'Abo and Brian Glover agreed to defer their fees, and thereby provided the security for future sales. 'I rang up sales agents and television companies to get an estimate of potential sales', explains Brooks, 'and their estimates turned out to be pretty accurate. This meant we had an excellent chance of paying back investors who were in first position for recoupment.'

Brooks is highly critical of the lethargic British film community. 'You just have to pick up the phone and get on with it', he says. The script was bought back from Prominent Features for £35,000 and the final production cost was £150,000 on a real budget of £650,000. Everyone was paid £20 a week including cast. There were heavy discounts from the labs and also from a facilities company, Furuma, who became an equity partner in the film.

To finance the film, Brooks, Jean and Sinyor raised £103,000 through a BES offering by City solicitors Gouldens (who also deferred all fees) and a further £20,000 from friends and acquaintances. The money was raised in a six-week period.

Pig Farmer had a six-week shoot, six days a week with ten-hour days. Post-production was twelve weeks and the shooting ratio was 12:1 with 2–10 takes on each set-up. The film went £30,000 over budget, which was covered through a personal bank loan for Vadim on the back of the promise of a foreign sales advance from Beyond International.

Once the film was completed, 'we pushed the hell out of it', explains Brooks. It was released by Electric in the UK on 6 screens in London and then widened to 20. It also won the International Critic's Prize at the Venice Film Festival. Market revenues were roughly as follows:

	Gross	Producer's share
UK theatrical	$1 million	$100,000
UK video	$0.5 million	$80,000
Channel 4	$125,000	$100,000
Foreign sales	$350,000	$200,000

The $0.23 million film thus earned producer revenues of around $0.5 million. This was below the 'real' production cost of $1 million, but enabled investors to be repaid and other parties to recoup half of their deferred fees. Over time, the library value of the film will push it towards break-even.

Brooks sees micro-budget film-making as the 'entry price' into the industry. 'It helps people move up a production grade. For example, our director of photography wasn't previously accepted by completion bond companies. Now he will be. Otherwise it would have taken him five years.'

European Producers

Being a producer is like mining for gold.
99% of the time you're digging shit.
It takes manpower and nerves to keep going.
Bernd Eichinger

CRITICS LIKE TO CONTRAST Hollywood's capitalistic producer-led industry with Europe's artistic auteur-driven community, but in fact the best of European films have been associated with intelligent entrepreneurs. Even classic auteurs like the 'Wunderkind' Wenders owe a huge debt to producers such as Anatole Dauman.

The main reason for the belittling of the role of the producer, is that the state has usurped his role. A good producer takes commercial and financial risks and plays an editorial role in guiding his film. If the state took this philosophy aboard, it would be required to pay much more attention to the track record and skills of commissioning editors and producers. Instead, commissioning editors and committee judges are usually drawn from outside the industry, and the role of the producer has been denigrated to that of technocrat.

Anatole Dauman describes the role of the producer as that of a father or 'guide' who must lead the director forward, without imposing his wishes or even letting the director know he is being guided. In place of such skilled producers there are now technocrats who either give total liberty to the director, or impose 'commercial' criteria which compromise the artistic vision.

There are still a few good producers in existence. Most are now linked to Europe's media groups, or have distribution deals with the American Majors, and many split their activities between local language films and Hollywood-style films with a US distribution deal.

Some of the leading producers are linked via the Club of European Producers (see membership list in Appendix C) but are far from representing a 'studio system' or integrated commercial industry.

European market cinema is not so much an industry, as a collection of individuals. Each producer has his own personal tastes, and broke into the industry in a different manner. The majority come from the war and pre-war generation and there is a critical shortage of good young producers.

THE TITANS

The 'Titans' who forged European cinema in the immediate post-war period are now gone, and many of the leading contemporary producers are edging towards retirement. This serves as a reminder that the crisis of European cinema could easily deepen in the near future.

PIERRE BRAUNBERGER (1905–90)

Braunberger wrote in his memoirs that his life was marked by three key encounters: with Irving Thalberg, Jean Renoir and Jean-Luc Godard. He was assistant to Thalberg in 1925 and said: 'To him I owe a very large part of what I was able to do afterwards. He was a true producer . . . total, complete, the *chef d'orchestre*.'

Braunberger set up Studio films in Paris in 1927, through which he produced many of the classic surrealist films of the epoch – including films by Man Ray, Luis Buñuel, René Clair and above all Jean Renoir. He shared Renoir's great admiration for German culture and produced several films in Berlin. But as Germany and France moved towards the Right, Braunberger and Renoir faced increasing hostility. They were both in Berlin the day of Hitler's election to power and had to flee to France.

During the Occupation, Braunberger was arrested and placed in a concentration camp, but escaped with his brother. After the war he played a key role in the 'new culture' that emerged in France and produced short films by many of the future Nouvelle Vague directors.

He believed that most directors have only ten years of creative excellence and felt that by the late 1950s French cinema had become mediocre, with the only talented directors being certain 'quality' directors such as Carné, Allegret and Clouzot as well as 'auteurs' such as Renoir and Bresson.

In the 1960s he produced many of the classic films of the French New Wave and helped design the new cultural subsidies. He nonetheless retained his distance from both the authorities and the major companies. 'In this profession which I love and which has impassioned me my whole life' he explained, 'I have always been badly viewed by the institutions and the leading houses. People don't like new things, and I dreamt only of discovery.' Braunberger was highly critical of the state system after 1968 which undermined the role of the producer and encouraged the idea that the director should do everything.

Braunberger was fondly regarded by France's leading directors who called him 'Pierrot' and 'Harlequin'. His definition of a producer was 'A man who reads a great deal, who goes to the theatre, café-theatre and the music hall, and who sees lots of films – he must be aware of all the artistic movements of his time. He must have ideas and imagination, insist that authors write their scripts under his supervision, choose the director and make sure that the shooting does not betray the original work (which is much more common than one believes). He must accompany the director during the editing, the release, and the promotion of the film and ensure that the ideas which inspired the film in the first place are given pride of place when the film is shown to the public.'

ANATOLE DAUMAN (B. 1925)

Dauman is perhaps the 'last tycoon' still working in European cinema. He has been compared to both Irving Thalberg and the Medicis and has nurtured some of the world's finest directors – Resnais, Godard, Bresson, Rouch, Varda, Marker, Borozcyk, Oshima, Schlondorff, Tarkovsky and Wenders. Elia Kazan said of him, 'In the light of his plentiful ideas, I started posing myself all sorts of questions . . . he took me to art galleries, painters' studios and restaurants that I never even suspected existed. The centrepiece of our programme was always the same – conversation.'

Anatole Dauman grew up in Poland within a wealthy Jewish family, with off-shoots in Russia. He came to Paris as a teenager and fought in the Resistance during the war. He then mixed with the community of writers and painters that formed around St Germain de Près in the immediate post-war era. He established Argos Films in 1949, taking as his company mascot the owl of Minerva – the goddess of wisdom.

Although Dauman is held up as one of France's finest producers and has been granted the Order of Merit, he has always felt himself to be an outsider. Half of the directors with whom he has worked have been non-French, and half of his revenues have come from abroad. He believes that much of the present cinema crisis derives from the domination of the market by parochial national monopolies.

Dauman began his career by producing short films. He brought together a community of film-makers and established key friendships, above all with his 'Dioscuri twin', fellow creative producer Pierre Braunberger. The two 'sons of Zeus' formed the nucleus of 'left bank' film-makers – Varda, Resnais, Marker.

The breakthrough for Dauman was in 1955 with a thirty-minute documentary by Alain Resnais on the concentration camps, entitled *Night and Fog*. Chris Marker collaborated on the film and the commentary was written by two poets, Jean Cayrol and Paul Celan. The film achieved worldwide acclaim and demonstrated a successful merging of poetry and reality, which is a hallmark of Dauman's films.

This critical and financial success provided the basis for a new film, which began as a documentary, but with a script by Marguerite Duras, became a poetic love story – *Hiroshima mon Amour*.

In the 1960s, Dauman produced two films by Godard – *Masculin-Feminin* and *2 or 3 things I know about her*. He greatly admired Godard's gift for insolence, ambiguity and seduction – even if this often caused him frustration during shooting – and says that he still expects Godard to give him his 'greatest cinematic moments'. Socially the two have not mixed since the late 1960s.

Many 'children' followed Godard, but it was Wenders who finally took him to the 'end of the world'. Dauman met Wenders through his ex-wife Pascale, and their three-film co-operation, beginning with *Paris, Texas*, elevated the Wunderkind to international status. Dauman refers to Wenders as the 'creature of the skies' and says that at the centre of his work is the fascination for 'watching – from the skies, observing dreams, seeing the soul' – like the owl of Minerva.

The results of *Until the End of the World* were disappointing and Wenders subsequently severed his relationship with Argos Films. Dauman concludes that perhaps the ultimate wish of all directors is patricide, and a caricature by Chris Marker features Dauman's severed head in front of a guillotine. 'When today's young directors unconsciously mourn the loss of the father, I understand' he says. He seems to share their grief.

ALAIN POIRÉ (B. 1919)

Alain Poiré has been the key production force for Gaumont over the post-war era. He joined the company in 1938, saying 'For me cinema was a way of dreaming . . . it was Hollywood.' He began producing during the Occupation, but maintained a low profile and lost family and friends in Auschwitz. In the late 1940s he was in charge of the French half of the Rank-Gaumont alliance, but was highly critical of J. Arthur Rank.

In the early 1950s, he set up Paris-Union Films with emigré producer Henri Deutschmeister, whom he described as 'Romanian by origin, German by culture and French by love'. They later established co-production ventures with MGM and Paramount, who offered up to 100% of finance in return for foreign rights.

Poiré's films include the most successful of French cinema such as *Le Corniaud* and *La Grande Vadrouille* by Gérard Oury. His idols came from music hall (Gabin, Raimu, Chevalier, Montand, Bourvil and Aznavour) and café-théatre (Louis de Funes, Patrick Dewaere, Gérard Départieu and Miou-Miou). This love is shared by his son Jean-Marie Poiré, who is one of the few French directors still committed to popular cinema.

Until the mid-1970s Poiré was the cornerstone of French commercial cinema. He has always placed a high emphasis on humour and mockingly describes his films as a mix of 'American-style burlesque and comedies' and 'sugar coated moralistic melodramas'. When Nicolas Seydoux became head of Gaumont in 1975, Poiré started to wind down his production activity, but he continues to make a small number of high profile films such as *Jean de Florette* with Claude Berri in 1986. His latest film is *Le Jaguar*, written by Francis Veber.

Poiré was extremely critical of the Nouvelle Vague and believed that its claim to 're-invent' the cinema was 'like trying to teach grandmother to suck eggs'. He blamed the 'nouvelle critique' for destroying both the 'dream' of cinema and its professionalism. 'There are many current directors who don't know how to write, edit or rewrite a line of dialogue', he wrote in his autobiography, 'They don't believe in giving the minimum of indications to their actors, and thus being auteurs of nothing, pretend to have made a "film d'auteur".'

RAOUL LÉVY (1922–66)

Raoul Lévy's buccaneering style was pure New York – hectic, modern, electric, excessive and cosmopolitan. He launched the French New Wave with Vadim's *And God Created Woman*. 'Lulu' was a Russian Jewish emigré, whose father was killed in Auschwitz. He lived a James Bond lifestyle, fascinated with gadgets, casinos, fast cars and beautiful women.

The so-called 'king of the schmoozers' created Trans-Mondial Films in 1947 and then became the French representative for an American producer, Edward Small. Lévy was obsessed with discovering a French super-star and made his name with Brigitte Bardot. He got Columbia to back *And God Created Woman* on the back of German actor Curd Jurgens and produced the film on an extremely low budget. On first run, it was assassinated by the critics in France, but after becoming a smash hit in the United States, it had a successful re-release in France.

Lévy then signed a multiple picture deal with Harry Cohn at Columbia – whom he knew through a cousin. He went on to make four more Bardot films including *En Cas de Malheur* (directed by Autant-Lara) and *La Verité* (Clouzot). He chose the best directors of the French 'quality tradition' and when the Nouvelle Vague came along, he called it 'a big joke'. He was opposed to the new state cinema, and refused a state film prize he was awarded.

His undoing was to embark on a mega-production *Marco Polo* (1964), starring Orson Welles, Anthony Quinn and Omar Sharif and directed by 'quality' director Denys de La Patellière. He had hoped to be financed by Columbia, but without Harry Cohn, he could no longer count on their support or advice. *Marco Polo* was a disaster and Lévy did not know where to turn. He tried to become a Nouvelle Vague style director, with *Je vous salue Mafia* using Raoul Coutard as his cameraman, but the film flopped.

On New Year's Eve 1966, Lévy retreated to Saint-Tropez – the location of *And God Created Woman* – and shot himself. Jean-Michel Frodon wrote his epitaph: 'His death felt like a metaphor for the end of a certain cinema, the "qualité française", whose last expression was *La Verité* and which was characterized by the alliance of artistic ambition and commercial objectives. This cinema was a partnership between commerce and creativity, and offered the chance to believe in a cinema which was both "cultural" and appealed to the general public . . . It has been buried by the film professionals and the media . . . and replaced by an incompatible divide between commercial cinema and the cinema d'auteur.'[1]

ALEXANDER KORDA (SANDÓR LÁSZLÓ KELLNER 1893–1956)

Korda was the central figure in the four-month 'spring' of Hungarian cinema in 1918–19 before the Horthy coup. Korda headed the central film organization along with László Vajda and Michael Curtiz. After the coup they left, along with his brothers and Emeric Pressburger, Béla Balázs, Bela Lugosi, Peter Lorre, László Benedek, Charles Vidor, and László Moholy-Nagy.

Korda then worked in Germany and Austria 1919–27, Hollywood 1927–30, Paris 1930–32 and then on to Britain in 1932, where he founded London Films with his brothers Zoltan and Vincent. One of his first films was *The Private Life of Henry VIII*, which lifted British cinema onto the international stage. He became a partner in United Artists in 1935 and during the war shuttled between England and America. His best-known films include *The Thief of Bagdad, The Third Man* and *The Tales of Hoffman*.

EMERIC PRESSBURGER (1902–88) AND MICHAEL POWELL (1905–90)

The Hungarian Emeric Pressburger began his career with Korda and left with him in 1919. He then worked as a top scriptwriter at Ufa in Germany alongside Anatole Litvak and Billy Wilder, before fleeing to France and then to England in 1936, where he was hired by Korda. Korda put Pressburger and Powell together in 1939, leading to classic films such as *The Spy in Black* and *Colonel Blimp* .

Powell was born in Canterbury and was always seen as a maverick within the British cultural establishment. He fell from grace after making *Peeping Tom* in 1960 and later went to work with Coppola's Zoetrope, from where he wrote in 1986, 'I have mirrored England to the English in my films. They have not understood the image in the mirror. I am writing these lines in a foreign country . . . because for the last ten years I have been made to feel an outcast by my own people. I was "too big a risk" and "too independent".'

MICHAEL BALCON (1896–1977)

Balcon founded Gainsborough Pictures in 1924, and was production chief at MGM-British 1936–38 and then at Ealing Studios. Balcon influenced filmmakers such as Hitchcock, made the classic Ealing Comedies, and via the Bryanston production company later launched the British New Wave.

His prime concern was always making 'national films'. When Ealing Studios were sold to the BBC in 1955, he erected a plaque saying 'Here during a quarter of a century were made many films projecting Britain and the British character.'

J. ARTHUR RANK (1888–1972)

Rank was a millionaire flour miller who began to be interested in film in the mid-1930s in order to promote Christian values. According to his biographer his 'greatest virtue of all was undoubtedly the fact that he knew nothing whatsoever about making films'. These moral and professional credentials meant that the British government considered that he was the ideal person to run the British film industry.

At the beginning of the war he bought Odeon and Gaumont-British at knockdown prices and the government considered giving him total monopoly over the film industry.

Rank boosted production during the war years and then laid plans for a world Major, Eagle Lion, at the end of the war. Despite a worldwide distribution and exhibition network and a UK trade ban by the Hollywood Majors in 1947, Rank was unable to build a profitable business.

Alain Poiré was particularly critical of Rank's leadership, commenting that 'the management of the company was not of great dynamism and "Sir J." did nothing to change this. He only wanted "yes men" who'd accept everything he said. He would not tolerate being contradicted, wouldn't listen, and consulted no one . . . this strange leader loved two things – to pose in the centre of young starlets as if in a harem, and organize giant congresses which wasted everyone's time but allowed him to talk pompously.'

In the 1950s Rank began to concentrate on light popular comedies such as the *Doctor* and *Carry-On* series. A Rank official booklet proudly boasted at the time that 'J. Arthur Rank frequently alters lines, touches up dialogue, or deletes scenes after talking them over with his wife or advisers, in order to avoid what he considers bad taste.' J. Arthur Rank began winding down production in the 1960s and died in 1972.

JOSEPH E. LEVINE (1905–87)

Joe Levine grew up in the Boston slums in an immigrant Jewish family. During the war he acquired the Lincoln Theatre in New Haven and began screening European art films and American exploitation pictures. In the immediate post-war years he imported films such as *Rome – Open City*, *Paisan* and *Bicycle Thief* and in 1959 scored a huge hit with the Italian film *Hercules*, which Warners released on 600 screens. Levine earned $4.7 million in rentals, against a $125,000 minimum guarantee.

Through his company, Embassy Pictures, Levine became a key figure in Hollywood-in-Europe with close ties to MGM. He established alliances with Lux, Titanus and Carlo Ponti (who in turn was allied with Georges Beauregard). With the latter, he produced a string of successful films including *Two Women*, *Bocaccio 70*, *Landru*, *Marriage Italian Style*, *Yesterday, Today and Tomorrow* and most famously *Le Mépris* by Godard.

Levine's most profitable production was *The Graduate*, which was produced on a tiny budget but proved to be a huge success. He later sold Embassy Pictures but returned from retirement to produce *A Bridge Too Far* in 1976, which he financed through international pre-sales – making a $5 million profit before even beginning the film. William Goldman, who scripted *A Bridge Too Far*, later wrote, 'Levine never stopped running throughout the 1960s, and long before *The Graduate* – his most prosperous enterprise – shattered everybody's concept of what the audiences were looking for in a hero, Levine had become the most famous and the most successful independent film producer in the world.'

SAM SPIEGEL (1901–85)

Sam Spiegel's Horizon Pictures in the UK stood alongside companies such as Carl Foreman's Open Road Films and Martin Ritt's Salem Films, as key vehicles for channelling Hollywood finance into British films. (Hollywood put up 43% of all UK production finance in 1962 and 71% by 1966.) This earned Spiegel a reputation as an American producer, but he was in fact a Polish Jew and only went to America to escape the Holocaust (using the pseudonym S. P. Eagle). He had worked in Europe with Billy Wilder and Otto Preminger, amongst others, and arrived in the US in 1939. By 1942 he had begun pre-selling internationally pictures, starting with *Tales of Hoffman* (1942).

In Hollywood, he produced classic films such as *On the Waterfront* (1954) and *The African Queen* (1952), and then moved to Britain where he started to set up a series of high profile Anglo-American productions, most notably *Bridge on the River Kwai* (1957) and *Lawrence of Arabia* (1962) with David Lean. Other classics included *Suddenly Last Summer* and *The Last Tycoon*. His last film was *Betrayal* (1983) made two years before his death.

The autodidact, Spiegel interfered extensively on his films, above all with the script, and often created great personal enmities with his directors as a consequence. Some described him as a 'monster', but all recognized his intuitive grasp of story-telling and his willingness to take risks.

DINO DE LAURENTIIS (B. 1919) AND CARLO PONTI (B. 1910)

The 'cat and the wolf' were the two giants of Italian cinema in the immediate post-war era. Ponti is Milanese, precise, rational and cautious. Dino is Neapolitan, extrovert, inventive and adventurous. The duo were trained under the state propaganda cinema of Mussolini, but when the Americans arrived their entrepreneurial spirit quickly chimed with Hollywood-in-Europe.

Dino in particular was never serene or calm. He would often call his associates at midnight with his latest idea. He lived on adrenalin and nervous energy – always looking for something bigger and better – and produced the first major Italian colour film, and the first film in 3D. Milos Forman later described him as 'a veritable dynamo, you're never bored with him'.

As a young man Dino was known as 'Dino de Parentis' due to his wealthy and well-connected family. He went to the state film school CSC aged eighteen and trained to become an actor. He then had bit parts in several films and aged twenty-two, teamed up with the then thirty-one-year-old Ponti.

Ponti was more reticent than Dino. He had trained as a lawyer and produced his first film in 1937. He worked hard, lived on the telephone and disliked parties or big social occasions. His wife Sofia Loren emphasized that while as a husband he was warm and compassionate, as a businessman he could be cold and brutal.

Both partners paid extreme attention to choosing the director and overseeing the script. They both constantly campaigned for greater discipline within the Italian film industry. Dino wrote in 1957, 'If there is a crisis, it is because Italy has too many amateur producers making too many bad films. Quality, not quantity is what counts.' He declared that his philosophy was 'to combine the industrial initiative with the inspiration of auteurs'.

One of their early hits was *Bitter Rice* (1949) starring Silvana Mangano, which featured brief nudity and Mangano dancing the boogie-woogie with Vittorio Gassman. Despite being the fifth biggest film of the year in Italy and a significant hit worldwide, the film provoked a scandal at home on all sides of the political spectrum and led to Andreotti's 1949 film law which introduced script pre-censorship and was designed to avoid more 'dirty linen' being shown.

By 1953, Ponti said 'today everyone intending to produce a film has to cross a minefield of political compromises'. The saviour for the duo was an alliance with the Americans, for whom they acted as line producers and also had production deals. It was via the Americans that they secured funding and international renown for 'art films' such as Fellini's *La Strada,* popular comedies starring Toto and super-productions such as *Ulysses* (1954) starring Kirk Douglas and *War and Peace* (1956) by King Vidor.

During the 1950s, the duo began to drift apart, partly as a result of Dino's marriage with Silvana Mangano in 1949 and Ponti's liaison with Sophia Loren. In 1957, the partners went separate ways.

Ponti divorced his wife and married Loren in Mexico in 1957. He was then vilified by the Italian church and press, who refused to recognize the marriage, and as a result he emigrated to Paris, where he established a pact with Georges de Beauregard and Joe Levine. In 1964 he took French nationality. On leaving Italy he said, 'Despite the fact that our films are recognized throughout the world as the finest and the best, our cinema is treated by the Italian establishment with utter disdain as if those who work there are some kind of circus clowns.'

After 1965, Ponti went solo and produced *Dr Zhivago, Blow Up, Profession: Reporter* and many other classic European films. One of his most controversial decisions was a refusal to pay up on Milos Forman's *Fireman's Ball*, because the final version was two minutes shorter than agreed in the contract. Claude Berri saved the film.

In Italy, Ponti continued to be hounded by the authorities. In 1979 he was sentenced in absence and fined $25 million for smuggling currency and art abroad. He denied the charges and said, 'I have always dreamed of the day that there would be a United States of Europe. In my opinion it's the only solution capable of resolving the present crisis of humanity, a crisis which is getting worse. In Europe, liberty and justice are more than ever placed in question. That is why I envisage for us a life between Europe and the United States. At the moment American cinema is filled with Italian names: Scorsese, Coppola, de Niro, Pacino, Puzo, Travolta, Minelli. There at least we will feel at home.'

Dino also suffered problems with the Italian authorities. In 1957 he established DDL with comedy star Toto and set up his own technical complex, Dinocitta, in Rome where he produced Italian-American co-productions such as *Barabbas* and *The Bible* as well as the Italian-Russian mega-production *Waterloo*. In 1961 alone he produced over twenty films, most of them in English, leading M. Raekin of Paramount to comment, 'A Dino de Laurentiis film is a Hollywood production in Rome exteriors.'

But as the Americans withdrew from Europe, Dino found it more difficult to work in Italy. He tried to work with the new state system, and established a pact with RAI in 1965 to produce *The Odyssey after Ulysses*. But the deal quickly fell apart because Dino couldn't work with the 'prudery, managerial moralism and public service values' of the RAI bureaucrats. Vittorio Bonicelli suggested that 'Dino loved the game of chance and the sense of power over the machine, which the TV couldn't give him.' Angelo Romano added, 'The co-operation with de Laurentiis could only be short-lived. His mercantile logic as a producer could not cohabit with an environment firmly anchored in the very European idea of "public service", which was pedagogical and directed from on high.'

By the late 1960s, Dino found that he had few friends in his home country, and in 1971 he sold his studios and moved to Hollywood. 'The political and economic situation kept getting worse' he later explained. 'By 1972 it became impossible. I was forced to come to the conclusion that if I was going to continue to make movies, I'd have to move to America. It's the only country in the world where you can work in complete freedom. Imagine trying to make *Serpico* in Italy with police co-operation. You wouldn't last one day.'

Dino then teamed up with Dutch financier Frans Afman and became a pioneer figure in American independent cinema with films such as *Serpico*, *Death Wish*, *Three Days of the Condor*, *King Kong*, *Flash Gordon*, *Dune*, *Ragtime* and *Year of the Dragon*, alongside European productions such as Bergman's *Face to Face* and *The Serpent's Egg*. He also played a key role in securing work in America for European talent – after winning a stand-off in 1978 against the New York guilds over the right of Swedish cinematographer Sven Nykvist to shoot *King of the Gypsies*.

Dino continues to produce pictures with the Majors and his daughter Rafaella (b. 1952) now works on both sides of the Atlantic and is co-producing two big-budget films for Universal, including the $80 million *Dragonheart* starring Sylvester Stallone. Dino's nephew Aurelio is also a key figure in Italian cinema.

LEADING CONTEMPORARIES

The ability of European cinema to continue to produce a small number of notable films a year, is mainly due to a handful of 'creative producers', many of whom launched their careers in the 1960s.

DAVID PUTTNAM (B. 1941)

The son of a star Fleet Street photographer, Sir David began his career in the Swinging Sixties as a bright light in the world of British advertising. He now stands at the heart of Britain's cultural establishment alongside Lord Attenborough of Richmond Upon Thames. He is a man with a 'mission', with a 'passion for my craft and the process of its growth into an art form which is capable of uniting, in peace, the family of man of which we're all part'.

Puttnam's formative years were the Hays Code 1950s, when Europe 'basked in the benign, positive and powerful aura of post-Marshall Plan concerned and responsible America'. In the 1960s, with his Paul McCartney lookalike haircut, he was one of the many working class wonders who invaded the British pop culture scene, and later commented 'I was rock 'n' roll up to my eyebrows.'

As a photographer's agent, Puttnam admitted, 'I've used representing photographers [like David Bailey, Terence Donovan and Terry O'Neill] to move on to bigger and better things.' In a certain way, he did the same in the film industry – capitalizing on the talent of 'outsiders' such as Alan Parker, Ridley Scott and Adrian Lyne.

'David *was* the British film industry in the late Seventies and early Eighties' says Michael Apted. He has been compared to Alexander Korda for his ability to internationalize UK films and to Michael Balcon for his suburban British mentality. His own role models are Balcon and Irving Thalberg, the classic creative producer.

The high and low point of Puttnam's career was his chairmanship of Columbia Pictures in 1987. 'I have been to the top of the mountain', he later declared. Puttnam accepted his Columbia post on condition that Coca-Cola accepted his commitment to 'quality movies'. 'I would never make a picture for purely commercial reasons', he said at the time. 'Take *Rambo* for example. Even if I knew *Rambo* was going to be as big as it was. I would never have made it. It's just not a film I would be interested in.'

Puttnam later declared in a British newspaper interview, 'I like a scrap. It's a working class thing. Screw you. I don't need any of you. I leave here in March, 1990. I have the date ringed on the calendar. If I make good movies and they don't work I will go with my head held high. Suck it and see.'

Many of Puttnam's objectives have since been embraced by Hollywood – the need to control budgets, to shift power away from the agencies and to produce more intelligent adult entertainment. But Puttnam's undiplomatic manner and moral mission brought him deadly enemies from within Hollywood's power elite.

After Columbia, Puttnam now seems somewhat war weary. He has shifted his attentions away from cinema and towards education and playing politics. Tina Brown has described him as 'The Lost Tycoon'.

Today Puttnam believes that the key to his success has been his advertising savvy. 'As a film-maker I'm an unreconstructed marketing man. I came up through advertising, it made me what I am. I knew how to package a film around two main elements and construct a strong soundtrack. A really good handle on marketing is invaluable. I was never frightened by money. At twenty-two I was negotiating advertising budgets bigger than the film budgets I handled ten years later. I also studied contract law at night school. My two careers up to then – advertising and a photographic agency – had worked out. I was very confident. I didn't even think of failure.'

Puttnam established his company Goodtimes in 1970, with Sandy Lieberson and backing from Evelyn de Rothschild and aimed to buy video rights to UK films. But Rothschild instead got hooked into film production. 'Sandy and I had good times in the Seventies. We were offering something different and were much more in tune with the times than most people, who were very old fashioned. We also worked with very talented professionals, like Jeremy Thomas. And our timing was good. There was a whole wave of talent trying to break through and we made it possible. If I'd started a year earlier, 1967–68, I would have been swept away by the Majors. But the Majors had just withdrawn and we were left with an open field. If I'd begun ten years later it would have been much more difficult because the special mix of talent that emerged in the 1960s would no longer have been available.'

Puttnam's first film, the £0.6 million ($0.9M) *Melody*, was written by Alan Parker and was based around the rights to seven Bee Gee songs. It was two-thirds financed by Edgar Bronfman Sr. on advice from his fifteen-year-old son (now head of MCA/Universal). The other third came from Hemdale (David Hemmings and John Daly). The second film, *The Pied Piper*, was helmed by French New Wave director Jacques Demy. 'For my second film I went with an eminent director' explains Puttnam, 'but I lost control over the film. I realised that wasn't the way for me.'

Puttnam considers that his breakthrough film was his third – *That'll be the Day* starring David Essex, which was semi-autobiographical. 'With my third film, I really became a producer' he says. 'I knew the terminology by then, we kept the budget low – £0.6 million – and I worked on the screenplay in detail with Ray Connolly. Again it was very music based. I had a terrific music deal [with Ronco], giving us a third of the budget plus promotional spending, and the album went on to be a great success. The rest of the money came from Nat Cohen at EMI. The next film was *Stardust* with the same elements and a slightly higher budget – $1.2 million. I got some money from Peter Guber at Columbia for US rights. He'd seen *That'll be the Day* and liked it.'

Puttnam then produced a couple of small pictures with Ken Russell before making *Bugsy Malone*, which was Alan Parker's shot at a Hollywood career. 'I'd always been good at bringing together investors' continues Puttnam. 'For *Bugsy*, which cost around $1 million, we had five investors – Paramount ($0.3M), Rank ($0.2M), the NFFC ($0.2M), Polydor ($0.1M) and some private money including £85,000 from Alan Parker.' Puttnam also secured P&A money (which Rank had refused to put up), by selling the Japanese rights for $75,000. *Bugsy*'s success at Cannes led to financing from Paramount for Ridley Scott's debut feature, the $1 million *Duellists*. Half-way through shooting Peter Guber asked Puttnam to head his production company in Los Angeles and produce *Midnight Express*.

'I'd tried to keep away from Hollywood and had deep reservations because I enjoyed my independence too much. Alan Parker always criticized me for it. He didn't have my heady dreams. He always wanted to crack the US market from the beginning. I don't know why.' The American experience was an eye-opener for Puttnam. His $150,000 fee was equal to the sum total of all his prior film earnings. And he saw how the Majors organized marketing and money management. 'I learnt how a film really gets pushed' says Puttnam. 'They spent more on promotion than production. In the UK, P&A was worth 10% of the budget. In comparison we were a one man and his dog operation.'

Puttnam returned to Britain a changed man. Not only did he have a renewed sense of moral mission after the traumatic experience of producing *Midnight Express*, he also had a much better understanding of how to hype a film. 'I took on board what I'd learnt in the States and was rewarded for it. By the time I got to *Chariots of Fire* and *Killing Fields* I'd nailed it down. I'd always been committed to a public service ethos, I now knew how to make it work for a relatively large audience. I knew that a radical film like *Killing Fields* would never be a mega movie but I consciously tried to maximize its appeal. Even with *Chariots of Fire*, I never thought it would do as well as it did.'

To make *Chariots of Fire*, Puttnam secured 50% of the budget from shipping millionaire Dodi Al Fayed. The film was released in the US by Warners and established a relationship that he has maintained ever since. Puttnam was also at the heart of Pearson's Goldcrest venture which was committed to quality films in the great tradition of David Lean. In 1985 he turned down an offer to run Paramount and then got the Columbia job.

The Columbia debacle and the collapse of Goldcrest led him to consider retiring from film in order to start a new phase in his career. But he kept his first-look deal with Warners and secured further backing from Japan's Fujisankei and merchant bank Country NatWest.

He has since produced films such as *Memphis Belle, Meeting Venus, War of the Buttons* and *Being Human* and has also tried to bring his marketing savvy to European producers through his position as honorary president of ACE, the European Film Studio. But he is convinced that Europe's public service tradition means that there will never be more than a niche industry on the continent. 'I've never set out to make a blockbuster,' he says. 'The closest probably is *Memphis Belle*. I've always been committed to entertainment with something to say. This leads to some compromises, sometimes they show through.' Puttnam is now spending much more of his energies on developing the World University Network on the Internet, as well as working for political associations and charities. He was awarded a knighthood in 1995.

JEREMY THOMAS (B. 1949)

Jeremy Thomas is president of the British Film Institute and son of veteran director Ralph Thomas, responsible for the *Doctor* series, and related to Gerald Thomas who directed many of the *Carry On* films. Despite these very British credentials, he is the most international of UK producers.

Thomas passed his childhood in film studios. He began working as a film editor and his first production was *Mad Dog Morgan* (1974) in Australia, followed by *The Shout* (1976) directed by Jerzy Skolimozski. He then partnered with music mogul Chris Blackwell in Recorded Releasing and in the 1980s produced a range of films including three films by Nic Roeg plus *The Great Rock'n'Roll Swindle, Merry Christmas Mr Lawrence*, and the $25 million *Last Emperor*.

Thomas is one of Europe's few producers who knows how to launch an international film and negotiate with the 'take no prisoners' Majors. He had a stand-off with MGM over Nic Roeg's *Eureka* (1982), which they had fully financed but were reluctant to release.

In 1988 Thomas signed a $120 million six-picture deal with Japan's Schochiku-Fuji, organizing sales through Glinwood Films and finance from Film Trustees. The latter was owned 33% by Thomas, 33% by Glinwood and the rest amongst foreign partners. Despite the early success of *The Last Emperor*, other films such as *The Sheltering Sky* and *Naked Lunch* underperformed and led to Film Trustees' liquidation in 1993 with $66 million in debts.

Thomas subsequently signed a first-look deal with UGC, and Terry Glinwood continues to advise on foreign sales. He also produces films outside this deal, such as Johnny Depp's directorial debut, *The Brave*.

SALLY HIBBIN (B. 1953) AND KEN LOACH (B. 1937)

Parallax Pictures is a worker's co-operative uniting Ken Loach, Sally Hibbin, Rebecca O'Brien, Les Blair and Sarah Curtis. They have been making some of the most innovative European films in recent years and also have the classic profile for attracting subsidy funds and critics' awards.

Sally Hibbin began her career writing books on the *Carry On* series as well as 'the making of' *007 License to Kill* and *Back to the Future*. At the same time she produced radical documentaries for *Eleventh Hour* on Channel 4 as well as campaigns for the GLC, VSO and other organizations. In 1987 she was asked by Ann Skinner of Skreba to work on the TV serial *A Very British Coup* (1988), which was the beginning of her film career. 'I was very lucky to team up with Ann Skinner' she says. 'I learnt a great deal from her. I was used to low-budget films and had never worked on a film with a 40–45 person crew. I had a very political background, and *Coup* taught me how to tell a story in a very populist way.'

She was then called by veteran director Ken Loach, who had recovered international prestige with *Hidden Agenda* in 1989. 'I was digging in the garden and heard the phone ringing', recalls Hibbin. 'It was Ken asking me if I'd produce *Riff-Raff*. My answer was "Yes" without even thinking about it. I'd always been a great admirer of Ken's work.'

Riff-Raff took eighteen months to get Channel 4 backing. The budget was trimmed down to $1 million. But the film helped relaunch Loach's career in Europe. Sally Hibbin followed the film through different festivals and began to establish a valuable set of European contacts. *Riff-Raff* was premiered in Vallodolid festival, and the following year there was a retrospective which established links with Wim Wender's Road Movies. The film was also declared European Film of the Year at the 1991 Felix Awards. The next films by Loach were *Raining Stones* and *Ladybird, Ladybird* with Channel 4, fully funded for £850,000 each film. *Raining Stones* was particularly important in strengthening contacts, following the Jury Prize at Cannes in 1992. This led to the $4 million *Land of Freedom* which was backed by a set of European co-producers including Road Movies and Enrique Gonzalez Macho in Spain, and also received support from Eurimages.

Parallax received Incentive Funding from the European Script Fund which Hibbin says 'transformed our lives'. The company supports new talent, including first-time director Phil Davis with *i-D* based on football hooliganism backed by British Screen, Channel 4 and German subsidy money. Other films include *The Englishman Who Went Up A Hill But Came Down A Mountain* and *Carla's Song*.

TIM BEVAN (B. 1959) AND ERIC FELLNER (B. 1961)

This duo is at the heart of PolyGram's film empire. They both began their careers in the music video business, through which they met PolyGram's Michael Kuhn. Tim Bevan's first film was the $1 million *My Beautiful Laundrette*

(1985), which launched him on the international scene. After a series of minor misses and hits, PolyGram decided in 1988 to take an equity stake in Bevan's production company, Working Title, as one of the main labels of their new film strategy. This required Bevan to shift gears towards more mainstream films and led to a rift with his producing partner Sarah Radclyffe, who left in 1992 to set up her own independent venture. Bevan then teamed up with Eric Fellner who had been at the heart of the MGMM music promo empire, and had produced a series of films in the late 1980s, most notably *Sid and Nancy*.

Bevan and Fellner are both committed to films with 'social edge', but their biggest hit to date is the romantic comedy *Four Weddings and a Funeral* (1994), produced by Duncan Kenworthy. This success led to a second romantic comedy, the $40 million *French Kiss* (1995) which grossed over $100 million worldwide. In 1996 they also released *Dead Man Walking* which is closer to their roots, and has been a surprise hit.

Working Title's track record at PolyGram has been uneven. The above successes have been mixed with significant disappointments such as *Moonlight and Valentino* and *Hudsucker Proxy*. But this is all part of the learning curve, as they move towards becoming fully fledged producers of big commercial pictures. Bevan says of his subsidy-style roots, 'I'm very happy not to need it any more. But it helped get me going. Channel 4 and British Screen were essential. You can't bite the hand that feeds you. *My Beautiful Laundrette* opened the international market to us. We followed the film around the world. The last ten years I've been working the circuit, building up contacts. It ain't easy. It's a very slippery pole. Everyone finds it difficult, especially with the agents. You have to find friends and build slowly.'

STEVE WOOLLEY (B. 1956) AND NIK POWELL (B. 1950)

Palace pictures was one of the most dynamic forces in British cinema in the 1980s but went crashing into bankruptcy in 1991 with total losses estimated as high as $38 million. Powell and Woolley set up the company in 1983, with Powell injecting $0.8 million of his own funds. The laconic Powell had previously been right-hand man to schoolfriend Richard Branson at Virgin, and the hyperactive Woolley had been running the Scala repertory cinema, part of the Virgin group.

> Since a child I'd been in love with the cinema [explains Woolley]. I started working at the Scala repertory cinema and had to fill an eclectic schedule of over eighty films a month. Soon I was programming seasons for the NFT and writing reviews for *Time Out* on cinema and rock 'n' roll. In 1980 Channel 4 wanted to buy Scala's premises near Tottenham Court Road. I did a deal with Virgin whereby I kept 10% of the value of the sale and moved Scala to King's Cross. Through the deal I also met Jeremy Isaacs and he commissioned a film show called *Worst of Hollywood*. It was produced by me, Chris Brown

and Michael Medved – before he became a right wing lunatic. We showed cult movies like *Planet 9 from Outer Space* and *They Saved Hitler's Brain* with Paul Webster playing Hitler's head in a jar. The series was very successful. Then I set up the video label with Nik Powell. Nik wasn't convinced about the movie business, but once he started mixing with the film crowd and seeing more cult movies he got hooked. We went round film festivals looking for hot titles, well before players like Miramax got into the business. We acquired films like *Evil Dead* and *Diva* at AFM as well as films by John Waters, Herzog, Lynch, Svabo. We worked with new people on the marketing and the press releases. We said the industry is dead, we're going to dictate our terms and control the entire process.

Releases such as *Evil Dead* sold a massive 50,000 video units in the UK. But Palace were attacked in Britain for selling video nasties and taken to court. 'Nik loved all that' says Woolley. 'He loves the scams, the ways of generating publicity.' Then Palace moved into theatrical distribution with films like *Diva* and carved out a healthy business. With their ear to the ground, they acquired UK rights to films like *Cinema Paradiso* on the basis of the rough cut. The logical next step was to start producing.

'I'd always wanted to build up a company as a family, with like-minded people', continues Woolley. 'Palace was a group of friends who didn't mind working late hours. Our first project was Neil Jordan's *Company of Wolves*. Everyone said it was too arty. Mamoun Hassan at NFFC had shown an interest, but in the end ITC bankrolled the film. They saw that we were doing business with obscure stuff and thought "these guys must know what they're doing".'

Palace used *Company of Wolves* to launch a production strategy while continuing to earn cash flow from their core business. 'You've got to have other sources of revenue' explains Powell, 'enough to cover your development costs and have the film far enough down the road to attract other investors.' From the beginning, Palace used their foreign contacts to set up their financing, using Woolley as the creative spark and Powell as the deal-maker. 'You need quite a sophisticated financial knowledge' says Powell, 'a very close link with an international sales agent and a first class relationship with your bankers. Ironically the Thatcher era forced producers like us to take Norman Tebbit's advice and get on our bikes. Ironically the Brits have been more active in doing this than anyone. We're good at combining cultures together. We don't have the cultural arrogance of the Americans or the French. We established a group of friendly distributors abroad – who later became the basis of Eurotrustees. For each film, they put up pre-sales money which established the film's value in the marketplace. We then went back to the British sources – basically British Screen and Channel 4 – to see if they were interested.'

The films that followed were perhaps not 'classics' but stood out as the few British films in the 1980s which rose above TV status – *Absolute Beginners* (with Goldcrest), *Mona Lisa* (with Handmade), *Letter to Brezhnev* (with Initial), *Siesta* and *High Spirits*. The financing strategy was always simple – name talent where available and a strong soundtrack. In 1989 they released *Scandal,* which was the biggest UK film of the year and generated huge video revenues. The film was bankrolled by Palace with support from Miramax. Palace then set up an LA division and started to diversify into the record business in Holland, satellite TV and even a chain of health-food stores. 'After starting out with me as the risk-taker and Nik as the conservative, the roles started to reverse', explains Woolley. 'We got into all these new areas, and spent less time on our core business. We stepped up production with films like *The Big Man, The Miracle, Shag* and *Rage in Harlem,* but many of the films flopped. We were caught in the gravitational pull of the Majors. When the recession hit we couldn't offload our businesses and we went belly up.'

Nik Powell had been a great believer in *The Big Man* starring Liam Neeson, with its 'epic feel' and soundtrack by Ennio Morricone. But the critics hated it. Adrian Turner described the film as typical Steve Woolley – fast cars, loud music and blow jobs. Woolley was initially angered by the comment, but says 'I began to think about it, and saw that all my films did in fact have those ingredients. Even *Interview with a Vampire* – if you substitute blood sucking for blow jobs. The real problem was that we'd built up a lot of jealousy and anger by starting up our company and saying "Fuck the industry". People were sitting in dark rooms waiting to pounce. They dumped on us from savage heights.'

Palace went bankrupt at their moment of crowning glory – with the success of *The Crying Game* in the US and with films like *The Player* and *Reservoir Dogs* lined up for UK distribution. Powell and Woolley lost their company and their library. From an eighty-person company they returned to a core staff of three and a half and established a temporary new venture called Matawa with a one-year first-look deal with PolyGram. They then renamed the company Scala Pictures and sold a 49% equity stake for $0.45 million to Chrysalis. They continue to make films that try to bridge the American and European film cultures. 'The problem for the Brits in Europe' says Woolley, 'is that we're seen as a Trojan Horse for American culture. The authorities have developed an antipathy towards the English language. At the same time the Americans see us as "too arty". Aesthetically I feel closer to Europe, but for business I prefer working with Americans. They're doers rather than talkers. A lot of people here want the money delivered on a plate. You only have to look at the way they learn their trade. At the BBC they're told how to make programmes and not how to sell them. I feel much closer to the Americans.'

After twenty-five 'unofficial' co-productions, the duo are making their first official co-production with support from Eurimages. 'We were never any good at filling in the forms' explains Powell, 'but we're getting better at it . . . The problem is that these subsidy boards often demand absurd conditions. For example, one of our films, *Hollow Reed*, was set in the West country and they wanted to impose a German script editor. It didn't make sense. It's these kind of bureaucratic rules that put producers like us off.'

Woolley and Powell aim to continue producing a mix of high-budget American films with quirky Euro fare. Their street background will mean that they will continue to irritate the critical establishment.

'The British film industry is very dynastic', sums up Oscar Moore of *Screen International*. 'They're all sons of sons of sons. Steve Woolley's seen as an outsider. But he's got exactly what the industry needs – raw talent and fresh ideas.'

DIETER GEISSLER (B. 1943)

Dieter Geissler began his film career as an actor working mainly in TV for German and British productions. 'I'd never wanted to be an actor all my life', he explains. 'One day, I met a young German director, Carl Laemker, who knew a nightclub owner interested in financing a short film. I said why not do a feature. We went for a couple of beers and the guy asked what the story was. Carl made something up, and he liked it. It was in February. He said, "When do you shoot?" I looked at my agenda and picked out a date at random – May 5th. He agreed to put up half the budget and I put up the rest. That's how I got started!'

Geissler's debut production was *48 Hours to Acapulco*, with him playing the lead alongside Christine Kreuger. The crew had all worked in short films and deferred their fees. The film was shot in Munich, Bavaria, Rome, Florence, Mexico City and Acapulco, all in six weeks. It was not a great success. But through showing the film at a festival at Utrecht, Dieter met a young Dutch director who had written a script, *Obsessions*, with Scorsese. Again Geissler played the lead in the film and was a co-producer. The film was a minor hit in Germany and No. 6 in the year in Italy.

On the back of this success I decided to quit being an actor and to start co-producing films with Italy [says Dieter]. Germany at the time was moving to either auteur films or sex films. Rome was the Hollywood of Europe and you could earn big money there. There was talent from everywhere. I relocated to Rome and got involved in co-producing Visconti's *Ludwig* (1973) with MGM. The film cost $4 million – a huge budget at the time. We had a prestigious cast including Romy Schneider and Helmut Berger and shot in castles. I then teamed up with Carlo Ponti to produce *What?* by Polanski which went on to win awards throughout the world. But despite the awards we didn't make much money on the movie.

Geissler also produced *State of Siege* by Costa-Gavras, and then returned to Germany in the mid-1970s 'when people started getting fed up of sex education movies'. The movie business in Germany was crumbling as the Majors withdrew their financing and state TV came in to back small cultural films. A large media group offered him the chance to run the TV division, which he says he thought about for two months before deciding to struggle on as a producer. In 1980 he acquired the rights to the *Neverending Story*. The book became a surprise hit and Dieter realized he needed a partner to cover the high budget needed to make the film. Bernd Eichinger wanted to acquire the rights from him, but instead they agreed to produce the film together with joint responsibility for the budget. The film was heavily dependent on special effects and was given an American feel. Warners gave a $12 million advance against rights in the US, UK, France, Scandinavia and Benelux, and sales agent PSO/Delphi put up an $8 million minimum guarantee for other territories. About $3–4 million was found in German subsidies and Eichinger's real estate partner had to mortgage two apartment blocks to fill the gap.

The film grossed $24 million at the US box office and $30 million in Japan, and performed very well throughout the rest of the world. It also sold well in video. Eichinger had the option to back the sequel but instead invested in *The Name of the Rose*. This left the franchise to Geissler and he has so far produced two sequels and an animation series, as well as establishing a special effects studio.

Neverending Story effectively launched Geissler's new company Cinevox, which he set up in 1982. 'I wanted to control my own destiny' he explains. 'I always kept the company small and concentrated on my own productions or co-productions. I keep total control of marketing and distribution and above all foreign sales.' Cinevox has offices in Munich, Berlin and Los Angeles and has a distribution deal with Warners for Germany, France and the UK, whereby Cinevox puts up P&A in return for a lower distribution fee. 'The relationship is excellent when we have a successful movie' explains Geissler, 'but when a film underperforms it tends to be dropped quickly whereas a smaller distributor might get more out it.'

Cinevox produces six to eight films a year, mainly US-German co-productions, typically shot in English but with a German director, crew and studio locat-ions, thus providing access to German industrial subsidies. Recent titles include *Knight Moves* and *Shattered*. Films are pre-sold through the LA office and are fund-ed like any American independent feature – except that they have the added advantage of European subsidies and status.

In 1992 a $30 million revolving loan facility was established with Hypo Bank and Berliner Bank, with Film Garantie Finance providing a completion bond and shortfall guarantees. But the scheme proved cumbersome and was dropped by Geissler in 1994 for more traditional discount financing on a film-by-film basis.

Geissler is also vice-president of the European Producer's Club, which informally represents European interests to the MPAA.

BERND EICHINGER (B. 1949)

Eichinger attended Munich film school between 1970 and 1973 and then founded Solaris Filproduktion in 1974. He became president and main shareholder of Constantin group in 1979 and now forms part of the Kirch business empire.

He began by making films by Wenders and Wolfgang Petersen, but his breakthrough was Uli Edel's $3 million *Christiane F* in 1980. Until the late 1980s he concentrated mainly on distribution, producing a film only every eighteen months. He now produces one to three German films a year plus one American production. For both kinds of film, he accesses German subsidies. For example, the English-language *Body of Evidence* directed by Uli Edel had $0.75 million in federal subsidies and further backing from the Bavarian film fund.

Eichinger is outspoken on the need to match budgets with markets and to produce better films. For German films he aims for a $3–5 million budget which will mainly recoup at home. For international films he looks for an American cast and a budget in excess of $20 million. He compares the two types of film to 'the difference between driving on a small country road or driving on the autobahn: the autobahn is faster, it is more dangerous and more cars are out there'. Eichinger's English-language pictures include *Neverending Story, Name of the Rose, Last Exit to Brooklyn, Body of Evidence* (with Dino de Laurentiis) and *House of the Spirits*. His German films include *Das Boot* (1981) and the recent smash hit *Der Bewegte Mann*.

Eichinger has an eclectic taste spanning quality literature to comic books, and emphasizes the role of development, on which he spends 10–20% of the production budget.

Many of Eichinger's films are based on an established literary property. This creates a narrative spine and also recognition in the marketplace. In the case of *The Name of the Rose* he joked that one of the main attractions of the film was that many people who had the book on their shelves had never read it.

Eichinger is very critical of the state of European cinema and the effect that subsidies have had since the 1960s. 'For years directors have been working like schoolteachers – writing red ink all over scripts and trying to write themselves. Any talented person doesn't want to be treated like that and disappears from the scene . . . The problem is that 80% of the people who make films in Europe don't know what they're talking about. But the system allows them to go on and on and on making movies. I don't understand why people like Jack Lang go round and get respect.'

Eichinger suggests that the way forward is to have backing either from a European media group or the Majors. 'A Major is like a big bear' he says. 'They will end up eating you, it's just a question of how round you are. If you go to sleep the bear will eat you. But as long as the bear is blocking the cave you're safe from other animals. If you can stay awake you'll be okay.'[2]

ANDRES VICENTE GOMEZ (B. 1943)

Andres Vicente Gomez is one of the leading forces in Spanish cinema and is now head of production for Sogepaq. He began his career aged seventeen working alongside Niels Larsen in distribution and then worked for two years for Elias Querejeta. In 1965 he set up his own company distributing American films into Franco's Spain. His first production was *White Comanche* (1969) starring William Shatner, which cost $3 million (at today's prices) and was co-produced with Westinghouse. The Spanish half of the budget was found through equity investors, with Andres providing 25% of the total.

'I come from a cosmopolitan background', explains Andres. 'I went to a French school as a kid, and was then sent abroad to learn English – something which was very rare at the time. As a distributor I was dealing with American films, foreign imports and re-issues of old classics by Keaton and Chaplin. I was constantly mixing with people from different countries. It was natural for me to try and build an international career.' Andres' second film was a co-production, *House of the Damned*, starring Donald Pleasance – which benefited from a Spanish subsidy but flopped miserably. He then produced *Treasure Island* starring Orson Welles in 1971 and in 1973 produced Welles' *F for Fake*.

Andres slowly familiarized himself with the market through production and distribution. 'In this business, you have to make lots of mistakes', he explains. 'The most important thing for a producer is to know the market for the films you are making. I've always had successes mixed with failures. Slowly you start to understand what makes people choose certain films and reject others. I spent the beginning of my career understanding the Spanish market. I learned about the international market in theory by importing films, attending festivals, and admiring the work of other producers. It's only since 1985 that I've begun to really develop into the international arena – and even now it's mainly in continental Europe. The Anglo-Saxon market is still very closed to me.'

Andres' films include *Matador* by Almodóvar, *Hay Carmela* by Carlos Saura and a variety of films with Fernando Trueba and Bigas Luna. His biggest financial liability was *Eldorado* (1987) by Carlos Saura, for which he provided the completion bond. The film ultimately cost 1 billion pesetas, and left him with huge debts which many felt he would never be able to repay. 'My problem has always been too much imagination', Andres explains. 'I will never be a rich man. There are always more projects than money.' His alliance with Sogepaq nonetheless gives him a much securer financial footing than before.

Andres has placed great emphasis on developing a viable independent production structure, which in 1994 had annual revenues of $15 million and overheads and development spending of $1.5 million. Andres was partnered with library holder Enrique Cerezo through much of the 1980s and had a distribution deal through UIP in Spain whereby he put up P&A costs and had a lower distribution fee.

'The leading European producers, such as Marin Karmitz or Dieter Geissler have their own integrated structures', he says. 'That's something which doesn't really exist in the Anglo-American model. I have always been a great believer that any company aiming for independence must do its own foreign sales, distribution expenses and have a direct relationship with clients which enables one to build up a volume of product and discount for failures.'

This structure is the basis for funding his films. 'My strategy for financing a Spanish film is like making a table with four legs' says Andres. 'One leg is national subsidies, another television sales, another video and theatrical and the fourth is foreign sales or co-production. You have to have at least three of the legs in place before starting production. The fourth can be covered by internal funds.'

Andres' deputy, Antonio Saura (son of Carlos Saura) explains that 'If we can hold the budget under $2 million we do the film domestically. Otherwise if we've got talent attached we talk to our friends, fish around a bit and for Spanish language, with the right talent, we can go up to $4–5 million. We're very producer led. We've got the rights to three of Spain's best-selling books, which we use to look for director and cast.'

Andres is now diversifying into English language production in the $12–15 million range. A breakthrough success for him was Fernando Trueba's *Belle Epoque* (co-produced with Cerezo) which won an Oscar for Best Foreign Language Film and grossed over $7 million in Spain. This helped him set up the finance for Trueba's first English-language film – *Two Much*.

CLAUDE BERRI (B. CLAUDE LANGMANN 1934)

Claude Berri is one of the few producers in France still committed to classic narratives and professional screenwriters. He was born into a modest family but has moved himself up into the highest social circles of French cinema. 'I became a writer-director because nobody wanted to give me work as an actor' he says, 'a producer because nobody wanted to back my films and finally a distributor because I was fed up waiting for others to do what I could do myself.'

Berri today stands at the heart of the Seydoux/Chargeurs/Pathé/Renn/AMLF empire, and is the power behind the throne in the powerful lobbying group ARP in 1987. Berri's long-time associate is his brother-in-law Paul Rassam, and via Paul's late brother Jean-Pierre he established close ties with the Seydoux family. French critic Jean-Michel Frodon comments, 'Berri has the sense of family, and even more of the networks that link together the children of the powerful and wealthy.'

The Berri galaxy includes Gérard Brach, Roman Polankski, Jean-Claude Carrière, Milos Forman, Jean-Jacques Annaud and Jean-Louis Livi. Berri was also one of the four founding members of Artmedia and was a close friend of Gérard Lebovici – a key figure in French cinema.

With Paul Rassam, Berri has also played an important role in American independent production. He was a key force in helping Coppola set up American Zoetrope in the 1970s, and since the early 1990s has been allied with Jake Eberts.

Berri established Renn productions in 1963 to make the short film *The Chicken* which won an Oscar in 1966. This success enabled him to produce *Le Pistonné* which was financed by Columbia and then *Mazeltov* which did moderate business in France but was a hit in America. He moved into distribution via AMLF-Paris in the early 1970s.

His early films were a mixture of autobiography and light comedy and met with mixed results. But distribution revenues from AMLF kept the company afloat, boosted by American films such as Coppola's *Apocalypse Now*. In 1978 Berri launched a new production strategy – expensive 'quality' films, based on literary adaptations. The first was *Tess*, directed by Polankski (his first film after fleeing the US), followed by *Jean de Florette, Valmont, Uranus, L'Amant, Germinal* and *La Reine Margot*.

LUC BESSON (B. 1959)

Luc Besson's life changed when at seventeen he was told he had to give up underwater diving. He decided instead to become a film director. He applied to the state film school but was rejected, so he moved to Paris and worked as an assistant on commercials and feature films. He slept on friends' floors and worked for a pittance. He then raised money to make a micro-budget film, which was mainly financed by a colleague of his father who ran a Club Med village and put up $40,000.

'I never had the "cinéphile" spirit' explains Luc, 'and I still haven't. I'd never been to the Cinémathèque, and never been attracted to that approach to cinema. What appealed to me was not studying films, but *making* them.'

Le Dernier Combat (1982) was shot with virtually no dialogue and demonstrated great visual talent. Luc even designed a makeshift steadicam for the shoot. The film won the Jury Prize at the Avoriaz film festival and ten other international prizes. It was released in seven screens in Paris, and established a small cult following which enabled the investors to recoup their money. Gaumont were so impressed, they gave Luc a producing deal which has led to some of the biggest French hits in recent years, including *Nikita* and *Le Grand Bleu*. His production company, Les Films du Dauphin, is now run by his father, Claude.

Luc makes one film every two or three years and personally designs the marketing campaign and follows the release throughout France. He has thereby become a youth icon. His father explains, 'Most of Luc's stories except for *Nikita*, were written by him as an adolescent. He takes a year off for the writing, with the financing already in place. He is a man of image and design. He reads a tremendous number of comic books and writes with the music for the film already in his head.'

Luc has provided a modern twist to popular French genres such as the 'policier' thriller. He is also one of the few French directors who pays great attention to production design, most notably using veteran Alexandre Trauner for his film *Subway*. Nonetheless, he is accused by French critics such as Michel Ciment as lacking in film culture, and his success and youthful style have led to severe jealousy and enmity within the French film-making community. 'Luc has many enemies' explains his father, 'but fortunately a small number of loyal friends. There has been a "renewal" in French culture in recent years which means that anyone like Luc trying to start out today will find it even more difficult.' The parochialism of the French market has encouraged Luc to move towards the English-language films, with the backing of Gaumont. He made *Léon/The Professional* in 1994 and the $80 million *Fifth Element* in 1996.

ALAIN TERZIAN (B. 1949)

Terzian is head of the Union of French Producers (which also includes Jean-Louis Livi and Alain Goldman) and has long campaigned for a more popular approach to French cinema. In 1992 he commented at length on the audience crisis:

> We are all responsible for this decline and loss in the seductive power of the majority of French films . . . the suicidal navel gazing of a great number of players in the sector is astonishing: everyone is complacent because of the panoply of aids whose very criteria have become completely arbitrary . . . this is especially true for the Avance sur Recettes where the decisions are often incomprehensible: the mode of operation should be clarified and not left totally to the discretion of a president who applies obscure philosophical rules. We've lost sight of the objective of these mechanisms . . . producers can no longer innovate and challenge people with new ideas, as they should do. Today, many mistakenly believe that their job is to avoid entering into dispute with any of the 'all-powerful' players of the sector . . . We have to restore the magic of the movies, the desire of the public, and above all make the best of our talent.[3]

Terzian was educated in politics and economics at elite school Sciences Po, and then by chance entered the film industry, beginning his career by producing films with several of the 'greats' of French popular cinema – Alain Delon, Jean-Paul Belmondo and Claude Lelouch. His idols are the great producers of the past – Mnouchkine, Dancigers, Silberman, Dorfman – and he is highly critical of the 'social security' producers of today. He believes that a great producer should combine a sense of adventure with humility and should have 'moral rights' over his films in order to bring greater professionalism and responsibility into the industry.

He also believes that the distinction between 'commercial' and 'author' cinema is absurd, and has himself produced a very eclectic range of films. His track record includes a series of films with Jean-Marie Poiré (son of Alain Poiré), and other hit comedies such as *Operation Corned Beef*. His greatest success to date was Poiré's *Les Visiteurs* (1993) which is the all-time most popular film in France, with over $80 million box office. Gaumont were not sure about the subject, but Terzian convinced them it was worth making. The film singlehandedly achieved almost half of the French box office for the year. Terzian also produced Poiré's most recent film, *The Guardian Angels* which grossed over $40 million in France.

MARIN KARMITZ (B. 1938)

Born in Romania, Karmitz emigrated with his family to France in 1947 and studied at the French state film school between 1957 and 1959. He played a vocal role in the events of May 1968, in support of revolutionary Maoism. He has since become a classic entrepreneur, albeit commited to quality auteur films.

In 1974 he took out a $100,000 loan to set up an arthouse cinema in a run-down part of La Bastille. He used this base to begin building up his own independent production and distribution outfit, MK2, which is today by far the most powerful Independent in France. He has a chain of 30 screens, and a distribution arm which caters for his product and also that of Alain Rocca's Lazennec. He also has a 180-title film library, a foreign sales division and even a niche distribution arm in New York. Financial banking has been provided from the Banque de Suez since 1980, supplemented by an injection of capital by the group GAN in 1992. In 1996 20% of the company was sold to Havas. With a full-time staff of 85, the total revenues of the group are over $45 million a year with healthy profits.

The cash cow of the Karmitz operation is exhibition and distribution. This allows him to make genuine equity investments in production and also run a development department which spends $1.2 million a year and considers over a thousand scripts. His highest profile production to date was Kiesloswki's $19 million *Three Colours Trilogy*, which enjoyed pre-sales of over 50% of the budget from outside France.

Karmitz has played a key role in providing managerial talent to the French industry, including Jean Labadie and Eric Heumann of Bac/Paradis, and Alain Goldman of Legènde.

PEDRO ALMODÓVAR (B. 1949) AND AGUSTIN ALMODÓVAR (B. 1956)

The brothers Pedro and Agustin have been working as a team since the 1970s – Pedro as the public face, Agustin the man behind the scenes. Their work is intimately connected to the creative flowering in Spain that arose in the immediate post-Franco era.

Pedro started his career by making three-minute experimental Super 8 films in the 1970s while he worked at Spanish Telecom. He was also intimately involved with the *movida* night club scene. His early films were 'happenings' involving performance artists in bars, with Agustin editing and Pedro providing the narration. The films were shown in art galleries or bars with a small number of friends.

Pedro's first feature *Pepi, Luci, Bom and other girls like Mom,* was shot at weekends between 1979 and 1981. 'It was like John Waters' first film' says Agustin. 'It was a co-operative with friends putting up the budget. Nobody was paid, everything was shot on location. The only cost was the 16mm negative. The team were all first-timers.'

The film was an underground hit and helped Pedro seek more traditional funding for his second film, *The Labyrinth of Passions* (1982) which was financed by art-house distributor, Javier de Garcillan, who believed in Pedro's work, and also needed a Spanish film in order to get a dubbing licence to release an American independent feature.

At this stage we were still running our office from our mother's bedroom [explains Agustin]. We only set up a production office for shooting. After *Labyrinth*, we made two films with Tesauro financed by TV and subsidy money and then made *Matador* with Andres Vicente Gomez. We saw that all producers did to raise finance, was to ask for subsidy and TV money so we decided to strike out on our own. We created El Deseo in 1986 to make *La Ley del Deseo* which was a co-production with Lauren films. We covered 80% of the budget through a state loan and 20% through guarantees from friends. We paid back everything in a year and *La Ley del Deseo* was shown in the Berlin Panorama and was repped in the US by René Fuentes of the Museum of Modern Art. Spanish films at the time were difficult to sell, especially a story involving three gay men. We were helped a lot because Spanish TV at the time was the least conservative in Europe. It's since changed a lot.

The smash hit for the brothers was their next film, the \$1.2 million *Women on the Verge of a Nervous Breakdown,* which they also co-produced with Lauren film and put up 70% of the budget.

The film was a record success in Spain, grossing \$8.5 million, and was sold worldwide by René Fuentes. This enabled them to produce the \$2.6 million *Atame* and secured a production deal with Ciby 2000.

Under this deal, Ciby guarantees a bank loan for 100% of the budget but only takes 20% of equity in return. This enables the brothers to hold off from demanding an advance subsidy and instead benefit from the potentially higher automatic subsidy which is based on box office performance.

Ciby also helps widen the international market for Almodóvar's films – especially in France – and also gives access to French subsidies. The first production under this deal was the $5 million *High Heels,* and with Ciby's help they have also been able to launch the career of young talents such as Alex de las Iglesias with *Accion Mutante.*

El Deseo is now a streamlined company housed in bright colourful offices in an apartment block in Madrid. Agustin is line producer and also oversees TV library sales, while foreign sales are made through Ciby.

The company aims to produce no more than two films a year and to spend around $200,000 a year on script development.

Pedro personally supervises the marketing for his films – which are released through Warners Spain. He collaborates with other artists on the production design, costumes and poster for the film.

Pedro also creates an enormous amount of publicity by himself. 'Pedro has lots of free promotion' says Agustin. 'He's a very active person. He talks a lot with the press and has become one of the best known people in Spain, like a rock star. He's a media phenomenon.'

Almodóvar has created considerable jealousy within the Spanish film community – where most film-makers have come up through the state system. He has been virtually ignored by the national Goya awards and his work is often dubbed 'kitsch' and 'superficial'.

Pedro himself says that he finds Madrid increasingly provincial but he does not know where to move to. He has made two more films with Ciby – *Kika* and *The Flower of My Secret* – but seems to have lost some of his early enthusiasm for the cinema.

'I am very bored with being Pedro Almodóvar' he explains. 'My early films were more fun to make. There was more hope, less responsibility and more surprises . . . I don't find nightlife as entertaining as I used to and, when I do go out I feel I'm repeating a situation I already know.'[4]

In 1996 Pedro announced he would be making his first American feature – a turn-of-the-century western, with gay undertones – adapted from Tom Spanbauer's *The Man Who Fell in Love with the Moon.*

His final film under his three-picture Ciby pact will be a Spanish-language version of Ruth Rendell's novel *Live Flesh* (with development money from the European Script Fund).

THE NEW GENERATION

The hope for European cinema lies in its young producers. A few dynamic individuals have proved that they can deliver powerful films which capture the views and tastes of the younger public.

ALAIN ROCCA (B. 1955)

Alain Rocca is one of France's leading young producers. He built up his company Lazennec by making short films and then made two breakthrough features by state film school graduates – Eric Rochant with *Un Monde Sans Pitié* and Christian Vincent with *La Discrète*. But he has found it difficult to maintain a consistent track record, and the second films by Rochant and Vincent both had higher budgets and both flopped. His most recent success was *La Haine*, which was an independent hit in France and also exported well internationally.

Rocca is severely critical of the present situation in France and believes that the sector is being taken over by large media groups, thereby squeezing out Independents. 'I have the impression that those who have the power to make decisions are less and less interested in the cinema' he says. Rocca was particularly critical of the policy of the Socialist government which encouraged either large media groups such as Canal+ or micro-independents based around a single auteur. Medium companies making three or four films a year find it very difficult to survive. He believes that there should be more pluralism in decision-making in France, and that funding bodies such as Avance sur Recettes are too 'anticommercial'.

Rocca had a distribution deal with Pan-Européenne, but when they were taken over by PolyGram in 1993, he switched to MK2. In recognition of the rising power of the media groups, in 1996 he established a joint venture with Le Studio Canal+ giving him an enlarged equity base of $2 million.

Rocca's financing strategy is crucially dependent on the 'supple' support of the IFCIC discounting system. He will start production on the verbal promises of the key buyers such as Canal+. His main objective is to establish an attractive library which can be used to build up his company equity and thus carve greater independence.

DOMENICO PROCACCI (B. 1960)

One of the most dynamic of Italy's young producers, Procacci made his debut production, the $0.5 million *Il Grande Blek*, in 1987. He set up Fandango films in 1989 and produces one or two films a year. After the death of Franco Cristaldi in 1992 he took charge of the $4 million *Flight of the Innocent* which won him major international recognition. He thereby established relationships with Australian distributor Giorgio Drascovic and the UK's Portobello Pictures. With the former he co-produced *Bad Boy Bubby* and *Epsilon*, and with the latter Jiri

Menzel's *The Life and Extraordinary Adventures of Private Ivan Chonkin* and began developing *The War Zone*. Procacci clearly sees the English-language market as his lifeline: 'Unlike actors, a producer is not limited by language or by cultural formation' he says. 'I'm lucky enough to be able to work in the English-language market and clearly, that's where my interest lies. It's still a real market, whereas the Italian market is closing up more and more.'[5]

DUNCAN KENWORTHY (B. 1949)

Producer of the smash independent hit *Four Weddings and a Funeral*, Kenworthy is British, but has had a very international career. He studied film in the United States in the early 1970s and then worked for four years in New York, two years in Kuwait and two years in Toronto. From 1983 to 1995 he was director of international production at the London office of the Jim Henson Company, where he was associate producer on *The Dark Crystal* and producer of the *Storyteller* TV series and *Seven Deadly Sins*. Since *Four Weddings* he has set up his own film company, Toledo Productions, with a first-look deal for family films with Jim Henson Pictures (which in turn has an output deal with Sony). He has recently produced the highly acclaimed TV series *Gulliver's Travels* for Henson and in 1996 received backing from Rank to produce *Lawn Dogs* set in Kentucky.

ANDREW MACDONALD (B. 1965) AND DANNY BOYLE (B. 1956)

The dynamic team behind *Shallow Grave* and *Trainspotting* which also includes the writer John Hodge and a core crew of production designer, director of photography, editor and actors such as Ewan McGregor.

Danny Boyle is an acclaimed television and theatre director. MacDonald is the grandson of Hungarian Emeric Pressburger, from whom he has inherited an antipathy towards the 'chatting classses' and public-service social realism. 'This is what my grandfather and Michael Powell always rebelled against in British cinema' he says. 'They, David Lean, all of them, were super-realists. That's all they were. Real cinema is about the imagination, about fantasy.'

Boyle and MacDonald's two films have been great successes. This has been due above all to PolyGram who provided 50% of the funding for the $1.5 million *Shallow Grave* (the rest came from Channel 4 and the Glasgow Film Fund) and who majority-funded the $2.5 million *Trainspotting*. The team now aims to make a $10 million American feature *A Life Less Ordinary* and also executive produce the $2 million *Twin Town*. They have turned down countless studio offers, including *Alien 4*.

Adam Dawtrey of *Variety* said of *Trainspotting*, 'It jabbed its needle straight into the aorta of British pop culture, tapping into the kind of youthful, aggressive spirit usually associated with the country's music scene rather than with its somewhat bookish, middle-class and middle-aged film establishment.'

JEREMY BOLT (B. 1965) AND ENRIQUE POSNER (B. 1962)

Ricky Posner was born in Columbia and moved to the US in 1986, working as assistant director for Cannon Films, and then from 1986–88 at niche New York distributor Cinevista, where he met Pedro and Agustin Almodóvar. In 1989 he moved to Madrid to work for El Deseo, and in 1992 set up his own venture, Filmania in alliance with José Vicuña of Warners Spain and financier Antonio Portero of Ibermer. In 1994 he allied with British producer Jeremy Bolt, and they have since enjoyed backing from Chrysalis and Pandora.

Jeremy Bolt made short films while studying English and philosophy at the University of Bristol. He then worked as driver to Ken Russell, and aged twenty-five produced an American-financed version of Henry James's *The Turn of the Screw* starring Patsy Kensit and Julian Sands. He is a founding member of the UK's New Producers' Alliance, where he declared his philosophy: 'We are about making films with commercial potential and we pursue that with confidence and aggression'. His first production was Paul Anderson's $3.5 million *Shopping* which was 40% financed by Channel 4, 20% from Screen Partners and the rest from German distributor NEF2, Japanese distributor Kazui and EMI (who paid $400,000 for the soundtrack rights).

The duo have been able to secure considerable backing from the European Script Fund including loans for *Uncovered, The Jam Factory* and *Vigo* and, since 1994, Incentive Funding. Their in-house funds enable them to bankroll production and also make a limited equity stake. If a film goes into production they will spend up to $200,000 on development. Otherwise they will limit their losses to $50–60,000.

Ricky explains, 'What's happening in England is fascinating. There's a great new wave of talent led by the New Producers' Alliance. I'd always admired partnerships like Nik Powell and Steve Woolley. Jeremy and I act as sounding boards for each other's ideas. By pooling resources we can hopefully avoid being dead by forty with no family life!'

Ricky's partner, Antonio Portero of Ibermer became involved in the film business as adviser to José Vicuña, head of both Warners Spain and film library Cinepaq (now 50% of Sogepaq). He also provided the production financing for Almodóvar's *Atame*. This experience showed him the limited potential for Spanish-language films. 'I don't know how Spanish producers make their films', he says. 'The numbers don't add up. People claim they have budgets of $2 million, which means they must be losing $1 million. We've decided to go the English-language route – with our first port of call being the sales agents such as Ciby, PolyGram, Bertelsmann, Cinevox, J&M, Canal+, Miramax, Sony Classics as well as the Majors.'

Posner's first production was the $6.5 million *Uncovered*, by Jim McBride, based on the Spanish best-selling novel *The Flemish Board*. The film was financed by Ciby 2000, a relationship established when Posner worked at El Deseo.

Both *Shopping* and *Uncovered* had disappointing results, but are part of the team's learning curve. The duo remain two of European cinema's brightest hopes for the future. 'Nobody pulls the wool over our eyes' says Posner. 'It's time for a new generation of producers. We hope that the business system in Europe can start gearing up to production needs. Nobody wants to do jigsaw puzzles, although for the immediate future we're probably condemned to it. Nobody wants to talk about how you make an industry out of this Babylon.'

ALAIN GOLDMAN (B. 1961)

Alain Goldman is the son of Daniel Goldman, the head of UIP in France. He previously was in charge of distribution for Marin Karmitz, but in 1988 his girlfriend, Roselyne Bosch, a journalist, wrote a screenplay for a film about Christopher Columbus. There was little interest in Europe, but through an American agent a deal was put together involving the Salkind brothers and Ridley Scott. The partners fell into dispute, leading to two different Columbus projects, and Goldman, with the help of CAA agent John Ptak, managed to put together the $43 million Ridley Scott project, *1492*, with pre-sales of $15 million to Paramount in the United States, $10 million to France (50% Gaumont, 25% Canal+, 25% TFi), an estimated $6 million raised by Pere Fages in Spain and a further $5 million in foreign sales through Odyssey. Ridley Scott also deferred his fees and thereby became a co-production partner.

The film flopped in the US, but was a huge success in France and also performed well in Spain and much of continental Europe. On the back of this project Goldman now has two rights deals – one with Gaumont, the other with TFi – and also a co-venture with Roland Joffé. Goldman brokered TFi's $14 million investment in Scorsese's *Casino* and one of his first productions is *Diabolique* (a remake of the film by Clouzot) starring Sharon Stone and Isabelle Adjani.

PAUL BROOKS (B. 1959)

Paul Brooks set up Metrodome to produce *Leon the Pig Farmer* (see case study in previous chapter) and used this success to make more ambitious films such as *Beyond Bedlam* and *Killing Time* (which was sold to Columbia-TriStar). 'We're part of what the new British cinema is trying to do' he says, 'make mainstream films with an edge . . . be bold, and perhaps controversial.' His company is linked to a bank, Union City Investments, and is listed on the Alternative Investment Market. Working capital is covered by a mixture of City money and private investors, which covers overheads and development.

Metrodome's second film *Beyond Bedlam* had over £0.25 million in foreign pre-sales and raised this amount through a BES offering. The rest of the £750,000 budget was covered through deferrals. 'The key thing for our films is international sales' explains Brooks. 'We found that comedy was very hard to sell, but low-budget horror was a much better bet. We pre-sold the film on the basis of the script and the package.' The horror theme presented problems in the UK. It had a limited release at the box office and then suffered from a UK video ban by the BBFC which limited further sales.

In 1996 Metrodome's projects focused on low-budget cutting-edge product located in the UK regions – *Darklands* in Wales, *Primetime* in Newcastle and *Sunset Heights* in Northern Ireland.

APPENDIX (A)

Financial Wizardry

OFF-BALANCE-SHEET FINANCING is a means of using government regulation to generate an additional 'unexpected' contribution to the budget. Certain techniques are specifically designed for the film industry, while many have been introduced for other economic areas, and then adapted to film. As former MPAA President, Eric Johnston, said in 1953:

> We have done such things as buy wood pulp in Scandinavia for kroner, shipped it to Italy in exchange for lire, and there we have used the lire to build or rebuild ships to go overseas to be sold for American dollars. We even raised a sunken French tanker in the harbour of Marseilles and repaired it, paying for it with French francs, and shipping it to the United States where it was sold for dollars. We have made Scotch-type whisky in Chile, sold it in America for American dollars. All in all, we have a very extensive organization constantly working to get our dollars over the hurdles that beset you nowadays in foreign trade.

The main areas of interest for off-balance-sheet financing are taxation, subsidies, blocked currency and debt swaps.

TAXATION

From a business point of view, all taxation is 'dead' money. To reduce the outflow of 'dead' money, taxpayers try to maximize the tax write-off for expenditure and minimize the tax rate for income. A film investment can sometimes help in this process.

The international context of the film industry means that tax breaks may be located anywhere in the world. Highly paid consultants keep a watchful eye on any favourable legislation or loopholes, and local tax authorities will often turn a blind eye at first and then tend to close up the tax break once its use becomes excessive.

The extensive use of tax breaks for film began in America in the early 1970s when the US government was trying to help many types of small businesses. Many of the tricks of the trade were invented at this time and then exported abroad.

The producer must prove to the tax authorities that there is genuine risk, while reassuring investors that there is no risk at all. Usually the producer tries to lock off the risk and in this way generate an 'automatic' saving which can fill a financing gap in the budget.

The main forms of tax break for an investor are limited partnerships, investment relief, capital relief, and gearing; and the main guarantees are buy-back guarantees, sales guarantees, sale-leaseback and non-recourse loans. Producers should also be aware of the advantage of tax havens.

LIMITED PARTNERSHIPS

In a limited partnership each investor has his own business unit with limited liability (i.e. he cannot lose more than the money he has put up). The partnership is a federation of these 'limited partners', managed by one or more 'general partners' with unlimited liability. The risk exposure of the general partners is usually limited through other measures. The advantage of limited partnerships is that investors participate in a single pool of capital, but cash flow, loans, revenues and assets are allocated as if each partner were a separate business. This offers considerable tax advantages, including gearing.

INVESTMENT RELIEF

An investment is a revenue-bearing asset. The simplest and safest form of asset is a bank account – it has a 'book value' and will earn interest. Other assets such as shares in a company are more risky – their book value and returns may change rapidly over time.

Any revenue earned from an investment asset is liable to income tax, and appreciation in the 'book value' of assets is also liable to capital gains tax. The cost of making an investment is not in itself liable to tax, although if its 'book value' declines this may reduce the capital gains liability from other investments.

Under a tax relief system, the investor is allowed to deduct a part of his investment against his yearly income, thereby lowering his tax bill. The most common example is mortgage relief for housing. Investment relief structures are designed by the government to encourage the development of certain sectors – small businesses, house ownership, and key economic sectors.

Under this system, the value of the asset acquired is greater than the cash investment made. For example, imagine a system with 50% income tax and 100% write-off for film investments. If the investor's taxable income is $100,000 he will normally retain $50,000 post-tax. If he instead makes a $10,000 investment, because of tax relief, his post-tax income is reduced by only $5,000.

	Taxable income	Tax bill	Post-tax income	Assets
Before	$100,000	$50,000	$50,000	–
After	$90,000	$45,000	$45,000	$10,000

The investor buys the asset at half price, with the government paying the rest. Even if the asset only returns half of its 'book value', the investor will have lost nothing.

Government regulation determines the percentage which may be written off against tax, the minimum and maximum investment and any special tax discounts for future revenues from the asset.

CAPITAL RELIEF

Any enterprise – from a sole trader to a giant corporation – requires capital equipment. This equipment depreciates in value over time, and the annual depreciation is a 'cost' which may be deducted against revenues. Tax legislation will specify the rate of capital depreciation and also the definition of capital equipment.

If the government wishes to encourage capital investment, it may step up the level of capital relief. For example, in Britain from 1979 to 1984 there were 100% capital allowances which were then used to generate investments in film, because film was accepted as capital equipment.

John Heyman explains that this came about because of a legal decision in the Court of Appeals in 1979 which declared that wallpaper designs represented part of the capital expenditure on the equipment for making the wallpaper. He then rang up a friend at the Treasury to see if a film negative could be accepted under the same definition. An official ruling declared that this was the case, and thus a film negative could be sold to a third-party investor, who could deduct 100% of the cost against their tax bill. The result was very similar to that of 100% investment relief, and generated a mini-boom in investment in British cinema which ended in 1984, when 100% allowances were withdrawn.

GEARING

Gearing means that the investor's tax write-off is higher than his cash outlay. Tax legislation tends to clamp down on gearing, but most tax-break schemes include a limited amount.

The simplest form of gearing, is where the government provides debt relief as well as investment relief. Subsidies and credit guarantees or soft loans can also be used for gearing. The investor thereby obtains a valuable asset at a lower price.

For example, imagine that the government automatically provides a matching loan against any equity investment and that there is both debt and investment relief. An investor puts up $10,000 and borrows $10,000. He thereby acquires a $20,000 asset which can be written off against tax. Post-tax income is thereby $50,000 – the same as it was before making the investment.

	Taxable income	Tax bill	Post-tax income	Assets
Before	$100,000	$50,000	$50,000	–
After	$80,000	$40,000	$50,000	$20,000

The more extreme the write-off, the less likely it is to be accepted by the authorities, and from a private investor's point of view is more likely to lead to a tax audit.

Graham Bradstreet provides a concrete example of gearing which was inspired by the financing of *A World Apart*, for which a corporate investor put up 25% of the budget. Bradstreet's model is based on the investor being subject to 50% corporation tax and making a $1 million investment. The rest of the $4 million budget is provided by other equity and sales, but the corporate investor is allowed to write off the full $4 million and thereby lowers its tax bill by $2 million – thereby actually increasing post-tax income as well as gaining a $1 million asset.

	Taxable income	Tax bill	Post-tax income	Assets
Before	$20M	$10M	$10M	–
After	$16M	$8M	$11M	$1M

This is an extreme example. In most cases, gearing amplifies the tax break, but does not produce a self-financing investment.

BUY-BACK GUARANTEES

The simplest way for investors to have their 'downside' risk protected is if a strong corporate parent guarantees to buy back their investment at a specific price. Buy-back guarantees are used in the offerings by the US Majors and also by the French Sofica system. Independents such as Island World also offered a 50% buy-back guarantee.

In this system the corporate parent guarantees a minimal return from the investment and usually limits the 'upside' benefits from hit films. When combined with a tax-break system, this protects investors and provides a source of cheap corporate finance.

SALES GUARANTEES

In order to benefit from a tax break the investor needs to prove that his investment is at 'risk' and therefore genuine. At the same time he will do his utmost to minimize that risk. The simplest way in which this can be achieved is through pre-sales.

If the producer pre-sells his films to third parties in his home country and abroad, he will then need to convert those sales into cash via a discount bank. He may instead look for equity investors who are willing to advance the money against promised sales.

The producer locks off the risk through pre-sales and thereby guarantees that the investors will be repaid. The investors therefore benefit from an immediate tax write-off and are also repaid a premium on their cash investment.

For example, in a 50% tax regime if an investor puts up $10,000 it will only cost him $5,000. He therefore only needs to be repaid that $5,000 plus a favourable rate of interest. Therefore if a producer wants to raise a $10 million budget, he may only need to repay, say, $8 million and thus produce an immediate 20% off-balance-sheet bonus.

NON-RECOURSE LOANS

Most film companies find it difficult to raise bank finance for their productions, and therefore it is very difficult to benefit from gearing. But if instead of a pre-sale, a buyer grants a loan, whose repayment is contingent on the film's success (known as a non-recourse loan), gearing becomes possible.

This technique was highlighted in a court case surrounding the production of *Escape to Victory* in the UK by Lorimar Pictures in the early 1980s. The UK-based Victory Partnership paid the $13 million budget through a $3.25 million cash investment and a $9.75 million non-recourse loan from Lorimar, to be repaid from the film's future revenues. Victory Partnership then declared the $13 million capital cost against their tax bill.

Had this been accepted this would in effect have generated a tax saving higher than their outlay, and Lorimar would have acquired the film for less than its true cost. The UK Inland Revenue took the case to court and declared it illegal.

SALE-LEASEBACK

A popular technique for acquiring capital equipment is through a leasing agreement. The purchaser buys the equipment in a series of instalments and deducts the cost of each instalment against taxable income. Sale-leaseback extends this principle. A company sells capital equipment to a third party and then buys it back through a leasing arrangement. This is a *refinancing* operation which generates a small immediate cash gain.

Sale-leaseback is popular in the aircraft industry and is also used in film. It is of greatest appeal when there are high capital allowances, which enables the third party to make an immediate write-off against tax. The leaseback agreement guarantees the risk of the initial sale, and ideally it should be backed by a strong corporate parent.

Imagine a corporate investor with $100 million taxable income a year liable to 50% corporate income tax. If the company acquires a $10 million film, its post-tax income only goes down by $5 million. The leasing payments therefore only need to cover this $5 million plus a favourable rate of interest.

This was how many film companies generated a tax break for their films in the late 1970s and early 1980s. For example, UK company Goldcrest regularly used this method. Goldcrest financed the film using the promise of a minimum guarantee from a US Major. The film was then sold to a third party, and 90% of the monies were deposited in order to guarantee the leasing payments. The leasing payments were actually made by the UK distribution arm of the US Major as a means of paying the minimum guarantee. In this way the US Major, Goldcrest and the third-party investor all shared a tax break. Goldcrest also benefited by channelling all funds via an offshore tax haven.

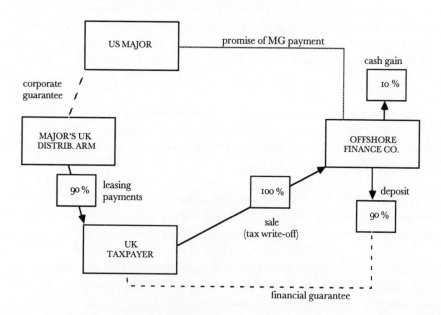

Source: David Norris, Marriot Harrison

The size of the cash gain depends on the rates of tax write-off and rate of interest. In the early 1980s it was as high as 20%, today it is around 4% and the paperwork invol-ved often means that producers don't bother.

TAX HAVENS

There are two kinds of 'tax haven' – those which benefit from low personal and cor-porate taxation, and those which have favourable double taxation treaties. The intelligent producer will aim to structure his economic activity to take advantage of both – in order to minimize both corporate taxation and the tax incidence on income.

Access to such tax havens depends on special relationships such as that between the UK and the Jersey Islands, between the Netherlands and the Netherlands Antilles and between Germany and Luxembourg.

Anti-avoidance legislation exists to prevent abuse of this system, and other countries will be wary of artificial structures that exist solely to avoid tax. For example, in recent years several countries, particularly Germany, have been unhappy for monies to flow from an 'onshore' company to the Netherlands Antilles.

To avoid such problems, the onshore distribution company must show that it is a genuine commercial operation and should retain some of the earnings to cover its opera-ting costs. In practice, this retention may be reduced to 3–4% and the rest can be remit-ted to a finance company based in a tax haven. Onshore taxes will only be paid on the 3% revenues, and the rest will be virtually tax free.

Special distribution companies may be set up in certain countries to benefit from specific loopholes. A recent example is the creation of a collecting agency in Hungary by the Dutch bank, Meers Pierson, to collect revenues from Japan, which has withholding taxes of 35% with most countries. Remittances to the UK have to pay 10%, but to Hungary only 1%.

TAX REGIMES IN DIFFERENT COUNTRIES

Although the general rules of 'tax shelter schemes' are universal, they have been applied differently in each country.

UNITED STATES

Investment tax shelters were significant in developing the 'New Hollywood' from 1972 onwards. Tax shelters were used by Roger Corman's AIP for *Futureworld* and *A Matter of Time*, but also by the Majors, in particular David Begelman at Columbia. In 1975 a multi-picture tax-shelter package was set up for Columbia Pictures and United Artists with titles including *Taxi Driver, The Man Who Would Be King* and *Sinbad and the Eye of the Tiger*. Investors bought $150,000, and through gearing wrote off $400,000 against their taxable income.

In effect, while Europe stepped up her cultural subsidies, the American government decided to pour money into their film industry through tax shelters. These 'automatic subsidies' played a critical role in re-capitalizing the Majors and helped establish Hollywood's hegemony over world cinema.

In 1976, the government cracked down on gearing in tax shelters, and attention switched to two new schemes – the 'investment tax credit' (ITC) and the 'small business administration' (SBA).

The ITC was not originally intended for the film industry, but after two key court cases by Disney in 1974 and 1976, feature films were accepted as capital assets with a useful life of three years and investors were allowed to write off an additional 6.66% against their investment as long as 80% of the picture was produced in the United States. In the mid-1980s some producers managed to exploit a loophole and push this extra write-off up to 10%. This served as a stimulus for independent production and also helped bring back runaway productions from Europe to the US.

The ITC achieved its full impact when combined with the SBA which was designed to promote small businesses, which were considered to be the main source of job creation. The government provided a generous loan system providing state loans of up to three times shareholder equity.

One of the first film ventures to use the SBA was International Film Investors (IFI) set up in 1977 by Josiah H. Child Jr and then Goldcrest chief Jake Eberts. IFI was a limited partnership, sold by E. F. Hutton, in which Goldcrest, Pearson and Electra each put up $1 million. A further $7 million was raised from investors with net worth of over $1 million, each of whom put in at least $150,000. Jake Eberts spent a year on the road at his own expense, but succeeded in setting up the partnership. IFI then borrowed $25 million in government loans, thus establishing an investment fund worth $35 million. E. F. Hutton received a fee and a small share of profits.

Investment funds aimed to spread their risks by investing in a portfolio of projects. Eberts recounts that his partner Jo Child told investors that if you backed enough projects you would be sure to find a hit, but as Eberts points out, 'The Cannon Group which built up a library of 900 titles in less than ten years and never had a major hit, proved that the theory simply doesn't stand up. It's like believing that you can beat the bank at roulette. Eventually you are bound to run out of money. My approach, then as now, was that you had to do both: put your money into a portfolio of films, but choose each film extremely carefully and make every effort you can to improve its chance of success.'[1]

Even the best managed investment has the further problem that most of the profits in the business are retained in distribution. It therefore makes much more sense to invest in a distributor than a producer.

In general, private investors have lost money in the film business. There are exceptions, such as *Rocky* or *Crocodile Dundee* where significant pay-outs were earned, but these are extremely rare. Jake Eberts' conclusion is that 'There's no place for private investors in the film business. It's a business for studios, distributors and exhibitors, but not private investors. They might as well throw their money down a rat-hole.'[2]

Tax-shelter schemes began to be withdrawn in the mid-1980s. Ironically, although they had been designed for smaller Independents, they played their most important role in re-capitalizing the Majors, especially Disney. In the 1980s $1.7 billion was raised in limited partnerships, over $1 billion of that for Disney, through Silver Screen Partners.

Disney established very strict clauses on the Silver Screen Partnerships. Partnership funds were allocated to specific films, but excluded from the high grossing animation pictures. The pay-back terms meant that the downside was protected but any upside profits on hit movies were severely limited. The corporate strength of Disney enabled them to provide a guarantee that the principal would be returned in five years even if the films flopped, and investors earned an average of 13–18% over five years.

Disney continues to use investment funds to finance its films off-balance-sheet. In 1990 they raised a $200 million Touchwood offering from Japanese investors who had significant tax breaks. In 1992 the company raised a further $400 million.

The main film partnership subscriptions in the US from 1981 to 1988 are listed below. The capital raised is quoted plus the net return on every $1,000 invested up until the end of 1990. A guide annual percentage return is also calculated, based on the assumption that the capital was fully repaid after five years and that the return quoted represents five years' earnings. (This is therefore only a guide and understates the percentage return after 1986.)

	Formation	Capital	$ return	% return
Delphi I	1981	60	842	13%
SLM I	1981	40	159	3%
Silver Screen I	1983	83	616	10%
Delphi II	1983	60	801	12.5%
Delphi III	1984	49	629	10%
Silver Screen II	1985	193	870	13%
Balcor	1985	48	611	10%
Delphi IV	1985	40	551	9%
Delphi V	1985	40	498	8.5%
Lorimar	1985	34	NA	NA
American Ent. I	1986	64	822	13%
ML Delphi	1986	63	398	7%
Vista	1986	69	0	0%
Silver Screen III	1987	300	949	14%
American Ent. II	1987	25	724	11.5%
Cinema Plus	1987	43	189	3.5%
De Laurentiis	1987	27	63	1.2%
Star I	1988	23	579	NA
Silver Screen IV	1988	400	462	NA

Not all investment funds were able to repay their capital, and even when they did, the returns were slight in comparison to other financial instruments. The withdrawal of the ITC sheme in 1986 and the 'crash' of 1987 signalled the death of most film limited partnerships. The main use of limited partnerships today is for micro-budget films backed by private investors.

The Majors have made little use of external investors since 1987, but in 1996, 20th Century Fox established a new $1 billion film financing package, arranged by Citicorp and mainly raised from the commercial paper market. The main attraction to Fox was that the deal removed production financing from the News Corporation balance sheet, creating a healthier profile for financial ratios.

American producers continue to look for 'off-balance-sheet' funding – both within the United States and abroad. If there's a loophole, they'll find it.

CANADA

In 1974 Canada introduced 100% capital allowances for all Canadian films and official co-productions. This was then reduced to 30% and was proposed to be abolished in 1996. There are still, however, means of generating slim sale-leaseback benefits from productions shot in Canada. One of the main specialists in the area is the Equicorp division of Alliance/MDP, which has a client list of 5,000 high net worth investors and 're-financed' forty films in 1994.

FRANCE

Perhaps the most famous 'tax shelters' in Europe are the French Soficas. As with every other aspect of French cinema, they are subject to extremely tight regulation.

The Sofica tax-shelter legislation was introduced in France in 1985, after studying the experience of the US, Germany, Australia and Canada. The initiative was in response to declining minimum guarantee payments from theatrical distributors in France. In 1985 minimum guarantees represented 24% of all French film financing, but by 1990 had fallen to 1.9%.

Originally, repayment of Sofica investments was expected to be derived from theatrical net profits, but in fact Soficas have come to depend upon long-run repeat television broadcasts for their revenue – and thus form part of the transition of the French film industry from a theatrically driven business to a tele-film industry.

A Sofica offers tax relief for the investment of both private individuals and corporations. A private individual investing in a Sofica may write off up to 25% of his taxable income (highest tax rate 58%), but cannot own more than 25% of the funds of any one Sofica, and the minimum investment is $6,000. A corporation investing in a Sofica may deduct 50% of the amount invested against its taxable income in the first year of investment.

In order to benefit from the fiscal advantages, the investor must tie up his investment for five to seven years. After this time the investor is likely to try to reclaim his investment. This can be achieved in two possible ways: gradual repayment of the investment through the Sofica revenues, or sale of equity to a third party (usually a media group) interested in the continuing long-term revenue.

The terms of a Sofica investment in an individual film are based on the principle that the Sofica will have a share of the first monies from the film up to a ceiling set by an agreed formula. In exceptional cases, where the film earns very high earnings (net profits exceeding the cost of the film), the Sofica may earn an extra 'bonus'.

A Sofica may only invest in films registered with the CNC and the combined Sofica investment may not exceed 50%. Since 1993, 20% of a Sofica's investments may be for foreign-language French co-productions.

Many of the initial Soficas were set up by banks and groups of private investors (e.g., there were two Soficas, SILAV1 and SILAV2 backed by surgeons and dentists) and were genuine risk investments often decided by financiers. The average performance of these Soficas was a marginal loss, even taking the tax break into account, and certain Soficas lost very considerable sums of money.

In reaction to this, the government introduced an amendment to the tax-shelter legislation in 1991 allowing a group to provide a corporate guarantee and own more than 25%. The main effect of the scheme is to provide a tax break for the main media groups. The tax break is split between the media group and the investor, generating an annual net return of 10–12% to the investor.

The new Sofica legislation has meant that far fewer funds go to independent producers. Even the 40% minimum required by legislation is principally invested in completed films or for independent producers linked to a group. This has angered some independent producers, and some commentators feel that if the system is over-abused by media groups it may actually be withdrawn.

Since 1985 the number of films backed by Soficas has been fairly constant at 40–60 films per year (40% of French production). Soficas often work together and 45% of films which received Sofica funding in 1993 were backed by two funds. Soficas are therefore a significant element in French film finance. In the early years, the average Sofica investment represented 20% of a film's budget, but are now closer to 12–14%.

The Sofica invests the bulk of its monies in its first two years of existence and aims to recoup its monies over the medium-term of four to five years. Recoupment is principally from the sale of the second and third French TV transmission rights. This has meant that the Soficas have been more selective in their investments because television re-transmission is not automatic, and the channels are increasingly focusing their library purchases on a narrowing circle of films which enjoy good ratings.

IRELAND

Ireland has become a haven of film production as the result of her Section 35 tax-shelter legislation, introduced by the Minister of Culture, Michael Higgins under the motto 'Imagination is our biggest resource.'

Section 35 was first introduced in 1987, but was made far more favourable in 1993. It allows investors to write off 100% of their investment against taxable income. In any three-year period, investors may invest up to $560,000 a year or make a $1.68 million investment in one film.

The lead production company for the film must be based in Ireland and 75% of the production must take place there. Section 35 investments cannot exceed 60% of the film's budget.

In practice, the scheme has worked using sales guarantees to lock off the risk, and then offer the subsequent tax break via the leading law firms to wealthy private investors and corporations in Ireland.

The law firm usually charges a 3–4% fee for the deal, and a further 10–12% cash benefit is generated for investors and for the producer. Since the investment risk has generally been minimal, the scheme has effectively worked as a 10% automatic subsidy for productions located in Ireland.

Productions that have benefited from the scheme include *Braveheart*, *Moll Flanders* and the *Scarlett* TV mini-series. Several producers have also used the scheme to establish a permanent Irish base, including John Boorman and Roger Corman.

The scheme boosted production in Ireland from four films a year in 1992 to 16, 18 and 18 in the subsequent three years. An average of $2 million of Section 35 investment is provided per film. The production boom, however, has placed a great strain on Irish crews and facilities and normally results in an increased production cost which thereby limits the advantage of the tax break.

BRITAIN

From 1979 to 1984 Britain benefited from 100% capital allowances. Since then, the main form of tax break has been the Business Expansion Scheme (BES), which was replaced in 1994 by the Enterprise Investment Scheme (EIS).

A special amendment in 1984 to the BES legislation made it suitable for the film industry, but was not exploited until the late 1980s. In the early years the scheme was used mainly for property companies. Relief was at the investors' top tax rate (maximum of 40%) with a maximum write-off of £40,000. Shares had to be held for five years and could then be sold free of capital gains tax.

The main problem for using the scheme for the film industry was that it had to be for a single trading film company and the maximum amount that could be raised in any one tax year was £750,000. As a consequence the BES was mainly used for micro-budget films, but also provided around 20% of the budget for Kenneth Branagh's *Henry V*.

The 40% tax break provided by the BES scheme made it much easier for micro-budget film-makers to raise finance. The new EIS scheme is far less favourable, mainly because tax relief is only available at 20%, although the maximum qualifying investment has been increased from £40,000 to £100,000. Companies can now raise share capital of up to £1 million. The scheme was also extended to non-resident UK taxpayers and to companies which are not resident in the UK but carry on a trade there. To date the scheme has proved to be of limited interest to film-makers.

LUXEMBOURG

The Luxembourg scheme was introduced in 1988 and is unique in that tax relief is granted as a certificate which can be sold to third parties, including foreign investors. But the lack of a film infrastructure in the country, the complexity of the scheme and the difficulty in trading certificates has meant that it has been of limited interest. The main US producer to use the scheme is Harmony Gold.

Investment has to be made in audiovisual companies. Therefore if a producer is seeking investment for a specific film, he must create a company for that film. The amount that can be written off is calculated by the following formula:

$$\text{the initial investment} \quad \times \quad \frac{\text{the company's audiovisual expenditure}}{\text{the company's paid-up capital}}$$

The eligible audiovisual expenditure is only for below-the-line expenditure invested in Luxembourg. The key crew must be of Luxembourg nationality but additional technical staff may be imported.

A tax relief certificate is issued which may be sold to up to three other individuals or organizations. Any one individual may write off up to 30% of their taxable income. Investors may be either companies or individuals. Corporation tax is 33% (48% with local taxes) and the top income tax rate is 56%.

GERMANY

Germany introduced tax-shelter legislation in the late 1970s which led to a flurry activity, including a considerable share of the financing of Steven Spielberg's *Close Encounters of the Third Kind*. Today there are no such tax shelters, but the country still has an attractive tax regime.

Michael Kuhn of PolyGram claims that without the German corporate tax system, he would not have been able to set up his film venture. (PolyGram also has a financing operation in Luxembourg through which it can channel sale-leaseback deals.)

AUSTRALIA

In 1981 generous new tax legislation was introduced allowing producers of Australian films and official co-productions to write off 150% of their production expenditure and claim 50% exemption from all revenues earned. These have now been reduced to a 100% immediate write-off.

JAPAN

Japan introduced tax-shelter legislation for film in the early 1990s which led to the MICO investment fund, and financing deals such as Disney's two Touchwood offerings. These investments generally underperformed, and the growing financial crisis in Japan led to a withdrawal of most tax breaks and a reluctance to invest in foreign media.

SUBSIDIES

Most subsidies are linked to cultural content and require a local producer to access them, but certain industrial subsidies are available if producers choose a particular location that the government wishes to promote. There may still be certain cultural limitations such as the NRW scheme, but these subsidies are often the best immediate way to generate a 'free' cash contribution to the budget. The catch is that often the location will result in other additional expenses, which cut out the subsidy gain.

Another form of implicit production subsidy is where state-owned facilities companies are willing to defer fees in return for equity and studio work on the film. A classic example is the Babelsberg studios – which has both private and state money backing it. The Eastern European countries are also particularly keen to attract foreign productions.

Relocating a film in order to benefit from subsidies should be done with care. It can compromise the artistic integrity of the film, or lead to unexpected problems and costs.

BLOCKED CURRENCY AND DEBT SWAPS

In the immediate post-war period, one of the main reasons for the Majors to relocate their productions to Europe and invest in European films was because they had revenues 'blocked' there. European governments placed limits on the amount of dollars that could be repatriated to America. In international finance this led to the Eurodollar market and the birth of the international capital markets. In cinema it led to Hollywood in Europe.

Blocked currency still exists in Eastern Europe and the Third World. These countries need hard currency, which opens up a number of schemes through which much greater spending power can be leveraged by locating production in these countries.

The Majors continue to suffer from blocked currency in some territories and are always interested in ways that this can be used to be converted into cash. For example, the opening scene in India for *Close Encounters of the Third Kind* took advantage of blocked currency in that country.

Debt swaps use the same principle and have been explored by UK producer John Wolstenhome, in a venture known as CODEM – Conversion of Debt into Equity. He describes his scheme as 'a constructive use of an appalling situation'. Eastern European and Latin American countries have high foreign debts and need hard currency to buy essential medicines and supplies. The producer is therefore able to buy a portion of their sovereign debt on the open market – at discounts of up to 80% – and then trade it with the debtor nation in return for a shopping list of film services. The debtor nation is also given a small equity share in the film, which may later bring in further hard currency.

Debt swaps are regularly used for shipping, property and ecological ventures. In the case of film, it can generate big savings – particularly in countries with well-established film infrastructures such as Russia, Poland and Bulgaria.

Wolsthenhome has established excellent contacts with the relevant government departments within these countries. He believes that debt swaps can provide up to 35% of the budget and are particularly useful for television productions where there are extensive below the line costs.

In 1992 Wolsthenhome also participated in the financing of the $8.6 million *Pampas*, brokered by the company International Link, for which a consortium of banks put up $5.15 million in Argentinian debt in return for equity in the film (guaranteed by pre-sales). The Argentinian government provided facilities in return.

Additional Profiles

IN THE MOVIES it is impossible to predict where the next big hit will come from. The Majors have locked up the mainstream business, but for foreign sales and European media, there continues to be a high diversity of companies. Certain leading players have been described in the main text. They are supplemented here by other players, who also have an important role in the business.

SALES AGENTS

A list of the main sales agents was provided on page 84. Leading players have already been described. Below is a mix of niche and crossover companies.

ADRIENA CHIESA

'We consider ourselves as a European distribution company although we happen to be based in Italy', explains Adriena Chiesa. The company represents eight to ten films a year from Italy, Germany and Spain. The emphasis is strongly on art films, and promotional strategy is heavily linked to achieving selection in international film festivals.

ALLIANCE/MARK DAMON PRODUCTIONS

Alliance is Canada's largest independent film distributor, with output deals with Miramax, New Line and Goldwyn. The foreign sales arm traditionally concentrated on niche titles, but in 1993 the parent company raised $25 million in new equity, signed a co-financing and distribution agreement with Universal and created a new production division, Le Monde, to make $3–4 million genre pictures.

The first high-budget production was the $30 million *Johnny Mnemonic* starring Keanu Reeves. The film was co-produced with indie veteran Mark Damon and led to a merger of the two sales divisions. 'About a year and a half ago we stopped producing the low-budget direct-to-video movies because the video market was collapsing all over the world', explained Damon in 1996. 'We began to sense that the overseas market was beginning to respond to specialised niche pictures.'

Damon is a veteran of the foreign sales business, having run one of the leading outfits PSO/Delphi and then Vision. Damon got MDP off the ground in the early 1990s through a $20 million loan facility from IMMO finance. He has also built up a forty-title library which has been folded into the new joint venture.

Damon would like the company to become a mini-major, producing six to eight films a year and controlling US/Canadian distribution. 'Quasi-alliances' have been signed with several studios including Sony and Universal, and in 1995 the company announced it would handle world rights for the next David Cronenberg/Jeremy Thomas picture. Off-balance-sheet funds are found through Alliance Equicap, which is a specialist in using foreign subsidies and tax breaks.

ATLAS

Dieter Mentz's company stands between niche and crossover. It caters for American action films and local movies, and is the only German member of AFMA. It also has a 450-title library – the largest independent library in Germany. Mentz is outspoken in favour of the free market: 'In 30 years I've never had a bank loan or a subsidy. I don't need gifts. I've even produced two or three films to prove to producer friends that you can get the money back if you make a film for the audience.' Mentz believes that things will change as the result of commercial television. 'Look at the success of RTL – they make fast paced programmes like the US and they have 10% as many employees as the public broadcasters.'

CAPELLA

Capella was founded in 1990 by German media group Deyhle/Baer which owns the German distributor Connexion. The company began with direct-to-video and niche films, but signed a $200 million partnership with Universal and Martin Bregman in 1995 which should push them towards the big time. They are looking to sign other deals with the Majors, and in 1996 teamed up with Morgan Creek in an unsuccessful bid for MGM.

CAPITOL

Capitol is run by Jane Barclay and specializes in 'international films with American star talent but European money'. Their strongest feature in 1995 was Polanski's *Death and the Maiden*. In the same year they struck a 50/50 co-production with Fox Searchlight for Christopher Hampton's *The Secret Agent* and hoped to continue the relationship.

CHRYSALIS

Chrysalis is the film division of the TV group headed by Mick Pilsworth. The film venture was established in 1993 with ownership of Red Rooster, a 49% stake in Nik Powell and Steve Woolley's Scala Productions and first-look deals with John Goldstone, Gary Sinyor, Jeremy Bolt, Richard Holmes and Stefan Schwartz. In 1994 Lyndsey Posner, who formerly ran Paramount's London office with Ileen Maisel, was appointed head of the division. She took a 45% stake in New York-based producer Mark Tarlov (*Serial Mom*), in return for which he gained 25% of the film venture. As part of the Tarlov deal a relationship was also established with his UK partner Cameron McCracken.

The Chrysalis strategy has not been able to come up with the films they had hoped for. In early 1996 Chrysalis ended their co-venture with Mark Tarlov and in September 1996 announced that they were closing down the film division, while maintaining their equity stake in Scala.

CINEPOOL

Cinepool is the feature film sales division of thirty-year-old Telepool which buys and sells for ARD, NHK and certain European producers. The film division was set up in 1989 and is run by Wolfram 'Wolfie' Skowronnek-Schaer. Many films are acquired at script stage. Typical projects are 'public service' films in the $3–5 million budget range. 'Our films tend not to be action or sex driven, but more high profile art projects, mainly Germanophone', explains Skowronnek. 'This niche has become very difficult in recent years. We sell to smaller niche companies and if it weren't for EFDO many of them would already be out of business.'

FILM FOUR

FFI is the theatrical sales arm of Channel 4 which began trading in 1993. FFI is also responsible for acquisitions for Channel 4's proposed UK theatrical distribution arm. Channel 4's films are niche films, with an average budget of $3 million. The most ambitious projects, *Four Weddings* and *Shallow Grave,* were sold to PolyGram in key territories.

GAUMONT

The French Major seemed to be outshadowed by UGC, Studio Canal+ and Ciby in the early 1990s but has since been establishing a stable of high-profile first-look deals. The comp-any has been frustrated by the dwindling foreign market for French films and has decided to place an increasing commitment on English-language features. The company nonetheless succeeded in making substantial pre-sales for Jean-Marie Poiré's next French-language feature *Guardian Angels,* on the back of the megahit *Les Visiteurs.*

In 1994 Gaumont put together Luc Besson's $16.6 million debut American feature *Leon,* with US rights sold to Sony for $5 million and key foreign rights sold to Largo/JVC. Gaumont is now financing *The Fifth Element,* starring Bruce Willis and budgeted $50–100 million, for which Sony has paid $25 million for US rights, JVC $10 million for Japanese rights and Tobis $10 million for German rights. Gaumont also has a development deal with Alain Goldman's Legende Productions, expected to deliver one or two English-language pictures a year. The first projects are remakes of *Les Diaboliques* and *En Cas de Malheur.* The former had a relatively disappointing $17 million box office in the United States (released by Warners), but grossed over $6 million in France.

Total foreign sales income has been boosted considerably by the venture into English-language production. Foreign sales rose from $10 million in 1992 to $30 million in 1994. Gaumont has also a successful television division run by Christian Charret, with English-language productions overseen by American Marla Ginsburg.

IAC/GOLDCREST

IAC was founded in 1976 and has raised the finance for over 65 independent films. It started as a sales agent in 1987 with Highlander II. It also handles library sales for sister company Bovino, which has library rights for southeast Asia to over 500 titles. In October 1995 the company merged with Goldcrest, which owns a 100-title library.

ICON

Mel Gibson set up his London sales office in 1995, headed by Ralph Kamp, formerly with Majestic and Lumière. Icon has a US deal with Warners and Paramount whereby they will alternately back its projects. With the success of *Braveheart*, the company is very well positioned. One of its first ventures will be *One Golden Afternoon* which they will be co-producing with Paramount after Pandora dropped out. Icon has also acquired a twenty-picture library from Kings Road.

LARGO

Largo used to be one of the leading independent production companies. It was set up in 1989 by Larry Gordon using a $100 million equity investment from parent company JVC. The company concentrated on action pictures, but lacked any really big hits despite a later injection of $125 million from JVC in equity plus extra loan finance.

In 1994, Gordon left the company to return to a standard studio deal. He had been frustrated by the $25 million budget cap imposed by JVC and signed a first look deal with Universal, where his first production was the $200 million *Waterworld*. JVC continues to be the main shareholder and new CEO is Barr B. Potter. The company now focuses on buying and selling rights. Largo signed a major output deal with MGM/UA in 1995 and has also signed a relationship with Ridley and Tony Scott who were formerly with Majestic/RCS.

LUMIERE

Lumière was formed in 1993 by the merging of French production and library arms, Initiale and IDA. The company is run by husband and wife Jean and Lila Cazes, and in 1996 was taken over by UGC.

Jean Cazes started building a French film library through IDA in 1987 and in 1991 bought the former Thorn-EMI 1400-title library from Weintraub for $57 million. The total Lumière library now includes 2000 classic films, 1500 television programmes and 400 half-hour animation programmes.

In order to maintain healthy library sales, the company aims to produce high profile European films and one or two high-budget American films a year. They have set up a $75 million credit line to do so. Recent films include *Leaving Las Vegas*, *Clerks* and *The City of Lost Children*.

MAYFAIR

Mayfair is the sales arm of the leading UK niche distributor which owns the Curzon Mayfair cinemas and since 1994 includes niche distributor Artifical Eye. Mayfair has long-standing relationships with producers Sarah Pilsbury and Midge Sanford and also with Merchant Ivory. The company merged with Canada's publicly quoted TMN Capital in 1995 which provided a new credit line. 'We want to broaden our financial base so that we can tackle bigger and more commercial films' explained Ian Scorer.

MK2

MK2 is France's leading niche distributor with a prestige exhibition circuit. The company enjoyed very significant sales on Kieslowki's *Three Colours Trilogy*. Sales were run by American John Kochman who has now moved to Studio Canal +. New head of sales is Sophie Bourdon.

OVERSEAS

Set up in 1980, Overseas is the foreign sales arm to US micro-indie First Look, which has the ambition to make bigger crossover hits. In 1994 the company set up a syndicated credit facility with Coutts & Co., Berliner Bank and Nat West using its 165-title library as security. In 1996 Overseas and First Look merged with venture capital fund EMAC in a deal worth $24 million. Overseas has used this stronger capital base to diversify into higher budget films as well as continuing with American indie films and European product.

PANDORA

The Pandora Group was set up by Luxembourg-based TV giant CLT in 1982 with a 50% equity stake. The film arm was set up in 1991 with the acquisition of Vestron, and a $70 million production fund, partly contributed by an equity investment from Barings bank.

Pandora already had a 700-title library, mainly of television programmes, and wished to boost library sales. In 1994 Pandora hired Ernst Goldschmidt from bankrupt Sovereign, and relocated production decisions to Paris. The company also set up a new extensive credit line. 'We like to be seen as a very active solidly financed European based company backed by important European banks with 13 years of existence behind us in film and television which have always been in profit', commented Goldschmidt.

Pandora originally aimed to produce classy English-language independent films in the $3–15 million range and also buy occasional foreign-language films such as *Like Water for Chocolate*. 'Sometimes we will work with the studios' commented Goldschmidt, 'but as far as I can see, they're not very keen to split rights at the moment and we want to be in a situation where we are in charge of a project.'

The company generally put up 30% of the budget in return for foreign rights, but recent losses have prompted the company to shift emphasis towards $15+ million pictures. Pandora president Christian Bourguignon explained in 1995, 'We are altering our target. The small British films have been very difficult for us. We certainly won't be abandoning this kind of picture but we will also be investing in projects that have better-known directors and bigger names in the cast. The question has been how to finance such films.'[1]

Pandora established a new $60 million credit line from Chemical Bank, adding to existing three credit lines worth $30 million. They tried to establish a multi-picture deal with Fox and then with Paramount. The latter fell apart over the debut film *One Golden Afternoon* and led to head of production Jonathan Taplin leaving the company. Pandora is now in a quandary as to where to access premium product. They announced in 1996 that they aimed to provide a bridge for world sales of Latin American pictures, and also have a nine-film production deal with Filmpact, a partnership of young producers Ricky Posner and Jeremy Bolt.

RANK

The UK distributor Rank has a series of co-financing deals with US companies including a $120 million six-picture deal with Jonathan Taplin, a six-film output deal with Savoy and a $75 million three-way deal with MGM and Live for a ten-film slate from Gladden Productions. These are financed through a $100 million revolving fund.

RYSHER

Rysher began as a successful independent television producer in 1991 and was taken over by Cox Enterprises in 1993. Cox owns six network stations with 7.6% coverage of the US. The takeover freed up production funds of $175 million a year for a new film venture. Rysher established US deals with Savoy, Warners and MGM and foreign deals with Village Roadshow in Australia, Entertainment in the UK, SACIS in Italy and Tele-Munchen for German TV rights. In 1996 Rysher sold international rights to three of its biggest pictures to Paramount, and also established a co-production relationship for further projects.

In April 1996 Rysher signed an output deal with Scripps Howards Productions, who own nine network stations with 8% coverage of the US. The deal gives them greater leverage in US TV.

SAMUEL GOLDWYN

Goldwyn is the foreign sales arm of the US indie distributor, and is now part of the Metromedia/Orion group. The company caters for in-house product and co-productions such as *The Madness of King George*. They have a London-based acquisitions executive.

SOGEPAQ

Sogepaq formed a joint sales venture with Iberoamericana in 1994, making them in effect the only Spanish Major. The company has over $11 million in capital and possesses a 1500-title library including world rights to over 250 Spanish films.

Andres Vicente Gomez is head of the company and acts 'rather like the president of production at a US studio'. The alliance has given Gomez the chance to step up his production plans. 'Sogetel will provide me with key financing . . . allowing me to devote more time to development and production of pictures'[2] he says. Under the deal, Gomez will oversee the production of 24–30 features costing $135 million between 1995 and 1997. This includes a series of $7–15 million English-language films, the first of which is a 50% commitment to Fernando Trueba's *Two Much* ($14 million), starring Antonio Banderas and Melanie Griffith and co-produced with PolyGram's Interscope. To cement the US link, the company set up an LA office in 1996 headed by Volkert Struyken, who previously worked with Frans Afman.

309

SPELLING/WORLDVISION/REPUBLIC

Aaron Spelling's company is one of the largest US Independents, traditionally concentrating in television. Republic was acquired by Spelling for $93 million in 1994 and produces its own theatrical features. Spelling also owns Worldvision which has a 10,000-hour TV library. The combined companies are part of the Viacom/Paramount colossus. In 1995 Viacom announced its desire to sell, but then shelved the plans.

Spelling has recently stepped up film production, including *Moll Flanders* by Stephen Frears and *The Usual Suspects*. In December 1995 Spelling signed a three-year pact with Trilogy Entertainment who contributed to the *Moll Flanders* project, and previously had a production deal with RCS/Majestic.

STUDIO CANAL+

The production, rights and foreign sales arm of France's pay-TV giant Canal+. It is now one of the largest sales houses of French-language product with films provided by Alain Sarde and Telema. The French market, however, is limited and it is very difficult to pre-sell, especially for unknown talent. Head of sales, Daniel Marquet (formerly with the Movie Company), explains, 'I am beginning to suggest to some of the buyers that we deal with – and there are really only 75 major buyers of French films worldwide – that they become more involved with pre-buying some of the smaller and less well-known directors we represent. I try to impress on people that although they know exactly what to expect from established directors such as Techiné, Sautet and Serreau, that they also need to invest for the long term. They need to invest in the re-development of French cinema.'[3]

In 1994 American John Kochman joined the company from MK2 and has used his international contacts to boost business. In 1995 one of the strongest sellers was *La Haine (Hate)* which clocked up $1.5 million in foreign sales.

THE SALES COMPANY

Established in 1986 by former Channel 4 sales chief, Carole Myers. The owners are British Screen, Zenith and BBC Worldwide (which replaced Palace in 1991). Myers excels at promoting niche films. 'I started out selling BFI films' she explains, 'which in those days you weren't supposed to be able to sell, because the BFI's remit was to give money only to things that nobody else would give money to!'[4] She continues to focus on smaller releases but has handled strong titles such as *The Crying Game* and *The Snapper*.

UGC

The French Major UGC began diversifying into English language production in the early 1990s with a $2 million development fund and six-picture deal with Jeremy Thomas in 1993, aiming to produce two pictures every eighteen months.

UGC also produced Kusturica's first American film, the $16 million *Arizona Dream* in 1992, and in 1995 announced a co-production venture with Fox Searchlight as well as production funding for an American film by Ken Loach produced by Jeremy Thomas. The UGC empire now includes Lumière and has formal links with Canal+.

EUROPEAN MEDIA GROUPS

Companies linked to the five main 'family groups' in Europe, were profiled in Chapter 8. There are many other important players in Europe. Over time, these companies may well establish formal links with the Big Five.

BONNIER

One of Scandinavia's biggest media groups. The company began in book publishing and has expanded into newspapers and magazines. The company owns Svensk Filmindustri, which has interests in exhibition, distribution and production and also owns the largest film library in Sweden.

BOUYGUES (TF1 AND CIBY 2000)

TF1 was privatized in 1987 when Chirac was briefly French Prime Minister. This was part of a general strategy to shift the balance of commercial television towards interests that were favourable to the Right (including placing Robert Hersant in control of La 5). The largest stake in TF1 (25%) was sold to construction magnate Francis Bouygues, with further 4% stakes sold to Berlusconi and RCS.

New chief executive Patrick Le Lay helped push TF1 to a 45% share of national ratings. The success of the channel is based on selling to 'la France profonde' – which means low-brow popular entertainment. The company invests in French cinema, as obliged by the law, and also has two rights ventures – Syalis for French films and Legènde (with Alain Goldman) for US films. The latter invested $13 million in Martin Scorsese's *Casino* and is partnered with Disney on the $42 million remake of *Un Indien dans la Ville*.

Parent company Bouygues also owns Ciby 2000 which is involved in production, French theatrical distribution and foreign sales.

CARLTON

Michael Green has built up Carlton Communications from scratch. The company began in hardware, and post-production, film processing and video duplication continue to provide over two thirds of the company's revenue.

Green was highly admired by Lady Thatcher, and some cynically suggested that the 1991 ITV franchise auction was designed for him. The shake-up in ITV allowed Carlton to acquire the jewel in the ITV crown from Thames. Green subsequently bought Central in 1994 for $1.1 billion and also owns 20% of Meridian and GMTV as well as 36% of ITN. This makes Carlton the biggest player in ITV.

Prior to the franchise auction, Carlton owned a 50% stake in Zenith Productions, a joint venture with Paramount, which it had to sell once it became a broadcaster. In 1992 Carlton bought a 10% stake of US indie mini-major Savoy for $15 million and in 1995 made a failed bid for the UK's MGM theatres, teamed with in-house management and PolyGram. In 1996 as part of ITV's renewed commitment to feature film production, Carlton set up a new film unit aiming to produce two films a year.

CECCHI GORI

Mario Cecchi Gori began in the movie business alongside Dino de Laurentiis and then set up his own production company in 1958. His son (b. 1942) has been producing films since 1960 and took full control of the company after his father's death in 1993.

Vittorio Cecchi Gori is a miniature version of Berlusconi, with strategic interests in exhibition, distribution, and pay-TV, ownership of the Fiorentini football team and election as Senator for the Popular Party (formerly the Christian Democrats).

Cecchi Gori has been trying to build up Tele Monte Carlo as a rival private TV station to Berlusconi, and in 1996 he announced a $410 million deal for exclusive soccer rights on free TV, but his bankers baulked at the deal.

EMI

EMI is one of the Big Six Majors and at various times has flirted with film. In 1996 Thorn EMI 'de-merged' – separating the music division (45% of total revenue) from consumer electronics. The music division could be acquired by a group interested in building a media empire.

EMI was active in the film business in the 1970s and early 1980s. In 1969 the company announced an ambitious production slate and throughout the 1970s secured studios, theatres and libraries, but failed to produce any big hits, the most successful being *The Deer Hunter*. In 1979 EMI was taken over by consumer electronics giant Thorn and decided to join hands with Lew Grade to form an American distribution company, AFD.

Grade was a veteran of ITV and had begun film production at the Cannes Film Festival in 1974, and over the next six years produced over 80 films, which despite superb salesmanship enjoyed very moderate success.

Grade and Thorn EMI had a UK distribution company and an exhibition circuit, and ventured forth into high-budget films. The result was disaster, culminating with the $35 million flop *Raise the Titanic* in 1981, which grossed only $8 million.

The Thorn-EMI empire was sold off in the mid-1980s with Lumière ultimately acquiring the film library (now part of UGC), and Cannon/Pathé and subsequently Virgin acquiring the MGM cinema chain.

EMI is unlikely to make any major investments in film in the near future, but if taken over it could be part of a wider film and multi-media strategy.

ENRIQUE CEREZO

Cerezo is Spain's mini-mogul. He bought up library titles throughout the 1980s to establish Spain's most valuable film library (over 1500 titles), filled with comedy classics produced during the Fascist regime. He has key interests in exhibition and distribution and was formerly partnered with Spanish producer Andres Vicente-Gomez. He also is vice-president of leading soccer team Atletico Madrid. Cerezo now has a new production partner, Pedro Costa, and in 1993 invested $7 million in production. Cerezo has also signed a joint venture with Antena 3 for the medium-budget English-language film *Death in Granada*, starring Andy Garcia.

FILMAURO

Luigi de Laurentiis (b. 1917) began working in the film industry alongside his brother Dino de Laurentiis. When Dino left for America, Luigi set up Filmauro in 1972, which he ran with his son Aurelio, who took full control of the company after his father's death in 1992. The company is vertically integrated with exhibition, distribution and production and has produced many Italian hits as well as the occasional American film such as *Leviathan* and *Son of the Pink Panther*.

GRANADA

Twenty per cent of the company's $3.35 billion revenue is earned in television, with ownership of Granada and LWT, and 24% of Yorkshire Tyne Tees, 20% of GMTV, 20% of ITN and 11% of BSkyB. Granada has occasionally invested in film productions, most notably with *My Left Foot* (1989) and *Jack and Sarah* (1995). In 1996 Granada's head of film production, Pippa Cross, announced a co-venture with Rank to produce a string of $3 million comedy films.

KINNEVIK

Kinnevik is the most important shareholder in private television in Scandinavia, and also has a rights library and a stake in production company Strix.

LUSOMUNDO

Lusomundo, headed by Colonel Luis Silva, is the Portuguese Major with a dominant position in exhibition, distribution, video and library rights. The company also has expanding interests in Spain.

NORDISK/EGMONT

Based in Denmark, owner of theatres, distribution, a substantial film library, and one of the main feature film producers in Scandinavia.

PEARSON

Pearson has traditionally had an eclectic mix of media interests combined with businesses in merchant banking, china, wine, oil and engineering. The company has been slowly shedding its slow-moving aristocratic image and has re-focused almost entirely on media, led by the likes of TV whizz kid, Greg Dyke, who is head of Pearson TV. Pearson has spent $1.6 billion in acquisitions since 1993, including $270 million for Grundy Worldwide and $465 million on California CD-ROM company Mindscape (which is expected to record a $71 million loss in 1996).

In late 1995 Pearson headed the consortium including MAI and CLT which won the Channel 5 licence with a $35 million bid. The company also bought American TV producer/distributor ACI for more than $40 million and in 1996 acquired the production interests of Selec-TV.

The company's key media interests include:

•	Print media	*Financial Times, The Economist* (50%)
•	Publishing	Longman, Penguin, Addison-Wesley
•	Theme park	Alton Towers
•	TV channels	Yorkshire-Tyne Tees (14.2%)
		TVB Hong Kong (10%)
		BSkyB (9%)
		Channel 5 (with MAI and CLT)
		Global alliance with BBC
		UK Gold and UK Living (15%)
•	TV production	Thames, Grundy, Reeves, ACI, Cosgrove Hall, Selec-TV
•	Film production	Euston Films
•	TV studio	Teddington Studios
•	Software	Mindscape CD-ROM, Extel, IDC

In the late 1970s, Pearson began flirting with the film business, and invested £100,000 in the Goldcrest development fund and then $500,000 in the US film fund IFI. After James Lee was appointed chief executive of Pearson Longman in 1979, the company stepped up its involvement, putting up 44% of the £8.2 million fund backing Goldcrest Films International.

Goldcrest was the great white hope of the British cinema in the early 1980s. The strategy of the company, like so many other European ventures, aimed to crack the US market. Despite the success of *Gandhi*, the company was unable to provide a consistent string of successes and ran aground on the flops of *Revolution, Mission* and *Absolute Beginners*. Goldcrest was sold to Masterman in 1987, having lost £34 million.

Pearson is now concentrating on the theoretically less risky areas of television and interactive software, but did make a failed bid for the MGM theatre chain.

PRISA

Prisa is Spain's leading media company, with 64% of the company's revenue earned from the national newspaper *El Pais*. The company also owns 20% of the UK newspaper *The Independent* and has a 25% stake in Canal+ Spain, plus 51% of Sogepaq, the Spanish Major.

Sogepaq brings together the forces of Spain's leading industry players, including Andres Vicente Gomez and José Vicuña (Warner Spain). In addition to production, there is a distribution joint venture with PolyGram as well as a foreign sales arm and important links to Canal+ Spain and the UCI/Alfredo Matas theatre chain Cinesa.

Under new chief Ele Juarez, recruited from PolyGram Spain, Prisa is stepping up its production plans and also looking for US partners in building multiplexes and launching English-language production. The company is in talks with Sony to make Spanish-language films.

RANK

The Rank Organisation was founded by J. Arthur Rank in the 1930s and by 1939 owned Pinewood, Denham and Elstree studios. With the outbreak of the Second World War the government waived anti-trust legislation to allow him to acquire two of the three largest circuits – Odeon and Gaumont-British, thereby becoming the UK's film tsar.

Rank established a network of theatres throughout the British Commonwealth and in 1944 created Eagle-Lion, 'a distribution organisation on the American model'. He set up distribution joint-ventures with Universal and United Artists, and in the UK even had the advantage of a nine-month boycott by the Majors in 1947. But Rank admitted in 1948, 'Many of the films we produced were not of a quality to ensure even reasonable returns . . . our plans to meet an unexpected and critical situation were too ambitious.'

By 1949 the company suffered a severe financial crisis, including a £16 million overdraft, and had to cut back its activities. In the 1950s Rank was at the forefront of rationalizing the country's film network, as the authorities believed that film would be replaced by television as the medium of the future. Cinemas became bingo halls and Rank switched from film production to running entertainment sites.

J. Arthur Rank died in 1972 and in 1980 the Rank Organisation announced withdrawal from UK film production. Rank suffered financial problems during the 1980s and by 1990 had accumulated a $1.4 billion debt load. In 1990 Warners appeared interested in acquiring 50% of Pinewood studios but later dropped out. In 1992 Rank sold Rank Screen Advertising and music venue Hammersmith Odeon.

In January 1993 a consortium known as Premier Media was established by Ileen Maisel and Graham Bradstreet to try to buy Rank's film and television interests for around $600 million. The bid was backed by Carlton's Michael Green and had a potential interest from Pearson. Bradstreet said that Rank is 'the last great vertically integrated company that can provide the bridge between US and Europe'. The consortium intended to use the company's exhibition strength to start up UK production but Rank said that it had no interest in selling.

In 1994 the company sold its 49% stake in Rank Xerox for $1 billion and invested the same amount in a joint venture with MCA for Universal Studios in Florida.

Rank now owns the Odeon Cinema chain (which represents a third of UK admissions), Pinewood studios, Rank Film Laboratories and Rank Video duplication, and has a distribution arm in alliance with Castle Rock/Turner. The company also has extensive interests in hotels, gaming and leisure activities – including a $410 million acquisition of the Hard Rock Café chain in 1996.

In recent years, the company has occasionally produced British films with Victor Glynn and has been active in investing in Hollywood films with a revolving $100 million production fund. In 1996 Rank announced a joint venture with Granada to produce a series of low-budget comedy films and also a plan to fully fund pictures up to $7 million. The first announced project is *Lawn Dogs*, to be directed by John Duigan and produced by Duncan Kenworthy. If the Arts Council adopts the proposed system of mini-studio investment funds, Rank would be a leading contender to receive subsidy monies.

RCS

Rizzoli Corriere della Sera is the largest publisher in Italy with a 19.2% share of the daily newspaper sector and a 25% stake of the magazine business. The company is controlled by Fiat, Italy's most powerful industrial group. Another key shareholder is Daniel Filipachhi, who sits on the Hachette board of directors.

In the past, Fiat boss Agnelli and RCS founder Angelo Rizzoli Sr. both played key roles in the Italian film industry. Rizzoli produced Max Ophuls' film *La signora di tutti* in 1934 and provided financial backing to Vittorio Mussolini's production company ACI-ERA during the war years. This established a link with a group of film-makers – Rosselini, Fellini, de Sica, Antonioni – whom Rizzoli backed in the post-war era.

After Rizzoli's death in 1970, Cineriz slowly withdrew from the cinema, and was finally sold to Berlusconi. Angelo Rizzoli Jr. is now involved in cinema through a separate production outfit, Erre Productions which produced *The Stolen Children*.

RCS has traditionally been very much Italian orientated, but began to expand internationally in the early 1990s. In 1991 it established equity stakes with Carolco (12%), TFI (4%), Carlton (6%) and set up Hannibal Films – a joint venture with Telemunchen to make TV mini-series. This international strategy was the only way forward for the group, since the domestic market was sewn up by RAI and Berlusconi.

But the company's international ambitions met with severe disappointments. The serious, hard-working and unbureaucratic RCS claimed to have a well thought out strategy but others claimed they were throwing money around. The Carolco investment had to be completely written off and Majestic suffered the departure of Guy East.

In 1995 RCS Editori announced a $500 million loss over the previous eighteen months, of which 20% was estimated to have come from film and television. This unusually high level of losses provoked a judicial enquiry focusing on alleged false company communications and illicit distribution of profits. Another European dream seemed to have bitten the dust.

UNITED NEWS AND MEDIA

The company was created in 1996, through a merger between United Communications (Express newspapers) and MAI which owns Meridian and Anglia TV, 14.9% of Yorkshire Tyne-Tees and is a leading investor in Channel 5. The company has a joint venture with Warners to build a $340 million theme park.

VIRGIN

Richard Branson's company which began in the music business is now much more involved in airlines. But in 1995 the company acquired the MGM UK cinema chain for $310 million. In the 1980s the company had been involved in production and distribution through Virgin Vision, which ultimately lost money. The company will now reinvest in its exhibition chain and also put some money into production.

Revenues and Contracts

The main text of this book has provided an overview of how revenue flows are negotiated in the movie business. This appendix provides a more detailed breakdown, divided into domestic revenues, foreign sales and Europe's legal framework.

THE REVENUE STREAM

Each step in the 'value chain' has a different deal structure, which determines how consumer revenues are divided between retailer, distributor and producer.

THEATRICAL REVENUES

Box office was traditionally the main source of revenue for films. Today it represents the minority of total distributor revenues, but because of accounting practices is still the main source of official 'production revenue'. For this reason the deals that are negotiated have a critical effect on net profits.

The distributor's share of the exhibitor's gross is known as 'rentals' and is normally negotiated under a *fixed percentage deal* which hovers between 45–50% of gross or under a *sliding scale* whereby the distributor's share goes up as grosses rise.

For blockbuster films the studios sometimes negotiate '*90/10 division over house floor*' where the studio guarantees the exhibitor's fixed costs (house floor or 'house nut') and receives 90% of all other revenues. In rare circumstances this is turned into a 'four wall' deal, where the distributor pays the house floor and then receives 100% of revenues.

DISTRIBUTOR DEDUCTIONS

The distributor will aim to recoup its investment in the film and allocate as much overhead and expenses to profitable films as possible in order to minimize net profit payouts. The producer has the right to check any deductions, and commission an audit of the accounts.

Distribution fee

The distributor incurs financial risks in distributing the film and in return will demand a fee. By far the most common is the *net deal* in which the distributor immediately deducts a distribution fee from rentals, typically 30% in the US, 35% in the UK and 40% for the rest of the world.

In certain cases the producer may be able to negotiate a *70/30 Major deal*, in which the distributor deducts promotion costs and any minimum guarantee (MG) payment, and then charges a 70% fee against all excess revenues (overages). A variation of this deal is a *sliding scale* under which the distributor's share of overages goes down as grosses rise. There is also the *50/50 Net deal,* where there is a 50/50 split of any net revenues after prints and advertising (P&A) and any MG has been recouped.

A well funded independent producer may choose instead to establish an output deal or *rent a studio* deal, under which they contribute part of the production and promotion costs and benefit from a lower distributor's fee. Both Castle Rock and Carolco had such deals with Columbia. The former was on the basis of a 17.5% distribution fee.

The best deal for a small independent producer is *first dollar gross* under which they get a fixed percentage, e.g. 30% of rentals, until P&A is covered and then a higher share. This is virtually never granted by the Majors. It is sometimes granted by independent distributors when there is no upfront minimum guarantee payment (see later).

Other possible deals include:

50/50 First dollar split. Instead of receiving a minimum guarantee, the producer receives 50% of rentals.

Modified gross deal. The distributor deducts promotion costs and a multiple of the theatrical minimum guarantee, and pays out any overages.

Distribution costs

The distributor has the right to recoup all distribution costs. The most significant of these are prints and advertising (P&A). In addition the distributor will charge for collections, dubbing, taxes, transportation and miscellaneous. There will also be a charge for royalties and residuals – particularly in television. These may be allocated either as a production cost or as a distribution cost.

A Major will often charge 10% overhead on top of P&A to cover the fixed costs of its marketing department.

Cross-collateralization

The Major will aim to deduct losses in one territory against gains in another. This means, for example, that if a film is a runaway success in a territory such as France but dies everywhere else, the French surpluses will be used to compensate for other deficits.

Even more serious, the distributor may try to deduct the losses from one film against the gains of another. Cross-collaterization can also be applied across different media, e.g. theatrical losses will be offset against video gains. The producer should try to limit all forms of cross-collateralization.

Minimum guarantee

The Majors are almost always involved in the production finance of a film and Independents will also often put up some production finance or pay an acquisition fee for the film. This investment is known as a 'minimum guarantee'. When the distibutor fully funds the film, the MG is equal to the 'negative cost'. The distributor will retain all revenues until the minimum guarantee is recouped.

VIDEO REVENUES

Video revenue is the main area of dispute in the calculation of net profits, since it is by far the most important revenue source and yet contributes only a small proportion of revenues. The video business is divided between sell-through and rentals.

Sell-through cassettes are sold at a 45–50% mark-up of wholesale price. For rental cassettes, video clubs pay the distributor a one-off elevated wholesale price.

From total wholesale revenues, only 20% is allocated to production revenue and is known as 'royalty'. The rest is kept in the video distribution arm to cover manufacturing and promotion. In the early years of video, where volume sales were low and unit costs were high, the 20% royalty seemed to be fair.

Today, where unit production costs are under $6 a cassette, it results in huge profits for the video distribution arm. Producers with very strong leverage can push their royalty up to 25% or 30% and limit distributor deductions.

The 20% production royalty is subject to a distribution fee and marketing costs. As a consequence of these accounting practices, although video represents 51% of total distributor's revenues, it will typically only contribute 20% of official production revenue. If all video profits were recorded in production revenue, then the volume of production revenue would double and almost 50% of films would earn net profits.

PAY-TV REVENUES

The Majors negotiate pay-TV deals with a sliding scale that goes up with box office success. There is a cap on the top pay-out of around $14–15 million. This was because in early years blockbuster hits such as *Ghostbusters* clocked up fees in excess of $30 million.

The Majors can negotiate far better terms than the Independents, who tend to be given flat rates. This was one of the main reasons that indies such as Miramax were keen to be taken over. The distributor takes a 30–40% distribution fee plus marketing and distribution costs.

FREE TV REVENUES

Films are sold to pay-TV and free television in 'packages' of 10–20 films. The distributor usually allocates these revenues on an equal basis to all the films in the package. Inevitably, this smoothes out the earnings of underperforming films. The average free television revenue per title for the Majors is $2–5 million. Distributor deductions are the standard 30–40% distributor fee plus minimal marketing costs.

NEGOTIATING A DISTRIBUTION DEAL

Most distributors aim to acquire all media rights for their territory, and will sell to third parties in areas where they do not have distribution. The fees with the Mini-majors will be comparable and in certain cases higher than the Majors. For the Classics and Micros they will tend to be lower, particularly when there is a low or zero minimum guarantee.

An illustrative range of percentage fees is:

% Fees	Major	Mini-major	Classic	Micro
US theatrical	30	27.5	20	20
US video	30	35	20	15
US pay-TV	30	25	22	15
US free TV	30	37.5	25	25
Foreign	40	37.5	20	20
Music/licensing	30	40	25	20

The exact fee will depend upon the elements of the deal. The independent produc-er should use a qualified lawyer to construct the distribution deal and pay particular attention to:

Minimum guarantee (MG). Value, timing and conditions of payment.

Distribution fee. Percentage fees by media.

Distribution expenses. Try to avoid indirect charges, overhead, etc. and set limit.

Promotion. Place minimum and maximum values for P&A spend. Approval rights for marketing campaign. Commitment to trailers.

Release pattern. Minimum number of screens.

Distributor approvals. Limit editing changes to those needed for ratings requirements. If there is a production MG, limit approval to key above the line talent.

Audit rights. Full right to audit all expenses.

Foreign sales. Prohibit flat-fee outright sales in seven key foreign markets.

Foreign taxes. Determine how foreign revenues are rapatriated and allow the producer access to any tax deductions.

Interest. Specify what monies are liable to interest payments.

Cross-collateralization. Prevent deductions for any other picture.

COMPONENTS OF NEGATIVE COST

Each Major will define negative cost differently. The main ingredients are production budget, overhead and interest. Other costs such as residuals, deferments and participa-tions may be allocated as distribution costs.

PRODUCTION BUDGET

This is roughly equally divided between the cost of the talent ('above the line') and the technical cost of producing the film ('below the line'). The average production budget for Hollywood releases is $20–25 million.

OVERHEAD

Each Major charges a premium over the production budget to cover their fixed costs. This varies from 12.5% on average at Columbia to 25% at Universal.

INTEREST

Studios will charge for advancing production monies, against future revenues. This is currently charged at 125% of US Prime. The size of interest payments depends on the production period of the film. On average it will be a 7% premium over production cost.

RESIDUALS

Minor talent will receive residuals payments, particularly from television exploitation. These costs may be allocated to distribution costs.

DEFERMENTS

Some films have deferment deals where talent will only be paid if film is a success.

GROSS PARTICIPATIONS

For big-budget pictures, agents try to negotiate talent deals which specify a salary fee against a fixed percentage of the gross (known as points). The deals normally are for theatrical gross only (or even just US gross) and may be before or after deduction of distributor's fees and costs.

These deals shunt all 'net profit' participants further down the line. Gross points can result in spectacular earnings, such as Jack Nicholson's reported $50 million earnings from *Batman*.

ADDITIONAL COSTS FOR INDEPENDENT PRODUCERS

In addition to the production cost, an independent producer must pay the following:

CONTINGENCY

The budget should include a minimum 10% contingency to cover unforeseen costs. Bankers and completion bond companies will insist on such a contingency.

PRODUCTION INSURANCE

The producer should take out production insurance for all the technical elements of the film: the camera, stock and processing and props, sets, locations and wardrobe.

There should also be comprehensive liability, life and accident insurance for cast and crew. Insurance costs were 3–4% of the budget, but as the result of recent star deaths (Brandon Lee, John Candy) rates have gone up.

ERRORS AND OMISSIONS INSURANCE

The producer must own all the rights to the film before being able to sell them. He or she must demonstrate that all talent appearances have been paid for, that there is chain of title on the script and original property and that all music and library images have been paid for. In the UK/US model, errors and omissions insurance is required to protect the producer against lawsuits alleging unfair competition, breach of contract or lack of rights clearances. No one will buy or show the film without such an insurance in place. This will require detailed documentation from the producer. The fee is normally 1–2%. The insurer will undertake clearance procedures to verify the following:

> Full copyright and 'chain of title' to the script and original property.
>
> Rights payments for all music and library images.
>
> Guarantees that there are not grounds for libel.
>
> Releases for all persons and real locations in the film, enabling full right to edit, modify, add and/or delete all material recorded.

On the continent, such clearance procedures are achieved through a lawyer, and declaration of chain of title through the state registry office.

INTEREST

The costs of a film are paid for before revenues are received. The difference will be covered by loans which incur interest. The budget should include a 10% interest reserve to cover these payments.

LEGAL FEES

All independent producers should consult a good lawyer to ensure that all of the above has been properly carried out. The top entertainment lawyers are at the heart of the movie business and can be instrumental in making a film happen. Legal fees for a film up to $3.5 million will be $15,000–30,000, an average of 0.7%.

DEFERRALS

Independent films often require deferrals of producer, cast or crew payments in order to balance the budget. These deferrals must be factored into the budget when calculating future break-even.

PARTICIPATIONS

Talent may well demand a favourable profit participation or share in the equity in return for fee deferrals. These should also be factored into the budget.

COMPLETION BOND

No third party will agree to finance a film unless they are sure it will be completed. Most Independents achieve this through a completion bond, although capital-rich companies such as Polygram or the Majors can guarantee completion in-house. The bond company guarantees that a film will be delivered on schedule, within budget and without substantial deviations from the approved script. It will meet any budget over-runs. This requires confidence in the track record of the producer and in the case of a first-time producer will require a 'godfather' executive producer.

The budget and all contracts will be carefully checked and the bond company will closely supervise production. If agreed cost and schedule requirements are not met, the bond company may at any time take control of the production and introduce draconian controls, including limiting the rights and payments of the producer. The bond company may also fire the director, but in practice this rarely happens, as it will jeopardize the creative integrity of the film.

To apply for a completion bond, the producer must submit an application form, final shooting script, detailed production budget, shooting and post-production schedule, chain of title, talent contracts and resumés, financing agreements and production insurance.

Most independent films are backed by completion bonds. In the early days fees were traditionally 5–6% of the production budget (including overages and interest). During the 1980s, competition pushed commissions down towards 1–2% with the balance to be paid only if the budget overran. This put considerable pressure on the bond companies, which led to the bankruptcy in June 1993 of one of the most prestigious bonding companies, The Completion Bond Company who had suffered high pay-outs on several films including *Malcolm X* and *Cliffhanger*. The bond market also suffered from harsher conditions in the insurance market, following $5 billion in losses at Lloyd's at the end of the 1980s.

The oldest bond company is the UK's Film Finances (established in 1950), which had a virtual monopoly of the bonding business until the early 1980s. In the wake of CBC's demise, the two main players are now Film Finances and International Film Guarantors, followed by smaller players such as Motion Picture Guarantors. The surviving companies have pushed their rates back to 5–6%.

NEGOTIATING A DEAL WITH A SALES AGENT

The sales agent will want exclusive rights to license a film over a specific period of time. The producer should specify approval rights over any distribution contracts entered into. The contract between the producer and the sales agent should specify the following:

Minimum guarantee (MG). Value, timing and conditions of payment.
Sales commission. Percentage fees by media.
Sales expenses. Avoid indirect charges, overhead, etc. Place cap on total value.
Promotion. Place minimum and maximum values for P&A spend. Approval rights for marketing campaign.

Foreign sales. Prohibit flat-fee outright sales in seven key foreign markets.

Foreign taxes. Determine how foreign revenues are repatriated and allow the producer access to any tax deductions.

Interest. Specify what monies are liable to interest payments.

An illustrative range of commission fees is as follows:

US theatrical	10–15% if the sales company sets up the deal
US video	10–15%
US network TV	10%
US pay-TV	20%
US cable	35%
Rest of world:	
All media	10–25% without MG
All media	25–35% with MG

It is important that the producer also does much of the running in terms of submitting to festivals and drumming up press interest. For key events this should be done in consultation with the sales agent.

The sales agent will be obliged to keep the producer informed of how his or her film is doing abroad. This is true even for films that may have been made many years ago and now lie in a sales agent's library.

The sales agent must produce a quarterly royalty report that will specify all payments made to the film – minimum guarantees, overages and television fees.

MARKET COSTS

The sales agent will have to pay to take the film to the leading three markets. These costs will be deducted as sales expenses from any revenues. The cost to take a film to Cannes is estimated to be as follows:

Low-budget market film	$10,000–$30,000
Mid-budget market film	$25,000–$50,000
High-profile or festival film	$125,000–$200,000
Official festival selection	$50,000–$200,000 (indie)
	$250,000 plus (studio)

(Source: *Hollywood Reporter*, Cannes 95)

This covers travel, taxis, hotel, marketing tools, trade advertising, screenings, office hire and parties. The costs at AFM and MIFED are slightly lower because there are no festivals or major press events.

This level of costs means that many independent and foreign-language films will not even have a market screening and will simply be available on videotape in a small office.

The micro-films are much more dependent on smaller festivals where they hope to build word of mouth and, at the minimum, secure a television sale.

MARKETING TOOLS

The sales companies send out marketing information about their films throughout the year, but they gear their main promotional push for the key markets.

The key tools are the poster and the press book. The press book will include a one or two page synopsis, filmographies of the leading talent, production notes, and full cast and crew lists. It is vital that the film also has good stills for the press book, posters and press coverage. Up to 2000 press books will be needed at a total cost of $5,000–$15,000.

The main objective of the marketing push is to attract the interest of the consumer press. To do this, they will try to create hype around the picture and will also need the presence of the stars. Some stars are very willing to tour round the world promoting a film, others are not. Usually the promotion conditions are specified in the talent's contract and represent about 30% of the total talent fee.

FOREIGN SALES REVENUES

Prices paid can be broadly categorized by the budget and elements of the film, and the size and wealth of the territory into which the film is sold. A guide to buying prices according to the film's budget was provided by *Variety* in 1990 (prices quoted in thousands of dollars):

Film budget

	$1–4M	*$4–8M*	*$8–12M*	*$12+M*
France	30–60	60–100	100–300	250–900
Germany	30–100	50–300	150–800	400–1000
Italy	25–50	50–100	100–350	350–1500
Spain	15–30	30–125	75–350	200–800
UK	30–50	50–175	175–500	500–1500
Japan	40–125	125–300	200–800	500–2000
Australia/NZ	25–35	35–100	100–225	200–600
World total	$0.3M–$1M	$0.7M–$2M	$1.5M–$5M	$3.5M–$12M

The world figures show the value of total sales if the film is sold in every foreign territory (i.e. everywhere outside the US/Canada). This demonstrates that as the budget goes up, so does the proportion of the budget covered by foreign sales. But this survey of prices also tends to underestimate values, particularly for high-budget films which often raise over $25 million in sales. A survey of MG prices in France in 1995 suggested the following average prices (in $ million):

	American Films				Non-American	
	$1-4M	*$4-8M*	*$8-12M*	*$12+M*	*Commonw.*	*For.-lang.*
France	0.04	0.3	0.75	2.5	0.35	0.06

The high acquisition prices for big-budget films (average $2.5M) demonstrate that since France is 7.5% of total world sales, it is quite possible to raise over $25 million in foreign pre-sales for a prestige title. Foreign-language films and other niche titles, on the other hand, will rarely be bought for more than $50,000 in a major territory except for the US, which may pay up to $1 million for a foreign-language film. Examples of recent acquisitions in France include the following:

	Duration	*Media*	*Buyer*	*MG*	*P&A*
Stargate (US)	12	C/V/TV	Studio Canal+	5	1.2
The Mask (US)	10	C/V/TV	AMLF	2.6	NA
Malice (US)	12	C/V/TV	Number One	2	0.7
Man without a Face (US)	10	C/V/TV	Bac	1.3	NA
Pulp Fiction (US)	10	C/V/TV	Bac	1.3	NA
Priest (GB)	15	C/V/TV	ARP	0.5	NA
Sirens (GB)	10	C/V/TV	CTV	0.15	0.15
La Scorta (It)	7	V	PolyGram	0.04	NA
Laws of Gravity (US)	10	C	FSF	0.01	NA
Vacas (Sp)	7	C/V	Colifilm	0.005	NA

Source: *Ecran Total*

Recent acquisition prices reported for the US include the following:

Film	*Year*	*Price ($M)*	*Buyer*
Crying Game	1992	1.5	Miramax
Kika	1993	0.8	October
Germinal	1993	1	Sony Classics
Simple Formality	1993	1	Sony Classics
Heavenly Creatures	1994	1.8	Miramax
Priest	1994	1.75	Miramax
Victory	1994	4	Miramax
Muriel's Wedding	1994	2.5	Miramax
Death and Maiden	1994	4	Fine Line
Jackie Chan film	1995	1	New Line
Ridicule	1996	0.8	Miramax

Source: *Variety*

PERFORMANCE OF FOREIGN-LANGUAGE FILMS IN THE US

In 1994 half of the foreign-language films released grossed under $50,000 at the box office, and only fifteen grossed higher than $0.5 million:

Film	Country	Box Office ($M)	US rank (No.)
*Eat Drink Man Woman**	Mexico	7.0	138
Belle Epoque	Spain	6.0	145
*Like Water for Chocolate**	Mexico	2.2	190
Kika	Spain	2.1	191
*Farewell my Concubine**	China	2.0	195
Scent of the Green Papaya	Indonesia	1.9	197
*Blue**	Fr./Poland	1.5	209
White	Fr./Poland	1.5	212
*Red***	Fr./Poland	1.3	217
*Reine Margot***	France	0.8	233
*L'Accompagnatrice**	France	0.7	239
Nuits Fauves	France	0.7	244
*Faraway So Close**	Germany	0.65	246
Cronos	Mexico	0.6	247
*Jamon, Jamon**	Spain	0.6	250

Source: *Variety* (* – released in 1993, 1994 gross only; ** – in continuing release)

EXPORTS OF EUROPEAN FILMS

Below is a list of the export figures for some of the top releases in recent years. The releases are divided by language and in order of export value. 'Home' box office is based on the home language territory (e g. UK/US for English-language releases).

Film	Fr	Ger	UK	It	Sp	US	Home	Export
Cinema Paradiso (It/Fr)	13.5	0.4	5	5	3	12	5	39
The Postman (It)	11	2	2	14	4	22	14	51
Caro Diario (It)	1.5	0.3	0.1	2.5	0.5	0.4	2.5	4
Like Water . . . (Mex)	1	1	0.7	2.5	3.2	21.5	–	37
Women on Verge (Sp)	5.2	1.7	0.7	4	8.5	7.2	8.5	24
High Heels (Sp)	9.4	0.4	1	5	6.8	1.8	6.8	22
Atame (Sp)	5.6	0.3	0.3	1	4.1	4.2	4.1	14
Kika (Fr/Sp)	2.5	0.6	0.5	3	2.5	2.1	2.5	11
Jamon, Jamon (Sp)	0.7	0.4	0.3	3.5	1.5	0.4	1.5	7

Film	Fr	Ger	UK	It	Sp	US	Home	Export
Four Weddings (UK)	35	34	45	8	8.5	53	98	145
The Bear (Fr)	43	7.5	3	7.1	5	24.5	28	78
Leon (Fr)	23	2.5	5.5	5.5	1	19.5	25	40
House of Spirits (Ger)	1.5	22	0.5	4.5	4	6.3	7	40
The Piano (Fr/Austla)	14	8	6	3	3	40	46	35
Damage (UK/Fr)	4.5	2.9	2.8	3.4	1	7.5	10	15
Until End World (G./Fr)	3.6	1.8	0.25	3.5	0.6	1	1	12
Crying Game (UK)	2	0.5	3.1	2.6	1	62.5	66	11
Cook, Thief (UK/Fr)	2.5	1.1	2	0.7	0.6	1.4	3	6
Orlando (UK + others)	0.6	1.6	2	2	0.6	5.2	7	6
Cyrano (Fr)	23	4	3.5	3	5	5.8	23	27
Nikita (Fr)	19	1.4	1.5	6.5	3	6.6	19	24
Delicatessen (Fr)	9	3.7	2.4	1.8	1.5	1.7	9	14
Indochine (Fr)	20	0.7	0.2	1	3	6	20	14
Red (Fr)	6	0.8	0.4	3	0.8	4	6	11
Les Visiteurs (Fr)	80	1.5	0.3	2	2.7	–	80	8
Blue (Fr)	7	1	0.7	1.5	1.5	1.7	7	8
La Reine Margot (Fr)	8	1	0.2	2	1.5	1.5	8	8
Double Vie . . . (Fr)	5	0.6	0.8	0.7	0.5	2	5	6
Toto le Héros (Bel/Fr)	4	0.58	1	0.8	0.5	1.3	4	5
Le Grand Bleu (Fr)	48	2.4	0.1	0.7	0.5	0.2	48	5
Nuits Fauves (Fr)	15	0.6	0.3	0.8	0.5	0.7	15	4
City of Children (Fr/Sp)	9	0.5	0.3	0.8	0.8	1	9	3
Germinal (Fr)	35	0.5	0.3	0.4	0.5	0.4	35	3
Man Bites Dog (Bel)	2.5	0.2	0.2	0.3	0.2	0.2	3	1
La Discrète (Fr)	10	0.2	0.1	0.4	0.25	0.2	10	1
La Haine (Fr)	15	0.3	0.4	0.5	0.6	0.2	15	2
Far Away So Close (G)	0.75	0.75	0.5	1	0.4	0.8	1	4
Der Bewegte Mann (G)	0.2	46	0	0.5	0.5	–	46	2
Europa (Fr/Den/Ger)	0.7	0.35	0.1	0.15	0.6	0.2	0	2

Source: *Variety*

ELIGIBILITY CONDITIONS IN EUROPE FOR A NATIONAL FILM

Each national cinema centre will have a different definition of a 'national film'. The basic ingredients include the following:

The producer must be resident or have his registered office in the home country. If from another EC state he must have a place of business in the home country.

The lead production company cannot be a subsidiary of an American or other non-EU company.

An original version of the film is recorded in the national language (double shooting in another language is permitted).

No more than 30% of the total shooting can be made abroad (this may be waived in light of cost factors).

The director must be a national citizen or part of the 'national culture' or a citizen of an EU member state. This can be waived if the scriptwriter or two leading actors, plus all other cast meets the above condition.

The first run of a national-language version of the film must take place in the home country.

At least 50% of the funding must be derived from the home country or EU member states. None of this 50% minimum may be provided by subsidiaries of American or other non-EU companies.

ELIGIBILITY CONDITIONS IN EUROPE FOR A CO-PRODUCTION

Each co-production must satisfy the official criteria of the co-production treaty signed between the participating countries. A bilateral co-production contract typically specifies:

The language in which the film is shot will be that of the majority country, which must provide over 50% of the budget. The minority country must provide at least 30% of funding. In both cases, funding must be sourced within the relevant countries and cannot be derived from American or other non-EU subsidiaries.

The lead producer must be clearly specified and come from the majority territory. The sales agent must be specified. The breakdown of rights, mandate of distribution and split of overages between the two countries must be specified clearly.

Each co-producer must receive a negative or inter-negative of the film. All prints destined for local release must be made in the home country.

The co-producers must be nationals and registered in their respective countries. They may not be subsidiaries of American or other non-EU companies.

The key creative and technical talent must be nationals of the two countries or drawn from the 'national culture'. The allocation of key posts between the two countries must satisfy a points system.

In the case of tripartite co-productions:

The majority co-producer may have a lower minimum investment and the smallest share may be reduced to 20%. Under certain conditions the third co-producer may make purely a financial contribution rather than technical or creative.

SAMPLE CO-PRODUCTION TREATY

A summary provided by Franco-Spanish lawyer Mercedes Perez-Desoy.

GERMAN-SPANISH CO-PRODUCTION TREATY

Authorization	Each co-production must be approved by the appropriate authorities of the two countries; Spain: ICAA. Germany: Bundesamt fur gewerblich Wirtschaft.
Application procedure	To be presented at least four weeks before start of principal photography: • the script • copy of acquisition of author's rights or option thereof. • 3 copies of the lists of cast and crew with nationalities attached. • 2 copies of the budget • detailed financing plan • shooting schedule including number of weeks, shots and locations. • 3 copies of the co-production contract between the relevant parties.
Producer	The contract must specify the line producer responsible for the production.
Financing shares	The co-production contract must specify the division of financing between the two countries. Neither country may provide less than 30% of the total.
The negative	The contract must guarantee the right to a negative or inter-negative for each co-producer.
Division of receipts	The contract must specify those territories (if any) for which one or other co-producer has exclusive rights, and for the rest the exact division of receipts between the co-production parties (in principle proportional to the financing shares).
Liability	The contract must specify the obligations of each co-producer in the case of budget overages (normally proportional to the financing shares, but can be limited for either party to 30%).
Cast and crew	The cast and crew must be residents of either Germany or Spain or represent part of one of the two countries' cultural expression. In principle the national division of cast and crew should be proportional to the financing shares. A director or leading actor may be chosen from a third country if this increases the possibility of commercialization.
Minimum role of minority producer	Either the director and assistant director or one screenwriter and leading actor, plus a sufficient number of secondary roles (the latter can in certain circumstances be waived).

Principal photography	Principal photography must take place between the two countries. Exteriors may be shot in a third country if required artistically and if approved. Studio shooting if made in a third country may not exceed 30% of all principal photography. The start date of principal photography must be specified in the contract.
Language	The shooting scripts must be provided in both Spanish and German.
Laboratories	The domestic prints must be made in a laboratory of that country.
Credits/ festivals	The film's credits plus all advertising and trailers must indicate the two countries of origin. The name and country of each co-producer must also be cited.
Int'l sales	The contract must specify the producer responsible for international sales.
Co-production with third countries	In the case of a tripartite co-production, if the third country is signatory to a treaty with either of the two main partners, he may benefit from the same co-production terms specified above. In justified cases the minimum financing share may be reduced to 20%.

MEMBERS OF THE CLUB OF EUROPEAN PRODUCERS

Presidents:	David Puttnam (UK) and René Cleitman (France)
Vice-President:	Dieter Geissler (Germany)

Founding Members:	Roberto Ciccuto, Leo Pescarolo (Italy)
	Yves Marmion, Alain Rocca, Toscan du Plantier (France)
	Sarah Radclyffe, Simon Relph, Jeremy Thomas (UK)
	Pierre Drouot, Dirk Impens (Belgium)
	Kees Kasander Denis Wigman (Netherlands)
	Bernd Eichinger, Günter Rohrbach (Germany)
	Andres Vicente Gomez, José Vicuña (Spain)

Notes

1   *Joe Public*

1   'An interview with Peter Gidal' by Peter Lehman, *Wide Angle*, Vol. 5, No. 2.
2   AD Murphy, '21 Fundamental Aspects of the Movies' (1990) Notes from Peter Stark Program.

2   *The Majors*

1   *Variety*, 21 March 1994.
2   *Variety*, 12 April 1993.
3   *Variety*, 23 October 1995.
4   Harold Vogel, *Entertainment Industry Economics* (Cambridge: CUP, 1990), p. 46.
5   *Variety*, 9 August 1993.

3   *What is Commercial?*

1   Mark Litwak, *Reel Power* (London: Sidgwick and Jackson, 1987).
2   Earl Shorris, *A Nation of Salesmen* (Dresden, Illinois: Avon Books, 1996).
3   Mark Litwak, *Reel Power*.
4   *Variety*, 15 November 1993.
5   Quoted in Mark Litwak, *Reel Power*, p. 47.
6   Connie Bruck, *New Yorker*, 9 September 1991.
7   Jon Boorstin, *The Hollywood Eye* (New York: HarperCollins, 1990), p. 3.
8   Quoted in Litwak, *Reel Power*.
9   Philip Rahv, 'Paleface and Redskin' in H. Beaver, *American Critical Essays* (Oxford: OUP, 1959).
10   Quoted in Mark Litwak, *Reel Power*.
11   Elia Kazan, *A Life* (London: André Deutsch, 1988).
12   Jon Boorstin, *The Hollywood Eye*, p. 57.
13   Michael Medved, *Hollywood vs. America* (London: HarperCollins, 1993), p.163.

4   *American Indies*

1   *Daily Variety*, 26 June 1991.
2   *Moving Pictures*, 26 May 1995.
3   *Variety*, 22 January 1996.

5   *Foreign Sales*

1   *Variety*, 18 December 1995.
2   *Variety*, 17 April, 1995.
3   *Moving Pictures*, 13 May 1994.
4   *Variety*, 30 November 1995.
5   *Variety*, 20 May 1994.
6   *Hollywood Reporter*, 16 May 1995.
7   *Variety*, 30 November 1992.
8   *Variety*, 29 March 1993.
9   *Variety*, 30 November 1995.
10   *Moving Pictures*, Cannes Preview 1995.

6   Independent Production

1   *Moving Pictures*, 16 May 1991.
2   *Variety*, 28 February 1994.
3   R. Corman, *How I Made 100 Movies in Hollywood* (New York: Random House, 1990).
4   John Russo, *Making Movies* (New York: Dell Trade, 1989).

7   Fortress Europe

1   L'ARP,*Vive le Cinéma* (Paris: Editions Austral, 1995) (My translation).
2   Quoted in Angus Finney, *A Dose of Reality* (London: *Screen International*/EFA, 1993), p. 20.
3   *Variety*, 24 January 1994.
4   *L'Expansion*, 16 July 1992.
5   *Variety*, 22 March 1993.

8   Europe's Media Barons

1   *Sunday Times*, 28 May 1995.
2   *Variety*, 9 October 1995.
3   *Variety*, 5 April 1993.
4   *Variety*, 28 March 1994.
5   *Variety*, 5 June 1995.
6   *Variety*, 19 December 1994.
7   *L'Express*, 28 August 1987.
8   *Le Film Français*, 17 May 1994.
9   *Financial Times*, 11 January 1995.
10 Jean-Claude Batz, 'A propos de la crise de l'industrie du cinéma' (paper delivered at Université Libre de Bruxelles, 1963), p. 6.

9   The Cultural Ghetto

1   L'ARP, *Vive Le Cinéma*, p. 162 (My translation).

10   The Subsidy System

1   J. P. Cluzel and G. Cerruti, 'Cluzel Report' (Paris: Ministry of Finance, 1992).
2   *The Guardian*, 5 December 1991.
3   Angus Finney, *A Dose of Reality*, p. 41.
4   *Variety*, 6 May 1996.
5   *Variety*, 12 June 1995.
6   Jean-Claude Carrière, *The Secret Language of Cinema* (London: Faber and Faber, 1995), p. 194.
7   *Variety*, 29 November 1993.
8   *Moving Pictures*, 18 May 1994.
9   *Variety*, 29 November 1993.
10 Personal interview.
11 Personal interview.
12 *Variety*, 29 November 1993.
13 EAVE training seminar 1991.
14 Personal interview.
15 Statement made in EU/US Seminar, Cannes 1995.
16 Personal interview.

17   Angus Finney's description of ACE, *A Dose of Reality*, p. 81.

18   Angus Finney, *A Dose of Reality*, p.79.

19   *Media Business File*, Summer 1994.

20   *Variety*, 11 March 1996.

21   *Acanews*, Cannes 1994.

22   *Moving Pictures*, 15 May 1994.

23   *Variety*, 21 November 1994.

24   A second edition, Angus Finney, *The State of European Cinema*, is published by Cassell, 1996.

11   Euro Production

1   Quoted in Andrew Yule, *David Puttnam* (London: Sphere, 1989), p. 115.

2   *Variety*, 30 October 1995.

3   J. P. Cluzel and G. Cerruti, 'Cluzel Report'.

4   *Moving Pictures*, Cannes 1995.

5   *Moving Pictures*, 14 May 1994.

6   *The Independent*, 6 October 1992.

12   European Producers

1   J. M. Frodon, *L'Age Moderne du Cinéma Français* (Paris: Flammarion, 1995), p. 185 (My translation).

2   All quotes from European Film College lecture 1994.

3   *Ciné-Finances*, 2 November 1992 (My translation).

4   *Sunday Times*, 1996.

5   *Variety*, 23 October 1994.

Appendix A

1   Jake Eberts and Terry Ilott, *My Indecision is Final* (London: Faber and Faber, 1990), p. 41.

2   Angus Finney, *A Dose of Reality*, p. 61.

Appendix B

1   *Variety*, 4 December 1995.

2   *Variety*, 27 June 1994.

3   *Screen International*, 12 May 1994.

4   *Screen International*, 26 May 1995.

Index